Recordkeeping, Ethics and Law

THE ARCHIVIST'S LIBRARY

Volume 4

Recordkeeping, Ethics and Law

Regulatory Models, Participant Relationships and Rights and Responsibilities in the Online World

by

Livia Iacovino
Monash University,
Melbourne, VIC, Australia

Springer

A C.I.P. Catalogue record for this book is available from the Library of Congress.

ISBN-10 1-4020-4691-X (HB)
ISBN-13 978-1-4020-4691-9 (HB)
ISBN-10 1-4020-4714-2 (e-book)
ISBN-13 978-1-4020-4714-5 (e-book)

Published by Springer,
P.O. Box 17, 3300 AA Dordrecht, The Netherlands.

www.springer.com

Printed on acid-free paper

Printed in the Netherlands.

To the person who nurtured my love of learning, my mother,
Elisabetta Gelsi-Simon-Kusinszky

1910-2002

PREFACE

Distributed networks such as the Internet have altered the fundamental way a record is created, captured, accessed and managed over time, and therefore who controls, has access to, and is responsible for its authenticity. Law and ethics provide the major sources of regulatory controls over participants in such networks. This book analyses the interrelationship of recordkeeping, ethics and law in terms of existing regulatory models and their application to the Internet environment. It proposes the legal and social relationship model as an analytical tool for identifying the rights and obligations of recordkeeping participants in networked 'business' transactions within communities of common interest based on trust. The model is also used to examine the legal concepts of property, access, privacy and evidence, with particular reference to its Internet context. As legal relationships have their basis in the law of obligations found in both common and civil law systems, as well as archival science, the model has a broad-based application.

The approach in this book has been to reconcile a number of archival traditions - the common strands rather than the differences, in particular concepts of identity, trust, acts, actors, and social relationships - as fundamental concepts to social regulation. It is therefore primarily directed to archives and records academics and practitioners (especially those working within the realm of electronic records), in order to provide them with a sound theoretical and practical knowledge of the legal and ethical dimensions of records created in distributed environments. However, it is also directed to other disciplines and professions in areas critical to the development of the information economy, such as electronic commerce and encryption policies. Thus policy makers, managers, corporate lawyers, business professionals, ethicists, probity officers and information technology disciplines are also a primary audience. Most importantly the book aims to further interdisciplinary bridges between those researching, teaching and working in ethics, law and archival science, thus specialists in the area of interdisciplinarity may also find the book a useful model of interdisciplinary analysis.

The book is a revised version of a PhD thesis, *Ethical-Legal Frameworks for Recordkeeping: Regulatory Models, Participants and their Rights and Obligations,* Monash University, Melbourne, 2002. While the original research focused primarily, but not exclusively on, the Australian legal context, the book has retained Australian examples where it was found necessary to illustrate a concept or model. In addition, examples from other jurisdictions have been added to provide an international perspective and as the basis for future comparative studies.

I would like to thank my family for their moral support throughout the completion of the book. Special thanks are also due to Associate Professor Terry Eastwood, University of British Columbia and Michael Piggott, The University of Melbourne for encouraging me to convert my PhD into a book, my colleagues at Monash University, in particular Professor Sue McKemmish, Frank Upward, and Dr Graeme Johanson, as well as the numerous thinkers and practitioners in the recordkeeping, legal and ethical professions who crossed my path in Australia and overseas, without whom the concepts in this book could never have reached fruition.

I would also like to thank Barbara Reed for her support. Finally, a special thanks to Lorna Frick for copy editing and formatting the text and to Rachel Salmond for preparing the index.

Livia Iacovino
Monash University, Melbourne, Australia
December 2005.

CONTENTS

FIGURES

INTRODUCTION

In the last decade of the twentieth century recordkeeping professions (archivists, records and information managers) began to re-invent themselves, largely, but not exclusively, in response to the change from paper-based to electronic recordkeeping systems. This is evidenced by the changing language of the recordkeeping professions, the recognition of related interdisciplinary research and knowledge, and the re-evaluation of recordkeeping theories and practices. However the process of re-invention is a continuous one and many recordkeeping concepts are being further refined as a result of the impact of the Internet and other communication technologies.[1]

---

[1] Although until recently there has been little recordkeeping research focused directly on the capture and retention of web transactions over time, one cannot discount the research on the preservation of metadata in electronic environments, the recreation of the record when the system and data are migrated and the maintenance of archival objects that move into other environments. For example, see Monash University, School of Information Management and Systems, Records Continuum Research Group, *Recordkeeping Metadata Standards for Managing and Accessing Information Resources in Networked Environments Over Time for Government, Social and Cultural Purposes* (hereafter referred to as RKMS), 1998-1999; University of British Columbia, School of Library, Archival and Information Studies, *International Research on Permanent Authentic Records in Electronic Systems 1:* 1999-2001 (hereafter referred to as InterPARES 1), and the Public Record Office Victoria, *Victorian Electronic Records Strategy*. The extent to which the findings of InterPARES 1 and RKMS apply in distributed environments is being addressed in the following research: Monash University, School of Information Management Systems, Records Continuum Research Group, with the University of California (UCLA) and National Archives of Australia, *Create Once, Use Many Times: The Clever Use of Metadata in eGovernment and eBusiness Processes in Networked Environments,* 2003-2005, and University of British Columbia, School of Library, Archival and Information Studies, *International Research on Permanent Authentic Records in Electronic Systems 2: Experiential, Interactive and Dynamic Records,* 2002-2006 (hereafter referred to as InterPARES 2).

The legal landscape has also changed, both locally and internationally. With the advent of electronic commerce, lawyers began to focus on the need to maintain evidence of contract formation, sender-recipient authentication, and message integrity in order to ensure the legality of the transactions, all of which have relevance to major recordkeeping concerns including reliability, authenticity, trusted systems, and in particular recordkeeping responsibilities in web-based business processes.[2] Electronic commerce highlighted the inadequacy of existing legal definitions of 'documents', 'writing', 'signature' and 'original', thus requiring lawyers to reconceptualise paper-based legal principles to accommodate electronic equivalents. The law is coming to terms with a world in which the record as an artefact is arcane.

Jurisdiction is essential to regulation. Electronic business via the Internet also complicates territorial jurisdiction and which law should govern an Internet transaction. Internet jurisdiction has brought to the forefront common legal and archival concerns for reliable and authentic records that may be stored anywhere in cyberspace.[3] The need to identify the recordkeeping roles and participants in Internet transactions (their competencies - which is their authority to act), is essential to ensuring that records are trustworthy, as well as that legal and social obligations are fulfilled.[4]

On the other hand, ethics provides a range of processes for understanding what motivates human behaviour, and has historical and continuing links with psychology, sociology and anthropology. It has had to provide new approaches to contentious issues, many of which are the product of technological innovation, for example genetic engineering and electronic surveillance. Ethicists have begun to focus on person-centred rather than rule or duty-centred behaviour to encourage the nurturing of honesty and other character traits that are conducive to responsible online

---

[2] Central Computer and Telecommunication Agency (CCTA), *Legal Issues and the Internet, Guideline* and *Legal Issues and the Internet, Reference Book,* HMSO, London, 1996, and Lars J. Davies, *A Model for Internet Regulation? Constructing a Framework for Regulating Electronic Commerce,* Information Technology Unit, Centre for Commercial Law Studies, Queen Mary and Westfield College, London, 1999.

[3] The extent to which recordkeeping regulatory models are still valid for online requirements is addressed in Chapter 7. Chapter 8 provides an alternative recordkeeping approach to legal regulation in cyberspace.

[4] The use of roles in Internet regulation has provided a useful approach for recordkeeping roles as articulated in Chapter 8, and draws heavily from Graham J.H. Smith et al. (eds), *Internet Law and Regulation: A Specially Commissioned Report*, F.T. Law & Tax, London, 1996.

behaviour. Ethical approaches based on personal and community relationships may provide a form of Internet self-regulation within limits delineated by community constituents.[5]

The importance of trust as a sociological phenomenon necessary for record authenticity has not been fully integrated into the recordkeeping-ethics-law nexus. Equally, professional ethics for recordkeeping professions has focused on their professional responsibilities rather than on the business participants and their ethical motives and actions. The ethical dimension pursued in this book is that of the parties involved with the creation of the record in its transactional and communicative nature, which includes, but is not exclusive of, the recordkeeping professional. Ethical issues should be extended to the analysis of the professional duties relevant to other professions or persons in the course of the activities and recordkeeping processes in which they engage. However, this hinges on what is the nature of a professional.[6] The idea of a profession which exists to provide a service in the public interest is no longer a central professional tenet.

New business models have altered the traditional controls on the behaviour of individuals within organisations which have been based on policy, guidelines, legal regulations, professional ethics, and corporate culture. These controls have also provided the basis for the recordkeeping practices of communities of common interest, such as professions. New behavioural models, in particular self-regulation with or without penalties, are particularly prevalent in distributed networks, such as the Internet, where legal jurisdiction is no longer clearly defined. The new behavioural patterns have highlighted problems with establishing and maintaining the evidential aspects of business activities required by the participants (physical and legal) to establish and fulfil their rights and obligations (ethical and legal).

It is within these new paradigms that are shaping and cross-fertilising the professional concerns of recordkeeping, ethics and law that an examination of their online context is addressed in this book.

---

[5] How to regulate behaviour in cyberspace has generated interest since the mid 1990s, as demonstrated by the evolution of computer ethics into a sub-branch of cyberethics. For example, see John L. Fodor, 'Human Values in the Computer Revolution', in *Social and Ethical Effects of the Computer Revolution,* ed. Joseph Migga Kizza, McFarland & Company, Jefferson, N.C., 1996, pp. 256-266.

[6] The change in status of the professional is a sub-theme addressed in Chapters 4 and 6.

Intellectual frameworks, interdisciplinary discourses and interrelationships

A number of models and perspectives have been used to integrate law and ethics with recordkeeping discourse.[7] Firstly the Australian postmodernist records continuum model provides a perspective from 'the continuum of recordkeeping processes that capture, manage, preserve and re-present records as evidence of social and business activity for business, social and cultural purposes for as long as they are of value, whether that be for a nanosecond or a millennium'.[8] The records continuum model as conceived by Frank Upward[9] is a powerful conceptual tool for analysing recordkeeping and its legal and ethical context.[10]

Secondly, an historical-analytical perspective, in particular from the viewpoint of the evolution of Italian archival science and diplomatics[11]

---

[7] The incorporation of relevant disciplinary discourses into archival theory and practice is a major conceptual construct adopted in this book.

[8] Monash University, Department of Librarianship, Archives and Records, Master of Information Management and Systems, *LAR5530 Managing the Records Continuum, Subject Book 1*, Module 1, Topic 1, Distance Education Centre, Monash University, Churchill, Victoria, July 1997, p. 3.

[9] See Frank Upward, 'The Records Continuum', in *Archives: Recordkeeping in Society*, eds Sue McKemmish, Michael Piggott, Barbara Reed and Frank Upward, Centre for Information Studies, Charles Sturt University, Wagga Wagga, NSW, 2005, pp. 197-222; 'Structuring the Records Continuum, Part One: Postcustodial Principles and Properties', *Archives and Manuscripts*, vol. 24, no. 2, November 1996, pp. 268-285, and 'Structuring the Records Continuum, Part Two: Structuration Theory and Recordkeeping', *Archives and Manuscripts*, vol. 25, no. 1, May 1997, pp. 10-35.

[10] Livia Iacovino, *'Things in Action': Teaching Law to Recordkeeping Professionals*, Ancora Press, Melbourne, 1998 and 'The Nature of the Nexus between Recordkeeping and the Law', *Archives and Manuscripts*, vol. 26, no. 2, November 1998, pp. 216-246.

[11] Most archivists in the English-speaking world are familiar with Italian diplomatics and archival science from the works of Luciana Duranti. See principally, Luciana Duranti, *Diplomatics: New Uses for an Old Science*, Society of American Archivists and Association of Canadian Archivists in association with The Scarecrow Press, Maryland and London, 1998. Aside from Duranti's writings, much of the Italian literature on diplomatics and archival science is not available in English. The following have been used in this book in their original language: Paola Carucci, *Le Fonti Archivistiche: Ordinamento e Conservazione,* Carocci, Rome 1998 (1983); *Il Documento Contemporaneo, Diplomatica e Criteri di Edizione,* Carocci, Rome, 1998 (1987); Paola Carucci and Marina Messina, *Manuale di Archivistica per*

provides a conceptual framework for integrating an understanding of law with recordkeeping, in terms of records satisfying the juridical requirements of a particular social system at a given point in time.[12]

Finally, a practice skills model that integrates ethics and law with the core knowledge and practice of the recordkeeping professions provides an additional approach. In order to relate law and ethics to these recordkeeping models it is essential to understand the principal issues that are, and have been addressed, within and across their respective domains of knowledge.

Recordkeeping, ethical and legal discourses

Postmodernism and the rediscovery of value provide two thinking paths, which are not irreconcilable, for addressing epistemological debates centred on fixed meaning as opposed to changing interpretation of concepts. These debates are evidenced in recordkeeping research which has constantly refined the meaning of a record. Recordkeeping questions centre on what data need to be 'fixed' in the record, what can change, and what can be lost with little or no effect on its integrity. The preservation of metadata that retains the record's evidential qualities is therefore a major concern to the archives and records community.[13]

For recordkeeping the issue of values is significant for appraisal practices. For example, why do we keep records beyond their immediate uses? Archivists have claimed that the use of functional analysis of recordkeeping systems is more objective than past methods based on 'secondary' record values. By deciding on which functions are more important than others or leaving appraisal to the needs of business, someone is still making value judgments. Recordkeeping practitioners are deluding themselves if they believe they have become more 'objective' in their practices; they have replaced one value system based on structural

L'impresa, Carocci, Rome, 1998, and Maria Guercio, *Archivistica Informatica: I Documenti in Ambiente Digitale,* Carocci, Rome 2002. For an Australian perspective on Italian diplomatics, see Livia Iacovino, 'Common Ground, Different Traditions: An Australian Perspective on Italian Diplomatics, Archival Science, and Business Records', *Archives and Manuscripts,* vol. 29, no. 1, May 2001, pp. 118-138.

[12] See Chapter 3 on diplomatics, archival science and law.

[13] See footnote 1. Chapters 2 and 4 critique those aspects of records research projects that are relevant to regulatory models and recordkeeping participants, (for example the capture of moral and legal person identity).

provenance with another - that of functionalism. There is no aspect of recordkeeping that is not affected by values.

As Bernadine Dodge points out, archival debates still centre on authenticity, accountability, evidence, authority, and history of progress.[14] She admits that 'archivists, through their professional practices, cannot avoid being part of the fabric of moral systems and ethical arguments'.[15] In fact she suggests restoring boundaries - temporal and spatial. This coalesces with the concern in ethical discourse to re-critique the role of positivism in general.[16]

Postmodernism is intrinsically problematic for ethics. Ethics is centrally concerned with norms and value systems; dualisms abound, for example good and bad, and right and wrong. Virtue ethics provides the main vehicle for a postmodern ethical perspective because it rejects positivism and its dichotomies of right and wrong, codified universal values and hierarchies of value found in Kantianism and utilitarianism; it places onto individuals and communities the responsibility of inculcating a sense of ethics. However, the insights of the 'moderns' are being re-interpreted. The modernists' perception of 'perfect' (what the law requires and punishes if one transgresses) and 'imperfect duties' (the duties to act for the right reasons) questions the interpretation of Kantian ethics as purely rule-based. The 'values' spurned by some postmodernists are being re-discovered as central to ethics.

The definition of ethics that is adopted in this book is one that focuses on the study of the principles of human conduct or human actions, as recordkeeping involves actors and agents that participate in 'business' and recordkeeping processes.[17] As Alasdair MacIntyre says, 'These actions

---

[14] Bernadine Dodge, 'Places Apart: Archives in Dissolving Space and Time', *Archivaria,* 44, Fall 1997, pp. 118-131.

[15] Ibid., p. 127.

[16] See Judith Squires (ed.), *Principled Positions: Postmodernism and the Rediscovery of Value,* Lawrence and Wishart, London, 1993.

[17] A dictionary meaning of ethics is the science of morals; also defined as rules of conduct; the science of human duty, and in its widest extent, it can include the science of law. From C.T. Onions, (ed.), *The Shorter Oxford English Dictionary on Historic Principles*, 3rd edn, 1994, Clarendon Press, Oxford, vol. 1, p. 685, 'ethics'. It is a 'rule-based' definition of ethics. However, ethics is not dependent only on rules; in fact if moral conduct is based on rules alone, ethics becomes almost redundant. The terms ethics and morality should also be distinguished, although some ethicists believe these terms are interchangeable. Noel Preston uses the terms interchangeably in *Understanding Ethics,* Federation Press, Leichhardt, NSW, 1996. G.E.M. Anscombe, 'Modern Moral Philosophy', in *Virtue Ethics,* eds Roger Crisp and Michael Slote, Oxford

must serve a purpose, which constitutes part or the whole of the moral agent's intention in doing what he [or she] does. The agent's purpose is only made intelligible as the expression of his desire and aims.'[18] Full ethical decisionmaking requires a moral agent who can rationalise and analyse what he or she does, not only as defined in rationalist-based theories, but also in theories which include emotion and character as motivating factors for ethical action.[19] The accountability of recordkeeping participants requires understanding their role not only as legal but also moral agents. In terms of recordkeeping participants, the question of their role as rational agents that operate on the basis of universally acceptable norms that require a person (physical or corporate) to be responsible for individual actions, is supported by the Kantian notion of the autonomous agent. In the online environment, communities of interest will have to universalise duties that impact on the global participants. Thus Kantian obligations have ongoing relevance to Internet communities.

Other definitions of ethics that are relevant to recordkeeping include John Charvet's ethical community, in which he states that, 'Ethical life depends on the sharing by a collection of persons of authoritative norms.'[20] The community element of ethical life is also consistent with a collectivity that forms the basis of a juridical system. Utilitarianism provides for notions of community and individual acts and their consequences, which have been influential on proportional punishment for criminal acts in legal thought. The execution of responsibilities of recordkeeping participants can be evaluated from their acts and intentions, as evidenced by the records themselves.[21]

The relationship of the external world (context) and how humans internalise it, of subject (human being) and of object (thing), and of changing social values, are ongoing ethical concerns that have also been raised in recordkeeping theory in relation to the relationship of the record

University Press, Oxford, New York, 1997, pp. 26-44 and Bernard Williams, 'Morality, the Peculiar Institution', in ibid., pp. 45-65, make a clear distinction between ethics and morality. They argue that if moral obligation is the dominant notion of morality, it drives out other ethical considerations.

[18] Alasdair MacIntyre, *A Short History of Ethics: A History of Moral Philosophy from the Homeric Age to the Twentieth Century*, 2nd edn, University of Notre Dame Press, Notre Dame, Indiana, 1998, p. 85.

[19] Ibid., p. xiii. Greek ethics had one set of principles only, modern ethics adopts 'reason' in various conceptions.

[20] John Charvet, *The Idea of an Ethical Community*, Cornell University Press, Ithaca, New York and London, 1995, p. 1.

[21] See Chapter 4 for the development of links between recordkeeping participants, acts and intentions.

(object or subject) with its creator (object or subject), and of the values placed on recorded information in different time-space settings. Descartes' division of the physical from the mental or spiritual, known as 'Cartesian duality', is rejected by the ethical demand theory which sets out to destroy the epistemology of subject and object.[22] Frank Upward in his records continuum model[23] also rejects the subject-object duality in which the record is the object. He elucidates how nineteenth century records were studied as 'objects', much the same as scientists studied the functioning of things. This observation is relevant to current computer paradigms that view documents as 'objects', albeit active rather than passive objects. The law has used the subject-object division in its understanding of electronic documents as 'non-physical' things in property law, and in relation to the legal bond between a person and a thing.[24] In terms of ownership of a record, postmodern perspectives provide an alternative view from that of legal concepts of property as object.

Upward's postmodern perspective in relation to recordkeeping in the online environment includes understanding records as logical rather than physical entities. This concept is relevant to the legal debate on the materiality-immateriality of records, including access to logical records in the Internet context.[25] He rejects the Jenkinsonian view of continuous physical custody of records and its relevance to their authenticity as a form of linear juridical control.[26] In the Internet context, he argues that the location of the resources will be of minimal interest to those using them.[27] Yet legal systems are very much concerned with linear ownership; if *where* no longer matters, the *who* and *how* of control over records to perpetuate authenticity is still very relevant.

---

[22] Hans Fink and Alasdair MacIntyre, 'Introduction', in Knud Ejler Logstrup, *The Ethical Demand*, University of Notre Dame Press, Notre Dame and London, 1997, pp. xvii-xviii. Logstrup and ethicists concerned with the ontological meaning of existence reject subject-object schema.

[23] Upward, 'Structuring the Records Continuum, Part Two', pp. 10-35.

[24] Simon Fisher, 'The Archival Enterprise, Public Archival Institutions and the Impact of Private Law', *Archives and Manuscripts,* vol. 26, no. 2, Nov. 1998, p. 358, endnote 12.

[25] Ibid. See also Chapters 5 and 7.

[26] The custody debate amongst archivists is an example of where the postmodern perspective provides a broader debate. A postmodern approach to recordkeeping does not confine the custody of records to boundaries between the creators and ultimate keepers.

[27] Upward, 'Structuring the Records Continuum, Part One', p. 282.

Although postmodernism has not had much direct impact on legal thinking and practice,[28] modern legal theories recognise the contingent aspects of legal rules and include broader conceptual frameworks for analysing legal issues, in particular the role of policy behind a law.[29] The postmodernist exposure of dualisms is evident in legal theory. Legal theory distinguishes between 'natural law' as a product of reason, principles and rules to promote peace in society, and 'positive law' as rules in force in an actual legal system. The two types of law are a form of legal dualism in which law is distinguished from ethics and morals. However, the legal terms of duty, rights and obligations are terms shared with religion and morality, which indicate that the origin of legal rules is found in ethical principles.[30] These definitions clearly demonstrate the tension between law as a system of coercive control over human behaviour as well as a means of binding communities together through mutual rights and obligations.[31]

The need to provide a scientific basis of legal discourse, through legal reasoning and structured language, has been taken up in Anglo-American scholarship, in particular by Albert Kocourek. His tightly structured approach to jural relations summarises the positivist jurisprudential interpretation of legal relationships, and is particularly useful to understanding terms used in diplomatics.[32] He describes jurisprudence as the science of law, which is conceptual in its elements and the conceptual structure is one of objective facts. This view of law survives in modern rationalist legal thinking.

The classification of law affects how it is administered. To some extent legal classification is based on historical accident, for example tort, equity and contract, all of which deal with obligations.[33] At least within Western

[28] Matthew Kramer, *Legal Theory, Political Theory and Deconstruction: Against Rhadamanthus,* Indiana University Press, Bloomington and Indianapolis, 1991.

[29] Bryan Horrigan and Brian Fitzgerald, 'International and Transnational Influences on Law and Policy affecting Government', in *Government Law and Policy: Commercial Aspects,* ed. Bryan Horrigan, The Federation Press, Leichhardt NSW, 1998, p. 7. Also Bryan Horrigan 'Contemporary Sources and Limits of Crown Immunity, Governmental Liability and Legislative Invalidity', in ibid., pp. 276-339. This article is a good example of the combination of broad policy with specific legal rules applied to an analysis of Crown immunity.

[30] C.G. Weeramantry, *An Invitation to the Law*, Butterworths, Sydney, 1982, p. 167.

[31] Legal dualism is relevant to Chapters 1, 2 and 3.

[32] See Kocourek's definition of jural relations in Chapter 3.

[33] J.E. Penner, 'Basic Obligations', in *The Classification of Obligations,* ed. Peter Birks, Clarendon Press, Oxford, 1997, p. 91. In *Hawkins v Clayton* (1988) 164 CLR 539 Deane J. said: '... The law of contract and the law of tort are, in a

legal thought the Roman taxonomy, as found in the *Justinian Institutes*, is considered by Peter Birks as an unsurpassed 'map' of the structure of law, in particular the classification of obligations.[34] Because the Roman taxonomy also deals with protecting property through obligations, and with the underlying nature of contractual and tortious obligations, it has much to offer in understanding ownership in records from the standpoint of the obligations of the parties in a legal relationship. The record has always been the manifestation of an obligation or a right, and not just a physical object.[35] However, it is in private law that legal theorists have found a coherent legal classification, by determining the scope and nature of legal obligations. Private law concepts of property and contract have become important at a time of government deregulation and privatisation, and also to online transactions.[36]

The law of obligations, as a composite right-duty obligation, is found in both the common and civil law systems. It has been the area of law that in recent years civil and common law lawyers have drawn from to accentuate

---

modern context, properly to be seen as but two of a number of imprecise divisions, for the purpose of classification, of a general body of rules constituting one coherent system of law', as quoted by R.E. Cooper, 'Foreword', in Fisher, *The Law of Commercial and Professional Relationships,* p. vi.

[34] Peter Birks, 'Definition and Division: A Meditation on *Institutes* 3.13', in *The Classification of Obligations,* ed. Peter Birks, Clarendon Press, Oxford, 1997, pp. 1-35. Jeffrey Hackney, in 'More than a Trace of the Old Philosophy', in ibid., pp. 123-155, points out the input of the civilian tradition into the common law in the nineteenth century. Reinhard Zimmerman, in *The Law of Obligations: Roman Foundations of the Civilian Tradition*, Juta & Co. Ltd, Cape Town 1990, makes it clear that in the law of obligations, at least at the structural level, the differences between the common and the civil law systems are not great. Simon Fisher, 'General Principles of Obligations', in *The Law of Commercial and Professional Relationships,* ed. Simon Fisher, F.T. Law & Tax, South Melbourne, 1996, p. 15, argues that the law of obligations has been a way of classifying legal questions, rather than relying on the common law structures of contract, tort, property and equity.

[35] See Chapters 5 and 7.

[36] See Simon Fisher's view of the application of private law to public law in, Fisher, 'General Principles of Obligations', p. 16. See also Simon Deakin, 'Private Law, Economic Rationality and the Regulatory State', in *The Classification of Obligations,* ed. Peter Birks, Clarendon Press, Oxford, 1997, p. 283.

their commonalties.[37] The notion of an obligation has obvious links to ethical obligations, and provides an important cross link between law and ethics. The re-evaluation of the Roman law of obligations within the common law framework of legal rights provides the backdrop to the renewed interest in legal rights and obligations as a common concern to Western legal systems. Apart from the relevance to the harmonisation of law within the European Union,[38] because of its conceptual and taxonomic nature, the law of obligations is a useful approach to global legal issues in the online environment.

The relevance of different legal systems to the universality of record-keeping principles, in particular in the area of diplomatics as the foundation of archival science, has been an issue of debate in the recordkeeping profession.[39] It is also relevant to recordkeeping research which is intent on finding a standardised methodology for maintaining the authenticity of records over time on a universal scale applicable to all legal jurisdictions. Rights and obligations evidenced in communities of common interest is one of the best 'authorities' for recordkeeping, a theme taken up in this book.[40]

In the 1990s, the Internet legal discourse included broad issues such as globalisation, democratisation, disintegration and arbitrage, as well as jurisdiction, conflict of laws, extraterritorial enforcement, harmonisation

---

[37] It could be argued that the higher the level of abstraction of concepts the more applicable they are to any environment; differences emerge at the micro-level where legal systems are applied.

[38] 'Today Roman Law has been replaced by modern codes. These codes, however, did not create new law from scratch, but rather, to a large extent, the rules of Roman Law which had been transmitted, were placed in a statutory framework which provided a modern, systematic order. Most important of all, Roman Law will have great significance in regard to the formation of uniform legal rules which further the process of political integration in Europe. It can serve as a source of rules and legal norms which will easily blend with the national laws of the many and varied European states.' Saarland University, Institute of Law and Informatics, *The Roman Law Branch of the Law-related Internet Project,* 'What is Roman Law?', 2005.

[39] See Chapters 1 and 3.

[40] See Chapter 1 on recordkeeping regulatory models. Chapters 6 and 8 provide recordkeeping examples from the government, business and health sectors. For authorities as recordkeeping warrants, see Richard Cox and Wendy Duff, 'Warrant and the Definition of Electronic Records: Questions Arising from the Pittsburgh Project', *Archives and Museums Informatics,* vol. 11, 1997, pp. 222-234.

and alternative dispute resolution.[41] There was a perception that within cyberspace, internal boundaries could be created by distinct communities, with a new civic spirit and a revitalisation of democracy.[42] However, the commercialisation of the Internet led to distinct business interests which pushed for legal certainties. Electronic commerce and signature legislation has provided a recordkeeping focus through electronic transaction and authentication requirements.

The major Internet legal discourse now centres on the extent to which current law is either applicable to or enforceable on Internet participants. The disappearance of territorial, geographic and political boundaries and the undermining of the application of laws based on the relationship of rule sets that apply to a physical-territorial space have been recognised as major legal challenges.[43] The breakdown in legal regulation of the Internet is evident from the early judicial failures to impose law on physical places. These failures included trying to shut down Internet servers where the court had jurisdiction, only to find that the server was simply moved elsewhere or ordering the Internet service provider to disable access to residents within that court's jurisdiction.[44] Despite lawyers rejecting the conception of the Internet as law-free, they have had to be pragmatic about the difficulties of enforcement of national laws.[45] It is not only a question of applying national laws; it is also a question about which country's laws

[41] In the 1990s, American law schools and subsequently the United Kingdom and Australia, established specialised law-related Internet subjects, legal centres and legal texts. For Internet legal texts, see for example, Edward A. Cavazos and Gavino Morin, *Cyberspace and the Law: Your Rights and Duties in the On-line World,* MIT Press, Cambridge, Mass., London, England, 1994, and Raymond A. Kurz with Bart G. Newland, Steven Lieberman and Celine M. Jimenez, *Internet and the Law: Legal Fundamentals for the Internet User*, Government Institutes, Rockville MD, 1996. More specialised books included Lance Rose, *Netlaw: Your Rights in the Online World,* Osborne McGraw-Hill, Berkeley, 1995.

[42] 'Preface', in Brian Kahin and Charles Nesson (eds), *Borders in Cyberspace: Information Policy and the Global Information Infrastructure,* MIT Press, Cambridge, Mass., 1997, pp. viii-ix.

[43] See for example, Brian Kahin and Charles Nesson (eds), *Borders in Cyberspace: Information Policy and the Global Information Infrastructure,* MIT Press, Cambridge, Mass., 1997.

[44] David R. Johnson and David G. Post, 'Rise of Law on the Global Network', in *Borders in Cyberspace: Information Policy and the Global Information Infrastructure,* MIT Press, Cambridge, Mass., 1997, p. 8.

[45] Anne Fitzgerald et al. (eds), *Going Digital 2000, Legal Issues for E-commerce, Software and the Internet*, 2nd edn, Prospect Media, St. Leonards, New South Wales, 2000.

to apply.[46] A failure in political will to enforce multinational treaties or policies, and differences in pre-trial prejudice and criminal law, have militated against a universal approach to Internet regulation.

Legal systems are not 'closed' and draw legal concepts from international and transnational legal systems linked to the globalising of both culture and the economy.[47] The Internet is proving to be another catalyst in finding cross-jurisdictional understandings of legal concepts and enforcement models. The loss of physicality in cyberspace is a further development of the materiality-immateriality debate which began with electronic records. The legal themes that are taken up in this book include the materiality-immateriality dichotomy in relation to property law, the emergent relevance of private law in terms of legal relationships, and the challenges to existing mechanisms to protect privacy, copyright and evidence in the online environment.

Although national and cultural differences have made an international archival discourse problematic, Eric Ketelaar argues that these differences should be evaluated until the commonalties are found.[48] The need for a global legal and moral language has also arisen in ethical and legal discourse, partly emanating from a need for universally-shared values in the online environment. Jurisprudential principles need to be re-evaluated, and a return to a conceptual understanding of the law which has been overlaid by local custom and procedure, may result from this process. Legal system types, as well as the universality versus contextuality postmodernist debate, are central to the role of national sovereign judicial systems over international jurisprudential principles. How legal rules are interpreted and liabilities attributed in different legal systems are also central underlying issues to the regulation of recordkeeping.

---

[46] Henry H. Perritt Jr., *Law and The Information Superhighway*, John Wiley, New York, 1996.

[47] Peter R.A. Gray, 'Saying It Like It Is: Oral Traditions, Legal Systems, and Records', *Archives and Manuscripts*, vol. 26, no. 2, November 1998, pp. 248-269 and Fisher, 'The Archival Enterprise, Public Archival Institutions and the Impact of Private Law'. Gray's article demonstrates the recognition of pluralist legal systems in Australia and Fisher clearly shows that lawyers take account of concepts from other legal systems.

[48] Eric Ketelaar, 'The Difference Best Postponed? Cultures and Comparative Archival Science', *Archivaria,* vol. 44, Fall 1997, pp. 142-148.

1 THE RECORDKEEPING-ETHICS-LAW NEXUS AND RECORDKEEPING REGULATORY MODELS

A nexus is a bond or tie between two or more things or concepts, while an interrelationship focuses on the points of interconnection between relationships. As the recordkeeping-ethics-law nexus bonds three conceptual areas or things, there are a number of interrelationships that make up the nexus, for example identity, trust and evidence. However, points of interconnection between areas of knowledge also depend on the framework which each discipline adopts to analyse its own concepts.

In legal theory there is often a question as to the relationship of law and morality, and whether 'institutions' or 'norms', or both, pre-empt the creation of a legal system.[1] Ethics, as the actions of free agents, or as the application of rules of codified behaviour within communities of common interest, may be viewed as separate from, or at least in addition to, positive law. How recordkeeping regimes ensure compliance with appropriate ethical behaviour depends on whether ethics is considered a set of rules, moral codes or norms (the 'law' conception of ethics rejected by virtue ethicists and ascribed to Kantians), or a system of personal choice of conduct, or a combination of both. The regulatory model that is adopted depends on how regulation is defined.

'Regulation' in the strict legal sense sets limits upon the manner in which a particular activity may be lawfully undertaken. Certain acts and procedures may be prescribed; others may be prohibited. Usually there is a penalty for a breach. There is an assumption that the law is enforceable.

The application of regulatory models to recordkeeping regimes takes into account both social controls and the law proper. 'Regulation' within a socio-legal view includes a range of normative systems. Professional and corporate ethics, and codes of conduct and practice, are a different kind of

---

[1] C.G. Weeramantry, *An Invitation to the Law*, Butterworths, Sydney, 1982, Chapters 1-2, 4, 7, 9-10 provide an historical, philosophical and conceptual study of legal systems, and the common law system in particular. Weeramantry's definition of a legal system includes the origin of laws in which religion and morality are included, while most general legal texts focus on a narrower definition of a legal system as a collection of rules only.

regulatory control on individuals and organisations; they are only 'legal' in a broad understanding of their place in a juridical system. Virtue ethicists would argue that codes of conduct are not a true form of ethics as they are used to control the ethical decisionmaking process of autonomous individuals. In this sense codes are a form of 'normative' ethics, that is they provide a rule or standard to be followed in ethical practice. They are a means of avoiding the complexities of regulation found in the legal system, and are also essential to providing a proper balance with 'black letter' regulation.

Existing recordkeeping regulatory models have included a place for 'self-regulation', defined in terms of approaches that do not rely on strict black letter law. In the Internet environment, self-regulatory models have been suggested for a number of areas. In actual practice, most schemes for the Internet are a hybrid of industry codes backed by legislation (see Chapter 7).

1.1 Law, ethics and regulation

The relationship between law and ethics is of central relevance to how individuals and communities regulate their lives, that is with or without coercion, in order to live within the bounds of socially acceptable behaviour, as well as to improve the quality of their lives. Both law and ethics grapple with similar issues. Are actions and motives causally linked?[2] Are consequences of actions, foreseeable and actual, the responsibility of the agent? Is negative responsibility, that is not doing something, as much a moral or legal issue as actually doing something wrong?

Law shares the terminology of duties, rights and obligations with one branch of ethics, that is deontology. In fact, in legal discourse, the notion

[2] Causation is an important jurisprudential concept. In Jeremy Bentham's utilitarian view of causation, a circumstance is considered material and relevant when it causes the consequences of an act (pain and pleasure, as defined by utilitarian theory, are derived from an act), and immaterial if this causal relationship is not there. Jeremy Bentham, *An Introduction to the Principles of Morals and Legislation, An Authoritative Edition by J.H. Burns and H.L.A. Hart; with a New Introduction by F. Rosen, and an Interpretive Essay by H.L.A. Hart,* Clarendon Press, Oxford, 1996, p. 80.

of an obligation is a form of moral recognition in the law.[3] Other terms, with which both law and ethics are concerned, include motives, will, voluntariness, internal or externally motivated behaviour, responsibility for consequences of action, and the role of ethics in legal regimes. The relationship of duty motivated by fear of sanctions or the volition to carry out an act without duress is at the core of the ethics-law nexus of morality. These terms are also essential to the nature of the record as an intentional document of action (see Chapter 4).

Rights in Western legal systems have been privileges, gradually granted legal recognition in both common and statute law. In the natural law theories of the seventeenth and eighteenth centuries, obligations were divided into 'perfect' and 'imperfect' duties, or natural and artificial duties, to differentiate between legal and moral duties. Thus the moral obligation differed from the legal one, in that it was discretionary, but nonetheless a praiseworthy act.[4] 'Perfect' and 'imperfect' duties split morality into an ethic of rule and ethic of virtue. Perfect duties were enforceable by the courts, imperfect duties were ruled by virtues and the agent had some discretion.[5] For Immanuel Kant, who was a follower of natural law theories, the chief connection to all duties, legal, moral or otherwise, was the concept of binding oneself.[6]

---

[3] A linkage between moral and legal obligations is endorsed in legal writings. See J.E. Penner, 'Basic Obligations' in *The Classification of Obligations,* ed. Peter Birks, Clarendon Press, Oxford, 1997, p. 120.

[4] These notions of natural rights are found in the writings of Hugo Grotius (1583-1645). For example, if a person had contracted with another person to perform a certain task then the person contracting had a right to the performance, and the person who agreed to the task had a perfect duty correlative to that right to perform it. If one is a beggar one has no right to alms, but a person has a discretion, an 'imperfect' duty, to give to the beggar and the motivation is relevant. Grotius's ideas as interpreted in Jerome B. Schneewind, 'The Misfortunes of Virtues', in *Virtue Ethics,* eds Roger Crisp and Michael Slote, Oxford University Press, Oxford, New York, 1997, pp. 178-200.

[5] Roger Crisp and Michael Slote, 'Introduction', in *Virtue Ethics,* pp. 18-19. Hume's distinction between natural virtues and artificial virtues, such as justice, can be mapped onto Kant's distinction between perfect and imperfect duties revived from theories of natural law.

[6] For example, one has a legal duty when a loan is taken out to the bank to repay it, but the basis of the repayment is that one has chosen to bind oneself to the laws of the government under which one is accountable. For Kant the obligation from the contract is due firstly to the government's laws and the legal system, and secondly to fulfil moral duties to others. Robert B. Louden, 'Kant's Virtue Ethics', in *Virtue Ethics, A Critical Reader,* ed. Daniel Statman, Georgetown University Press, Washington, D.C., 1997, p. 294.

English jurists and philosophers moved away from notions of natural rights after the French revolution. Jeremy Bentham rejects theories based on natural law or natural rights which suppose that there are rights, duties, and obligations apart from those embodied in positive law.[7] For Bentham, rights, duties, and obligations exist only in a particular context. According to his theory of logical fictions, obligation is a fiction.[8] Logical fictions include legal rights, duties, obligations, trusts and powers.[9] His position can be summed up as: for every right that the law confers on one party, it imposes on some other party, a duty or obligation. But there may be laws that command or prohibit an act, that is impose duties that generate no rights. Duties may be extra-regarding or self-regarding. The only motive for obeying rules is the pleasure to be found in obedience or pain in disobeying them.[10] The individual discovers his aims and his desires from within a set of rule-governed relationships to others. The goals are partly specified for him, and then he has choices to make. This is the essence of the legal positivist view.

[7] The common law system as it is known today has been largely rethought and reformed by Jeremy Bentham. To William Hearn, another anti-natural law jurist, a duty is defined as a command of the state. See William Edward Hearn, *The Theory of Legal Duties and Rights: An Introduction to Analytical Jurisprudence*, F.B. Rothman, Littleton Colorado, 1990 (1883), pp. 4-5, p. 53, and Chapters 4, 6, and 7. Hearn presents a strong representation of the common law positivist legal school of the late nineteenth century, which has been brought into question by the liberal legal rights theorists in the twentieth century and beyond.

[8] H.L.A. Hart, 'Bentham's Principle of Utility and the Theory of Penal Law', in *Jeremy Bentham, An Introduction to the Principles of Morals and Legislation, Jeremy Bentham, An Authoritative Edition by J.H. Burns and H.L.A. Hart; with a New Introduction by F. Rosen, and an Interpretive Essay by H.L.A. Hart*, Clarendon Press, Oxford, 1996, p. lxxxvi. The distinction between real and fictitious entities in Bentham's work arises because of his opposition to the language of natural law and natural rights followed from his distinction between real and fictitious entities: real entities are those that can be known empirically, and complex ideas and concepts may be analysed in terms of real and fictitious entities which comprise them (hence the term 'legal fiction').

[9] F. Rosen, 'Introduction', in Jeremy Bentham, *An Introduction to the Principles of Morals and Legislation, Jeremy Bentham, An Authoritative Edition by J.H. Burns and H.L.A. Hart; with a New Introduction by F. Rosen, and an Interpretive Essay by H.L.A. Hart,* Clarendon Press, Oxford, 1996, p. xxxvi.

[10] Alasdair MacIntyre, *A Short History of Ethics: A History of Moral Philosophy from the Homeric Age to the Twentieth Century,* 2nd edn, University of Notre Dame Press, Notre Dame, Indiana, 1998, p. 235 and p. 227.

Bentham's ideas were very influential in the common law system, in particular the laws of evidence. His understanding of human behaviour and motivation for actions provided a unifying concept of morals and law, with the legal system as the primary motivator for ensuring individuals took other people's interest into account.[11] Law is heavily based on utilitarian thought, the notion of what is best for the community, and the avoidance or punishment of harm.

Within the structure of the common law system, the law of equity as a source of English law based on close fact scrutiny, and the assessment of individual merit, has been described as the moral adjunct to the formal general law.[12] Therefore, a less strict application of law on the basis of individual need is part of the common law system.[13] The notion of rules that can apply to both how we judge acts as ethical or unethical, or that if followed lead to ethical actions, is a central question both within and among a range of ethical theories.[14] Can actions be judged as classes of action or only in relation to individual acts? For example, is murder always wrong? Rules have been accepted as useful for ethical decisionmaking in practical cases, but should they be regarded as moral principles which justify particular actions?

Jurisprudential concepts owe much to ethics, but within a legal system these concepts become codified and less amenable to change than ethics. For example, criminal law does in fact take into account moral motives of agents, the *mens rea* (the guilty mind), that is, the intention to carry out the criminal act. Bentham in particular, through intentionality and consciousness, contributed to the exposition of *mens rea* as a constituent of criminal responsibility. The 'rule of law' or the fear of law may stop murder, but within all ethical theories it is insufficient for a truly ethical society to exist.

Kant did not see rules as the only defining aspect of ethics. Roger J. Sullivan, in *An Introduction to Kant's Ethics,* states:

---

[11] Hart, 'Bentham's Principle of Utility and Theory of Penal Law', p. xciv. The 'rule-utilitarian' approach of Bentham has been criticised by 'act-utilitarians' for its mechanistic approach to ethics. See also Matti Häyry, *Liberal Utilitarianism and Applied Ethics*, Routledge, London, New York, 1994, p. 44.

[12] Joshua Getzler, 'Patterns of Fusion' in *The Classification of Obligations,* ed. Peter Birks, Clarendon Press, Oxford, 1997, p. 177.

[13] Ibid., pp. 180-181. Getzler also lists some of the literature on this theme on p. 181, footnote 110.

[14] Eighteenth century European philosophy was centrally concerned with what kind of warrant is appropriate for moral rules. MacIntyre, *A Short History of Ethics,* p. 148.

> The appreciation to which Kant refers comes down to an attitude that should lie behind and encompass all our more specific duties. *Rules cannot totally define our lives.* In government and business, for example, an unjust person will always be able to find loopholes in even the most carefully stated professional or civil codes. Kant knew this, and for that reason he held that above all we need an underlying commitment to the moral law that will, as it were, fill in the legislative loopholes.[15]

Kant believed that certain acts such as lying had to be wrong because if everyone lied there would be no way of knowing the truth. Thus truth telling is a universal duty. The need for assumed trust and truth is essential for social groups to survive. To make life within a community of benefit to everyone, a shared understanding of what is good or bad or unjust or just is required.[16]

Kant's doctrine of law concerns 'duties of outer freedom', or 'juridical obligations'; that is, the legal system can coerce obeying the laws, but it cannot enforce reasons for obeying it; moral motivation cannot be legislated. Thus even those who do not have a moral character will have to obey the law.[17] 'Inner duties' cannot be coerced. They arise from an ethical society, a community that affirms each other's worth.[18] He contrasts the terms moral (juridical duties) and ethical (non-juridical duties); but he also uses the term moral to include both juridical and ethical duties. The notion of duty or obligation does not exclude the moral intention or good will of the moral agent. Rights derive from corresponding duties that the state enforces. Kant uses 'right' in its legal sense to mean a legally enforceable claim against others. The advantage to Kantianism is that duties coupled with rights bond human relationships. Kantianism on the surface fits best with legal positivism because of its emphasis on duties, actions and the centrality of law operating universally.

---

[15] Roger J. Sullivan, *An Introduction to Kant's Ethics,* Cambridge University Press, New York, 1994, p. 95. [Emphasis added.]

[16] Fernando Leal, 'Ethics is Fragile Goodness is Not', in *Information Society: New Media, Ethics, and Postmodernism*, ed. Karamjit S. Gill, Springer, London, New York, c1996, pp. 78-89.

[17] Sullivan, *An Introduction to Kant's Ethics*, p. 24.

[18] The duty to develop one's own moral character first is the linchpin of the Kantian system of duties. 'For I can recognize that I am under obligation to others only in so far as I, at the same time, obligate myself'. Sullivan, *An Introduction to Kant's Ethics,* p. 416, quoting from *The Doctrines of Virtues*, trans. Mary J. Gregor, Philadelphia, Pennsylvania Press, 1964.

Utilitarians regard individual rights and entitlements as subservient to general welfare.[19] However, in Peter Singer's cooperative model which is a form of utilitarianism, individual social relationships in communities of interest are taken account of within a societal collectivity.[20] Rights, rather than duties, are emphasised in contractarian rights-based theory. As a theory on its own it is inadequate for social relationships without the correlative duties imposed by another's rights.[21]

An obligation dictates what has to be done, and may leave no place for ethical considerations which depend on character. From a number of ethical standpoints, an obligation to do something, as a positive claim, must allow the moral agent a choice.[22] One strand of virtue ethics is 'role-relative, the possession and exercise of which tends to enable a person to achieve those goods, which are internal to practices'.[23] Ethical duties in relation to various 'roles', for example a doctor, teacher, judge, politician, or parent, and the duties emanating from these roles, are made manifest in social relationships. The obligations and rights between parties are based on mutual respect and trust rather than as a result of the pressures of legal sanctions, a theory which draws heavily on 'the ethical demand' or in

---

[19] Louden, 'Kant's Virtue Ethics', p. 287. Classical utilitarians are concerned with maximising the social benefits for the whole community. See Häyry, *Liberal Utilitarianism and Applied Ethics*, pp. 135-138. The rights-based liberal view of utilitarianism provides a balance between individual needs and that of the needs of others.

[20] The minimisation of pain or harm and the maximisation of happiness for the majority take into account the suffering of an individual, for example a disabled child is best left to die than allowed to grow up and suffer. A duty view would place the absolute sanctity of the individual life above that of considering the consequences of pain from disablement. Preferential utilitarianism considers the consequences from satisfying as many preferences as possible for an individual. Peter Singer, Radio Interview, Margaret Throsby, ABC Classic FM, 10 AM, 22 August 2001.

[21] John Charvet, *The Idea of an Ethical Community*, Cornell University Press, Ithaca New York, London, 1995, pp. 193-197.

[22] The lack of freedom to choose opens up issues of determinism. See Bernard Williams, 'Morality, the Peculiar Institution', in *Virtue Ethics,* eds Roger Crisp and Michael Slote, Oxford University Press, Oxford, New York, 1997, p. 46.

[23] Daniel Statman, 'Introduction', in *Virtue Ethics, A Critical Reader,* ed. Daniel Statman, Georgetown University Press, Washington, D.C., 1997, p.15, quoting from Alasdair MacIntyre, *After Virtue*, 2nd edn, London, Duckworth, 1985, p. 191. This is further explored in Chapter 6 in relation to professional ethics.

some ethical theories 'the ethical command'.[24] The notion of 'duty' has long been associated with the notion of the duties of office, but has been generalised into a notion of what a person *ought* to do in personal ethical situations.[25] It is also the association made with the official in public office, and the trustworthiness of records emanating from office as a public duty.

The issue of rules of any kind is problematic in many ethical systems. Knud Logstrup, within the ethical demand theory, finds a place for law, morality and convention. Law imposes limits on the ability of one person to take advantage of another person, but there are no clear boundaries.[26] On the other hand, in virtue ethics the character of the individual person provides the warrant for following or not following rules.[27] The focus on character traits means voluntariness becomes less important, and this is problematic in law, in which intention is relevant to responsibility.[28]

Liberty, rights and property are central in ethical and legal theories. Natural law theorists define these in terms of the law of reason and natural justice, while utilitarians like Bentham dismiss these terms completely, and replace them with utility, human psychology and a theory of action. From the liberal utilitarian view the law has a very limited role in enhancing moral behaviour.[29]

The legal and ethical aspects of actions are not easy to disentangle, and will in fact often overlap. However, law and ethics need not be in opposition; they can and should complement each other as a system of control over human behaviour. Ethics, unlike law, is also about choice of behaviour. One can choose to ignore ethics; one cannot ignore the law because of penalties for not obeying it. The attempt to balance rules and

---

[24] See the influence of Levinas's ethical command on Logstrup's thought in Knud Ejler Logstrup, *The Ethical Demand*, University of Notre Dame Press, Notre Dame and London, 1997, Chapter 2.

[25] MacIntyre, *A Short History of Ethics*, p. 236. In Aristotelian ethics, the notion of 'good' is tied to the function one has in society, and how well one performs one's role. Duty is linked to specific roles individuals play in society which when divorced from desire become a mere duty. MacIntyre demonstrates how in the eighteenth century the concept of duty as moral goodness became associated with the concept of vocation. He argues that when duty is detached from office, the concept of duty becomes inappropriate for personal use.

[26] Logstrup, *The Ethical Demand*, p. 54.

[27] Harold Alderman, 'By Virtue of a Virtue', in *Virtue Ethics, A Critical Reader,* ed. Daniel Statman, Georgetown University Press, Washington, D.C., 1997, pp. 145-164.

[28] Statman, 'Introduction', in *Virtue Ethics, A Critical Reader,* p. 14.

[29] Häyry, *Liberal Utilitarianism and Applied Ethics*, pp. 165-166.

what is 'right' is found in applied ethics, in particular the codification of ethical standards.

Law and ethics are therefore essential to the central purpose of recordkeeping as evidence of actions between human beings, the circumstances and intentions surrounding those actions, the rights, duties and identities of the participants.

1.2 Recordkeeping regulatory models

1.2.1 The warrant and juridical models

The 'warrant' and 'juridical' models have been the major models that link regulatory controls with recordkeeping concepts. Luciana Duranti has defined the juridical model[30] in terms of both ethical and legal rules, in which a legal system consists of rules, laws or practices a given society's institutions sanctions and enforces. It includes rules and codes which may not always be strictly part of positive law.[31] Juridical systems as defined by Duranti emphasise the pervasiveness of the legal system:

> Because a legal system includes all the rules that are perceived as binding at any time and/or place, no aspect of human life and affairs remains outside a legal system.[32]

A number of the ethical theories support the juridical view. These include communitarianism which views virtues as drawn from the internal practices of the community and contractarianism in which the authority for moral norms derives from reciprocal cooperation and mutual respect of community members.[33] Rule-based theories such Kant's moral (juridical)

---

[30] 'Juridical' is a term widely used in civil law systems to describe a legal system in which rules bind social groups and regulate the legal facts dealing with social and legal relationships. Luciana Duranti says: 'Juridical thinking is not universal other than as philosophy of the law. Jurisprudence, being the study of a specific juridical thinking, is necessarily conditioned by time and space'. Luciana Duranti, 'Medieval Universities and Archives', *Archivaria*, vol. 38, Fall 1994, p. 40. The term 'juridical system' and many associated concepts are found in diplomatics.

[31] Luciana Duranti, *Diplomatics: New Uses for an Old Science*, The Society of American Archivists and Association of Canadian Archivists in Association with The Scarecrow Press, Maryland and London, 1998, p. 61.

[32] Ibid.

[33] Charvet, *The Idea of an Ethical Community*, p. 171.

duties and ethical (non-juridical) duties, grapple with the many forms of social governance that are incorporated within the juridical system.

Although the juridical system is based on a particular European theory of law, it can be used as a conceptual model for understanding the socio-legal context of recordkeeping; a means of exploring legal issues and their relationship with records; an implementation model which can be applied to regulating an industry; a particular theory of law that includes all the rules which are recognised as binding within a given socio-legal system; a framework for the relationship of law and recordkeeping in societies that have oral laws and oral recordkeeping; and a role for ethics and self-regulation 'rediscovered' in modern business practices.[34] It is a model that has claimed to provide universal principles that cut across all juridical systems. The juridical model builds on the concept that all legal systems exist to enforce and protect the rights and obligations of individuals and groups in the system, and that records participate in actions that are recognised as binding within that system.

The University of Pittsburgh's Electronic Evidence Research Project has provided an alternative means of establishing the legal and social mandates for recordkeeping that are supported by 'warrants',[35] such as professional regulations, standards and best practices for ascertaining the functional requirements for recordkeeping. The Pittsburgh team believed that the functional requirements they had proposed for recordkeeping would not, on their own, carry weight, but that organisations or individuals would comply with them if their 'authority' derived from their own best

---

[34] Livia Iacovino, *'Things in Action': Teaching Law to Recordkeeping Professionals*, Ancora Press, Monash University, Melbourne, 1998, Chapter 4 and p. 136, Figure 4.

[35] 'Warrant' is a term borrowed from librarianship, which refers to a means of classifying a subject area from the literature of that subject area. 'Literary warrant' is E. Wyndham Hulme's theory of library classification which propounds the idea that classification systems should utilise the literature of a subject for forming the basis of a class. 'Social' and 'legal' warrants are sub-categories of the literary warrant. Wendy Duff, 'The Influence of Literary Warrant on the Acceptance and Credibility of the Functional Requirements for Recordkeeping: A Dissertation Proposal' (unpublished draft), University of Pittsburgh, 1995, p. 11. Wendy Duff's research tested the effect of statements of 'literary warrant', that is statements from laws, regulations, standards established by one's own profession or industry, on lawyers, auditors and information specialists' evaluations of a set of functional requirements for electronic evidence. See Wendy Duff, 'Increasing the Acceptance of Functional Requirements for Electronic Evidence', *Archives and Museum Informatics*, vol. 10, no. 4, 1996, pp. 326-351.

practices.[36] As David Bearman, the leading researcher of the Pittsburgh team, explains, 'if professionals in our society were made more aware of the functional requirements for recordkeeping as expressed in recommended practices of their own profession (which are themselves grounded in law), they would be more inclined to take responsibility for the adequacy of their recordkeeping practices.'[37]

The warrant-based recordkeeping model recognises that recordkeeping requirements may vary from country to country, industry to industry, and discipline to discipline. The model is a relativist notion of the need to create and maintain records. The sources included for recordkeeping mandates range from literary works to professional codes of practice, which appear on the surface to claim a greater ambit than juridical sources.[38] However, during the course of the Pittsburgh Project, it narrowed the literary warrant to businesses and professions excluding warrants for personal recordkeeping, in practice aligning it more closely with the mandates used in a juridical system.[39] The warrant model emphasises the importance of recordkeeping habits amongst 'communities', an essential aspect of trustworthy records, which in the communitarian variant of virtue ethics is described as 'those goods which are internal to practices'.[40]

1.2.2 Comparative aspects: the juridical and warrant models as implementation models

Apart from the use of different terminology, the juridical and the warrant-based approaches are not in conflict and can in fact be complementary. As the juridical approach is grounded in legal principles which include not

---

[36] David Bearman et al., in 'The Warrant for Recordkeeping Requirements', in *University of Pittsburgh, Recordkeeping Functional Requirements Project: Reports and Working Papers, LIS055/LS9400*, School of Library and Information Science, University of Pittsburgh, Pittsburgh, 1994 expressed the Pittsburgh team's initial findings which justified the need for 'warrants'.

[37] Ibid., p. 1.

[38] Richard Cox and Wendy Duff, 'Warrant and the Definition of Electronic Records: Questions Arising from the Pittsburgh Project', *Archives and Museums Informatics,* vol. 11, 1997, pp. 222-234.

[39] Further research significantly found that the legal warrant was the most influential, and the information technology warrant was the least important. Wendy Duff, 'Harnessing the Power of Warrant', *The American Archivist*, vol. 61, Spring 1998, p. 98.

[40] Alasdair MacIntyre, *After Virtue*, 2nd edn, London, Duckworth, 1985, quoted in Daniel Statman, 'Introduction', in *Virtue Ethics, A Critical Reader,* p. 15.

only codified law but also other rules and codes that a given group has sanctioned, it theoretically does not exclude the wider social and moral mandates for recordkeeping which the warrant-based approach is predicated upon.

Diplomatics, including the notion of juridical systems, uses terms that have been codified over centuries. The terminology it adopts is analogous with many legal terms, due to its teaching in law schools. The sources for the recordkeeping mandates are largely, but not exclusively, from legal sources, that is statutes and codes. The diplomatics approach is particularly suited to verifying who is legally responsible for an action, whether the records have emanated from a competent authority, who created and who owns the records, the 'form' of the record prescribed by the legal system and whether the records are part of the normal course of business. In particular, diplomatics provides rigorous rules for analysing the responsibilities of parties involved in the action recorded.

It could be argued that the differences in the two approaches derive from the type of legal system in which they developed, that is the juridical approach derives from precepts in Roman law and is therefore suited to civil law systems and cannot be applied to countries which have common law systems. As has been argued above, the juridical system is a conceptual construct. It is not based on a specific legal system. The role of recordkeeping in underpinning legal relationships is recognised as much in the common law as in civil law systems.[41] Therefore, differences in legal system types is not central to either the warrant or juridical-diplomatics models.

The warrants referenced by the Pittsburgh Project and the principles of archival science and diplomatics are the basis for equally valid implementation models for establishing recordkeeping regulatory requirements.

1.3 Implementing regulatory models for recordkeeping regimes in specific organisational contexts

Recordkeeping regimes, which take into account the attributes of a juridical system and its regulatory sources, provide a framework for identifying legal and ethical recordkeeping requirements in specific organisational contexts. Two recordkeeping regulatory models - juridical and warrant - can be applied within a records continuum view of

---

[41] See Chapter 3.

regulation, that is one in which the legal ramifications of recordkeeping are multi-dimensional.[42]

1.3.1 Regulatory environment

Recordkeeping is regulated in different organisational contexts by a range of sources, from laws, customs, standards, ethics, and best practices of professions. 'The big picture' at a global level should also be considered, particularly if the organisation transacts internationally. These sources provide the context for understanding the function and purpose for requiring records to be created and maintained within the needs of the organisation and related professions themselves.[43] For example, the regulatory environment in a common law system can be established from positive law and its authoritative sources: statute (legislation) and case law (common law); professional, personal and corporate ethics; and industry codes of conduct and practice as sources of regulatory control that may prescribe recordkeeping requirements explicitly or implicitly, but more importantly controls that are sustained by records as proof of action.

Records are in fact the products of the regulatory environment. All organisations operating within a socio-legal system will have legal requirements and obligations with which they must comply. An organisation or person may be established and given powers in legislation to carry out duties and in turn enabling legislation may place duties on them which will impinge on recordkeeping. The notion of the 'regulatory environment' as part of the recordkeeping regime is included in the international records

[42] Frank Upward explains the basis of the recordkeeping-based activity model represented by four axes and four dimensions in, 'The Records Continuum', in *Archives: Recordkeeping in Society,* eds Sue McKemmish, Michael Piggott, Barbara Reed and Frank Upward, Centre for Information Studies, Charles Sturt University, Wagga Wagga, NSW, 2005, pp. 197-222. Livia Iacovino, 'Recordkeeping and Juridical Governance', in *Archives: Recordkeeping in Society,* eds Sue McKemmish, Michael Piggott, Barbara Reed and Frank Upward, Centre for Information Studies, Charles Sturt University, Wagga Wagga, NSW, 2005, pp. 262-266 provides a juridical analysis of Upward's model.

[43] Livia Iacovino, 'The Nature of the Nexus Between Recordkeeping and the Law', *Archives and Manuscripts*, vol. 26, no. 2, Nov. 1998, pp. 232-236 and Iacovino, *'Things in Action'*, Chapter 5 provide a range of legal principles that are relevant to recordkeeping in the Australian context.

management standard.[44] The standard proposes a jurisdictionally-based analysis of legal and ethical requirements specific to the business processes of an organisation. Its conceptual basis is the warrant-based model.

1.3.2 Categorising and identifying regulatory sources

Identifying the regulatory controls for recordkeeping involves locating relevant legislation, legal considerations and codes in relation to each function and activity of the organisation and complying with them by capturing and maintaining records for an appropriate time span. Most substantive law (law which regulates rights, duties and liabilities among citizens and government), and procedural law, may obligate recordkeeping in a range of human endeavours.

There are a number of ways of classifying regulatory controls for recordkeeping requirements of organisations in a specific context. One way of identifying and classifying legal requirements is to follow the international records management standard, *ISO 15489-2: Information and Documentation - Records Management*.[45] The categorisation used here breaks down the ISO categories differently. The divisions are not mutually exclusive; it is simply a convenient way of thinking through the legislation and relevant codes for different industry contexts.

Regulatory law for recordkeeping can broadly be categorised as that which relates to:

- recordkeeping standards found in records/archival and other legislation (for example Freedom of Information and privacy), supported by procedural laws, particularly the laws of evidence;
- universal legislation affecting all organisations or organisation types (for example tax laws), some of which may have mandatory recordkeeping requirements with penalties, or may be required by implication, that is as proof of an undertaking;
- entity-specific statutes which establish a specific body (for example a statutory authority or a public body which is generally subject to the administrative law) or a particular type of organisation or entity (for example a company or incorporated association) which may also stipulate the creation of specific records peculiar to that legal form of

[44] See *ISO 15489-1, Information and Documentation - Records Management*, ISO, 2001, Part 1, General, 5 Regulatory environment and 6 Policy and responsibilities, 6.1 General.

[45] Ibid.

organisation or imply a need to create records to support accountability to that legislation;

- industry or profession-specific legislation (for example medical and legal practice legislation) which may prescribe records or require them by implication;
- legislation of regulatory organisations which may have recordkeeping provisions;
- common law considerations which affect particular industries should also be taken into account; and
- relevant codes of ethics for a particular industry as well as general codes (for example records management standards, industry codes and technical standards).

Identifying the specific regulatory requirements in relation to each business function and activity is recordkeeping best practice.[46]

1.3.3 Records retention

The nature of a business activity will activate the need to create records to operate a business. The records continuum view considers the role of the record beyond its purely business use to include its value in the collective memory. Do legal requirements help us decide which records to keep?

Recordkeeping is a contingent activity. The social and organisational functions of records need to be analysed before a business can decide what to document and how long to keep it, and why. That is:

- Is there a business need for a record of particular actions?
- What is the calculated risk of not creating the record?
- Once it is in the recordkeeping system should it be disposed of having regard to appropriate laws or procedures?
- Does the business need to prove how it made a particular decision?
- How does the business identify statutes and regulations that do not prescribe records but that require evidence to be enforceable?

Corporations, for example, are subject to a number of evidentiary requirements, but evaluate business and legal risks on the basis of their specific activities. Product liability claims have resulted in huge

---

[46] An example of a methodology for identifying business requirements is the National Archives of Australia and the State Records Authority of New South Wales, *DIRKS (Designing and Implementing Recordkeeping Systems) Manual: A Strategic Approach to Managing Business Information*, Commonwealth of Australia, 2000.

compensation awards in the United States, Europe and Australia. Documenting all the processes in the production of the product is important to being able to pinpoint what went wrong, when, and who was responsible. A blood bank needs to keep records of donors to be able to trace batches of donated blood that might be infectious. The industry or entity context will determine how regulation is viewed and the risks associated with the decision to create or not create records.[47]

Legislation which prescribes the creation, form, retention, and data accuracy of information and records, has been included in the list of categories that identify regulatory sources (see 1.3.2 above 'Categorising and identifying regulatory sources'). Some of this legislation is universal to all organisations (for example taxation laws) or it may be included in laws that also set standards for recordkeeping and information (for example archival legislation); some legislation is specific to the legal entity type (for example corporations law), and some is industry-specific. There may be penalties if they are not complied with. Thus the law has both a direct and an indirect influence on the type of records captured and maintained.

Increasingly many records management practitioners are coming to the view that recordkeeping legal requirements are not based on simple legal prescription but depend on linking particular activities and processes to a number of legal requirements. The need for records as evidence derives from their creation in the context of a transaction or process and their retention as evidence of that transaction and process.

In law one makes a prediction as to a likely legal outcome in a particular set of circumstances. A legal strategy for recordkeeping has to consider a course of action which will suit a number of circumstances. In addition, there are other binding rules within specific organisational contexts that affect recordkeeping that a strictly black letter law approach would exclude. Before a regulatory regime for recordkeeping at an organisational level can be put into place, the political, social, legal and technological

[47] Risk management is important to recordkeeping compliance. In the 1990s David Bearman argued that records management should be presented in risk management terms. David Bearman, 'Archival Data Management to Achieve Organisational Accountability for Electronic Records', *Archives and Manuscripts,* vol. 21, no.1, 1993, pp. 14-28. In Australia, the application of risk management to appraisal and disposal of records has been questioned by the archival community. In the 'Heiner affair', which involved the destruction of records of potential use in legal proceedings, risk management emerged as an unsatisfactory appraisal tool. Chris Hurley, 'The Shredding of the "Heiner" Documents: An Appreciation', RIMOS, 1997.

environment in which the organisation operates, must be researched and captured as recordkeeping metadata.

The implications of the ethics-law nexus to implementing regulatory models includes both ethical frameworks as well as legal compliance provided by the juridical and warrant regulatory models. Legal obligations are only one set of reasons why we make and keep records. There are other obligations on recordkeeping participants which are revealed by focusing on the relationships that arise through the transactional nature of recordkeeping processes themselves. In fact, the law-recordkeeping nexus is not so much about what laws regulate or control recordkeeping but rather how records support legal and social relationships.

2 IDENTITY, TRUST, EVIDENCE AND THE RECORDKEEPING NEXUS

Records as evidence of human actions are a central point of interconnection between recordkeeping, ethics and law. Records involve a number of participants or actors, who may be parties to a transaction, or agents representing another party, with a number of roles. The legal system recognises organisations as legal persons, and over time the principle of their potential liability for their acts has emerged. The identity of the participants is therefore essential to how a record is defined.

In archival theory, identity has been defined by the corporate entity, organisation, legal or natural person that created the records. Person identity is of particular significance in trust relationships and is one element of the requirement for record authenticity. The nature of person identity is also tied to community identity which may be ethnic or religious, as well as professional, familial, or service related. Understanding how communities bond together has become important in a global environment, in which the relationship between sovereign states is being replaced by relationships between individuals, social groups or businesses. The nature of community as a means of providing identity, a value system and trust affects the reliability and accuracy of its records.

2.1 Identity and trust in communities of common interest

2.1.1 The nature of community

The nature of community is central to jurisprudence and ethics. Communities as social groups that perpetuate identity through a common value system are the basis of both legal and ethical systems. As analysed in the previous chapter, in the juridical view a legal system emerges when a community of persons enforces the notion of obligation. An organised community is a social (juridical) system that maintains its own identity and rules, but may also exist within a dominant culture. The community consists of organised groups that have the power to enact and interpret law, as well as to impose sanctions when the law is broken. These groups also need collective memory to ensure their survival.

Community, in one form or another, is fundamental to an individual's reference point for ethical practice. In Aristotelian ethics, community was associated with the state. The moral philosopher, Alasdair MacIntyre, argues that Christianity broke the nexus between state and community. In the eighteenth century, Hegel defined communities as 'collections of individuals'. These individuals had their own passions and ends that depended on the social structure in which they found themselves.[1]

From a philosophical point of view, community has its own focus in utilitarianism and its variants of communitarianism and contractarianism, but individual action or intentions rather than community remain more relevant in deontological theories. The communitarian version of virtue ethics is dependent on what is 'right' within a community, which is then transposed to all human practices.[2] This supports the interpretation of the 'warrant' as the identification of recordkeeping requirements for communities of practice, while diplomatics universalises from practice what the nature of records is all about.

Community is defined by the contractarian John Charvet as the sharing by a collection of persons of authoritative norms governing their social cooperation as a matter of reasoned choice under ideal conditions. The norms have been disembedded from a specific society, and have taken on a universal character.[3] Each individual has a set of equal individual rights built into the community structure. Although Kant is concerned with individual action, his moral philosophy does include a conceptual structure for a community life that can be shared by everyone. The universal duty is the collective good.[4]

Community as sharing, that is the 'other-regarding' nature of humans, is also fundamental to utilitarian ethics, and central to the moral dimension of a social relationship. Jeremy Bentham's community is 'the sum of the

---

[1] Alasdair MacIntyre, *A Short History of Ethics: A History of Moral Philosophy from the Homeric Age to the Twentieth Century*, 2nd edn, University of Notre Dame Press, Notre Dame, Indiana, 1998, p. 199.

[2] Ibid., pp. xviii-xix and p. 148. MacIntyre uses the term 'good' functionally; certain things or people are good, that is they are well fitted for certain roles or functions.

[3] John Charvet, *The Idea of an Ethical Community*, Cornell University Press, Ithaca, New York and London, 1995, p. 193.

[4] Roger J. Sullivan, *An Introduction to Kant's Ethics*, Cambridge University Press, New York, 1994, Chapter 5. 'Every rational being must act as if by his maxims he were at all times a legislative member of the universal kingdom of ends', p. 84. For Kant everyone obeys fundamental laws not group interests.

members who composed it,' rather than individuals. Even in the most self-interested business relationships, a common good is beneficial to all parties concerned. Some business ethicists define community as the corporation, but one that operates for the social good as well.[5]

On the other hand, Peter Singer proposes a cooperative community as a means of encouraging the best of human evolved behaviour, based on a range of social practices enforced by a system of rewards and punishments from peer esteem to government policies.[6] The community has its own system of rewards based on punishing what causes harm and rewarding what benefits. However, group standards of what is good or bad behaviour can also be used for evil purposes, and is a flaw in the utilitarian conception of community.[7]

Thus communities operate to support their own interests, but must also recognise the need for universal moral principles. Recordkeeping practice has needs that are specific to a community of interest, but through experience has arrived at general principles, which are reflected, for example, in records standards and professional codes of practice.

2.1.2 Community, identity and value systems

Community is not only defined through common standards but also through the exclusion of others.[8] Dominant groups use their standards to exclude others. Specific communities or groups provide what is termed a 'logic of identity' linked to 'otherness', as opposed to 'togetherness'.[9] For Iris Marion Young, 'a social group exists and is defined as a specific group only in social and interactive relation to others'.[10] In this approach it is not

---

[5] Robert C. Solomon, 'Corporate Roles, Personal Virtues: An Aristotelian Approach to Business Ethics', in *Virtue Ethics*, A Critical Reader, ed. Daniel Statman, Georgetown University Press, Washington, D.C., 1997, pp. 205-226.

[6] Peter Singer, *A Darwinian Left, Politics, Evolution and Cooperation*, Weidenfield and Nicolson, London, 1999.

[7] See Logstrup's ethical demand in Knud Ejler Logstrup, *The Ethical Demand*, University of Notre Dame Press, Notre Dame and London, 1997.

[8] David Harvey, 'Class Relations, Social Justice and the Politics of Difference', in *Principled Positions: Postmodernism and the Rediscovery of Value*, ed. Judith Squires, Lawrence and Wishart, London, 1993, pp. 85-121.

[9] Iris Marion Young, 'Together in Difference: Transforming the Logic of Group Political Conflict', in *Principled Positions: Postmodernism and the Rediscovery of Value*, ed. Judith Squires, Lawrence and Wishart, London, 1993, p. 124.

[10] Ibid, p. 130.

the group as otherness, but as specificity and variation. In 'togetherness in difference' a group must see itself in the wider society. Community is seen as inclusive of many communities.

'Humanity' in the sense of the unity of the species as a community, to which modernity has given a special meaning, is challenged by 'universal human values' which continue to respect diversity. 'Radical pluralism' is suggested as an alternative, which allows one to choose different identities, but includes a cluster of values to guarantee moral pluralism.

Francis Fukuyama's community is cultural, formed not on the basis of explicit rules and regulations, but a set of ethical habits and reciprocal moral obligations internalised by each of the community's members. Rules and habits give members of the community grounds for trusting one another.[11] The relevance of community is also found in sociological theory and in particular in Anthony Giddens' structuration theory, where it is essential to memory traces, which include records.[12]

In archival theory, the nineteenth century concept of state had a powerful influence on how recordkeeping context was interpreted, and how records were described and organised.[13] It was an all-embracing concept for those citizens who had attained political and legal rights. Community was used more in a moral sense, and the term society had a restricted meaning that only included those with power. Society has become an inclusive term, encompassing all humanity, and the state the legal representation of specific societies. So although the term global community as inclusive society is widely used, community can also be a group with the same values, rather than as a legal jurisdiction or society as a whole. Communities of interest operate within a larger community, which is society. Community cannot be divorced from the social and political context of its time and place.

The term community is important to a value system, to group identity, to legal and ethical responsibilities and the regulation of recordkeeping participants identified by community affiliation.

---

[11] Francis Fukuyama, *Trust: the Social Virtues and the Creation of Prosperity*, Penguin Group, London, 1995, p. 21.

[12] Frank Upward, 'Structuring the Records Continuum, Part Two: Structuration Theory and Recordkeeping' *Archives and Manuscripts*, vol. 25, no. 1, May 1997, pp. 10-35.

[13] Livia Iacovino, *'Things in Action': Teaching Law to Recordkeeping Professionals*, Ancora Press, Monash University, Melbourne, 1998, Chapter 2.

2.1.3 Communities of common interest

Communities of common interest can be defined as organised interest groups, professional groupings, occupations and industries, as well as families and like-minded individuals, rather than as social or political classes. Their driving force is their collective self-interest. The notion that every activity is a business or an industry (including humanitarian work), is a competing notion with that of community, that retains a sense of civic virtue, found in Aristotelian ethics and echoed in professional ethics.

The concept of communities of common interest has potential relevance to a global environment as communities cut across national and legal jurisdictional boundaries. They have their own methods for enforcing behaviour. Communities of interest do not exclude universal values that should be adhered to in addition to their specific values.

2.1.4 Communities as boundaries

Within the juridical view a boundary is clearly defined by the rules sanctioned by the community. In the warrant approach, boundaries are also defined by way of organisational or professional groupings.

Geographic boundaries are both cultural and political.[14] In law, the notion of a legal boundary as 'jurisdiction' is central to the application and enforcement of laws. In the online environment, the apparent dissolution of boundaries and the increase in communities communicating across boundaries has become part of the Internet culture. Boundaries and the lack thereof are also used as metaphors, in particular in 'cyberspace'. The 'borderless' cyberspace is often construed to mean that legal and social rules no longer apply. The issue is really the difficulty of detection of illegal activity and the enforcement of laws when detection occurs.[15]

2.1.5 Trust and communities of common interest

Trust in its ordinary meaning is 'confidence in or reliance on some quality or attribute of a person or thing, or the truth of a statement'.[16] If the search for truth is an element of trust, in a postmodern sense it must consist of many truths. In the legal context the search for truth is also, at least for

---

14 'Culture' has its linguistic roots in land, as the notion of 'to cultivate'.

15 See Chapter 7.

16 *Oxford English Dictionary*, Oxford University Press, New York, 1971, vol. 2, 'trust'.

civil cases, based on the concept of probability, not on absolute truth. In the Benthamite interpretation of common law, trust is tied to power and imposed legislatively.[17] Jeremy Bentham has defined trust in a legal sense as an act which one party in the exercise of some power or some right which is conferred on him, is bound to perform for the benefit of another. Trust is therefore always directed to someone else, rather than for oneself, whether considered from the ethical or legal standpoint.[18] Powerful institutions have used alleged 'truth' from documents to legitimise their power.[19] The misuse of documentary evidence necessitates caution as to its objectivity.

Francis Fukuyama argues that trust is a social virtue dependent on bounded contexts. There are variations found in societies and communities. Trust is built over time. A social and political scientist, Fukuyama looks at how the economy of a country operates in what he terms high trust and low trust societies. Economic activity is considered a part of social life, and can only be understood in its social context, that is as part of the human need for 'recognition' which is beyond material needs.[20]

> Thus, economic activity represents a crucial part of social life and is knit together by a wide variety of norms, rules, moral obligations, and other habits that together shape the society... a nation's well being, as well as its ability to compete, is conditioned by a single, pervasive cultural characteristic: the level of trust inherent in the society.[21]

Trust is a social virtue dependent on the norms of communities of common interest, such as familial, professional, business, or recreational communities. The assumption that underlies his hypothesis of trust within a community is that of shared moral beliefs. Thus if we adopt Fukuyama's

[17] Jeremy Bentham, *An Introduction to the Principles of Morals and Legislation, An Authoritative Edition by J.H. Burns and H.L.A. Hart; with a New Introduction by F. Rosen, and an Interpretive Essay by H.L.A. Hart*, Clarendon Press, Oxford, 1996, p. 205.

[18] Ibid., p. 205, footnote e2 'on powers and rights to power but not conversely'.

[19] Heather MacNeil, *Trusting Records: Legal, Historical and Diplomatic Perspectives*, Kluwer, Dordrecht, 2000, pp. 11-12 summarises Lorenzo Valla's exposure as a forgery the papal claim to temporal power in the document known as the 'Donation of Constantine'.

[20] Fukuyama, *Trust: the Social Virtues and the Creation of Prosperity*, section 5, and in particular, pp. 335-336. Fukuyama makes it clear that there are many factors that affect industrial structure besides culture, but that the importance of culture is often underestimated by economists.

[21] Ibid., p. 7.

definition of trust then the concept of community must imply trust amongst its members.

> Trust is the expectation that arises within a community of regular, honest, and cooperative behavior, based on commonly shared norms, on the part of other members of that community. Those norms can be about deep 'value' questions like the nature of God or justice, but they also encompass secular norms like professional standards and codes of behavior. That is, we trust a doctor not to do us deliberate injury because we expect him or her to live by the Hippocratic oath and the standards of the medical profession.[22]

Trust is also 'social capital' that enhances the economy.[23] It is the community that dictates the level of trust and economic wellbeing. Social capital, the 'crucible of trust', rests on cultural roots. Culture and social structure are used synonymously. Culture is an 'inherited ethical habit'.[24] An ethical habit can be an idea or a value, or it can consist of an actual social relationship, for example, family, friend or neighbourhood. Culture can change, albeit slowly.

Fukuyama proposes a close relationship between trust and informal rules. 'Spontaneous sociability', that is the ability to engender trust, is a subset of social capital. Social capital minimises our dependence on law.[25] Those who do not trust each other cooperate under a system of formal rules, which are negotiated, litigated, and enforced. It is a substitute for trust. He admits that contemporary society is a contractual one (as recognised by Max Weber) which uses laws to replace trust. [26] The private law of contract increases the cost of legal transactions but claims are guaranteed by legal coercion. Rules of contract do away with the need for trust in modern business. The more rules dominate the less trust is required. 'There is usually an inverse relationship between rules and trust: the more people depend on rules to regulate their interactions, the less they trust each other, and vice versa.'[27] Inward obligation is replaced by external

[22] Ibid., p. 26.

[23] The examples Fukuyama provides are based on companies that did well because of the high level of trust amongst workers.

[24] Ibid., p. 34.

[25] Ibid., p. 335.

[26] Ibid., p. 222. Fukuyama uses Max Weber's thesis on rules and laws which involves the tripartite division of authority: traditional (inherited from longstanding cultural sources); charismatic (for example a leader chosen by God) and bureaucratic (ordered rationality, fixed rule and laws). For Weber rights and duties are rule-bound. Contract can be a 'status contract' based on tradition or a 'purposive contract' for the sake of a specific economic exchange.

[27] Ibid., p. 224.

law. From a liberal capitalist view, Fukuyama argues for less government intervention on the basis that communities can be successful on their own. He supports the view of human behaviour as basically 'social' rather than 'legal' in the coercive sense.

Adrian McCulagh's definition of trust has four elements, which include Fukuyama's behavioural trust. They can also be located in recordkeeping theory. They are:

Trusted organisations, for example public authorities and banks in which transactions are with known organisations. This is an archival principle found in Roman and common law. The public authority provides the trustworthiness (see 2.3 below, 'Rules of evidence and trustworthy records').

Trusted technology involves trusting the outcome created by a process on the basis of existing classification schemes for security and trust. Security is important to the generation of the key pair for digital signatures, signing mechanisms, and identity. Signatures, their function and validation are central to diplomatics and law.

Behavioural trust is important in understanding the ambit and use of legislation in low trust or high trust societies. In the Internet context when low trust societies deal with high trust societies, which measure of trust can be used? Levels of trust are found in the juridical environment and are central to the regulatory context of recordkeeping (see Chapter 1).

Legal trust relates to digital signature and other framework legislation, which should sufficiently cover trust.[28] The legal framework may be insufficient to engender trust (see 2.2.3 below 'Electronic documents and trustworthy records').

Trust is also a 'saleable commodity', that is of economic value because it is essential to consumer confidence in electronic commerce.[29] Confidence in the truthfulness of a record is also an essential characteristic of a trustworthy record.

The social, economic, legal and technological elements of trust all contribute to trustworthy records.

---

[28] Adrian McCulagh, 'Ecommerce a matter of TRUST', in *Electronic Commerce: Net Benefit for Australia?*, *The 1998 Information Industry Outlook Conference*, the Australian Computer Society, Canberra Branch, Canberra, Australia, 7 November 1998, pp. 15-29.

[29] Cedric Israelsohn, Delphi Consulting Australia, 'Where is the Technology Taking Us? Current Office Technology, Knowledge Management: the Hype and the Reality', Paper presented at *Doing Business Electronically: Electronic Commerce and Recordkeeping*, Recordkeeping Systems and the Records Continuum Research Group, School of Information Management and Systems, Monash University, Canberra, November 1999 (unpublished).

2.2 Trustworthy records: diplomatics, Italian archival science and the records continuum model

2.2.1 A trustworthy record

When a record is said to be trustworthy, it means that it is both an accurate statement of facts and a genuine manifestation of those facts. Record trustworthiness thus has two qualitative dimensions: *reliability* and *authenticity*. Reliability means that the record is capable of standing for the facts to which it attests, while authenticity means that the record is what it claims to be.[30]

Heather MacNeil focuses on two qualities of record trustworthiness - reliability and authenticity - concepts found in diplomatics and Italian archival science. The reliability of the record is associated with the degree of control exercised over its creation procedures and completeness of intellectual form. Authenticity is linked to a record's mode, status, and form of transmission, and the manner of its preservation and custody. MacNeil concedes that record trustworthiness in archival science has been built around the Weberian model of bureaucracy that relies on rules and regulations to control the actions of record creators.[31] However, social trust founded on informal rules of community, business and professional expectations, is also essential to reliable and authentic records.

Trust in a social context is concerned with faith in someone or something while identity is defined as a condition or fact that a person or thing is itself and not something else. In the records continuum model identity is multi-dimensional; it can be personal, corporate, professional, group or collective identity. In archival science, record identity refers to: who wrote the record, who received it and when.[32]

As the reliability of a record is closely linked with a person's or entity's role in record creation, identity has to be defined in relation to roles. It is possible to identify in a single physical or juridical person different roles and multiple identities. Law, conventions and societal mores may define

---

[30] MacNeil, *Trusting Records*, p. xi. MacNeil's interpretation excludes the importance of social trust embedded in communities of common interest and wider political aspects. Nevertheless, it provides one of the clearest examinations of record trustworthiness in notarial legal systems, and also its application to common law.

[31] Ibid., pp. 110-111.

[32] See InterPARES 1 Project, Authenticity Task Force, *Final Report*, 28 October 2001, University of British Columbia, Vancouver, 2001, 'Appendix: Requirements for Accessing and Maintaining the Authenticity of Electronic Records', pp. 1-15.

these roles. Legal identity is evidenced in juridical information, for example birth records or group identification in oral societies. Corporate legal identity is found in incorporation details, and company or business numbers. Personal identity is also based on the notion of roots and identity of geographic place and personal experience.[33] Identity and community are co-dependent concepts. In modern governments, tax file, healthcare, business or company and licence numbers are used to uniquely identify a physical or a juridical person in a specific context. Unique identifiers can also be used to link records within and across systems.[34]

Recordkeeping trust includes control over information about the identities in the transaction, their intentions and relationship to statements of fact, and verification of content or of a procedure by way of signature and/or seals and witnessing. Traditional recordkeeping ways of proving identity are derived from diplomatics, archival science and law, through documentary form, provenance, notarial seals, and other mechanisms of proof of identity.[35] Validation of the parties to a transaction or the authors and recipients has been dependent on control over record creation. The circumstances of creation of records were assured by bureaucracies having authority and delegation clearly assigned; that is, procedural controls on the record writers and record keepers. In addition, the authority of the document was derived from the technical form of its composition, its documentary form, including signing and dating.[36]

---

[33] Examples of identity based on geography include Italian author Claudio Magris' works on Istria and Central Europe, for example, *Danubio*, Garzanti, Italy, 1990 and *Un Altro Mare*, Garzanti, Italy, 1991, and Robertson Davies' character Connor Gilmartin who rediscovers his Welsh roots in *Murther and Walking Spirits*, Sinclair-Stevenson Ltd., London, 1991.

[34] See Chapter 8.

[35] In diplomatics, notarial validation attested to the signatures of persons who took part in the issuing of the record (author, writer, countersigned), and to the signatures of the parties and witnesses to the action, while corroboration explicitly referred to the means used to validate the record. In countries that did not use the notarial system, seals were used to validate the author and were also used as a substitute for a signature. See 'Validation/Attestation: Notarial validation of a signature is dependent on the use of a prescribed form and the professional role of the person validating the signature. The validation of a signature does not validate the content of a document to which it is affixed'. InterPARES 1 Project, Authenticity Task Force, *Template for Analysis*, 7 Nov. 2000, University of British Columbia, Vancouver, 2000.

[36] Paola Carucci, *Il Documento Contemporaneo, Diplomatica e Criteri di Edizione*, Carocci, Rome, 1998 (1987), p. 28.

'The fact that a document is signed by a notary does not mean that the statements in it are true in themselves, but they are true in law.'[37] The signing by a third party is a validation not of the truthfulness of the contents, but proof of authorship. Elements of record identity in the notarial system essential to its authenticity include dating and signing of documents. In Roman legal practice each document was written by an authorised scribe or notary and dated (sometimes even the time of day) as the exact time was considered essential to its authenticity. A copy of the document was kept by a public authority. The notary in his own hand appended his name and signum drawn with a pen. Thus signing was done by professionals and not by parties to the action. If a dispute arose the notary could be cross-examined, or if he/she was dead, reference to other documents signed by him/her could be used to verify the notary.[38] The modern equivalent to notarial practice is the trusted third party (TTP), important to authentication of authors online.

Seals have had a number of functions over the millennia,[39] but the most important one for recordkeeping has been to identify the persons and validate the action in the record. The process of sealing provided validation of the action by witnesses adding their seal, ownership/attribution of authorship of contents of documents and of property, preservation and security of the contents by sealing, evidence of place (sometimes), and identification of authorising authority. A combination of digital signatures, encryption and other secure methods of transmission have replaced the function of seals in the online world. However, the authenticity of an electronic record relies on more than just the authentication of the recordkeeping participants; it requires the preservation and continuing accessibility of the record in a form that is trustworthy.

---

[37] M.T. Clanchy, *From Memory to Written Record: England 1066-1307*, Blackwell, Cambridge, Massachusetts, 1993, p. 305.

[38] Ibid., pp. 304-308. England and Northern Europe did not adopt the Roman notarial system based on Roman legal practice which required that all documents be dated, written by an authorised notary, and a copy registered with a public authority. Why England did not adopt the notarial system, but applied other continental bureaucratic procedures is unclear.

[39] Gertrud Seidmann, 'Personal Seals in Eighteenth and Early Nineteenth Century England and their Antecedents', in *7000 Years of Seals*, ed. Dominique Collon, British Museum Press, London, 1997, p. 153. Even today in China, Korea and Japan signatures do not have the same legal status as in the West, thus the seal has continued importance in some parts of the world.

2.2.2 Documentary form and trustworthy records in diplomatics and archival science

Written records have not always inspired trust in their contents. In England until the thirteenth century, memory was often considered a superior tool to a written record for proving past events. The development of 'form', that is acceptable rules for structuring information in written documents, contributed to trusting their content, and was particularly significant in countries that adopted the notarial system.[40]

'Documentary form' is the way a message is laid out and structured in a document. Documents are recognisable in a given society as types, for example contracts, permits and receipts, which have evolved into their existing form as a result of legislative and administrative procedures and the technology available to produce them.

Form is relevant to trustworthiness and predictability. If the system in which a person lives accepts records in a particular form, one is likely to trust them; that is, by force of habit. The elements of documentary form have always been important for ensuring that the record is reliable - that its content can be trusted, and that it is authentic - that it has not been tampered with, either intentionally or accidentally.

The importance of form as proof of a legal act, found one of its most sophisticated developments in diplomatics, culminating with the work of twelfth century Italian jurists. As translated from Cesare Paoli, 'a document is a written testimony (witness) of a fact of a juridical nature compiled following specific forms, which aims to achieve faith and the force of proof'.[41] It had three elements: written testimony; the juridical nature of the act in the content of the document; and the form, which gives the document determined requisites of faith. In the common law system different legal forms have also depended on the nature of the legal action.[42]

---

[40] Clanchy, *From Memory to Written Record*, Chapter 9.

[41] 'Una testimonianza scritta di un fatto di natura giuridica, compilata coll'osservanza di determinate forme, le quali sono destinate a procurarle fede e darle forza di prova'. Carucci, *Il Documento Contemporaneo*, p. 28, quoting from Cesare Paoli, *Diplomatica*, Sansoni, Florence, 1942, p. 18. See also Paola Carucci, *Le Fonti Archivistiche: Ordinamento e Conservazione*, Carocci, Rome, 1998 (1983), p. 26.

[42] Joshua Getzler, 'Patterns of Fusion', in *The Classification of Obligations*, ed. Peter Birks, Clarendon Press, Oxford, 1997, p. 173. An example of the importance of 'form' in common law practice in late medieval England is the use of writs which were essential to distinguishing the kind of action enforced.

In diplomatics, documentary form is defined as 'the complex of rules of representation used to convey a message'.[43] In the InterPARES 1 project it has been further refined as:

> … the rules of representation according to which the content of a record, its administrative and documentary context, and its authority are communicated. Documentary form possesses both extrinsic and intrinsic elements.[44]

The extrinsic elements of documentary form are the elements of a record that determine its material make-up and its appearance. Elements of extrinsic documentary form include human language, presentation features such as text, seals, logos, and letterheads. The intrinsic elements of documentary form are the elements of a record that convey the action in which the record participates and its immediate context. Elements of intrinsic documentary form include the name of the writer and author, the recipient, date of generation, receipt, and signature.[45] How they are laid out is also meaningful.[46]

One of the underlying assumptions of diplomatics is that it decontextualises and universalises the elements of documentary form, thus establishing a method that can be used in any juridical system and in any time-space. The absence of certain elements raises doubts over the record's authenticity.[47]

Documentary form as developed in diplomatics has been used to verify the authenticity of a record. In Luciana Duranti's words:

> At the core of diplomatics lies the idea that all records can be analyzed, understood and evaluated in terms of a system of formal elements that are universal in their application and decontextualized in nature. The essential assumption of diplomatics is that the context of a document's creation is made manifest in its form, and that this form can be separated from, and examined independently of, its content. Thus, diplomatists view records conceptually as embodying a system of both external and internal elements, consisting of

---

[43] Luciana Duranti, *Diplomatics: New Uses for an Old Science*, The Society of American Archivists and Association of Canadian Archivists in Association with The Scarecrow Press, Maryland and London, 1998, p. 134.

[44] InterPARES 1 Project, Authenticity Task Force, *Template for Analysis*, p.1, 'documentary form'.

[45] Ibid., pp. 1-2.

[46] 'The way in which elements are aggregated gives you the documentary form. This is meaningful. So, we need to consider documentary form [and presence/absence of elements within this], not just whether elements are present or absent.' Authenticity Task Force, InterPARES Meeting, Minutes, April 2001 (unpublished).

[47] MacNeil, *Trusting Records*, pp. 20-22.

> a) *acts*, which are the determinant cause of record creation, b) *persons*, who concur in record formation, c) *procedures*, which are the means by which acts are carried out, and d) *record form*, which binds all the elements together.[48]

Thus the document's form binds together the determinants of the record's creation, the persons involved, and the procedures by which the act is carried out. So although diplomatics is being applied at the document level, it does not isolate the document from its procedural and regulatory environment.

2.2.3 Electronic documents and trustworthy records

In contemporary diplomatics as presented by Paola Carucci, any written thing is a document. All kinds of testimonies on any media have been adopted in relation to the contemporary document and have required a re-assessment of their evidentiary value.[49]

For twentieth century documents, Carucci finds all the basic elements are still relevant. These include the elements of the document important to its juridical character and its authenticity, which are there from the time of creation of the document, and include firstly the author, the addressee, the text, signature and date; secondly registration and authentication; and thirdly the elements of classification, registration of the protocol and archival signs that identify the place of the single document in the archival series.[50]

Diplomatics has assisted in understanding the internal structure of the archive. Carucci points out that what is defined as a document in archival science is much less restrictive than in Italian law and diplomatics, in which the definition is linked to very formal elements of a document and a very narrow definition of a legal act. A procedure may include all kinds of documents, not just the formal ones. Importantly, documents that may not

---

[48] Luciana Duranti, 'The Archival Bond', *Archives and Museum Informatics*, vol. 11, 1997, p. 215.

[49] Carucci, *Il Documento Contemporaneo*, pp. 92-97. Any written thing as a document in contemporary diplomatics conforms with the legal acceptance of any 'form of record' in Australian 'reformed' Evidence Acts, for example, *Evidence Act* 1995 (Cth), definition of a document, in the Dictionary, s 3, Part 1, Definitions, 'document'.

[50] Carucci's elements found in twentieth century documents are some of the elements identified as benchmark requirements for the authenticity of electronic records maintained by the creator in the InterPARES 1 project. See further discussion in this chapter.

originally be legal documents, may be used as proof of some fact in a legal process.[51]

Archival science connects the entire working of an institution and its functions rather than focusing on the individual document which is the subject of diplomatics. In diplomatics the document takes part in successive phases of an action, which forms part of a procedure. Procedure is a series of acts that fulfils a final action or goal of the administration or organisation.[52] Building on Carucci's definitions, a procedure is a part of the context of creation of the record and its reliability. Its modern equivalent is 'work processes' that many organisations employ and have previously employed under the guise of procedure, which follow internal and external rules in order to achieve a 'business' outcome, within a regulatory framework. Control over a record is particularly difficult in a distributed electronic environment where the procedures are often found in workflow software. There is a need to explicitly retain procedures and other reference documentation that ensures the reliability of the record, which in diplomatics was embedded in the document itself.[53]

The elements of archival analysis derived from contemporary diplomatics are powerful tools for ascertaining both structural elements and procedural controls needed for trustworthy electronic documents.[54] These elements can also be defined as recordkeeping metadata elements.

[51] Carucci, *Il Documento Contemporaneo*, p. 31.

[52] Ibid, pp. 47-48. In Italian public law there are specified phases, such as an introductory phase, a preparatory phase, and a deliberative phase that ensure the act is effective and not in conflict with an existing law.

[53] Case studies used in the InterPARES 1 project revealed that elements of record identity are found in the procedural controls over records creation. See Anna Gibson, 'Overview of the Diplomatic Analysis of Electronic Records within the Canadian Automated Patent System (TechSource)', in *How Do You Know It's the Real Thing?, Preserving Authentic Electronic Records: Preliminary Research Findings*, Proceedings from an International Symposium, 17 February 2001, University of British Columbia, InterPARES and the Italian Government Cultural Office, Vancouver, August 2001, p. 65.

[54] Paola Carucci has articulated the application of Italian diplomatics to twentieth century paper, but not electronic, documents. Luciana Duranti and her colleagues further developed contemporary archival diplomatics in the electronic environment. See the University of British Columbia (UBC) Project 1994-1997, 'The Preservation of the Integrity of Electronic Records'; and the InterPARES 1 project which has adopted a typology of the electronic document based on elements of documentary form that need to be captured and preserved over time. For further articulation of the electronic document, see Maria Guercio, *Archivistica Informatica: I Documenti in Ambiente Digitale*, Carocci, Rome, 2002.

In paper documents they have been more readily visible on the face of the document itself. Whether or not web documents need to more visibly demonstrate these elements to engender trust is as much a cultural as a recordkeeping issue.[55] In an electronic document, 'form' has a logical rather than a physical structure. It includes the document's appearance (which includes fonts, styles embedded in code), the data itself (not all of which may be visible and includes metadata about the document's creation), and relationships between the data presented. Do web 'forms' engender trust on appearance alone? What about metadata held by websites which are not evident to the user? What about the document's routing information held by servers? In the paper world, registration systems created and maintained much of this kind of metadata. For practical reasons of identification of transacting parties, recordkeeping metadata has to be incorporated into web-authored documents. The elements of documentary form or recordkeeping metadata in electronic recordkeeping and archival descriptive systems are unlikely to be visibly manifested as part of the record. They have to be deliberately captured and inextricably linked to the record.

Research based within the diplomatics and records continuum paradigms in relation to trustworthy electronic records have addressed how best to preserve their authenticity. In the Australian records continuum thinking the need to deliberately capture recordkeeping relationships has animated ongoing research in the recordkeeping metadata communities. In *Recordkeeping Metadata Standards for Managing and Accessing Information Resources in Networked Environments Over Time for Government, Social and Cultural Purposes* (RKMS), records are defined as active participants in business processes, which have contextual data essential to their

---

[55] For example, on websites 'form' includes PDF format which captures and freezes an image of a document in conventional form; HTML documents which have structural features that allow the document to link to other HTML documents. The ways the links are made are not apparent to the user. Depending on browser software the 'look' of the document may vary. Capturing the dynamic form of a web page is problematic. The evolution of web documents from static to dynamic, to automated applications include Document Type Definition (DTD) which provide their logical structure and their layout; use of schema which are 'a set of rules for constraining the structure and articulating the information set of XML documents', and machine validation of instance documents, for example, 'everything I send to you will be in that format' used for exchanging information. Web 'forms' are an emerging aspect of diplomatics. Notes from Distributed Systems Technology Centre, 'W3C Update', Seminar, 17 November 2000, Monash University.

reliability and authenticity. This contextual data must remain with the record over time if its evidential qualities are to remain probative.[56]

The RKMS project's objectives in terms of the metadata to be captured provide elements that ensure the record's reliability and authenticity over time. These are:

> Unique identification of records; authentication of records; persistence of records content, structure and context (involving maintaining records with fixed content, ensuring that their structure can be rendered, and maintaining sufficient context to preserve their meaning over time and beyond their context of creation); administration or resolution of terms and conditions of access, use and disposal; tracking and documenting of recordkeeping event history; discovery, retrieval and delivery to authorised users together with other types of information resources through common user interfaces; interoperability in networked environments.[57]

The project provided for situations in which the metadata which is not persistently linked to the record as object may be captured into record-specific systems.[58]

RKMS is particularly designed for metadata in distributed environments such as the Internet.

> When records move beyond the boundaries of the local domain in which they were created, or, as is increasingly the case in networked environments, they are created in the first place in a global rather than a local domain, then this kind of metadata needs to be made explicit - i.e. captured and persistently linked to the record. This is essential so that users in the broader domain can uniquely identify, retrieve, and understand the meanings of the records.[59]

---

[56] See Monash University, School of Information Management Systems, *Recordkeeping Metadata Standards for Managing and Accessing Information Resources in Networked Environments Over Time for Government, Social and Cultural Purposes*, 1998-1999.

[57] Sue McKemmish, Glenda Acland, Nigel Ward and Barbara Reed, 'Describing Records in Context in the Continuum: the Australian Recordkeeping Metadata Schema', *Archivaria*, vol. 48, Fall 1999, p. 11.

[58] Ibid., p. 31.

[59] Ibid., p. 7. Monash University, School of Information Management Systems, Records Continuum Research Group, with the University of California (UCLA) and National Archives of Australia, *Create Once, Use Many Times: The Clever Use of Metadata in eGovernment and eBusiness Processes in Networked Environments*, 2003-2005. This research project is developing a proof of concept prototype to demonstrate how standards-compliant metadata can be created once in particular application environments, then used many times to meet a range of business purposes.

The InterPARES 1 Project, on the other hand, proposed that degrees of record authenticity can be presumed by the preserver if benchmark requirements have been met by the record creators, with additional verification undertaken by the preserver where these requirements appear insufficient to presume authenticity.[60] The more requirements that are satisfied, the more probable is authenticity. Benchmark or threshold requirements for *identity* are the intrinsic elements of documentary form (author, addressee, writer and originator, dates, the name of the action or matter, its status of transmission, its archival bond and indication of attachments). The *integrity* of a record is its soundness (condition is unimpaired), and completeness (possesses all necessary parts). The integrity cannot be absolute, but has to be seen in relation to its purpose, creation and use. Thus an electronic record does not have to replicate the exact number of 'original bits' as long as certain formal elements are there. The project proposed preserving the record as a digital object (a set of digital components which consists of the procedures and the record).[61]

To maintain the authenticity of the record the preserver must meet another set of requirements which are termed 'baseline'. The foundation for the preserver depends on the creator having undertaken certain procedural controls. The preserver must verify authentic copies, provide archival description and document the reproduction process.[62] The relationship between the records acquired and those reproduced involves maintaining the minimum elements of identity. Integrity may have been compromised by migration, tampering, or a system's inability to preserve identity. A level of acceptable 'corruption' is necessary in the electronic

---

[60] InterPARES 1 Project, Authenticity Task Force, *Final Report*, 28 October 2001, 'Appendix: Requirements for Accessing and Maintaining the Authenticity of Electronic Records', pp. 1-15. InterPARES' requirements for authenticity were mapped to other standards, for example, the ISO *Records Management Standard* in terms of reliability, integrity and authenticity but the ISO standard is concerned with record creation rather than preservation over time. From a continuum perspective the elements of reliability would remain the same over time.

[61] The InterPARES 1 Preservation Task Force concluded that it is not possible to preserve an electronic record as a stored physical object: it is only possible to preserve the ability to reproduce the record. InterPARES 1 Project, Preservation Task Force, *Final Report*, 25 July 2001, University of British Columbia, Vancouver, 2001, p. 5.

[62] Heather MacNeil, 'Providing Grounds for Trust: Developing Conceptual Requirements for the Long-Term Preservation of Authentic Electronic Records', *Archivaria*, vol. 50, 2001, pp. 56-67.

environment. Whether all elements of authenticity need to be present could be interpreted as a risk management decision.

In the InterPARES 1 project, a dedicated preservation system controlled by a trusted third party, for example an archival authority, guarantees the authenticity of the record over time. In other approaches, such as the Pittsburgh University's functional requirements for recordkeeping, authenticity is based on different communities' needs, and the responsibility for preservation depends on the 'warrants' of the community. InterPARES also acknowledges different juridical requirements. The presumption of authenticity relies to some extent on circumstantial evidence. The level of acceptable authenticity will depend on the laws of evidence of the jurisdiction in question, and the social mechanisms of trust within the communities that rely on those records. For example, the Italian legal system does not accept the same level of presumption of authenticity of electronic records as found in Australia and Canada.[63]

RKMS, Pittsburgh, and InterPARES 1 all rely on social mechanisms of control for digital authenticity, through the role of preservers, whoever they may be.[64] Record authenticity requires the preservation of the elements of record identity and integrity to attribute responsibility for obligations to recordkeeping participants. The presumption of authenticity includes a community of common interest and its continuing need for social trust and evidence.

Authenticity is linked not only to what is an original or a copy, but also with social concepts of faithfulness, trust and truth. What are the core elements that render an object something other than what it purports to be? What is intrinsic to the object and what depends on external knowledge, for example the technology used to create it, and the legal system in which

---

[63] Gigliola Fioravanti, 'Italy's Legislative Framework for Electronic Documentation', in *Authentic Records in the Electronic Age, Proceedings from an International Symposium*, ed. Luigi Sarno, Istituto Italiano di Cultura Vancouver and The InterPARES Project, Vancouver Canada, 2000, pp. 94-107. The high risk of document fraud in visa and citizenship decisions is recognised in Australia and also calls for higher authenticity requirements. See *Electronic Transactions Act* 1999 (Cth) s 4.

[64] Peter B. Hirtle, 'Archival Authenticity in a Digital Age', in *Authenticity in a Digital Environment*, Council on Library and Information Resources, Washington, D.C., 2000, pp. 8-23. Hirtle explains that the Pittsburgh project did not set out to identify functional requirements for authenticity; like RKMS it assumed automatic capture of metadata for recordness. Rather than an archives authority ensuring authenticity over time, specific communities would do so.

it was created? The meaning of authenticity in relation to information (oral or recorded) is discipline-specific.[65] Jeff Rothenberg suggests that some disciplines have *a priori* needs for authenticity. For archivists, documentation about the record, such as provenance, and in modern parlance metadata, are essential to authentic records.[66]

Trust is not an absolute, but a subjective probability assigned case by case.[67] 'Trust in the maker or warrantor of a claim is not necessarily binary; in the real world, we deal with levels of confidence or degrees of trust'.[68] Authenticity is a process of examining and assigning confidence to a collection of claims. Clifford Lynch argues that technology on its own will not suffice to provide trust; instead there is a need for business models to support it, as well as social and legal constraints. He disputes that technology, in particular cryptography, will solve problems of authorship and record integrity. A simple integrity check, such as a message digest that accompanies a digital object as metadata, serves as an effective mechanism to ensure that the object has not been corrupted, but it does not prove the reliability of the record. Perfect copies can be pirated, but they are not authentic because their provenance is different from the original.[69] Provenance, unbroken custody and trusted systems must operate together. Provenance must include the origin of the object and the relationships between objects.

Lynch defines identity to include the management of the documentation about the evolution of trust, the identity management infrastructure, and policies of certificate holders that support the assertions of authenticity. He supports the view that a community will establish its own trust rules that will authenticate data. All technological solutions involve a trusted third party; a form of transferred risk to a trusted party.[70] This supports the communities of interest model and their own 'trust' rules that will evolve in an online context.

---

[65] 'Introduction', in *Authenticity in a Digital Environment*, Council on Library and Information Resources, Washington, D.C., 2000.

[66] Jeff Rothenberg, 'Preserving Authentic Digital Information', in *Authenticity in a Digital Environment*, Council on Library and Information Resources, Washington, D.C., 2000, pp. 51-68.

[67] Ibid., p. 56.

[68] Clifford Lynch, 'Authenticity and Integrity in the Digital Environment: An Exploratory Analysis of the Central Role of Trust', in *Authenticity in a Digital Environment*, Council on Library and Information Resources, Washington, D.C., 2000, p. 40.

[69] Ibid., pp. 32-50.

[70] Ibid., p. 48.

Arguments over whether authenticity and related concepts change in a digital environment, and whether characteristics such as medium, can play a role in a digital context where all digital objects are a bitstream, have emerged at forums dedicated to their discussion.[71] As authenticity is clearly related to ensuring something, in this case a record, remains unchanged from what it was originally, it deals with preserving particular attributes over time. The preservation of record identity and integrity requires trusted third parties, which in information communities have included archivists and librarians, to continue their roles.[72]

Authentication and certification methods as articulated in the information technology environment are concerned to ensure that the identity of a person or entity is what it claims to be at the time of the transaction. In diplomatics, authentication is a declaration at a specific time by a juridical person entrusted with the authority to make such a declaration.[73] Identity as expressed in the records continuum model, modern diplomatics and research which derives from them, have broader requirements of identity than those found in authentication frameworks. The identifiable record is not just the persons in the transaction but other essential attributes, that have to be maintained through time, or at least for more than their immediate use.

Current authentication regulatory frameworks are inadequate to support record authenticity. A Public Key Infrastructure (PKI), which is a hierarchical organisation of certification authorities invested with the competence to authenticate the ownership and characteristics of a public key, is only effective if there is a continuity of the chain of trust guaranteed by those certification authorities.[74] As private sector organisations take on

---

[71] Even if the medium is not of central relevance to electronic records, records still need to be preserved as physical objects. See Guercio, *Archivistica Informatica*, p. 25.

[72] See Research Libraries Group and Online Computer Library Center, *Trusted Digital Repositories: Attributes and Responsibilities, Final Report, May 2002*, RLG, Mountain View, California, 2002.

[73] 'Authentication is understood as a declaration of a record's authenticity at a specific point in time by a juridical person entrusted with the authority to make that declaration. It takes the form of an authoritative statement (which may be in the form of words or symbols) that is added to or inserted in the record attesting that the record is authentic'. InterPARES 1 Project, Authenticity Task Force, *Final Report*, 28 October 2001, p. 3.

[74] For example in Australia, the initial recommendations for a statutorily based central root registration authority were rejected by the federal government. A root certification authority supports the certification of subordinate intermediate certification authorities and holds root cryptographic information. Third party

the role of certification authorities, there are no mechanisms in place to guarantee the continuity of the chain of trust in the event that the organisation ceases to exist.[75] Bodies with certifying power to issue the software, keys and certificates for digital signatures will hold metadata necessary for establishing the reliability of the records. Who controls the keys? Who retains the certificates? How will they remain linked to the record for authenticity over time?[76]

In the recordkeeping context the participants need to know the identity of those with whom they are dealing to trust the content of their communications. Thus data that provides identifying information is essential recordkeeping metadata that must be persistently linked to, or

---

independence with an archival authority playing the role of gatekeeper was not considered. See National Office for the Information Economy, *Establishment of a National Authentication Authority*, A Discussion Paper, 19 August 1998, Commonwealth of Australia, 2000.

[75] Anne Picot, 'Uncovering the Mysteries of Digital Signatures. A Discussion of What Signatures Really Stand for and How They Should be Managed in the Digital Environment', in *Convergence, Joint National Conference, Conference Proceedings*, the Joint National Conference of the Australian Society of Archivists and the Records Management Association of Australia, 2-5 September 2001, Hobart, pp. 251-259.

[76] Stephen Wilson, 'Current Issues in the Rollout of a National Authentication Framework?', in *Electronic Commerce: Net Benefit for Australia?*, The 1998 Information Industry Outlook Conference hosted by the Australian Computer Society, Canberra Branch; Canberra, Australia, 7 November 1998, pp. 5-13. Digital keys are either held in a repository of certification keys or the certification body creates a certification certificate which is checked for each transaction. The need to preserve the means of authenticating the record across technological obsolescence via the use of a digital signature is subject to debate. See Jean-François Blanchette, 'Digital Archiving Strategies for the Long Term', in *E-archiving for Posterity, Electronic Record Keeping and Long-term Preservation of Digital Data*, One-Day International Conference, University of Leuven, 26 June 2003, Technologische Instituut, Antwerp, 2003, pp. 1-12. Digital signatures and their continuing validity for record authenticity may depend on preserving their related infrastructure. See InterPARES 1 Project, Authenticity Task Force, *Final Report*, 28 October 2001, p. 45. The National Archives of Australia advises preserving recordkeeping metadata that indicates the validity of signatures at the time of their use or that government agencies that need to revalidate digital signatures consider maintaining a key management plan. See National Archives of Australia, *Recordkeeping and Online Security Processes: Guidelines for Managing Commonwealth Records Created or Received Using Authentication and Encryption*, May 2004, pp. 20-21.

part of, the record. In addition, identity metadata is essential for the enforcement of rights and obligations, both moral and legal.[77]

2.3 Rules of evidence and trustworthy records

Theories of knowledge are at the heart of evidence rules and of the trustworthiness of records within legal systems. Evidence law reflects the fundamental way a legal system seeks to understand the truth. The notion of a trustworthy record is therefore tied to the principles of evidence in a legal system. In this sense it is a cultural phenomenon (for example extracting evidence by torture), and open to the postmodernist critique of relativism.

Heather MacNeil has argued that truth, established by reasoning from the relevant evidence, not as certainty, but a matter of degree, is part of a theory of epistemology, founded in the eighteenth century Lockean tradition of rationalist empiricism. Rational empiricism provides that the probable existence of fact is based on the theory of logical relevancy, which is expressed in terms of the relationship between evidence and probability. The concept of 'inference' or inductive evidence in rationalist empiricism means inferring one thing from another, as opposed to one thing being or not being what it seems or pretends to be. Evidence theory is therefore connected to the development of probability theory and the separation of the observer from the event recorded, clearly embedded in Cartesian metaphysics which separates the physical and the mental, and the internal and external perception of things. An inference from one fact may change the inference from another fact. Chains of facts and inferences provide and overarching framework in which assessments of trustworthiness of evidence in general and documentary evidence in particular are made.[78]

Over the centuries Western legal systems have evolved criteria and methods for establishing the trustworthiness of records as evidence clearly traced back to Roman law and later developments.[79] These rules embody

---

[77] See Chapter 4.

[78] MacNeil, *Trusting Records*, pp. 23-26.

[79] Luciana Duranti, 'Archival Science', in *Encyclopedia of Library and Information Science*, vol. 59, supplement 22, 1997, pp. 1-19 examines the roots of archival science in Roman law which became part of all legal systems of Europe through education, and the association of archival knowledge with law which provided for its separation from the philological disciplines. The major codification of Roman law and its revived study in the twelfth century

much of what recordkeeping theory refers to as recordkeeping metadata or elements of documentary form, in particular at the record creation and capture stage. Form also played a vital part in legal procedure in so far as particular kinds of documents were used to trigger legal actions, such as writs.

Concepts of record trustworthiness in archival science which originate from Roman law are also found in the evidence laws of common law countries, for example the ancient records and the best evidence rules.[80] In Roman law there were two concepts of particular relevance to trustworthy records, the concepts of 'perpetual memory' and 'public faith'.[81] Public faith in society as a whole is 'community as society' in Aristotelian terms. The relationship of these concepts to recordkeeping principles can be traced to the function of public records as collective memory providing social continuity. The public place in which records were kept formed part of the seat of government and also contributed to the trustworthiness of the records.[82] The Roman law of evidence reinforced the privileged status accorded to government documents and invested them with public faith.

In Italian law the probative value of public records has a much wider ambit than that of the common law (see 2.4.1 below 'Public records as evidence'). Documents made by private persons, such as contracts, which the common law would consider in the private sphere, are public documents if authenticated by a notary. Notarised records of a private transaction are not part of the common law tradition. The fact that a document was a notarial document gave it probative value equivalent to a

influenced the English common law. The principles of evidence, equity and natural justice were already enshrined in canon law. See also Saarland University, Institute of Law and Informatics, *The Roman Law Branch of the Law-related Internet Project*, 'What is Roman Law?', 2005.

[80] For example in Australia, the *Evidence Act* 1995 (Cth) s 152. 'Ancient records' and the best evidence rules have their origin in what MacNeil calls the 'antiquity' criterion. The more removed the records were from the past the more impartial they could be considered. MacNeil, *Trusting Records*, p. 3.

[81] Luciana Duranti, 'The Concept of Appraisal and Archival Theory', *American Archivist*, vol. 57, Spring 1994, pp. 328-344, 'Archives as a Place', *Archives and Manuscripts*, vol. 24, no. 2, Nov. 1996, pp. 242-255, and 'Reliability and Authenticity: The Concepts and Their Implications', *Archivaria*, vol. 39, Spring 1995, pp. 5-10.

[82] The purpose of the 'archival place' as guaranteeing authenticity has its origin in Greco-Roman times. The word archives derives from state power, government and authority. See Ole Kolsrud, 'Developments in Archival Theory', in *Encyclopedia of Library and Information Science*, vol. 61, supplement 24, 1998, p. 92.

public record, that is public faith ('publica fides') and witnessed the rights and obligations of private citizens. Thus a public document was defined as one that emanated from a public authority (including a notary) as opposed to a private citizen.[83] Private documents depend on proof of the signature on the document, which can be denied by the signer, and the onus of proof is on the person wishing to use the document as evidence. If the signature has been authenticated by a notary or public official it also has probative value. Since 1997 Italian law has recognised a digital signature as having the same legal efficacy as a hand-written equivalent.[84]

2.3.1 Documentary evidence within the common law system

The laws of evidence are part of the common law[85] which have been modified and added to by statute.[86] The term 'documentary evidence' rather than the term 'record' is used in the common law to distinguish it from 'oral evidence' which is testimony given in court by witnesses. The courts have dealt with documentary evidence as a special category.

The way the common law system developed, legal obligations arising from actions were initially evidenced orally in front of witnesses rather than via written documents.[87] As a centralised system of justice developed in England towards the end of the thirteenth century, written documents began to be used for legal purposes. In the nineteenth century the need to identify the intent of parties to the action increased the need to process

[83] In the Italian legal system documents of public authorities all have probative value. The probative efficacy of the document within the Italian legal system, starts with a public act which following set requirements of law is either executed by a notary or a public official which attributes public faith to the contents of the document. Elements of record identity include the signing as author, the date and place of act, the declaration by the parties and others to the facts that the public official is witness to. Unless there is a legal challenge to its validity, a judge is bound to consider true what is stated in the document. However there is a process that a third party can instigate to contest the validity of an official act. Carucci, *Il Documento Contemporaneo*, pp. 67-71.

[84] Paola Carucci and Marina Messina, *Manuale di Archivistica per L'impresa*, Carocci, Rome, 1998, pp. 41-42.

[85] The examples in this chapter are mainly from Australian jurisdictions.

[86] In Australia, the laws of evidence apply to the jurisdictions of all courts, state and Commonwealth. Different courts may apply different rules often via the statute establishing the particular court. Other tribunals may or may not apply rules of evidence. Documents from outside Australia may not be admissible. J. D. Heydon, *Cross on Evidence*, 5th edn, Butterworths, Sydney, 1996, p. 6.

[87] Duranti, 'Reliability and Authenticity', p. 5.

more facts.[88] Documentary evidence began to supplement oral testimony and in some instances supplant it.

Despite the fact that the rules of evidence in the common law system can be traced back to the thirteenth century their modern developments are based on the decisions of the common law judges of the seventeenth and eighteenth century, which include the 'hearsay' rule. The courts developed various tests to make sure that documents were trustworthy. The common law rule requiring the production of the original document and documents as 'hearsay' were rules of particular relevance to records.

Documents as hearsay

In common law systems the principal source of evidence is the oral testimony of witnesses which can be tested by cross-examination to find 'judicially determined truth' to prove alleged facts.[89] The nature of the English adversarial system, depends on direct evidence as the most reliable source, that is the live oral testimony of the witness as opposed to hearsay evidence. The rule against hearsay has been defined as, 'an assertion other than one made by a witness while testifying in the proceedings is inadmissible *as evidence of any fact asserted'*.[90] A witness can only give evidence of facts of which they have personal knowledge. This is prima facie evidence. The party against whom testimony is given has a right to cross-examine the witness. Thus a statement made by someone other than the witness giving oral evidence is generally not admissible because the person who actually makes the statement cannot be cross-examined about it.

Documents are classed as hearsay. They infringe hearsay when they are tendered as evidence of the truth of the facts stated. Courts traditionally excluded documentary records as evidence as it was not possible to subject documents to cross-examination. However exceptions to the hearsay rule in certain circumstances allowed the 'contents of the documents', that is statements, to be accepted as legal evidence if certain requirements were met, such as the duty to record and if their accuracy and reliability as information sources could be demonstrated (see 2.4 below 'Record reliability and authenticity and the principles of evidence').[91]

---

88 Getzler, 'Patterns of Fusion', pp. 187-89.

89 R.A. Brown, *Documentary Evidence in Australia*, 2nd edn, LBC Information Services, North Ryde, NSW, 1996, p. 1.

90 Heydon, *Cross on Evidence*, p. 815.

91 Ibid., pp. 46-59. The body of exemptions to the rule against hearsay are so comprehensive and detailed that almost anything can be an exception. For this

Statutory provisions have gradually broadened the scope for admissible documents. In common law countries evidence statutes now have a range of document-admitting provisions which overlap with respect to any one piece of evidence.[92]

Principles of admissibility, weight and relevancy

The document may be put in evidence as a chattel (material object), 'a thing' or 'real evidence' bearing an inscription, or else as a statement, the inscription on a thing.[93] While documentary evidence admissibility provisions admitted the statements in a document in lieu of direct oral evidence and not the document as a whole, many common law provisions admitted the entire document, particularly public documents. When treated as a statement, the document is testimonial evidence, and the maker of the statement is treated as a witness. Parts of the contents of the document might not be admitted or they may be treated as circumstantial evidence, that is, any fact from the existence of which the judge or jury may infer the existence of a fact in issue.[94] The general rule is that all relevant evidence is admissible subject to exceptions, documents being one of them.

Another distinction that has to be borne in mind with rules of evidence is between admissibility and weight or value. For example, a document may be ruled inadmissible and one which is admitted may be given no weight or value because other evidence is led which disproves the facts which it supports. Weight can affect admissibility as this is related to the relevancy of the matter under consideration, but generally it is not taken into account.[95]

Evidence that is relevant to the issue before the court is admissible subject to numerous exceptions, including hearsay, opinion, character and conduct. Although it would appear logical that all relevant evidence is admissible, in law it may not be admissible if it falls into an exclusionary rule. Thus admissibility and relevancy are treated as separate concepts.

---

reason documentary evidence in practice has been as important as oral evidence in the common law system's rules on evidence. Heydon claims that even if it is argued that documents are more accurate than oral evidence, they do not suit the adversarial system because the opposing side can always bring in a witness to dispute the contents of a document.

[92] Brown, *Documentary Evidence in Australia*, Chapters 9, 12 and 13. Documents can be admitted under business or specific computer records provisions, or as reproductions.

[93] Ibid., Chapter 6. Document as 'thing' still appears in the Australian 1995 evidence legislation, and 'representation' replaces 'statement'.

[94] Heydon, *Cross on Evidence*, p. 16 and p. 49.

[95] Ibid., p. 97.

The two main types of evidence are 'prima facie' (sufficient unless outweighed), and 'conclusive'. The extent that a record can provide conclusive evidence as opposed to prima facie may depend on the level of its reliability and integrity.

2.4 Record reliability and authenticity and the principles of evidence

In the recordkeeping context the trustworthiness of the record depends on its reliability (is the content true/accurate?) and authenticity (is the record what it claims to be?). Reliability is never an absolute, but rather there are degrees of reliability due to the dependence of accurate content on individual 'truthfulness'. The degree of reliability of the contents of a record depends on how much is captured of the identity of the persons involved in the record's creation, their credibility, their authority (their competencies), and the consent of parties to the transaction. Validation or certification of the parties to a transaction or the authors and recipients depends on controls in the record crcation process. Authenticity depends on ensuring that the record's reliability has not been compromised by tampering during or after transmission.[96]

The relationship between record reliability and admissibility/relevancy on the one hand, and authenticity (identity and integrity) and best evidence rules/weight on the other, has been examined by Heather MacNeil. Legal rules relating to authentication and the best evidence rule address whether the record is genuine, while rules on reliability deal with whether the facts are trustworthy and are dealt with as an exception to the hearsay rule. MacNeil says: 'Whereas the documentary exceptions to the hearsay rule are concerned with the reliability of a record's contents, the authentication and best evidence rules are concerned with its identity and integrity'.[97]

A definition of legal evidence is 'data that tend to establish some alleged fact', admitted into legal proceedings and relevant to a specific case.[98]

[96] The elements of authenticity in archival science have been considered absolute; a record was either authentic or it was not. See Duranti, 'Reliability and Authenticity', pp. 5-10. In the electronic environment the InterPARES 1 Project has modified record authenticity to mean circumstantial evidence that may provide a presumption of authenticity, through attributes that establish its identity and integrity. See InterPARES 1 Project, Authenticity Task Force, *Final Report*, 28 October 2001.

[97] MacNeil, *Trusting Records*, p. 46.

[98] Brown, *Documentary Evidence in Australia*, p. 8.

Evidence is the means of proving or disproving a fact, what may be introduced, that is, what is admissible, and what standard of proof is necessary, that is, the quality, integrity and quantity of evidence. John Dyson Heydon states: 'The legal burden of proof is the obligation of a party to meet the requirement of a rule of law that a fact in issue be proved (or disproved) either by a preponderance of the evidence or beyond reasonable doubt, as the case may be',[99] while 'the evidential burden is the obligation to show, if called upon to do so, that there is sufficient evidence to raise an issue as to the existence or non-existence of a fact in issue, due regard being had to the standard of proof demanded of the party under such obligation'.[100]

Rules relating to the burden of proof depend on the substantive law, especially those allocating the burden of proof, and are often expressed in the language of presumptions, for example 'the presumption of innocence is simply another way of saying the burden of proving the guilt of the accused is unconditionally allocated to the prosecution'.[101] The degree of proof will depend on the type of case (criminal or civil) and the area of law.[102] Thus the standard required for the identity and integrity of the record will not be universal for all areas of law, as noted in the InterPARES 1 benchmark requirements for authenticity.

Heather MacNeil has found that no uniform standard has been developed in Canada for measuring acceptable degrees of trustworthiness or necessity, but rather a case-by-case basis has emerged.[103] In Australia declarations made in the course of a business duty have been treated as an exception to the hearsay rule if recordmaking was regular. Records made

---

99 Heydon, *Cross on Evidence*, p. 190.

100 Ibid., p. 191.

101 Ibid., p. 188, footnote 2.

102 In the Australian legal system one of the distinctions is between civil and criminal cases. The most important difference, so far as evidence is concerned, is that the 'onus of proof' (who must come up with the proof) varies in each case. In criminal cases guilt must be proved 'beyond reasonable doubt'. In civil cases it is necessary to prove something on 'the balance of probabilities'. Heydon, *Cross on Evidence,* Chapters 4 and 5. However, the test for admissibility is not in principle different between a civil or criminal case and should not change the degree of record reliability required.

103 MacNeil, *Trusting Records*, p. 37, examines the two interconnected tests for trustworthiness in the hearsay rule: cross-examination and confrontation. Documents as out of court assertions have been admissible in situations when a witness could not be cross-examined, thus exceptions to the hearsay rule needed to meet two conditions: circumstantial probability of trustworthiness and necessity.

subsequent to a duty to an employer are likely to be reliable as they arise from professional duty, which parallels the notion of trust in the creator in archival science.

2.4.1 Documentary exceptions to hearsay and record reliability

Public records as evidence

There are many important aspects in terms of how the common law adduced written evidence in public documents in terms of their reliability. These included: the maker of the record had a duty to record, the public nature of the document, retention or an intention to keep a record, public inspection availability and contemporaneity of record creation. Acts recorded must have been performed for the document to have any validity.[104] As in diplomatics, the record had to accurately represent the actions it witnessed.

Document and record as evidence

Statutory definitions of a document and record have centred on their physical characteristics rather than function.[105] A document has been

[104] In common law there has not been a simple categorisation of what constitutes a public record and when it is admissible. Not all records created by a public authority are considered public records, for example a register from a public authority not prescribed by law may be excluded; if it is a requirement of a statute then it more likely to be a public document, such as statutory records of a corporation. There have also been other requirements, for example public accessibility. A ship's passenger list or the internal working papers of a government department have been excluded as public documents in cases where they were not open to the public or made for public access. Public documents that fall under 'judicial notice' do not have to be proved. The 1995 Australian Evidence Acts do not accord public documents with any special status in being admitted as evidence, which has simplified the complex common law approach. See Brown, *Documentary Evidence in Australia*, Chapter 4 and Heydon, *Cross on Evidence*, Chapter 17, section 2.

[105] The *Archives Act* 1983 (Cth) s 3 (1) defines a record as a document (consisting of any written or printed material) or object (including a sound recording, coded storage device, magnetic tape or disc, microform, photograph, film, map, plan or model or a painting or other pictorial or graphic work) that is, or has been, kept by reason of any information or matter that it contains or can be obtained from it or by reason of its connection with any event, person, circumstance or thing. In the *State Records Act* 1998 (NSW) s 3(1), record means 'any document or other source of information compiled, recorded or

defined through case law as a physical thing or *medium* (this may apply to an electronic document as it is stored on some sort of medium; it would include objects), on or in which *data* (data as fact, opinion, information as the subjective interpretation of the data), are more or less permanently *recorded* (it is capable of being retained, but there is no inference of permanence), in such a manner that data can subsequently be *retrieved* (with proper equipment). There is no need for direct human intervention in the creation of a document.[106]

However, a document which stores data and is retrievable is not a record. A number of English cases shed further light on what constitutes a 'record'. These suggest that to qualify as records, a document must be the product of a process and must give effect to a transaction or act such as a contemporaneous register of information supplied by those with direct knowledge of the facts (see also 2.4.1 above 'Public records as evidence').[107] The higher probative value given to a record that was documented at the time of action, rather than subsequent to the event, that is, the proximity of the documentation with the action, is more likely to ensure that it is accurate. This principle is also found in diplomatics.[108] In fact, the way documentary evidence has been admitted has depended on features of a trustworthy record.

Statutory and common law exceptions to hearsay

All Australian jurisdictions until the passing of the 1995 *Evidence Acts*, except Western Australia, had equivalent statutes to the *Evidence Act* 1938 (UK) which had allowed certain kinds of hearsay statements in documents to be admissible in civil cases. For example the former NSW *Evidence Act* 1898, Pt 11A, s 14B dealt with evidence of statements in documents that clearly needed to be authenticated 'in writing' by the 'maker'. Although these documentary exceptions were directly linked to facts on which direct oral evidence can also be given, the statements in documents that could be admitted had to be made by a person who had personal knowledge of the thing recorded, or the document had to form part of a record made contemporaneously in which the person had a duty to record and had no motive to misrepresent the information in it. The US Federal Rules of

stored in written form or on film, or by electronic process, or in any other manner or by any other means'.

[106] Brown, *Documentary Evidence in Australia*, p. 9.

[107] Ibid., p. 35.

[108] See Chapter 3 on documents which coincide with the act (*ad substantiam*).

Evidence 902 contain similar provisions.[109] The reliability of the record was linked to the duty or office of the person creating it, the deontological duty of the professional, and a record's place within a system.[110]

The relationship of trust with the professional duty to record honestly is supported by case law, in particular *Ares v Venner* in the Supreme Court of Canada which restated and expanded the common law exception to hearsay by adapting it to modern recordkeeping.[111] Although nurses were present and could be cross-examined, their notes passed the test of trustworthiness and necessity because in a hospital where a patient's health is at stake every effort would be made to keep records accurate; it was the nurses' duty to keep notes, there was no motive to misrepresent and notes were likely to be a better test of the events than their memory. The notion of the reliability of a professional's records associated with professional duty, is relevant to trust and professional relationships.

Business records as evidence

'Business records' and also 'bankers books' are particularly important in the way documentary evidence including computer records have been accepted as evidence, and what they reveal about features of a trustworthy

[109] US-InterPARES Project, *Findings on the Preservation of Authentic Electronic Records*, Final Report to the National Historical Publications and Records Commission, 2002, pp. 74-75.

[110] The Canadian common law exception to the hearsay rule for admitting declarations made under a business duty parallels the Australian one. The Canadian requirements include the duty to act and to record the thing done, the necessity that the declarant had observed the act, the act must have been completed and the declarant must have made the statement contemporaneously with the act. MacNeil, *Trusting Records*, p. 39. See also Brown, *Documentary Evidence in Australia*, Chapter 8 and Heydon, *Cross on Evidence*, Chapter 18.

[111] *Ares v Venner* in the Supreme Court of Canada in 1970, a medical malpractice case made two changes to the common law exception of hearsay in Canada. It eliminated the need for a declarant to be deceased, and opened the door to allow recorded opinions in court as long as they fell within the declarant's normal scope of duty. However, it did not affect general principles of testimonial evidence which required demonstration of personal knowledge. See MacNeil, *Trusting Records*, pp. 39-40. See Australian cases in Ian Freckelton, 'Records as Reliable Evidence: Medico-legal Litigation', *Archives and Manuscripts*, vol. 26, no. 2, Nov. 1998, pp. 270-293, in which in a number of medical negligence cases, records were acknowledged by the courts as superior to the memory of the patient.

record.[112] In the US Federal Rules of Evidence, business records exceptions allow 'records of regularly conducted activity' to be an exception to hearsay.[113] Business records provisions in most Australian jurisdictions are defined in terms of 'the statement must have been made in the course of or for the purposes of the business'.[114] 'A record of a business' is broadly defined in most evidence legislation which specify that the records are to be kept by and for an organisation in respect of its business, which is also the internationally accepted definition of a record.[115] It is still the statements and not entire documents that are admitted, and the document must form part of a record of a business.[116]

In Australia, the judgment in the New South Wales Court of Appeal in *Albrighton v Royal Prince Alfred Hospital* established the principle that since businesses must keep reasonably accurate records if they are to stay in business, these records are likely to be sources of sufficiently reliable information to be acceptable as legal evidence. The judgment provided an exposition of the operation of the business records provisions found in Part 11C of the NSW *Evidence Act* 1898. Hope JA stated that:

> Any significant organisation in our society must depend for its efficient carrying on upon proper records made by persons who have no interest other

---

[112] The admissibility of bankers' books of account has existed in evidence legislation in every Australian state except the Commonwealth. They are no longer found in the 1995 Evidence Acts as they are covered by the business records provisions. Through case law bankers' books of account have been extended to all kinds of banking records, not just financial ones. Business records provisions have a number of advantages. They dispense with problems relating to the admissibility of originals as copies, definitions of a document are broader than in the general admissibility provisions for documents, and business is also generally defined to encompass most human activities, including government, corporate and community activity. Case law referenced in Brown, *Documentary Evidence in Australia*, Chapter 12 indicates that computer records have been admitted under business provisions if it could be demonstrated that they were a regular part of the recordkeeping of the business.

[113] US-InterPARES Project, *Findings on the Preservation of Authentic Electronic Records*, p. 75.

[114] *Evidence Act* 1898 (NSW) s 14CE(4). The two business records models adopted in Australian evidence legislation are summarised in Brown, *Documentary Evidence in Australia*, Chapter 9.

[115] 'Records: information created, received and maintained as evidence and information by an organisation or person, in pursuance of legal obligations or in the transaction of business'. From *ISO 15489-1, Information and Documentation - Records Management*, ISO, 2001, Part 1, General, p. 3.

[116] Heydon, *Cross on Evidence*, p. 1055.

> than to record as accurately as possible matters relating to the business with which they are concerned. In the everyday carrying on of the activities of the business, people would look to, and depend upon, those records, and use them on the basis that they are most probably accurate … No doubt mistakes may occur in the making of records, but I would think they occur no more, and probably less often, than in the recollection of persons trying to describe what happened at some time in the past. When what is recorded is the activity of a business in relation to a particular person amongst thousands of persons, the records are likely to be a far more reliable source of truth than memory. They are often the only source of truth.[117]

The records of business transactions that the creator relies on 'in the usual and normal course of business', and which are not self-serving, are presumed reliable.

Computer records as evidence

Evidence rules, like the principles of diplomatics and archival science, attribute to all recorded information the *capacity* to be used as evidence, that is, any documentary trace of a fact or event may be admitted as legal evidence.[118] Therefore if an electronic document forms part of the normal

[117] *Albrighton v Royal Prince Alfred Hospital* [1980] 2 NSWLR 542 as quoted in Philip Sutherland, 'Documentary Evidence', in *The Principles of Evidence*, 94/43, *Papers presented for the Continuing Legal Education Department of the College of Law, 9 July 1994*, Sydney, CLE Department of the College of Law, Sydney, 1994, p. 32. See also *Canada Evidence Act* (1985) in which records are not self-serving evidence; they have to be made in the 'usual and ordinary course of business', not just prepared by a business organisation. Canadian provincial business records provisions also require records to be made at or near time of event. MacNeil, *Trusting Records*, pp. 40-42.

[118] Duranti, *Diplomatics: New Uses for an Old Science*, pp. 5-6. In diplomatics, the term evidence has a very specific meaning. Diplomatic analysis of a document provides a source of proof of facts for evidence, which is distinct from the document as an instrument of action. Evidence as a relationship between a fact to be proven and the facts that are used for proof is both broader and more specific than a record. Carucci provides a narrower definition of a document than Duranti from the point of diplomatics as opposed to archival science. See Carucci, *Il Documento Contemporaneo*, p. 28. Evidence as inference by examining documentary traces is analysed by Heather MacNeil in *Trusting Records*, pp. 23-26. The notion of document as memory trace of an event which can be used to prove a legal right is recognised in the first dimension of the records continuum model, even though the trace does not have record attributes until it is associated with metadata. See Frank Upward, 'Structuring the Records Continuum, Part Two:

course of business it is as likely to be admitted (or statements/ representations from it) as evidence as any other document in any format.

Computer records have been recognised in most Australian jurisdictions either by inserting legislative provisions which are directed to the admissibility of computer evidence or by demonstrating that computer records are a business record.[119] In the United States, Federal Rules of Evidence also admit computer records as business records.[120]

Computer records have been considered copies of originals which needed to meet a number of conditions to be admissible. The admissibility of computer records in Australia includes the following general principles: the computer has been used regularly to store or process the information in question, the computer operated properly at the time the document was created, the document reproduces or derives from information supplied by the business, and it is a routine not programmed process.[121] Electronic records challenge these presumptions in that modifications may have taken place before a record is taken out of a live system into another one.[122]

The problem with electronic data as evidence is that it is not fixed to a specific event or action which can be proved by data representation. For example a letter produced by a word-processing program will not automatically be linked to a document on the same subject matter. Even if the document is captured in a document management system, it may only provide successive versions of a document but not evidence of which version was sent, who authorised it, and if it was received. Email that is admitted as evidence that is clearly not part of a recordkeeping system is an example. However at the same time the weight given to it may diminish as a result of the lack of proof of procedural controls (see 2.4.3 below, 'Evidence legislation and record trustworthiness').

Structuration Theory and the Records Continuum', *Archives and Manuscripts*, vol. 25, no. 1, May 1997, pp. 10-35.

[119] Victoria and Queensland have computer-specific sections as well as business records provisions in their evidence legislation. See *Evidence Act* 1958 (Vic) s 55B and *Evidence Act* 1977 (Qld) s 95.

[120] US-InterPARES Project, *Findings on the Preservation of Authentic Electronic Records*, p. 75.

[121] Brown, *Documentary Evidence in Australia*, Chapter 13.

[122] 'Explicitly recognize that the traditional principle that all records relied upon in the usual and ordinary course of business can be presumed to be authentic needs to be supplemented in the case of electronic records by evidence that the records have not been inappropriately altered.' InterPARES 1 Project, Strategies Task Force, *Report*, December 2001, 'Principle 12', p. 5.

In *Armstrong v Executive Office of the President*,[123] the District Court of Columbia held that under the United States' *Federal Records Act*[124] a 'record' can include material 'regardless of physical form or characteristics', including an e-mail, if it was 'made or received by an agency of the United States under Federal law or in connection with the transaction of public business.'[125] The court determined that once a document in an electronic form is designated as a 'public record', it should be preserved by the relevant agency 'as evidence of the organisation, functions, policies, decisions, procedures, operations, or other activities of the Government or because of the informational value of the data in them.'[126] Importantly it was the relationship of the email to the business of government that made it a public record.[127] This interpretation may not necessarily hold in other jurisdictions.[128]

---

[123] *Armstrong v Executive Office of the President*, 810 F. Supp. 335, at 340-41 (D.D.C. 1993). The case involved inter alia, a question of adequacy of recordkeeping guidelines and instructions with regards to the management of public records in electronic form.

[124] 44 U.S.C.S. § 3301.

[125] *Armstrong v Executive Office of the President*, 810 F. Supp. 335, at 340 (D.D.C. 1993).

[126] Ibid. In the *Armstrong* case the District Court found that the defendant's recordkeeping procedures were arbitrary and capricious because there was no adequate management program or supervision by recordkeeping personnel of the staff's determination of record or non-record status of computer material. Moreover the guidelines did not provide sufficient guidance to determine what was a federal record that must be preserved or destroyed.

[127] David Bearman, 'The Implications of *Armstrong v the Executive Office of the President* for the Archival Management of Electronic Records', in *Electronic Evidence: Strategies for Managing Records in Contemporary Organizations*, Archives and Museum Informatics, Pittsburgh, 1994, pp. 118-144.

[128] In European Union member states, the legal ownership of email in an organisation is unclear. Although the employer determines the purpose of the email system and is the controller with obligations under Directives 95/46/EC and 97/66/EC, there is no clarity in relation to employees' private sphere and their right of confidentiality. Henrik W.K. Kaspersen, 'Data Protection and E-commerce', in *eDirectives: Guide to European Union Law on E-Commerce: Commentary on the Directives on Distance Selling, Electronic Signatures, Electronic Commerce, Copyright in the Information Society, and Data Protection*, Kluwer Law International, Dordrecht, 2002, p. 142. The EU position on human rights and privacy law is unlikely to consider employees' personal email on a business system as business records. This needs to be compared with the very different approach to monitoring employees' email in the United States, upheld in case law on the basis of employers owning

The *Armstrong* case has been important case law regarding not only email but the nature of electronic records in general. It provided a definition of email as a record ('an account made in an enduring form, especially in writing, that preserves the knowledge or memory of events or facts' and 'something on which such an account is made').[129] The court emphasised the need for retaining metadata (header, transmission data, time, sender and receiver) for the email to be considered a record. Importantly it noted that a paper copy is not an equivalent counterpart of an electronic record, and that creation and storage of electronic records should be in recordkeeping systems; the rights of final disposition or retention - who can destroy an electronic record - must be observed; preservation and access to electronic records must be maintained; login files, passwords, audit trails, performance tests, pre-migration files, and old documentation are all needed for evidential reconstruction. The subsequent case, *Public Citizen Inc v John Carlin,* challenged the right of the National Archives and Records Administration (NARA) to instruct government agencies to destroy electronic records if paper versions included all the relevant metadata (as designated in *Armstrong*) and were kept in an official recordkeeping system or in an electronic recordkeeping system as designated by NARA.[130] The court again took the view that a paper copy is not an equivalent to the electronic record. Thus, in relation to electronic records the US cases established limited guidelines for reliability (ie requirements for recordkeeping agents, time and place, and links to related messages) and for authenticity (that a paper copy of an electronic record is not an authentic copy, and that original functionality of the live system must be maintained).[131]

2.4.2 The best evidence rule and record integrity

The best evidence rule, that is, the production of an original record has been a safeguard of record integrity, in particular in the era when

---

employees' computer systems. Milton Babirak et al., 'Electronic Commerce in the USA', in *E-Commerce in the World: Aspects of Comparative Law*, Brussels, 2003, p. 318. See also Chapter 5.

[129] *Armstrong v Executive Office of the President*, 810 F. Supp. 335, at 342 (D.D.C. 1993).

[130] *Public Citizen Inc v John Carlin*, 2 F Supp 2d 1 DDC, 1997. On 6 August 1999, the Court of Appeals for the District of Columbia Circuit reversed its decision and upheld the Archivist's rule.

[131] MacNeil, *Trusting Records*, pp. 77-85. US-InterPARES Project, *Findings on the Preservation of Authentic Electronic Records*, pp. 76-77.

hand-copying or re-setting type could produce errors. In looking at the best evidence rule, which is now largely abolished in common law jurisdictions by statute changes,[132] an important point is that the legal view of an original document was not the first version but the one accepted by the parties involved in the transaction and the one they operated under.[133] The notion of the 'original', the first, complete record capable of achieving its purpose, is also a central diplomatic tenet.[134]

The best evidence rule is based on the notion that 'primary evidence' is the best evidence available; 'secondary evidence' is evidence that suggests better evidence exists. However, the common law developed rules for secondary evidence relating to the contents of the original as well as prima facie presumptions about when a document was written or sent and how to deal with missing documents. Rules governing secondary evidence, that is, how the court dealt with admitting evidence that was not original or that substituted the original allowed copies in certain circumstances to be admitted.[135] The original rather than a copy could prove the truth of the contents, but copies were acceptable under certain circumstances, for example, via testimony, certified copies, or specific statute.[136]

---

[132] The best evidence rule was abolished in Australian federal courts and in the Australian Capital Territory in the 1995 Commonwealth Evidence Act and also in the 1995 NSW Evidence Act. See National Archives of Australia in cooperation with the Attorney-General's Department, the Office of Government Information Technology and the Tasmanian Department of Premier and Cabinet, Information Strategy Unit, *Records in Evidence, The Impact of the Evidence Act on Commonwealth Recordkeeping*, Commonwealth of Australia, 1998, p. 8. The requirement for the original paper record (or an acceptable copy) is still applied in Australia where there is a risk of fraud if an electronically generated record is accepted as proof of a fact. The *Electronic Transactions Act* 1999 (Cth) requires 'original' paper documents for citizenship claims, but electronic communications are acceptable where there is no suspicion of fraud.

[133] Brown, *Documentary Evidence in Australia*, p. 17.

[134] 'An original record is defined as the first, complete record, which is capable of achieving its purposes (that is, it is effective). A record may also take the form of a draft, which is defined as a temporary compilation made for purposes of correction.' Authenticity Task Force, *Final Report*, 28 October 2001, 'Appendix: Requirements for Accessing and Maintaining the Authenticity of Electronic Records', pp. 1-15, footnote 10.

[135] Brown, *Documentary Evidence in Australia*, Chapter 6.

[136] Heydon, *Cross on Evidence*, p. 82 and p. 1144. The original record in court proceedings in the case of a telegram is the one handed in at the post office but for the receiver the message received is the original.

In the Australian *Evidence Act* 1995 (Cth) s 47(2) 'a document that is not an exact copy of the document in question but that is identical to the document in question in all relevant respects' and s 48(1), proof of content provides for tendering the original document, or a copy produced by a device that reproduces the contents of documents such as a computer printout, photocopies, copies that have been scanned, are as good as the original or a business record. The legal acceptance of a copy that is identical in all respects translates into the electronic context where the original will always be a copy or reproduction.[137]

Statutory exceptions to the common law to deal with reproductions, such as microfilm, have been interim steps by the legislature to grapple with records in different formats.[138] The courts had tended to resist statutes which accepted machine-copies whether in the form of sound/visual recordings, for example audio and videotapes, computer output or computer records. Machine-produced documents were usually considered real evidence, that is, a physical thing, and had to be proved by persons programming the computer that the computer had been working properly at the time the printout was made.[139]

The admissibility requirements for photographs are a good example of integrity issues. These included the requirement that the print was an accurate print from the negative and that the negative had not been retouched. There were two methods to prove these aspects; either by tracing the custody of the film from the moment of taking the shots until production in court, or by identification of the ultimate print through oral or other evidence of the scene recorded. The photographer may be called as witness but this was not essential for the admissibility of photographs. Depending on the provisions under which they are admitted, a similar approach has been adopted by the courts for films and videos. Proper custody figures in most of these cases. The admissibility of photographs reveals features of record trustworthiness; it needed evidence of the competence of the person creating the record (record identity) and

---

[137] 'In common language, *copy* and *reproduction* are synonyms. For the purposes of this research, the term reproduction is used to refer to the process of generating a copy, while the term copy is used to refer to the result of such a process, that is, to any entity which resembles and is generated from the records of the creator.' Authenticity Task Force, *Final Report*, 28 October 2001, Appendix, footnote 10.

[138] Brown, *Documentary Evidence in Australia*, Chapter 9; Heydon, *Cross on Evidence*, pp. 1142-1154. Business records provisions in Evidence Acts of all Australian jurisdictions from 1976 onwards included computer output in terms of their creation in the course of a business activity.

[139] Heydon, *Cross on Evidence*, p. 29 and p. 839.

evidence of the accuracy and tamper-proof features of the photographic process (record integrity).

2.4.3 Evidence legislation and record trustworthiness

The changes to the rules of evidence in common law countries such the United States, Canada, United Kingdom and Australia[140] in recent years have provided for more avenues to introduce documentary evidence into legal proceedings, including electronic records.

The 1995 Australian Commonwealth and New South Wales Evidence Acts provide good examples of the acceptance of documents in all formats, including electronic, to be tendered as evidence in court without the previous process of proving their status.[141] Rather than being concerned with the physical format of the document, knowledge about how the records were created and maintained proves their content, which conforms to recordkeeping elements of reliability and trust that are concerned with procedural controls over the creation of records in systems.

The legislation expands the admissibility of hearsay evidence, including documentary evidence, by narrowing the hearsay rule, extending the exceptions to that rule, abolishing the original document rule, and replacing it with simpler means of giving evidence of the contents of documents, including documents held in computer and other non-paper forms. It provides for easier proof of, and presumptions about, business and official records, and the use of mail, fax and other means of communication and allows for pre-trial procedures enabling litigants to test the weight of documentary evidence that might be given in proceedings.[142] The substantial use of presumptions in the 1995 Australian evidence legislation

[140] For example, in Australia the *Evidence Act* 1995 (Cth), the *Evidence Act* 1995 (NSW) and the *Evidence Act* 2001 (Tas). As these reforms preceded the advent of Internet commerce, they address electronic records as evidence but not in the context of the online environment.

[141] Document is defined in the *Evidence Act* 1995 (Cth), s 3, Dictionary, as 'any record of information' and s 3, Clause 8, Part 2, Dictionary, a document includes 'any part of the document; or any copy, reproduction or duplicate of the document or any part of the document; or any part of such a copy, reproduction or duplicate'.

[142] National Archives of Australia, *Records in Evidence*, p. 7. Business records provisions are simplified and integrated within Evidence Act 1995 (Cth).

include presumptions that enable documents, regardless of format, to be acceptable as evidence.[143]

Abolition of the original document rule

The abolition of the original document rule (*Evidence Act* 1995 (Cth) s 51) does not completely detract from the need of either party to prove that the record is what is purports to be, and that its identity and integrity have not been compromised. Elements of identity of the record covered in the legislation include proof of posting; date of receipt of articles sent by post; time and sending of and identity of persons who have sent and received messages by fax, email, telegram, and transmission and receipt by persons of lettergrams and telegrams.

As the Commonwealth commentary states:

> While the 'original document rule' has been abolished, it is still necessary for parties *to authenticate evidence of the contents of documents* given by one of these alternate ways. For example, in relation to a document in writing that is signed, it remains necessary to lead evidence (if the point is contested) that the signature appearing on the document is *the signature of the person who has purported to sign it*. In the case of computer records, it is necessary to give evidence that the *computer output is what it purports to be*.[144]

There is a presumption that procedural controls over record creation were in place, and that the identity of the parties is known, but the onus is on the opposing party to challenge the proof.

> While there are several provisions of the Acts facilitating this authentication process, the Acts also set out procedures under which litigants may test the authenticity of evidence of the contents of documents that is or might be led under one of the alternate ways in a proceeding. In the usual case, these procedures would be used by a party against whom evidence of the contents of a document is or might be led in a proceeding.[145]

---

[143] *Evidence Act* 1995 (Cth) Part 4.3, s 146 and s 147 relate to presumptions that enable documents, regardless of format, as long as they form part of the records belonging to or kept by a person, body or organisation in the course of, or for the purposes of a business, and that are produced by processes, machines or other devices that function properly, to be acceptable as evidence. The rationale being that if a business depends on the records they must be reliable computer documents. The presumptions can be challenged. See Brown, *Documentary Evidence in Australia*, pp. 376-377.

[144] National Archives of Australia, *Records in Evidence*, pp. 11-12. [Emphasis added].

[145] Ibid., p. 12.

The *Uniform Electronic Evidence Act* Canada adopted in 1998 takes the opposite approach to the Commonwealth Evidence Act in that the proponent of the electronic evidence has the burden to prove the trustworthiness of the record as opposed to the opponent who has to disprove the trustworthiness of the evidence. In addition common law and statutory business records exceptions to the hearsay rule are unaffected by the Canadian Evidence Act.[146] In Australia under the Commonwealth Act the opposing party has to specifically instigate procedures before a legal proceeding commences if they wish to test the authenticity of the documents. This may lead to court orders against the party leading the evidence who may be compelled to produce an original document, or allow the examination of a copy, or call a person who manages the recordkeeping system to give evidence, or in the case of a computer or similar document, that a party be permitted to examine and test the way in which the document was produced or had been kept. Section 171 of the *Evidence Act* 1995 (Cth) continues with the notion of a responsible recordkeeper who can provide relevant evidence on how a business or any specialised records have been maintained. This would suggest that in order to ensure that the presumptions can be supported, a common practice of audit trails, time stamping, procedures for routine checking of the accuracy of the storage processes, and document malfunctions are kept.[147]

Even if the original document rule has been abolished, businesses need to have reliable systems because their opponents can challenge both the reliability and the authenticity of the records.

2.4.4 Record as process and evidence law

The evidentiary nature of records derives from their creation in the context of an action and their retention as evidence of that action and related processes, and it is this connection that makes records potentially relevant to a range of legal disputes if they arise, but they are not created to specifically serve that purpose, that is, they are not self-serving.

Modern evidence law has shifted its focus away from the record as a material object to a record as the outcome of reliable business processes. Evidence legislation and case law reveal that records that are part of a system of recordkeeping, in possession or control of a business which has a responsible recordkeeper, are likely to be admissible under business

---

146 MacNeil, *Trusting Records*, p. 54; p. 134, footnote 137.

147 National Archives of Australia, *Records in Evidence*, pp. 16-17.

records rules.[148] For example, the business records provisions in evidence legislation define records in terms which relate to their existence as part of recordkeeping systems. These provisions no longer define documents in terms of their physical attributes.

The 1995 Commonwealth and New South Wales Evidence Acts and the various business records provisions found in the Evidence Acts in all Australian jurisdictions view records as part of a trustworthy system in order to presume the document is reliable. Heather MacNeil points to the Uniform Law Conference of Canada (ULCC) in 1997 and how it justified the special rule for electronic evidence based on its special vulnerability to undetectable change. The best evidence rule was inappropriate, and the notion of an 'original document' moved to a 'system' view. The ULCC stated that 'the integrity of the record-keeping system is the key to proving the integrity of the record, including any manifestation of the record created, maintained, displayed, reproduced or printed out by a computer system'.[149] The presumption of integrity is based on the integrity of the computer system that produced the record at the time of admitting the evidence.

Records as evidence for legal proceedings require evidence of competencies of the creators (identity), and evidence of permissions to use the record so that they have not been altered (integrity). The nature of the legal system and how documents have been used in, or relate to, legal proceedings, the definitions of documents and records in the laws of evidence, including their relevance to electronic evidence, all have to be taken into account in determining the trustworthiness of the record.

Standards of record trustworthiness operate on informal social rules of communities of common interest, societies that trust records, the technologies that produce them, political and economic environments that may be more or less conducive to trust and the way the legal system has trusted records as evidence.

---

[148] An example of case law in which the reliability of a record was enhanced by the fact that it formed part of a recordkeeping system is found in, *Tubby Trout Pty Ltd v Sailbay Pty Ltd* (1993) ACLR 195 FC. This is a particularly interesting judgment in terms of whether a letter formed part of the records of a particular business, the opinion being that it had to form part of a record system kept by the business to meet requirements of reliability. Section 1305 of the Corporations Law was considered in conjunction with the *Evidence Act* 1905 (Cth) ss 7B, 7H. See also National Archives of Australia, *Records in Evidence*.

[149] As quoted in MacNeil, *Trusting Records*, p. 52. In Canada the 'system' is defined to include features that are not embedded in the computer system itself.

A trustworthy record depends in part on trustworthy record creators whose identity depends on the trust that communities of common interest provide through social, legal, and procedural controls. It is a two-way dependence as community is also dependent on identity as either 'togetherness' or 'otherness'. Social and legal controls are relevant to social relationships that are formed by an act that has legal and social consequences. Before the advent of electronic communication it had not been necessary to document every aspect of the relationship, as elements of trust and identity have been part of the social fabric of any community. In the online context these social and legal controls have to be documented as part of the record (whether as metadata, recordkeeping or archival description) and inextricably linked to the record to which they relate. They are not in themselves new concepts because diplomatics, archival science and records continuum principles provide for identifying elements of trust, either through documentary form, procedure, or as metadata captured by the record, system, entity, and policy-directing bodies. In addition evidence law in the quest for proof and certainty, have developed rules for authenticating records that depend on reliable recordkeeping systems. On the other hand, access and privacy rights may interfere with the record's identity and integrity and the evidence of rights and obligations that arise from legal and social relationships.

3 LEGAL AND SOCIAL RELATIONSHIPS AND THE RECORDKEEPING NEXUS

In the previous chapter it was established that a culture of trust depends on a community's value system, which in turn is essential to how it regulates itself. Legal and social relationships are a particular way of exploring the recordkeeping-law-ethics nexus from concepts found in archival science, modern recordkeeping concepts, jurisprudence and ethics. The notion of social relationships as networks that form the basis of a juridical system, in which documents witness the relationships, is a central tenet of archival science. The initial reason for the preservation of documents has been to confer certainty on relationships between persons in a given society. This usually means that documents that preserve rights and power have been considered the most important.[1] Social relationships are also bound by ethical considerations sanctioned by their own 'communities of interest' within norms of a universally acceptable moral community. The legal and social relationship model can be applied to a record as 'a business transaction' that creates, alters and 'destroys' the relationship, that is equally relevant to electronic transactions. The model is also predicated on the need for an approach that cuts across a number of legal and normative systems and can have universal application, but particular legal systems will of necessity contextualise the concept.

[1] Paola Carucci, *Le Fonti Archivistiche: Ordinamento e Conservazione*, Carocci, Rome, 1998 (1983), p. 52.

3.1 Legal and social relationships: jurisprudential and ethical dimensions

3.1.1 A legal relationship as a jurisprudential concept

'The notion of a legal relationship is a shorthand way of saying two persons are related by some act, event or dealing'.[2] From a recordkeeping view the event, act or dealing automatically triggers a transaction or a series of transactions within a business process (see Fig. 1, A Simple 'Business' Transaction). As a result of the transaction, the persons participating are related to each other, legally and socially. Legal relations in the strict sense only apply to acts as facts, which have a legal consequence, recognised by the legal system.[3] Although Simon Fisher's definition above does not differentiate the event from the act, it is useful to distinguish between them, using the Kantian notion of an act which involves acting intentionally, and thus accepting responsibility for the act, from an event, which does not include a human element of choice.[4]

---

[2] Simon Fisher, 'General Principles of Obligations', in *The Law of Commercial and Professional Relationships*, ed. Simon Fisher, F.T. Law & Tax, South Melbourne, 1996, p. 17.

[3] In jurisprudence the abstract definition of a legal relationship is referred to as a 'jural relation'. There is no systematic treatment of the term 'jural relation' in most Anglo-American legal writings. Although Roman law did not have a term for jural relations, a number of German writers in the 1860s included the concept in legal treatises. For Albert Kocourek the jural relationship is the rule of law applied to social events that have a legal consequence. Since the law does not govern every possible situation of fact it follows that a jural relation, likewise, does not attach to every situation of fact. He defines 'legal relations' as actual or assumed relationships, and 'jural relations' as the abstraction of the juristic elements of a legal relation. Albert Kocourek, *Jural Relations*, 2nd edn, The Bobbs-Merrill Company, Indianapolis, 1928, p. vi, p. 31 and pp. 75-76, footnote 3. An example in civil law systems of the term 'legal relationship' is in the Italian 'rapporto giuridico' defined as 'every interpersonal relationship regulated by law'. G. Leroy Certoma, *The Italian Legal System*, Butterworths, Sydney, 1985 pp. 19-20.

[4] See Chapter 4. Kant differentiates an act as a human ability from an event as a fact which an animal can trigger because there is no requirement for a motive or an intention. Events within the Kantian view are relevant to the movements of animals only. Processes in computers may be seen as events or acts, the former raising the question of accountability for the outcomes of the processes. For a discussion on outcomes of automated machines as agents, see Chris Reed, *Internet Law: Text and Materials*, Butterworths, London, 2000, p. 181, footnote 8.

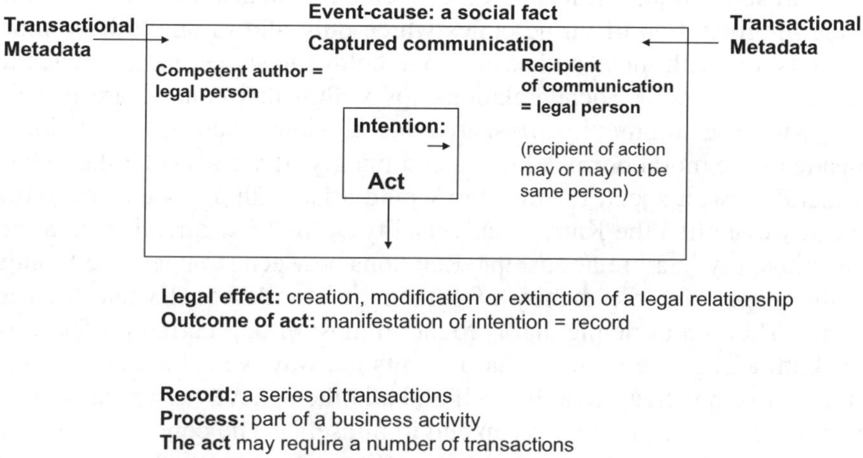

Fig. 1 A Simple 'Business' Transaction

3.1.2 An ethical dimension of a legal relationship

A number of ethical principles, including Kantian duties, 'virtues' in virtue ethics, the notion of trust in the 'ethical demand', and rights-based ethical theories, are relevant to the nature of legal and social relationships. Rights and duties are prevalent in the deontological tradition, and for this reason this form of ethics lends itself to the notion of reciprocal rights and duties, which is also the basis of legal relations. It is therefore appropriate to view legal and ethical elements as a composite part of social relationships, even if in practice the legal aspects are sanctioned under different rule-systems.

If legal relations in the strict sense only apply to acts as facts which have a legal consequence recognised by the legal system, facts which create rights and obligations of no direct legal consequence, are simply social relationships. If we take the view of law as classified by judicial remedies rather than rights and obligations, only litigation or the threat of litigation can clarify the legal rights of parties to the action.[5] An ethical dimension

[5] Jane Stapleton, 'A New "Seascape" for Obligations: Reclassification on the Basis of Measure of Damages,' in *Classification of Obligations*, ed. Peter Birks, Clarendon Press, Oxford, 1997, pp. 193-231.

has no place in judicial remedies unless it is built into the kind of remedies available, for example damages in unintentional torts.

Do all social relationships involve an ethical dimension? If we subscribe to the interpretation of virtue ethics which only allows one to have moral relationships with those with whom one holds the same moral views, then the answer is 'no'.[6] Social relationships within this context are possible only within a community of shared moral views, and are very limited outside of the moral norms of one's community. If we consider the 'ethical demand' view, a social relationship would arise with anyone or everyone. And if we applied the Kantian universality of the 'categorical imperative', it would apply in all relationships. Relations between strangers are founded on the respect for the dignity of persons in Kant's equal value for each person. This is a principle that is found in most of the 'caring professions'. It is both a negative norm in that it limits the way we act against persons, but it is also positive, 'treat himself and all others, never as a means, but in every case at the same time as an end in himself'.[7] The core element of the Kantian rational position is the universality requirement: the necessity to move from seeing the world and the interests of others purely from one's own point of view to seeing both one's own and others' interests from a position of impartiality between them.[8]

Is ethics a normative system that uses different sanctions from the law? In Chapters 1 and 2 on the nature of communities and how they are regulated, it was clear that social norms are enforceable outside of legal rules. 'Extra-legal' norms also affect how legal relationships are created and performed. This is evident in areas of law which try to regulate behaviour, like anti-discrimination legislation.[9]

---

[6] According to virtue ethicists who ascribe to the social practice school, there is no shared set of moral concepts in society. This means that each of us has to choose both with whom we wish to be morally bound and by what ends, rules, and virtues we wish to be guided. These two choices are linked. In choosing certain ends or virtues over others certain moral relationships are possible and others impossible. Alasdair MacIntyre, *A Short History of Ethics: A History of Moral Philosophy from the Homeric Age to the Twentieth Century*, 2nd edn, University of Notre Dame Press, Notre Dame, Indiana, 1998, p. 268.

[7] Roger J. Sullivan, *An Introduction to Kant's Ethics*, Cambridge University Press, New York, 1994, Chapter 4, and p. 67.

[8] John Charvet, *The Idea of an Ethical Community*, Cornell University Press, Ithaca New York and London, 1995, p. 122.

[9] Simon Fisher, 'Introduction', in *The Law of Commercial and Professional Relationships*, ed. Simon Fisher, F.T. Law & Tax, South Melbourne, 1996, p. 8.

3.1.3 Trust and social relationships

Trust is a social concept essential to social relationships.[10] The notion of trust as an ethical demand in human relationships is the central tenet of Knud Ejler Logstrup. The ethical demand of Logstrup presupposes that all interaction between human beings involves a basic trust. Logstrup places the emphasis on person-to-person relationships, placing ethical relationships into a specific time and space. The demand does not change, while law and social norms are forever changing. For Logstrup trust relationships do not depend on law. One takes care of the life which trust has placed in our hands to serve their interest, so exploiting a person with whom we have a relationship would be unethical. This responsibility is not limited in the way in which the responsibilities assigned to the holder of a particular position or office are limited in archival science. It is not possible to know ahead all the responsibilities. It is not derivable from or founded upon any universal rule or set of rights.[11] It is a one-sided demand, so that we can never be in a position to demand something in return for what we do. In this sense it is not a reciprocal relationship as in the legal and social relationship model, but an alternative view.[12]

In a recordkeeping context the one-sided demand would mean assessing the ethical action for each event and divorcing it from legal requirements. It is difficult to apply to organisations because the ethical demand theory is concerned with individual action only. However the notion of trust is also essential to the reciprocal view of legal and social relationships.

3.2 Legal relationships and the law of obligations

The 'law of obligations' provides an area of common concern to two major legal system types, that is, the common law and the civil law legal systems. This makes it an ideal tool for the online environment which must search for legal and recordkeeping principles that are not tied to a specific legal system. There are however differences in the way that the two legal system

[10] Trust is considered a 'natural' motive by David Hume, and it is not found in Aristotelian virtues. Roger Crisp and Michael Slote, 'Introduction', in *Virtue Ethics*, eds, Roger Crisp and Michael Slote, Oxford University Press, 1997, p. 24.

[11] Hans Fink and Alasdair MacIntyre, 'Introduction', in Knud Ejler Logstrup, *The Ethical Demand*, University of Notre Dame Press, Notre Dame and London, 1997, p. xxxiv.

[12] Logstrup, *The Ethical Demand*, p. 123.

types have developed an approach to the law of obligations, which significantly affect convergence.

Although the common law recognises a number of commercial and professional relationships, the nature of which determine the rights and obligations of the parties concerned, Simon Fisher argues that it does not provide a systematic treatment of the 'law of obligations', as found in civil law systems.[13] The range of remedial actions in common law has not been reduced to a rational system of legally-regulated relationships.[14] This difference also accounts for a less integrated theory of law with recordkeeping theory in common law countries than that found in civil law countries, in particular Italy, where records have been defined in relation to legal acts.

3.2.1 Roman law origin of the law of obligations

Simon Fisher finds the roots of the law of obligations in Roman law.

> One of the central elements of the Roman legal system was its highly systematic and structured approach to private law. As part of this highly systematised approach, Roman private law was divided into a trichotomy of *persons*, *things* and *actions*. In turn, the law of 'things' subdivided further into the law of *property* and the law of *obligations*. So the inspiration for the recognition of 'obligations' as a discrete or stand-alone legal category is the ordering and systemisation which Roman law imprinted on the very concept.[15]

Persons, things (property and obligations) and actions are all elements of legal relationships and components of record creation as defined in diplomatics, as well as entities used in conceptual recordkeeping models (see 3.3.3 below, 'Recordkeeping and the jurisprudential concept of a legal relationship').

---

[13] Fisher, 'General Principles of Obligations', p. 17. Fisher's book provides a systematic treatment of commercial and professional relationships by focusing on the law of obligations.

[14] Joshua Getzler, 'Patterns of Fusion', in *Classification of Obligations*, ed. Peter Birks, Clarendon Press, Oxford, 1997, p. 168.

[15] Simon Fisher, 'The Archival Enterprise, Public Archival Institutions and the Impact of Private Law', *Archives and Manuscripts*, vol. 26, no. 2, Nov. 1998, p. 335.

A legal relationship is in fact an obligation.[16] The obligation could be perceived from one side as a right of the 'obligor', and from the other, as a duty of the 'obligee'. Fisher quotes Zimmerman's definition, 'a two-ended relationship which appears from the one end as a personal right to claim and from the other as a duty to render performance.'[17] Legally it is devoid if one person entitled to demand performance from another cannot enforce the claim or gain compensation from its failure. Thus a legal obligation includes a legally recognised right of one person to the performance of a duty by another person, which the law will have a remedy for if a breach of the duty occurs.[18] As correlatives, the right and the duty constitute a legal bond. Morally, an obligation is only enforceable if the community that approves or disapproves the action has a system for its recognition and enforcement.

3.2.2 Origin of the law of obligations in common law

Given the status in common law legal systems of the individual in society, within groups, in the family or in corporations, law and custom derive obligations for the individual, *which are autonomous of his will*, while civil law legal systems attributes the fountain of obligations to contract and to *the will of the individual*. These differences affect property concepts, agency, and negligence.[19] The restriction in the Italian law of legal

[16] Simon Fisher, 'Preface', in *The Law of Commercial and Professional Relationships*, p. vii. In Roman law the obligation was a relationship between persons, a personal tie, the 'obligatio est iuris vinculum'. Puntschart, a nineteenth century German jurist, draws his ideas from Roman law in which legal norms relate to persons, things, the relations of persons to things and to persons. Persons are tied to persons, and persons to things which create legal bonds. This is the jural bond, 'juris nexus' and the 'juris vinculum' which runs throughout the whole system of Roman law. Kocourek, *Jural Relations*, p. 403. However, according to Simon Fisher the notion of obligations binding persons is also found in common law judicial references. See Fisher, 'The Archival Enterprise', p. 330, footnote 7; 'In Brett v Barr Smith (1919) 26 CLR 87 at 97, Higgins J said "obligation" involves binding'.

[17] Fisher, 'Introduction', *The Law of Commercial and Professional Relationships*, p. 7.

[18] Fisher, 'General Principles of Obligations', p. 15.

[19] Francesco de Franchis (ed), *Law Dictionary, English-Italian*, vol. 1, Giuffre, Milan, 1984, pp. 65-66. Common law systems did not develop a general theory of obligations. Rather it is a composite of the law of contract and the law of torts. But a peculiar characteristic of the common law arising from its feudal

relations to voluntary actions of the subject is relevant to the notion of the will of the individual as an essential element of the 'legal act' in the diplomatics analysis of what constitutes an archival document (see further discussion below, 3.3 'Recordkeeping theory and legal relationships').

In the common law system the master-servant relationship is the earliest formulation of a legal relationship.[20] The law of torts in the common law system is particularly concerned with legal relations, the law of obligations and consequently with acts, facts and events. In the Anglo-American tradition rights are part of what the relationship is about, the correlatives of rights and duties.[21] An alternative view of the law of obligations in common law is to focus on remedial action or damages rather than the claimant's rights or position centred on the level of judicial intervention that is justified to ensure both parties are protected. Thus the courts consider the remedies first and then conclude the rights of the plaintiff.[22] In diplomatics the nature of the juridical act and its legal effects, the notion of the will to create a record, lead to obligations and/or rights, in which the document stands as testimony of those rights and obligations.

3.2.3 Civil law obligations and its common law counterpart

Fisher has synthesised the Roman law understanding of obligations into the common law recognition of legal relationships. The law of obligations in the civil and the common law system finds its genesis within private law. The civilian notion of obligation unifies bodies of law which the common law has kept distinct despite occasional judicial references to the

---

origin is the concept of relation, not as a result of the voluntary autonomy of the subject but arising from a legal regime of obligations.

[20] Danuta Mendelson, *Torts*, 3rd edn, Butterworths Casebook Companions, Butterworths, Sydney, 2002, pp. 143-146. The master's legal responsibilities, as head of the household, for his servants' and children's actions provide the origin of the employer's vicarious liability for employees' actions during the course of employment.

[21] Kocourek, *Jural Relations*, p. 41.

[22] Getzler, 'Patterns of Fusion', p. 168. 'To tie' in the Roman law of obligations is 'ligare'. By contrast to Fisher, Getzler argues that in English law to have an obligation can only mean to owe a duty to another. The classification of law by remedies is espoused by Stapleton, 'A New "Seascape" for Obligations', pp. 193-231. She recommends that every type of obligation should have one type of remedy.

notion of obligation.[23] Roman law makes property an obligation, and an obligation is a composite 'right-and-duty thing'.[24] Property in common law refers to a 'thing in action' or a 'chose in action' as an assignable right that is intangible.[25] Thus ownership is an intangible thing which arises from the relationship between two persons, a concept that has applicability to ownership of records, not as objects but as right-duty things (see Fig. 2, Law of Obligations: Comparison of Roman and Common Law). The jural bond is central to the Roman legal method, to Fisher's legal model and to archival science as formulated from diplomatics. The jural act ties the parties in the action. The right of ownership is 'the sum of legal powers which spring from the ownership bond to use a thing for all the purposes of the person which can availably be realized'.[26] Rather than the view of ownership as a right or a bundle of rights, it is a legal bond between a person and a thing as relationship. Rights are derivative from this bond.

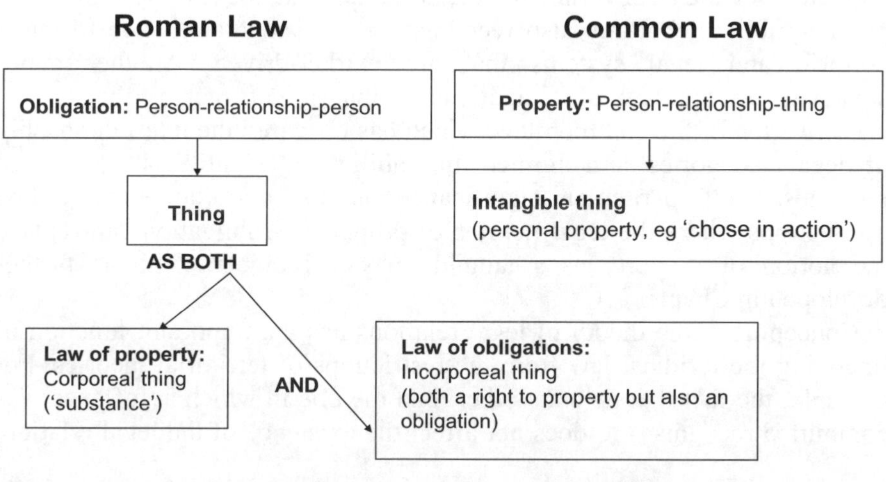

Fig. 2 Property Law and the Law of Obligations: Comparison of Roman and Common Law

[23] Fisher, 'General Principles of Obligations', pp. 16-18. Roman law divided obligations into four subsets; contract, quasi-contract, delict and quasi-delict. In modern civil codes there are conceptual linkages to the Roman law divisions.
[24] Fisher, 'The Archival Enterprise', p. 336.
[25] See 'chose in action' in Chapter 5.
[26] Puntschart's analysis as interpreted by Kocourek, *Jural Relations*, p. 43.

Property is not the only source of obligations. In the Roman taxonomy, contract and tort are also sources of obligations as is the distinction between voluntary and involuntary obligations. The effects of obligations in Fisher's analysis of common law can be divided into primary consequences, which place the obligee under a duty to perform or discharge an obligation, that is the substantive obligation, and the secondary consequences which arise when the obligation is not performed. This is the remedial obligation. For example, if a contract is not discharged, the substantive obligation may lead to civil action for damages as a remedial action. A tort obligation may involve a duty of care and a remedial action may include damages awarded for negligent behaviour.[27] Sanctions apply to legal relations based on legal rules.[28]

Fisher demonstrates how the law of obligations can also transcend the private-public law divide. Although essentially grounded in private law because of its origin in the Roman law of obligations, Fisher believes it applies equally to public law.[29] Given that social activity is now largely regulated outside of government, a legal model that does not depend on the private-public dichotomy also recognises a fundamental change to many political and legal systems that are market-driven. Another major advantage to the law of obligations is that it cuts across the subject classification of the common law, which has obscured the interrelationship of legal categories and limited the ability to identify a variety of remedies.[30] Of particular significance is its importance to online transactions where the legal notions of property as obligation can replace the notion of property as a tangible physical object. (This is further developed in Chapter 7.)

Conceptually the theory of legal relations has the important function of liberating the juridical law from the restrictions of territorial theories. For example, the fact that no state other than the one in which an offence was committed recognises it, does not affect the existence of the legal relation.

---

[27] The extent to which common law lawyers agree on the nature and origin of contract and tort has been much debated, see Fisher, 'General Principles of Obligations', pp. 19-21.

[28] A sanction has been defined as 'inflicting a specific evil upon a specific person in consequence of a specific act or omission.' Kocourek, *Jural Relations*, quoting Terry, p. 343.

[29] Fisher, 'General Principles of Obligations', p. 16.

[30] Peter Birks, 'Editor's Preface', in *The Classification of Obligations*, argues the need to constantly revise the taxonomy of law. See also Ernest J. Weinrib, 'The Juridical Classification of Obligations', in *The Classification of Obligations*, pp. 37-55.

Similar sanctionable legal relations will exist in other jurisdictions; only the remedies may differ.[31]

3.2.4 Characteristics of a legal relationship

If an event or act that triggers a transaction or a series of transactions gives rise to a legal relationship in which the transacting parties have rights and obligations, it is important to recognise the elements of the relationship.

For both Kocourek and Fisher the characteristics of a legal relationship are:

- two legal persons, and
- an act or event (that is facts), and
- a definite legal effect following the act.

For example, a visit to the doctor is an event in which two legal persons, the patient and the doctor, are legally bound by the occurrence. The act requires a 'meeting of minds', and an intentional decision to have the event occur.

Definitions of acts, facts, persons and things

The capability to claim an act from another is called a 'right' (in the strict sense). The capability to act against another is called a 'power'. In Kocourek's model a claim is the preferred term for a right; a capability to claim acts from others or the power to act against others requires *persons* and *acts* (see Fig. 3, Kocourek's Model of Jural Relations).[32]

---

[31] Kocourek, *Jural Relations*, pp. 234-237.

[32] Terms used in Figure 3 include: *nexal line*: one way only in a legal relationship; *acts*: legal result of the relationship; *claim*: a legal capability to require a positive or negative act of another person; *immunity*: a legal capability (that is, a legal advantage) to prevent a positive act or negative act of another, for example immunity from arrest is a claim not to be arrested; *privilege*: legal capability to decline an act toward another; *power*: a capability to act with legal effect toward another; *right* is often used for a privilege as the term for the side with the legal advantage in all types of jural relations and *ligation* or tie is the servient side of the relationship. A *duty* as a claim corresponds to a right. There can be no right without a duty, but there can be a duty without a right.

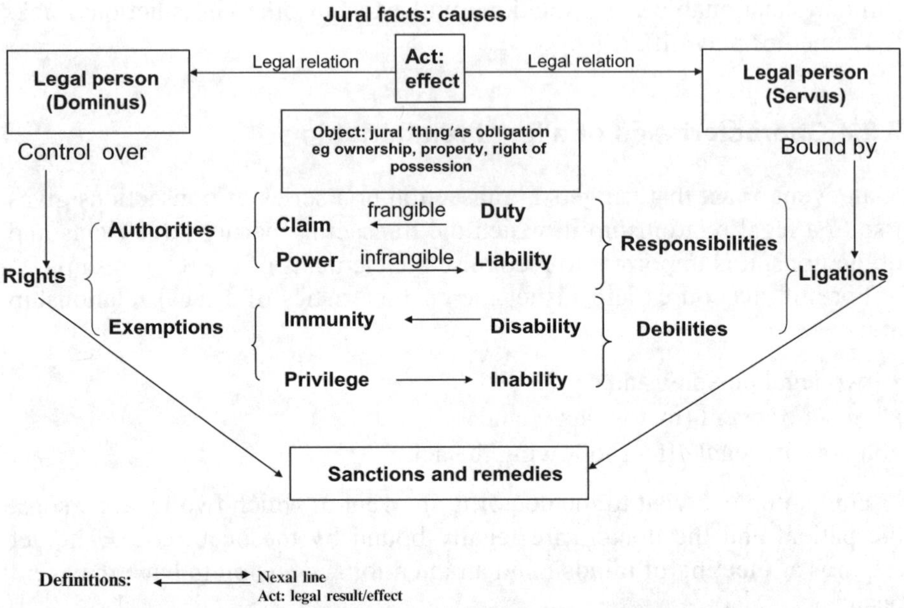

Fig. 3 Kocourek's Model of Jural Relations

Based on Albert Kocourek, *Jural Relations,* 2nd edn, The Bobbs-Merrill Company, Indianapolis, 1928, p. 21, Table 1.

Figure 3 represents Kocourek's model of a legal relationship which divides rights and ligations into specific sub-types. The model consists of a *dominus* (holder of the relation), who has the active right, and a *servus* (bearer) of the relation, who has a passive claim. Complex jural relationships, for example one debtor with two creditors, result in two relationships.

For Fisher, the two persons or parties are referred to as the obligor and the obligee. He defines an obligation as both a right and a duty which creates a legal bond, that is the legally recognised right of one person and the duty to be performed by another (Fig. 4, Fisher's Model of a Legal Relationship). For example, a doctor has a duty to provide a medical service to the best of his/her ability; the patient has a right to the service remaining confidential. *Acts*, together with *events*, bring jural relations into existence, modify or extinguish them.

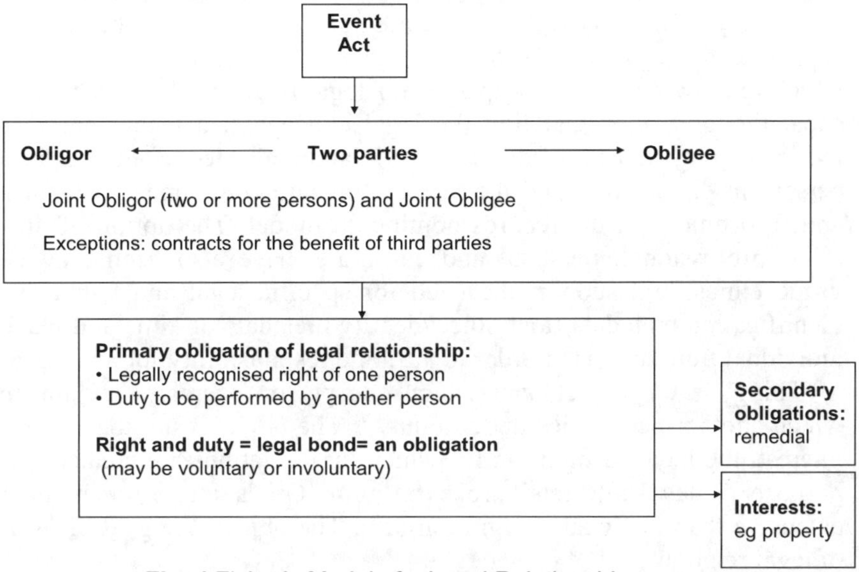

Fig. 4 Fisher's Model of a Legal Relationship

According to Fisher 'a legal person is "an entity on which a legal system confers rights and imposes duties". That is, this definition of "legal person" positively connects the idea of legal personality to whether or not the supposed legal person is capable of assuming obligations (that is, a composite right-and-duty thing)'.[33] 'Legal personality' is the sum total of the legal relations of a person, which includes the sum total of the legal rights (claims and powers) and ligations (duties and liabilities). Human beings and legal persons (personae) can be separate entities. Legal persons may antedate and post-date the life of human beings.[34] Examples of a legal

[33] Fisher, 'The Archival Enterprise', p. 330, quoting from *Butterworths Concise Australian Legal Dictionary*, Butterworths, Sydney, 1997, 'legal person'.

[34] Kocourek, *Jural Relations*, p, 227, footnote 1. There is an issue as to whether jurists consider a human being as representing a legal person. In European codes a human being is a legal person. In Anglo-American law legal persons can antedate and post-date legal relations. Generally in Anglo-American law legal personateness requires a human being, a group, a succession of human beings or an anticipated or retrospective human being. A corporation for example can be immortal. In Roman law, complexes of objects and legal relations can be legally personified. In common law some material things are personified. Kocourek defines physical personateness as a social fact, while legal personateness is a legal fact.

person include a human being (living, dead, or unborn), corporation, and an agency. Basically different kinds of legal persons have different capacities for legal relationships. A legal person (persona) is any entity to which the law attributes a capacity for legal relations. It is these different capacities and roles that link the legal concept of a legal person to the recordkeeping concept of the 'author' in archival science and the 'juridical person' in diplomatics, and the 'actor', 'organisational units', 'organisation' and 'institution' in the records continuum model. The notion of different roles, professional, personal and corporate, have also been drawn from virtue ethics, and support the need for specific legal and human person identification metadata (and other identity metadata on time and place) for individual transactions in order to attribute responsibility for an action.[35]

'Thing' is the object over which one person exercises a right and to which another person lies under a duty.[36] The object is not the same as the interest, the legal recognition for which jural relations are created. For the purpose of law 'interests' are extra-jural. One's interest may be more extensive than the legal recognition of it. The object (thing) itself is a kind of legal relation.

The act is the dynamic element of the legal relationship which is also necessary for record creation. There are various analyses of the nature of an act which are central to attributing responsibility for the act. The physical act alone requires an exertion of the will, for example attending a clinic in order to be examined. In Kant, the will and the action are one, that is, if one wills an action one finds the means to carry it out. In addition, an accompanying state of consciousness that one is carrying out an act is needed. In relation to categories of liability, even particular kinds of consciousness are categorised as intentional and unintentional acts. Intentional acts can be malicious or intentional without malice. Non-intentional acts also have categories. Criminal law also attempts to classify states of mind. A doctor unintentionally omits particular procedures which harm the patient; evidence of the unintentional action may be relevant to a liability claim.

The consequences that follow an act also work as motives or drivers for further acts. Kocourek does not believe that attempting to define intention

---

[35] See Chapter 4 and the analysis of the Monash Recordkeeping Metadata Schema, which introduces the term 'agent' to encompass the four terms of Upwards records continuum model, that is, person/actor, organisational unit/workgroup, organisation/corporate body, and social institution.

[36] Kocourek, *Jural Relations*, quoting Holland, p. 305. Things are further explored in Chapter 5.

is useful and instead concentrates on outcomes. This contrasts with Kant and the virtue ethicists, for whom motive rather than outcome is central to action. Intention and motive are important to ethical and legal responsibility, and to whether parties intended to create a record.[37] The notion of will is also found in diplomatics. Recordkeeping metadata which identifies the legal author who has permission from the socio-legal system to create the record is also likely to be a more reliable one. For example, the doctor's professional qualifications and standing will affect both the intention and motives of his acts; acts (as events which are willed) are necessary for record creation.

The manifestation of the will is through some outward expression of the act, which in most cases has been the record. Accountability is provided by the evidence of the relationship of the actor to the event, and the application of a standard to measure this objective relation. The primary issue for courts is what is done and the secondary issue is the cause.[38] Business transactions as the outcome of events triggered by actions of consenting persons are therefore relevant to providing evidence of both primary and secondary aspects of legal liability. For example, the doctor's act may have resulted in the patient being harmed, even if unintended; the motive may have been to help the patient, and the cause of the harm may have been due to an untried medical procedure.

The qualities of legal relations are relevant to bringing many kinds of records into existence. A fact triggers an event which involves initially at least two parties. The record has no continuing legal significance if the legal persons cease to exist. Conceptually the qualities of a legal relation are not tied to a specific legal system. Records as 'things' create, modify or destroy rights and obligations of parties in transactions.

The act and liability

Legal consequences of legal relations are evidenced in business transactions. The act, for purposes of liability, is the legal concept of a result. There are two kinds of liability: the occurrence of an objective harm or no harm, for example a breach of a contract is actionable without proof of a harm. Acts may be positive or negative: acts of commission and acts

[37] Intention and motive in record creation are further developed in Chapter 4.

[38] Kocourek, *Jural Relations*, p. 266. There are three types of theory on the nature of an act. The act as a muscular contraction (or a series of such contractions); the act as consisting of muscular contractions, surrounding circumstances, and the consequences; and the act as a legal concept the result of either a bodily movement or attributable to its absence (the latter is Kocourek's view).

of omission, for example not warning of a danger is an act of omission common in medical negligence. The act as liability has application to all jural consequences that are attributable to legal persons through the activities of human beings.[39] The record will provide circumstantial evidence of the consequences of action.

It has always been difficult to base any sort of responsibility on a particular state of mind. In the area of strict liability for an act, the irrelevance of motive is apparent and it is one of the most notable differences from the ethical point of view of responsibility, in particular the Kantian view of motive and act. Rights, powers, claims and duties are used as a means of ascertaining legal liabilities, and are also put forward in ethical systems. Ethical duties may be self-imposed or imposed by others, and ethical rights can be defined by referring to the duties that moral agents do and do not have towards themselves and others. The 'other-regarding' duties underlie both negative and positive rights, which can be owed either by particular individuals or groups (*in personam* rights) or by moral agents in general (*in rem* rights). In legal contexts the *in personam* rights are positive (the positive action of someone to repay a debt), and the *in rem* rights are negative (general duty not to steal). Generally legal rights that are linked to duties of positive assistance are restricted to particular individuals.[40]

The system of rights and duties which a legal and/or ethical system has adopted is relevant to identifying rights and obligations of recordkeeping participants in relation to specific legal relationships.[41] In addition, legal relations deal with things as rights, so although property is an object, it is equally a legal relationship. This supports the view that records are right-duty things that create, modify or destroy the rights and obligations of parties in transactions.

---

[39] Ibid., pp. 268-269; p. 276.

[40] Matti Häyry, *Liberal Utilitarianism and Applied Ethics*, Routledge, London, New York, 1994, pp. 135-145. Moral rights include a licence or permission to choose a course of action only if there is a negative duty not to choose. The absence of duty to refrain from courses of action is also called a privilege or liberty in philosophic-legal literature, but a licence applies to anyone. Häyry defines 'claim rights' as negative and positive claim rights.

[41] See Chapter 6.

3.3 Recordkeeping theory and legal relationships

3.3.1 Diplomatics and archival science: the document as witness to social relationships

The Roman law concept of legal relationships is central to diplomatics. Diplomatics has been defined by Pratesi in terms of a science that has as its objective the critical study of the document.[42] It is the study of single documents, mainly their formal aspects, to understand their juridical significance, both in relation to their creation and their legal effects.[43] Legal relations are concerned with the creation of legal obligations and their effects. Archival science includes the wider study of the institutional context of documents because there is often deviation between the law and its practice, that is, the legal apparatus and society.[44] Diplomatics, even more than archival science, explicitly includes the identification of the juridical person involved in the creation of the record, notions of volition in recordmaking, acts, and facts.

In diplomatics, social relationships which are witnessed by the document are provided with legal certainty because they are recorded in a particular form that is recognisable to all the participants in the social system in which they live.[45] The record participates in the legal relationship between persons, facts and effects, as grounded in the jurisprudential discourse of the law of obligations.

'The document is defined as "evidence"' because the document is retrospectively analysed as a source for proving facts'.[46] The subtle shift from evidence to testimony in the nineteenth century occurred when diplomatics began to be considered an auxiliary science of history, and archival science widened the role of records to include their social function.[47] It illuminates Paola Carucci's definition of a document as testimony and witness of events, which unlike evidence of a legal fact, is

---

[42] 'La scienza che ha per oggetto lo studio critico del documento'. A. Pratesi as quoted in Maria Guercio, *Archivistica Informatica: I Documenti in Ambiente Digitale*, Carocci, Rome, 2002, p. 19.

[43] Paola Carucci, *Il Documento Contemporaneo, Diplomatica e Criteri di Edizione*, Carocci, Rome 1998 (1987), p. 28.

[44] Ibid., p. 31.

[45] See Chapter 2 on documentary form.

[46] Luciana Duranti, 'Introduction', in *Diplomatics: New Uses for an Old Science*, The Society of American Archivists and Association of Canadian Archivists in association with The Scarecrow Press, Maryland and London, 1998, pp. 5-6.

[47] Luciana Duranti, 'The Archival Bond', *Archives and Museum Informatics*, vol. 11, 1997, p. 214, footnote 15.

inclusive of memory of social events that can serve a number of purposes.[48] Carucci emphasises that even when the juridical effects have gone, records are important for historical research, as well as having continuing probative value. Thus Italian archival science is concerned as much with the social dimension of records as their legal context.[49]

3.3.2 The juridical act as a legal relationship in diplomatics

A juridical system in Italian diplomatics only attaches juridical significance to the acts and facts that have a legal consequence. This accords with the legal theory on legal relations as expounded by Kocourek. The legal status of acts and facts can vary over time and space, or within a legal system, or in different legal systems. Carucci speaks of a plurality of legal rules historically determined.[50]

Both Carucci and Duranti support the institutional conception of law, in that the legal phenomenon does not consist of just rules of conduct, but is embedded in an institution, that is a social body set up around communal needs, and with power to achieve these needs. These rules give certainty to legal relations but they operate in a social context which recognises those rules and which at the same time has an organisational principle from which the norms derive, that is the capacity to confer 'juridicalness' to the rules. The juridical act ('l'atto giuridico') is an act of the will directed to produce a specific juridical effect.[51] To have legal effect the will of a legal

[48] Paola Carucci, *Le Fonti Archivistiche: Ordinamento e Conservazione*, Carocci, Rome, 1998 (1983), p. 25.

[49] Carucci, *Il Documento Contemporaneo*, p. 66.

[50] Ibid., p. 38.

[51] Ibid., p. 40. In a legal definition in Francesco de Franchis (ed), *Law Dictionary, English-Italian*, Giuffre, Milan, 1984, vol. 2, p. 410, 'atto/i', the act or action and the document are synonymous, which does not accord with Carucci's differentiation between the act and the document. 'Atto' is translated as 'act', 'action', 'remedy', 'measure', and also as the document itself, instrument, deed, paper, proceedings, record or certificate. Reference is made to different kinds of acts including administrative acts for which there is no direct equivalent in the common law, except for 'judicial review of administrative action'. A public act in Italian law is also the document. The closest common law equivalent to an act is the instrument which is a formal document of any kind, such as an agreement, deed, charter, or record, that is drawn up and executed in technical form (see *Azevedo v Secretary, Department of Primary Industries and Energy* (1992) 35 FCR 284 at 299-300). See also various Australian state Instruments Acts. The function of a record or a document, in common law legal discourse, has meant primarily the instrument as a record of a legally significant or legally

person has to be communicated to the recipient(s) of the act. Thus there is an immediate legal relationship between two persons. The procedures required to give legal effect to the act depend on the type of act (or acts) and dictate the content and form of the documents.

The juridical act is a concept found in Italian private law. When a public act is involved it may fall under public or private law. What distinguishes the juridical act from the fact is the human element, which is in line with the Kantian notion of human will. Italian jurists have classified legal acts in a number of ways. Of particular relevance is the classification by relationships, which include relationships between states, between states and public entities, and between states and private entities, which can be extended to the legal rights and responsibilities of recordkeeping participants.[52]

The elements required for the act to have legal effect are the will, the content, and the purpose that have to be intentional, as distinct from the motives of the parties. Unlike common law systems, the Italian law of legal relations is restricted to the voluntary actions of the subject.[53] Communication or declaration to the person who is the recipient of the action and the publication to the general public, for example in an official gazette, makes it efficacious in front of third parties.[54] This is an example of the legal relationship of the ordinary citizen with the government or state, which is captured by the record.

In Italian legal language the word 'act' indicates both the behaviour of the legal persons, that is the manifestation of the will that produces the legal effects, and the document, which is the written testimony in which the will takes form and is manifested externally.[55] Each act has to be externalised, that is, perceptible to the subjects to whom it is directed. The law will often stipulate how this should be done, for example it must be in

---

recognised transaction, for example a will or a contract. Thus it has been less pervasive than in the civil law system. It has not had the transformation to other legally significant documents as in diplomatics; see the categories of dispositive and probative records as outlined in this chapter.

52 Carucci, *Il Documento Contemporaneo*, p. 43.

53 *Law Dictionary, English-Italian*, vol. 1, 1984, pp. 65-66.

54 In discretional acts the motive which determined the will of the party to act must appear on the document or be referenced by other acts. Carucci, *Il Documento Contemporaneo*, pp. 40-41.

55 Ibid., p. 65. Although the act ('atto') is the documentation of the act ('documentazione del fatto'), Carucci distinguishes the juridical act ('atto giurdico') that creates, modifies or extinguishes juridical situations from the document that transmits the memory of the act and its juridical effects.

written form.[56] The document and the act do not have to coincide. This is due to the fact that not all juridical acts require a written form to be effective.[57] When the act requires a written form to put the act into effect, it is said to be *ad substantiam,* or dispositive, for example a contract, and the document coincides with the act. As in evidence law, its proximity to the act increases its probative value. If the act precedes its documentation and requires a written form as proof that the act took place, it is *ad probationem* (probative, for example a death certificate).[58]

Dispositive and probative records are therefore required by the juridical system, that is, they relate to an act that is lawful in that system, which is a juridical act. Duranti classifies other types of records as those that support a potential legal fact but are not required by the juridical system, and may be used in litigation, that is, narrative (may only relate to informal workings) and supporting records (exist as records only in relation to a business activity). Some facts are considered juridically relevant, others are juridically irrelevant, that is, they are recognised as either binding or not binding within a given legal system.[59] In diplomatics, as in law, the only socially relevant acts are juridical ones.

Despite the Italian legal context, it is possible to extract some general recordkeeping principles from types of juridical acts, if they are analysed in terms of their function. For example the 'administrative act' is similar to an administrative activity that any entity, public or private, must undertake to achieve its goals.[60]

---

[56] Carucci, *Le Fonti Archivistiche*, p. 19 and p. 26; Carucci, *Il Documento Contemporaneo*, Chapters 2 and 5. In Italian law and diplomatics the technical definition of what constitutes a document includes a 'written form'. In common law in Australia there are similar legal requirements for legal processes that must be 'in writing' to meet probative tests in evidence and procedural law. In Australian law written form has been caught up with the document as paper. The shift to 'any record of information' to ensure that any carrier or medium is a document is found in the *Evidence Act* 1995 (Cth), s 3, Dictionary, Clause 8, Part 2.

[57] Carucci, *Il Documento Contemporaneo*, p. 42.

[58] Ibid., p. 28. Duranti uses the terms 'dispositive' and 'probative' respectively in her translation of *ad substantiam* and *ad probationem*.

[59] Duranti, 'The Archival Bond', p. 214, footnote 15.

[60] 'Administrative acts' are classified by procedure. The cessation of an act is distinguished from the cessation of its legal effects. Some effects of the act may continue much longer and its probative value may arise unrelated to the original aim of the act. In civil law systems the public entity is superior to the private one. Carucci, *Il Documento Contemporaneo*, p. 46; pp. 53-58.

3.3.3 Recordkeeping and the jurisprudential concept of a legal relationship

From the above analysis it can be seen that Italian diplomatics and archival science are imbedded in the civil law system.[61] However, it appears from the view of legal theorists such as Fisher that the generality of concepts as adopted in the civil law system are not in conflict with the common law, which has underlying principles and concepts founded in Roman law, a sub-stratum of the civil law system.[62] In fact, according to Fisher, the law of obligations is 'enjoying a modern renaissance, including within the common law legal system and its proponents are going back to its Roman legal roots for inspiration and exegesis of the taxonomy of the law of obligations even in common law legal systems'.[63] The law of obligations has its basis in private law, as does the legal act as manifested in the document in diplomatics.

In the common law system, apart from the narrow definition of an act as a legal instrument, the 'act', as in the civil law system, is an element of a legal relationship (contractual, professional, fiduciary) which legally binds persons as result of the act, and has a definite legal effect, that is, an act is a relationship between persons.[64] The record can be conceived as an outcome of a process arising from the legal relationship, and consists of an interrelationship of the act, the persons, and the legal and social effects. The act in diplomatics is always part of a procedure. It may be easier to focus on the procedure, which involves a series of activities or processes to achieve an end, such as the provision of a social service (which is the act). If an act is understood as the trigger to a procedure, which is built on legal and business requirements that creates a relationship between persons, and thus reciprocal rights and duties, it is applicable to recordkeeping in any legal system.

---

[61] Other civil law jurisdictions have not been analysed in this chapter, in particular the Dutch and German legal systems that have been pivotal to archival theory.

[62] Some substantive rules, and more importantly concepts and ways of reasoning, developed by continental legal scientists, based on the Roman legal tradition, influenced the English legal system. Saarland University, Institute of Law and Informatics, *The Roman Law Branch of the Law-related Internet Project,* 2005.

[63] Fisher, 'The Archival Enterprise', p. 335. The law of obligations facilitates the cross-border flow of legal information and concepts as lawyers strive to speak a common lexicon or at least draw upon terms familiar to readers in foreign legal systems.

[64] See also footnote 51 in this chapter on an act as a legal instrument in common law. Not many common law lawyers adopt legal relationships as a taxonomy of law. Two proponents are Albert Kocourek and Simon Fisher.

Archival science as developed in the European romance countries incorporated diplomatics. However, definitions in diplomatics of 'juridical persons', 'fact', 'act', 'will' and 'effects' within a juridical system, are concepts found in ethics and the jurisprudential discourse of both the common and civil law system, and in particular in the notion of a legal relationship, which is manifested in the juridical document.

The diplomatics terms of particular relevance to legal and social relationships are:

- *Juridical person* is the author of the action.
- *Legal facts* (natural or social facts) are facts or events of life which give rise to legal consequences in human and corporate relationships, for example a birth (natural fact), or an agreement for sale (social fact). For example, the death of a person leads to property inheritance.
- Legal facts or events, in which human activity or the *will* is relevant, are both *human acts* and *legal acts*.[65] *An act is a fact* originated by a will to produce the effect or desired consequence; that is the act is a type of fact. For example, I want to arrive early to my destination (the will) and I drive into another car and the car is damaged (fact). The legal effect/consequence is that I am sued (action is speeding/reckless driving).
- A *legal transaction* is a specific type of act, that is, it is directed to a defined effect, for example the execution of a will.

The distinction between voluntary and involuntary obligations, the latter being duties imposed by law whether one intended a particular outcome or not, found in the common law notion of obligation, provides for a more expansive interpretation of legal relations as obligations, and consequently its application to a greater range of relationships and recordkeeping contexts.[66] So rather than diplomatics being irrelevant to the common law or other legal systems, it needs to be adapted to each legal system.

The 'legal bond', another characteristic of a legal relationship, is transposed in archival science to the 'archival bond', the documentation of

---

[65] In diplomatics and in Italian civil law, human acts are distinguished from natural facts. In juridical acts, the human act is distinguished from a fact, because there is an intention that legal consequences take place. Carucci, *Il Documento Contemporaneo*, pp. 37-38 elaborates on facts ('fatti') and juridical acts ('atti giuridici').

[66] 'Will' theory and voluntary and involuntary obligations are further explored in Chapters 4 and 6.

an entity made manifest in classification and registration codes.[67] The 'archival bond' is the logical connection between documents arising from the same activity. Maria Guercio has described the purpose of the 'archival bond' in terms of the document that has meaning only in relationship with other previous or subsequent documents that take part in a business process.[68] It is through the archival bond that the 'recordness' of the document emerges. Archival science, unlike legal systems and diplomatics, moves away from individual documents to linking documents on the same matter or activity. It takes 'records' and assesses their functions in terms of their relationships.[69] Thus in archival science the representation of legal relationships moves beyond those recorded in the individual document, to aggregations of related documents.

3.3.4 'Business' transaction as a legal relationship

There are a number of definitions of transaction in archival science and recordkeeping theory. Luciana Duranti defines a transaction from the diplomatics point of view in the following way:

> According to diplomatics, a transaction is a special type of act (i.e., an exercise of the will aiming to create, change, maintain, or extinguish a situation) that aims to change the relationships between two or more parties. Diplomatically, transactions are embodied in dispositive records (whose written form is required ad substantiam) and attested to in probative records (whose written form is required ad probationem), but they may only incidentally relate to supporting and narrative records.[70]

[67] Carucci, *Le Fonti Archivistiche*, p. 19. The 'archival bond' ('vincolo archivistico'), is also defined in the glossary of *Le Fonti Archivistiche*, p. 230 and in, Paola Carucci and Marina Messina, *Manuale di Archivistica per L'impresa*, Carocci, Rome, 1998, pp. 45-46.

[68] Maria Guercio, 'Definitions of Electronic Records, the European Perspective', *Archives and Museums Informatics*, vol. 11, 1997, p. 222; *Archivistica Informatica*, pp. 37-45; Duranti, 'The Archival Bond', p. 217. Duranti describes the archival bond as 'the expression of the development of the activity in which the document participates'.

[69] 'Archival science examines records as aggregations, rather than as individual entities, and studies them in terms of their documentary and functional relationships and the ways in which they are controlled and communicated'. Duranti, 'The Archival Bond', p. 213, footnote 3.

[70] Ibid., p. 216, footnote 9.

Thus, in diplomatics, a transaction is 'an act capable of changing the relationships between two or more persons',[71] essentially the legal definition of a legal relationship, expressed in Anglo-American terms as 'an act or agreement, or several acts or agreements having some connection with each other, in which more than one person is concerned, and by which the legal relations of such persons between themselves are altered'[72] while the Australian legal definition focuses on a commercial view as: 'carrying out negotiations, dealings or affairs usually in the context of business'.[73] Thus according to most legal (and diplomatics) definitions, a transaction changes the legal relationship of the parties concerned. This supports the need to capture the transactions that document the changed state of the parties to an action.

In 1990 in defining an electronic record for ease of comprehension and control, David Bearman suggested that transaction should be synonymous with record. A record-transaction is 'information, communicated to other people in the course of business, via a store of information available to them'.[74] Unlike diplomatics and law it does not include the notion of a change in the relationship of persons involved in the transaction.

---

[71] University of British Columbia, School of Library, Archival and Information Studies, 'The Preservation of the Integrity of Electronic Records', 1994-1997, Template 1. See also Certoma, *The Italian Legal System*, p. 31.

[72] Henry Campbell Black, contributing authors, Joseph R. Nolan and M.J. Connolly, *Black's Law Dictionary: Definitions of the Terms and Phrases of American and English Jurisprudence, Ancient and Modern*, 5th edn, West Pub. Co., St. Paul, 1979, 'transaction'.

[73] *Butterworths Business and Law Dictionary*, Butterworths, Sydney, 1997, p. 446.

[74] 'Glossary', in *Management of Electronic Records: Issues and Guidelines*, United Nations ACCIS, New York, 1990, p. 185. See also Chapter 2, 'Electronic Records Management Guidelines: A Manual for Policy Development and Implementation', in United Nations Advisory Committee for Coordination of Information Systems, *Management of Electronic Records: Issues and Guidelines*, United Nations ACCIS, New York, 1990, pp. 17-70, in particular 'record-transaction' defined on p. 35. Sections A, B, and C of Chapter 2, pp. 17-34 are reprinted in a shortened form as David Bearman, 'Electronic Records Guidelines: A Manual for Development and Implementation', in *Electronic Evidence: Strategies for Managing Records in Contemporary Organizations*, Archives and Museum Informatics, Pittsburgh, 1994, pp. 72-116. In this article Bearman restates his definition of a record-transaction: 'Records are recorded transactions. Recorded transactions are information communicated to other people in the course of business via a store of information available to them. While this definition is more explicit than the one archivists have traditionally used with paper records, it is consistent with the concept that a record is created by an official action of receiving or sending

The 'atomic' nature of transactions in diplomatics fits within the definition of jural relations outlined in Kocourek's legal model, which is much narrower than Fisher's application. It excludes other social, political, economic and organisational contexts in which a record operates. In archival science 'context shifts the analysis away from the record itself to the broader structural, procedural, and documentary framework in which the record is created and managed'.[75]

Transactionality as adopted in the record continuum model is defined in terms of the many types of social interaction from individual communications to corporate transactions, to social and business activities and relationships that are documented in records at all levels of aggregation. Thus the strictly 'legal' transaction is only one kind of transaction. The ethical dimension of social relationships which are inclusive of legal relationships, and the communities of common interest that operate across society, provide for a broader reading of the record, in tandem with the transactional one.

Clearly, then, 'business' transactions that form the basis of a dynamic relationship between the parties involved in a business or social activity are essential to the *creatibility,* the facts that bring legal relations into existence; the *alterability,* the changes to a claim or to an enforceable right; and the *destructibility,* the cessation of legal persons destroys legal relations.

It is the act as a relationship between persons that is at the heart of the relevance of the application of legal relationships to recordkeeping processes. Legal and recordkeeping concerns coalesce in identifying the legal person responsible for the act, the intention of the participants, the event, and its consequences.

3.3.5 The records continuum and the jurisprudential concept of a legal relationship

The emphasis in diplomatics on the formal elements of the document has obscured the dynamic nature of the legal relationship represented in the juridical act. Within the records continuum model legal relationships exist as the initial transactions of actors and acts. The transaction is not the same

information', p. 94. For a discussion of the evolution of Bearman's view of records as communicated transactions see, Sue McKemmish, 'Constantly Evolving, Ever Mutating': An Australian Contribution to the Archival Metatext, PhD Thesis, Monash University, 2001, Chapter 1.

[75] InterPARES 1 Project, Authenticity Task Force, *Final Report*, 28 October 2001, University of British Columbia, Vancouver, 2001, p. 8.

as a legal transaction used in diplomatics and law, but is defined to encompass social and organisational activity. However, Frank Upward's model broadens the business transaction from its legal context in which it is created and captured (the first dimension), its characteristics (second dimension), to specific legal requirements which may be satisfied by recordkeeping system functionality or other approaches (third dimension). These link to who can control, own, and regulate recordkeeping and how records are pluralised via legal and social mandates (fourth dimension).[76] It provides a rich context to the initial transaction, that protects rights and obligations of business participants by ensuring that systems and organisations retain sufficient evidence of the event.

Peter Scott's notion of relationships amongst records and between records, and their contexts of creation and use, has been articulated by Sue McKemmish within the Australian records continuum thinking.

> The object of Scott's own quest was a system that could reconstruct recordkeeping systems in their legal, functional and organisational contexts at any given point in time, a system that was capable of generating for users multiple views 'on paper' or 'on the screen' of a complex reality that has always been conceptual rather than physical.[77]

It must be remembered, however, that recognisable form has provided legal certainty, which the electronic world is searching for. The juridical act, inextricably linked with procedure, and the document as its representation, could translate into current computer object-oriented technology, in which a record as a digital object encapsulates related procedures and workflow. The process of arriving at a contract, for example, as well as the contract itself, can be captured as record.

Both Italian archival science and the records continuum model go beyond the legal notion of a legal relationship, to embrace social relationships, and their contexts of creation. However, the focus on the transaction which requires authentic representation of dynamic relationships, supports recordkeeping developments in which records need to have layers of metadata to indicate what the record represents and how it is to be re-represented.

---

[76] See Livia Iacovino, 'Recordkeeping and Juridical Governance', in *Archives: Recordkeeping in Society*, eds Sue McKemmish et al., Centre for Information Studies, Charles Sturt University, Wagga Wagga, NSW, 2005, pp. 262-266.

[77] Sue McKemmish, 'Are Records Ever Actual?', in *The Records Continuum: Ian Maclean and Australian Archives First Fifty Years*, eds Sue McKemmish and Michael Piggott, Ancora Press in association with Australian Archives, Clayton, 1994, p. 187.

Records and their metadata capture both business and recordkeeping processes.[78] The business process can be derived from implicit metadata in the records, that is, the implementation of rules, responsibilities, and the workflow in a business procedure. Is this different from the procedure captured in a document's structure in the paper world? In diplomatics the document participates in an action, which forms part of a procedure. In electronic systems individual documents often lack a link to their procedural context. Carucci argues that documentary and administrative procedures or workflow must be captured by electronic systems.[79] The relevance of procedural context provides an important bridge between diplomatics-archival science and the records continuum approach to metadata and record context.

The records continuum model, and the research projects which adopt its framework, include high-level societal contexts, as well as group identity, in which individual rights and obligations, compete with the 'public interest', a theme taken up in the following chapters.

3.4 Legal and social relationships and current recordkeeping concepts

Legal and social relationships are dynamic processes in which records actively participate as evidence of the relationships. Entities and documenting relationships provide the core of the records continuum approach to documenting recordkeeping, as 'complex relationships

---

[78] 'Metadata, which can be generically defined as "structured data about data", is simply a new term for the type of information that has existed in records and archives systems throughout time - indeed records managers and archivists have always been metadata experts. Traditional archival finding aids, index cards, file covers, file registers, the headers and footers on paper documents, and all of their computerised counterparts are rich in metadata that helps recordkeepers to identify, describe, authenticate, manage and provide access to records. More recently, specific sets of records and archives metadata have been standardised, such as the records management metadata specified in the US Department of Defense Design Criteria Standard for Electronic Records Management Software Applications'. Sue McKemmish, Glenda Acland, Nigel Ward and Barbara Reed, 'Describing Records in Context in the Continuum: the Australian Recordkeeping Metadata Schema', *Archivaria*, vol. 48, Fall 1999, p. 4.

[79] Carucci and Messina, *Manuale di Archivistica per L'impresa*, pp. 43-44 and p. 80.

between records and context'.[80] However, a record does not have to be conceived as an entity with attributes and relationships. It may in fact be a set of relationships. These relationships not only evidence one set of legal rights and obligations but in fact evidence the ever-changing legal relation between the parties involved.

3.4.1 Record as object, process and as a right-duty 'thing' relationship

Recordkeeping is concerned with the routines and processes involved in keeping records. The records are the outcomes of the recordkeeping and the business processes. They can be conceived as objects or things that represent actions and transactions. Recordkeeping is itself the 'business of recordkeeping': what to create, capture and keep and not to keep.

The word 'object' has been defined in archival science, ethics, law, recordkeeping, information management, and computer science. In archival science a document is 'any material object held in an archive'.[81] The subject includes the creator of the object, which is the record. In ethics, the relationship of subject (the moral agent) and object (external world) are also central to many ethical viewpoints. However, postmodernist readings see the record as the subject and mover of the action, rather than a passive object to be managed.[82]

The common law legal system, like the civil law, has been concerned with documents at a 'micro' level.[83] As a legal 'object' documents have a capacity to evidence transactions, to be 'probative', that is to have the capacity to prove or disprove the existence of a transaction or event. The 'probative value' of evidence means the extent to which the evidence could rationally affect the assessment of the probability for the existence of a fact in issue. The legal system provides the rules of recognition to enable transactions to take place. However, the definition of probative in diplomatics is tied to requirements of form and proximity to action.

[80] Chris Hurley, 'The Making and Keeping of Records: (1) What Are Finding Aids For?', *Archives and Manuscripts*, vol. 26, no. 1, May 1998, p. 74.

[81] Carucci, *Le Fonti Archivistiche*, p. 25.

[82] In Frank Upward's reading of the records continuum model, the record is not an object but a subject or participant in society. In some ethical theories the subject is a physical person who relates with an external world of objects (known as Cartesian duality). For ethicists like Logstrup the subject as a person does not stand outside the external world.

[83] See Guercio, *Archivistica Informatica*, p. 19.

In law, documents and records have been defined as legal objects or things, and this has made the translation of the function of the record in law to an electronic environment all the more difficult. However, the importance of systems and controls over record processes in the laws of evidence of a number of countries, have to some extent moved away from the document as a material object.

In computer science, 'object' is a key concept in object-oriented technology, in which it is a set of software bundles of data and related methods. The record, using object-oriented programming, has been defined as an encapsulated object, or 'digital object,' which carries with it its entire recordkeeping context.[84] At the same time, it is the product of process. Thus it can be conceived as object and as process. Within records continuum thinking, records as described by Barbara Reed, are both 'agents of action in business processes', as well as 'contextualised data' and 'objects'.[85]

The technology definition of object captures the essence of a record as an object that encapsulates its processes, and gives a renewed meaning to the record as object. Jeff Rothenberg calls it a 'digital informational entity', which he describes as a single composite bitstream that includes the core content of the entity, including all structural information required to constitute the entity from its components, its contextual information that is meaningful, and a perpetually executable interpreter that renders the core content of the entity from its bitstream in the manner intended.[86] However if a record is a set of relationships, it is the relationships that have to be preserved, unless the record entity captures the outcome of a

[84] Victorian Electronic Records Strategy, *Final Report*, Public Record Office Victoria, 1998.

[85] Barbara Reed, 'Metadata: Core Record or Core Business?', *Archives and Manuscripts*, vol. 25, no. 2, Nov. 1997, pp. 221-222. The Monash Recordkeeping Metadata Schema defines a record object as the smallest unit of recorded information controlled by a records system. A record object may be a whole record or a component of a record. McKemmish, Acland, Ward and Reed, 'Describing Records in Context in the Continuum', pp. 14-15.

[86] In actual practice there are no effective mechanisms for preserving digital entities. 'There is as yet no viable long-term strategy to ensure that digital information will be readable in the future. Digital documents are vulnerable to loss via the decay and obsolescence of the media on which they are stored, and they become inaccessible and unreadable when the software needed to interpret them, or the hardware on which that software runs, becomes obsolete and is lost'. Jeff Rothenberg, 'Preserving Authentic Digital Information', in *Authenticity in a Digital Environment*, Council on Library and Information Resources, Washington D.C., 2000, p. 54.

relationship (like a document in diplomatics that documented an entire action, its procedure and its participants). There are a number of conceptual approaches as to how a record is represented that significantly affect how computer systems preserve an authentic record. There is as yet no viable long-term strategy to ensure that digital information will be readable in the future.[87]

If an obligation can be defined as incorporeal, and fundamentally a legal and social relationship between two persons, that is as a composite right-duty, then the record, as an outcome of a process of interaction between legal persons, is a 'thing as a relationship', as well as encapsulating the process. A contract is a good example. It is not the 'contract' alone that evidences its validity or the rights and duties of the contracting parties. It is the process of arriving at an agreement, when it was made, and under what conditions. The record is evidence of the ever-changing legal relation between the recordkeeping participants.

In this chapter the record is conceived as an outcome of a process arising from a legal relationship, which also has an ethical dimension, and consists of an interrelationship of the act, the persons, their intentions, and the legal and social effects of the act. This view is supported by the analysis from jurisprudence, ethics and diplomatics, in which the act is always a relationship between persons that changes their relationship. In diplomatics the document takes part in a procedure as successive phases of an action. Procedure is a series of acts that fulfils a final action or goal of the organisation. The procedure affects the content and form of the record,

[87] Persistent object preservation which involves preserving digital objects outside of their software environment by encapsulating the document and metadata into a form that can be viewed indefinitely, is technically feasible and has been recommended in some recordkeeping research projects on the long term preservation of electronic records but has not been extensively tested, and is a highly complex area of computer science. For example University of Pittsburgh, *Reference Model for Business Acceptable Communications* (BAC Model), 1996, defined records as dynamic, self-managing metadata encapsulated objects. Monash University, School of Information Management Systems, *Recordkeeping Metadata Standards for Managing and Accessing Information Resources in Networked Environments Over Time for Government, Social and Cultural Purposes* has been informed by Pittsburgh and other recordkeeping projects in which metadata elements are embedded in, and encapsulated or persistently linked to, information objects so that records function as evidence of action. The Victorian Electronic Records Strategy (VERS) is a scaled down version of Pittsburgh's BAC model. The VERS prototype is an XML document type; all components of the record are encapsulated in one object and are software independent.

and procedural controls contribute to the reliability of the record. The act, as the trigger to a procedure, built on legal and business requirements that create a relationship between persons, including reciprocal rights and duties, is applicable to recordkeeping in any legal system. In the records continuum model, the act, the persons and the effects gain layers of context which convert a document into a record. Essentially legal and social relationships are conceptual tools for analysing legal and ethical rights and obligations of recordkeeping participants, which as we will see in the following chapter may not necessarily be represented in formal metadata schema.

4 RECORDKEEPING PARTICIPANTS: LEGAL AND ETHICAL RESPONSIBILITIES

In Chapter 3 it was established that legal relations are all about rights, claims, duties, immunities and liabilities of legal persons which arise from acts which trigger a set of processes which have a legal consequence and are 'caused' by social facts which may be external to law. When a business transaction has a legal consequence the parties to the transaction and possibly third parties have taken part in evidencing (creating, modifying or extinguishing) a legal relationship. The notion of a legal relationship in law is an atomic aspect of human activity and in its narrow juristic interpretation includes only two persons and excludes third parties, unless they are acting as an agent for the parties.[1] It eliminates the web of relationships that a transaction operates within, or in fact any communicative act (oral or captured in a material form). If we define legal persons as also moral persons, then socio-legal relations also include persons that have control over or responsibilities for acts that have a moral effect. The motives and intentions of these persons have to be taken into account if records are to have any degree of reliability. Can recordkeeping metadata capture legal persons and their compliance with legal and ethical responsibilities?

Circumstantial evidence of the facts, persons involved and their intentions, regardless of outcome, required by law and ethical systems to attribute responsibility, rely heavily on the recordkeeping metadata elements of delegation, mandates and authority, captured and retained in recordkeeping systems. To ensure the participants are legally and morally accountable, recordkeeping metadata needs to capture the elements of person identity, and relationships between persons in order to establish rights and obligations in relation to recordkeeping transactions.

---

[1] In common law, the 'law of agency' has developed special rules on the agent's role. See Simon Fisher, *Agency Law*, Butterworths, Sydney, 2000.

4.1 The act-circumstances-motivation-intentionality in law, ethics and recordkeeping

The 'will to act', that is 'volition', and the notion of 'intention', are components in law necessary for attributing complete or partial liability. In the exposition on diplomatics the notion of volition was a requirement for the creation of a record, that is, the intention to create a record is essential for a record to be created. Civil law systems attribute the fountain of obligations to the will of the individual which explains the requirement of the 'will' of the juridical person in diplomatics to give validity to the transaction. Paola Carucci notes that Italian law includes motivation as the manifestation of the will, but the motive itself cannot be expressed, only its result in the act.[2] Thus the effects of the act as captured in the record evidence the actual motive of the moral agent, which is relevant to many ethical theories. The record witnesses ethical and legal consequential action.

In diplomatics, the outcome of the act, as the manifestation of the intention of the participants, is also evidence of legal and social responsibilities for the act and its consequences. The distinction regarding voluntary and involuntary acts in the common and civil law systems were noted in Chapter 3, in particular the requirement for consent in obligations in the civil law system. However, even if the common law in civil cases (as opposed to criminal) does not always require intentionality for the liability of an act, it cannot be excluded in terms of ascertaining moral responsebility.

4.1.1 The act-circumstances-motivation-intentionality in common law systems

Jeremy Bentham defines an action as an act of the body or mind, and an act of the mind is an act of intellectual faculty or will. The will depends on motivation, which in turn leads to an action. Every act and therefore every offence will have different effects according to the nature of the motive which gave birth to it. He defines motive as anything which influences the will of a person to act or to refrain voluntarily from an act on an occasion.[3]

---

[2] Paola Carucci, *Le Fonti Archivistiche: Ordinamento e Conservazione*, Carocci, Rome, 1998 (1983), pp. 42-43.

[3] Jeremy Bentham, *An Introduction to the Principles of Morals and Legislation, Jeremy Bentham, An Authoritative Edition by J.H. Burns and H.L.A. Hart; with*

English lawyers follow Bentham's doctrine regarding two forms of intention. Simple acts may in most cases be done either intentionally or unintentionally and may have consequences that are intentional or unintentional.[4] The distinction is not used as a constituent of criminal offences or measures of seriousness of an offence. As a consequentialist theory, moral value and disvalue of actions depends wholly on their outcome, so no distinctions are made between harm that is brought about as a means to an end and the same harm brought about as a foreseen by-product or second effect of the action.[5]

An intention to do what the law forbids is generally a necessary condition of liability for punishment (excluding unintentional torts or cases of strict liability). Bentham argues that if the act is unintentional, to apply the law is simply inefficacious; an intentional offence creates a secondary evil, as a person is more likely to offend again.[6] The distinctions in forms of intentionality are very important in the exposition of *mens rea* as a constituent of criminal responsibility. Therefore cognitive and volitional factors involved in the structure of intentional action are important in criminal law.

Bentham does not consider the 'goodness' or 'badness' of intention as relevant, only its effects or motives. Intentionality is only in part a matter of will; it is also a matter of the awareness of 'consciousness', the existence of those circumstances, which determine what consequences the act will have. These distinctions help illuminate the concepts of mistake, heedlessness and negligence which are important for the determination of legal responsibility. Consciousness of the circumstances is also relevant to the intentionality of the act, but is not included in Bentham's analysis.[7]

'The general tendency of an act is more or less pernicious, according to the sum total of its consequences.' Consequences have to be 'material' (an

---

a New Introduction by F. Rosen, and an Interpretive Essay by H.L.A. Hart, Clarendon Press, Oxford, 1996, pp. 96-97.

[4] H.L.A., Hart, 'Bentham's Principle of Utility and the Theory of Penal Law', in Jeremy Bentham, *An Introduction to the Principles of Morals and Legislation,* p. xcix. Bentham adopts the terms 'intentional' and 'unintentional' to avoid the use of the terms 'voluntary' and 'involuntary' (used by Aristotle) due to what he considers as their ambiguity.

[5] Ibid., p. ciii. 'The doctrine of double effect' challenges an outcome approach.

[6] For Bentham an unintentional act should be excused from punishment, as it does not serve as a deterrent. Strict liability does not follow Benthamite reasoning. It does not take account of excuses and punishes equally those that have control over their acts as much as those that do not.

[7] Bentham, *An Introduction to the Principles of Morals and Legislation,* Chapter VIII, Of Intentionality.

important term in common law), that is relevant to pleasure and pain, or have some evidentiary quality.[8] The intention, with regard to the consequences of an act, depend upon two things: the state of the will or intention, with respect to the act itself, and, the state of the understanding, with regard to the circumstances which it is or may appear to be, accompanied with.

> In every transaction, therefore, which is examined with a view to punishment, there are four articles to be considered. 1. The *act* itself, which is done. 2. The *circumstances* in which it is done. 3. The *intentionality* that may have accompanied it. 4. The *consciousness*, unconsciousness and false consciousness, that accompanied it. The two other aspects that are relevant to the act and its punishment are: *motive* or motives which gave birth to it and the general *disposition* which it indicates. Acts may be negative and positive, e.g. to strike or not to strike is relevant to material differences with regard to consequences.[9]

The circumstances of an act may be explicitly stated as distinct from the act (for example, lying while on oath). The causal linkage Bentham makes is between a circumstance that is material (pain and pleasure from the act), a cause that brings about the consequences, and one that is immaterial if this causal relationship is missing. In the Benthamite framework the consequences of an act are events. Types of circumstances central to consequences are: criminative, exculpative, extenuative and aggravative circumstances. Those that bear a material relation with the offence are evidentiary circumstances.[10] It can be argued that circumstantial evidence may be found in a record's creation (metadata in the record) and includes evidence of the person's role as well as the act. This is the notion of competence, or duty to record found in law on documentary evidence (see Chapter 2).

Consent is necessary for certain acts, that is, one must have an intention to consent. Informed and express consent have been defined (in relation to the principles of privacy) as:

> Free and informed agreement with what is being done or proposed. Consent can be either expressed or implied. Express consent is given explicitly, either orally or in writing. Express consent is unequivocal and does not require any inference on the part of the organisation seeking consent. Implied consent

[8] Ibid., p. 74.

[9] Ibid., pp. 75-76. There are three states of consciousness: consciousness, unconsciousness and false consciousness.

[10] Ibid., pp. 80-83.

> arises where consent may reasonably be inferred from the action or inaction of the individual.[11]

Consent is relevant to acts that have contractual consequences, and must also be captured in recordkeeping metadata.[12]

4.1.2 Moral action and intention: the recordkeeping dimension

For Kant action is both the will and the act.

> An action has to be an intelligent movement, that is guided by a conception of the environment and it has to make a change externally by way of making a change in the actor. It has to have *intentional content*, that is be subject to a norm of efficiency, which includes a standard of success or failure. In the sense of the norm of efficiency a computer system could be said to act *intentionally* but *not intelligently*.[13]

---

[11] Office of the Privacy Commissioner, Australia, *National Principles for the Fair Handling of Personal Information*, revised edn, January 1999, Human Rights and Equal Opportunity Commission, 1999.

[12] Australia, Senate, *Electronic Transactions Bill 1999,* Revised Explanatory Memorandum, 30 June 1999, p. 20, 'consent'.

[13] [Emphasis added]. For Kant the will and the action are one, that is, if one wills an action one finds the means to carry it out. From Christine Korsgaard, Professor of Moral Philosophy, Harvard University, 'Human Action and Normative Standards', Guest Lecture, the Australian Catholic University, Christ Lecture Theatre, Melbourne, Friday, 14 July 2000.

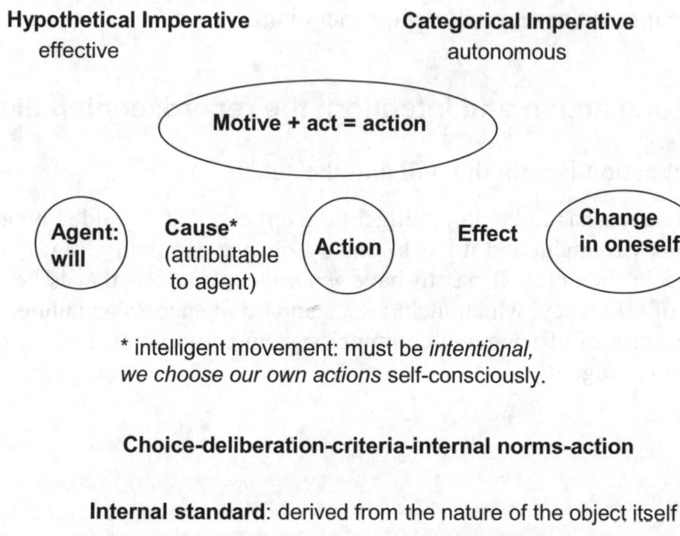

Fig. 5 Korsgaard's Kantian Model

The Kantian action involves conscious causality. Human action is the self-conscious causality or self-determination of a person. We do not act just from instinct, but rather we create our own forms of the world[14] (see Fig. 5, Korsgaard's Kantian Model and Fig 5.A, Korsgaard's Kantian Model and Diplomatics). Thus the document as the archival document or record requires the intentional action of the author to attribute to it 'recordness', that is, the author must know a record is being created. In diplomatics will and volition are found in the identity metadata on the competent author. The record provides the evidence of the intention of the author as well as its results, that is, it is evidence of the action, in the Kantian sense.

[14] Ibid.

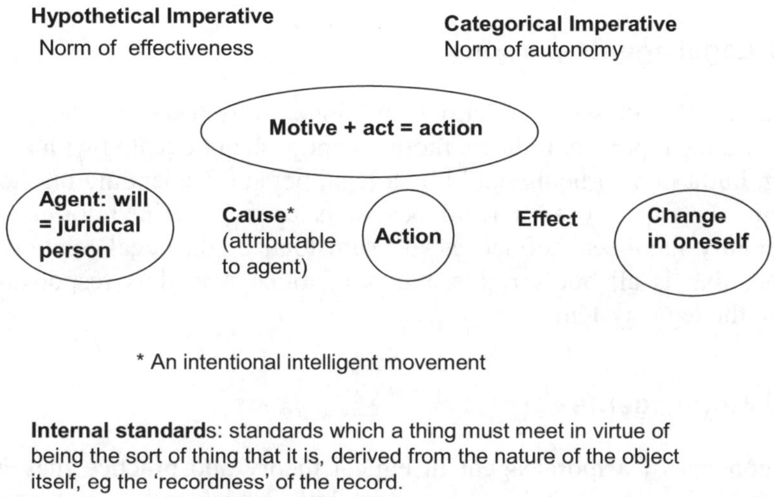

Fig. 5.A Korsgaard's Kantian Model and Diplomatics

The record must document an intentional act that results from a business-social process in which the participants, as moral and legal actors (physical or corporate) take part, and have specific rights and obligations arising from their act.

4.2 Moral actors, agents and legal persons

Actor is a term used in law not so much as a legal term but to describe the different roles a legal person may undertake, while an agent acts on behalf of other legal persons. In ethics, actors or persons are human beings who are either moral agents or moral patients. Kant extends the moral agent to corporate entities but it is still within the notion of individual moral action. The definitions of person and agent in law are therefore generally not the same as in ethics, but do at times overlap. In recordkeeping theory including diplomatics and the European tradition the term actor as the person who undertakes the act in which the record participates, and the terms author, creator, and agent have their own meanings tied to legal origins. Thus to incorporate moral agency and legal persons into recordkeeping concepts of actor and agent, it is necessary to examine their meanings from the perspective of ethics and law.

4.2.1 Legal agents-persons

In the legal and social relationship model introduced in the previous chapter a legal person, unlike a moral agent, was not equated with a human being, but a human being could be a legal person. Depending on the legal system our capacity as a legal person is usually defined for us. Legal personality has been defined as the sum total of the legal relations of a person, that is all one's rights and obligations, and thus responsibilities within the legal system.

4.2.2 Moral agents

The concept of a moral agent in ethical theory and practice may be the person acting on behalf of another but is generally the individual responsible for an ethical action. 'Moral agents' are defined as autonomous persons who are aware of their own capacity to make ethical judgments and moral choices. 'Moral patients' are not fully autonomous persons, and can only be passive decision-makers. They may include young children, unconscious human beings, the mentally retarded and the senile.[15] In the Kantian view, 'persons' are human beings, but with duties with regard to other beings, including animals, that are still duties to themselves.[16]

The notion of a moral agent can be extended to corporate bodies. For example, Kant describes states as 'moral persons', with the same obligations toward each other as any other persons.[17] If everyone is a moral agent, a corporate entity, both as a legal entity and as a community of persons, has moral agency. From a legal and moral view the corporation is an autonomous entity or artificial person, responsible for its actions. It is also responsible for its own members. It is a community in its own right, as

[15] Matti Häyry, *Liberal Utilitarianism and Applied Ethics*, Routledge, London, New York, 1994, pp. 109-110; p. 143.

[16] Roger J. Sullivan, *An Introduction to Kant's Ethics,* Cambridge University Press, New York, 1994, pp. 62-63, footnote 6.

[17] Ibid., p. 20.

well as consisting of employees and shareholders who have rights and obligations within the corporate community.[18]

In classic utilitarianism the agent is neutral, as the welfare of each individual is given equal weight, but moral agents themselves do not have to be equally concerned with everyone's good; the obligation of each agent depends on achieving good consequences. In virtue ethics, on the other hand, what counts as virtue in the ordinary sense, embodies a concern for self and other, understood as applying to a class of persons.[19]

In specific legal and social relationships moral permissions that are based on deontology will be directed at favouring the other party, or parties, to whom one has a duty. For example, the doctor has a duty to ensure that the patient's treatment is of benefit to the patient, and to his/her family. On consequentialist grounds moral permission emanates from all parties affected by the action, that is, the doctor's treatment benefits society as a whole.

Rights-based ethics also incorporates the moral agent, firstly as a result of rights of one party arising from the duty of the other party, and secondly from pre-existing rights. In virtue ethics the nature of 'role' and the virtues that predicate the role, permit the moral agent to behave in a particular way.

Ethics involves making individual decisions as an autonomous moral agent, not merely accepting socially established conventions.[20] 'Deontic' person-appraisal is a method used to judge people for either acting or for refraining to act, thereby attributing blameworthiness or praiseworthiness. In this approach the moral worth of persons is defined in relation to specific acts. In 'aretaic' appraisals, physical persons are assessed, not in terms of how they act but their overall moral worth.[21] This latter view has relevance to a person's overall trustworthiness, and in the online environment or when there is a need for the continuous certainty of trustworthiness in transactions, overall moral worth may be a preferable method to a duty-centred one. In recordkeeping activities trustworthiness is

---

[18] Kenneth Goodpaster, 'Concepts of Corporate Responsibility' in *Just Business: New Introductory Essays in Business and Ethics*, ed. Tom Brogan, Random House, New York, 1984, pp. 292-322.

[19] Michael Slote, 'From Morality to Virtue', in *Virtue Ethics, A Critical Reader*, ed Daniel Statman, Georgetown University Press, Washington, D.C., 1997, pp. 128-144.

[20] Logstrup's position in, Knud Ejler Logstrup, *The Ethical Demand*, University of Notre Dame Press, Notre Dame and London, 1997, Chapter 2.

[21] Philip Montague, 'Virtue Ethics: A Qualified Success Story', in *Virtue Ethics, A Critical Reader*, ed. Daniel Statman, Georgetown University Press, Washington, D.C., 1997, pp. 194-204.

captured in person metadata, that is, the attributes of the legal and moral authority of recordkeeping participants.

4.3 Legal and moral accountability

4.3.1 Autonomy and character

Accountability, responsibility and blame are concepts relevant to both ethics and law. Blame and responsibility are component parts of accountability. Accountability for a deed means one is responsible for its cause, deserves blame, and is liable to compensate the person affected or harmed. To be responsible one has to be free to make a moral decision. The moral agent is one that is capable of reasoning and making choices intentionally.[22] Autonomy and character are decisive factors for responsible moral action.

The social determinist view of autonomy is one that allows an individual to choose a set of values within a particular society, as a choice within a plurality of views. The relativist view argues that the right to choose within a liberal society is limited by the fundamental values of a specific society. An alternative view of autonomy is that of prudential rationality, that is, organising one's life to maximise the good in it, as summarised by John Charvet:

> If we think of the autonomy of self-conscious reason-giving beings as a matter of the degree to which reasoned deliberation prior to choice occurs, then we must allow that autonomy is present even in the most elementary choices by an agent of one good over another, and is expanded as the agent develops its powers of reflection on the good-making properties of the natural and social worlds and builds this understanding into the characteristic responses to life's options.[23]

In Kantian ethics the notion of a purely rational moral agent rests on the principle of the law of autonomy. The 'categorical imperative' that we act only on maxims which we are able to treat as universal has to be read with the requirement to treat other persons as rational autonomous beings.[24]

---

[22] Alasdair MacIntyre, *A Short History of Ethics: A History of Moral Philosophy from the Homeric Age to the Twentieth Century,* 2nd edn, University of Notre Dame Press, Notre Dame, Indiana, 1998, p. 85.

[23] John Charvet, *The Idea of an Ethical Community*, Cornell University Press, Ithaca New York and London, 1995, pp. 81-82.

[24] Sullivan, *An Introduction to Kant's Ethics,* Chapter 3.

Through the categorical imperative, maxims can be identified as right, independent of the consequences of following those maxims.[25]

Today the term autonomy is used in psychology to designate the 'self-actualising' self-directed person. This is more how Kant used the term prudential.[26] It is also used today as an absolute right of persons to make their own decisions and to control their own lives without interference from others, and in the patient-doctor context has developed a special meaning (see Chapter 6). The contemporary uses have some relationship with Kant's meaning of the term. The conviction that the autonomous person is responsible for individual moral actions rules out coercive interference from others. Outside of this, Kant's reasoning is far more restrictive than contemporary notions of autonomy. For Kant 'autonomy' denoted our ability and responsibility to know what morality requires of us and to act accordingly. It is not a norm to satisfy our desires; in fact it is 'the supreme limiting condition of all subjective trends'.[27] The obligations to others are not based on their rights but on our prior obligations. Autonomy is an obligation. For this reason Kantian deontology reinforces the notion of obligation as defined in legal relations.

4.3.2 Moral character and moral agency

In social sciences a person's character consists of inherited qualities modified by acquired habits and other external influences such as family and education. From this perspective, a person's character is explicable in terms of prior causal factors. For a free will proponent like Kant, inherited attributes can make the notion of moral character meaningless, as we would not be free to exercise our agency because it was causally determined. Kantianism places responsibility for our own character on individuals. Humans have an innate predisposition to a morally good character; thus human moral agents cannot be irrevocably evil. However, morally correct actions do not mean a morally good character, even though in acting dutifully we must have moral sentiments.[28] In virtue ethics the

[25] Ibid., pp. 125-126. According to Kant, when we deliberate and act, we are free from determination by any prior or concurrent causes outside of our reason. A free will is one that acts only on general maxims that can at the same time be laws for all other free wills.

[26] The prudent man, more or less refers to 'practical intelligence' from the medieval Latin 'prudentia'. Ibid., p. 79.

[27] Ibid., p. 128.

[28] Ibid., pp. 130-144.

character of the agent is decisive in moral action and will affect his/her choice of action and determine its value.

4.3.3 Voluntary and involuntary actions

Within a legal system the emphasis is on ascertaining the chain of responsibility for an action. Is it possible that all actions are determined by causes independent of the agent's deliberations and choices, so that no actions are voluntary? For virtue ethicists it is only voluntary actions that are praiseworthy or blameworthy.[29] What does emerge about voluntary action in ethics is a positive sense that choice and deliberation play a key role but not every human action is preceded by deliberation. Deontological ethics searches for rules for specific moral judgments.[30]

In common law the distinction between voluntary and involuntary actions, or intentional and unintentional acts is found in the differences in responsibility in contract and tort law.[31] While in the theory of contract law the intention of the parties is an element of contract formation, in practice a contract is inferred from conduct, as an expression of intention.[32] The record also infers intention from the action recorded. The voluntary or intentional aspect is not always relevant to legal liability. A strict liability standard in product liability would mean that the vendor is liable for an injury caused by its product whether or not he or she is at fault. Negligence defence would require proof of reasonable conduct. Tort law compensates for harm, but someone has to be responsible for the harm. Where does foreseeable harm enter? Both law and ethics will hold a person responsible for events that are outside of their control. Taking control even of events that appear outside of one's control is essential to moral agency, as well as

---

[29] MacIntrye, *A Short History of Ethics,* pp. 68-71. For virtue ethicists 'involuntary' is contrasted with 'deliberate' rather than with 'voluntary'. An action is non-voluntary when it is done under compulsion or ignorance. Compulsion covers cases when an agent is really not a free agent. In law the theory of 'causation' is a jurisprudential discourse in its own right.

[30] Sullivan, *An Introduction to Kant's Ethics,* pp. 37-39.

[31] Aristotelian ethics distinguishes between voluntary and involuntary actions. Aristotle does not get into later riddles of philosophy on free will. MacIntrye, *A Short History of Ethics*, p. 70.

[32] *Halsbury's Laws of Australia*, vol. 6, Butterworths, 1999, Part 3, 'Theories of Contract' and Part 7 'Intention to Create Legal Relations', pp. 196,043-196,051.

to legal liability.[33] Circumstantial evidence of the facts, persons involved and their intentions, regardless of outcome, required by law and ethical systems to attribute responsibility, rely heavily on the recordkeeping metadata elements of mandate, delegation and authority, captured and retained in recordkeeping systems.

4.4 Recordkeeping participants: legal persons and moral agents

Recordkeeping participants include moral and legal actors, that are also legal persons and moral agents, as defined above.

4.4.1 Recordkeeping professional responsibilities

Although business and recordkeeping processes have a number of participants, the recordkeeping professional has a special role as an independent third party.[34]

A model for defining the exclusive expertise of the recordkeeping professional which supports legal and ethical rights and obligations can be defined with reference to the role of the recordkeeper as the trusted preserver of the memory of society, specifically responsible for:

- ensuring that organisations and individuals create and capture records of their actions, so that they can fulfil their obligations and enforce their rights or that of their descendants;
- determining how long records need to be kept for business, legal and cultural purposes;
- ensuring that organisations and individuals manage their records over time using appropriate preservation strategies;

[33] 'Moral luck' refers to the fact that many aspects of a person's conduct and the circumstances in which that conduct occur may be out of their control. These are philosophic questions that tort lawyers, as well as ethicists, tackle. Peter Cane, 'Retribution, Proportionality, and Moral Luck in Tort Law', in *Law of Obligations: Essays in Celebration of John Fleming*, eds Peter Cane and Jane Stapleton, Clarendon Press, Oxford, 1998, p. 142.

[34] In the current environment this role may appear in new guises such as that of a trusted third party in electronic transactions, including that of a certification authority for issuing digital signatures, or as a 'cybernotary', a theme that is taken up in Chapters 7 and 8.

- providing appropriate access and security controls to prevent the inappropriate use of information;
- maintaining the corporate memory of organisations or persons; and
- contributing to collective identity and cultural continuity by carrying records through time and space.

These activities gave rise to the professional ethical and legal obligations of the recordkeeping professional.[35]

4.4.2 'Business' participants' responsibilities

The recordkeeping participant is defined more broadly than recordkeeping professionals, and includes actors as moral agents and legal persons in business transactions, within a network of relationships. Although the recordkeeping professional has a professional responsibility to ensure that systems keep records, other business employees are also responsible for the records of their activities. In the *International Records Management Standard*, responsibilities are articulated as:

> Records management responsibilities and authorities should be defined and assigned, and promulgated throughout the organization so that, where a specific need to create and capture records is identified, it should be clear who is responsible for taking the necessary action. These responsibilities should be assigned to all employees of the organization, including records managers, allied information professionals, executives, business unit managers, systems administrators and others who create records as part of their work, and should be reflected in job descriptions and similar statements. Specific leadership responsibility and accountability for records management should be assigned to a person with appropriate authority within the organization. Designations of the responsible individuals may be assigned by law.
>
> Such responsibilities should include statements such as:
>
> (a) Records management professionals are responsible for all aspects of records management, including the design, implementation and maintenance of records systems and their operations, and for training users on records management and records systems operations as they affect individual practices.
>
> (b) Executives are responsible for supporting the application of records management policies throughout the organization.
>
> (c) Systems administrators are responsible for ensuring that all documentation is accurate, available and legible to personnel when required.

[35] See Livia Iacovino, *'Things in Action': Teaching Law to Recordkeeping Professionals*, Ancora Press, Melbourne, 1998, Chapter 4 on law as an integral part of the knowledge of the recordkeeping professional.

> (d) All employees are responsible and accountable for keeping accurate and complete records of their activities.
>
> Archival authorities may be involved in the process of planning and implementing records management policies and procedures.[36]

Clearly there are many individuals in an organisation responsible for accurate recordkeeping in addition to recordkeeping professionals.

4.4.3 Business participants as legal persons and moral agents in recordkeeping processes

> Business or personal actions should be captured as records and linked with metadata which characterize their specific business context when they commit an organization or individual to action, render an organization or individual accountable, or document an action, a decision or decision making process.[37]

Recordkeeping responsibilities are not only attributable to the recordkeeping professional but also to all business participants involved in business processes that give rise to records. From a transactional and process perspective of recordkeeping there has to be a number of participants. Both diplomatics and the records continuum model provide approaches that are developed here for the purpose of attributing responsibility to business participants that depend on the data that captures their responsibilities and their actions.

4.5 Recordkeeping research projects: identifying the responsibilities of recordkeeping participants

In applying the legal and social relationship model to the rights and obligations of parties to a business transaction, the identity of the authors and recipients found in the 'intrinsic' elements of diplomatics adopted by the University of British Columbia's *International Research on Permanent Authentic Records in Electronic Systems 1* (InterPARES 1), and 'actors and agents' as defined in the Monash University's Recordkeeping Metadata Project (RKMS), and where and when their rights and obligations

---

[36] *ISO 15489-1, Information and Documentation - Records Management Standard,* ISO 2001, 6.3, 'Responsibilities'.

[37] Ibid., 9.1 'Determining documents to be captured into a records system.'

begin and end, depends on the recordkeeping model adopted by these research projects.[38]

Both research models have been concerned with modelling conceptual requirements for the preservation of authentic electronic records over time, but within intellectual frameworks that arrive at different strategies for their creation and retention.

4.5.1 InterPARES 1 and recordkeeping responsibilities

InterPARES 1 in its early development adopted the diplomatics concept of the requirement of the 'intent to communicate' as necessary for a record to exist. Even when there is system to system communication, a juridical person is responsible for each system - there is an intent to communicate between the juridical persons responsible for the systems.[39] This element is central to the notion of ethical responsibility (see above).

Of relevance to recordkeeping responsibility in this project has been:

- the assignment of responsibility for record creation and record keeping to juridical persons, and
- control (legal and physical) of records over time.

In the life cycle approach that supports the InterPARES project there is a shift in responsibility for protecting the record's integrity from the creator to the preserver, that is, a neutral third party, usually an archival authority once the business purposes of the records have been exhausted, that ensure their authenticity over time. This view involves the physical transfer of records, whether paper or electronic, from the creator to the

---

[38] In the Monash Recordkeeping Metadata Project, *the people (agents) entity class* includes natural and legal persons, for example, individuals, work groups, corporate bodies, and social institutions: 'People or agents (as-actors, as-organisational units, as-corporate bodies/organisations, as-social institutions).' Sue McKemmish, 'Constantly Evolving, Ever Mutating': An Australian Contribution to the Archival Metatext, PhD Thesis, Monash University, 2001, p. 332, footnote 26. In the InterPARES 1 project the persons participating in a transaction are physical and legal persons who are identified through the intrinsic elements of documentary form and take part in the action of the record. They are not defined as metadata elements, as metadata is restricted to data outside the documentary form. See InterPARES 1 Project, Authenticity Task Force, *Template for Analysis*, 7 Nov. 2000.

[39] InterPARES 1 Project, Authenticity Task Force, *Template for Analysis*, 'Intellectual Form', 21 May 1999. This earlier version of the template is not on the public website.

preserver, and is referred to as the 'custodial model'. For example, different parties are accountable for different recordkeeping activities. 'The creator is accountable for its action *through* its records, the preserver is accountable *for those* records'.[40] However, this assumes some way of knowing when the creator is no longer responsible, or a statutory or administrative procedure that arranges for this to take place. Outside of the public sector private entities may come and go, and must be targeted to keep authentic records. It is a strategy that has become technologically difficult.

The transfer of records from a creator to a preserver is one strategy for preserving the elements of authenticity of the record over time.[41] Evidence law has had rigorous requirements for a record's admissibility because of hearsay rules that considered a document had to have been in 'proper or unbroken custody' to be authentic. Archivally this is termed as 'continuous custody' and has supported a preserver, such as an archival authority, who can take long-term custody of the record.[42] Changes to evidence law in a number of countries have placed more responsibility onto the business creators to ensure that electronic systems have been operating correctly, and that they have been maintained, so that businesses have become 'preservers'.[43]

The issue is that *someone* has to be responsible for the long-term preservation of records arising from legal and social relationships. *How* this is done will depend on recordkeeping good practice which takes into account the juridical system or systems in which it operates.[44]

---

[40] Luciana Duranti and Heather MacNeil, 'The Protection of the Integrity of Electronic Records: An Overview of the UBC-MAS Research Project', *Archivaria,* vol. 42, Fall 1996, p. 62.

[41] Australian recordkeeping research which operates within the continuum framework, considers a range of strategies for the long-term preservation of records. The advantage to the records continuum view is its greater flexibility in this regard, as it does not have to be read as a complete integration of all recordkeeping responsibilities by the creator, although this reading of the model is also possible. The fourth dimension can be read as the independent third party whether that is the archival authority or some other accountability mechanism. It is a question of the 'role' of a preserver, which can be taken by the same physical person but with different legal status.

[42] Iacovino, *'Things in Action'*, pp. 95-96.

[43] See Chapter 2, 'Rules of evidence and trustworthy records'.

[44] The fact that the custodial model is followed in many North American national public archival institutions, but until recently has not been favoured in Australia, is an implementation issue that is not addressed in this book. In March 2000 the National Archives of Australia announced that it accepts

4.5.2 The Monash Recordkeeping Metadata Project: the concept of mandate and recordkeeping responsibilities

In the Recordkeeping Metadata Project developed by Monash University, the concept of a mandate in relation to an agent provides the main tool for identifying and capturing recordkeeping legal and ethical responsibilities.[45] Mandates are associated with the related business activity, which is linked to the people-agent doing the business. In the early development of the project, mandates were not all inclusive, and were differentiated from law, policies and business rules.

> The elements defined in the Recordkeeping Metadata Scheme identify and describe significant features of the business contexts in which records are created, managed and used. They identify and describe the people or agents involved, and the records themselves. *They also link business contexts to the people or agents doing the business and the records that document it, and they reference the mandates, laws, policies and business rules that authorise and control business activity.* They enable description and management of recordkeeping actions, e.g. the processes which fix the content of records, enable their forms to be re-presented and rendered over time, manage their physical preservation, classify and index them. They enable the stringing together of related records, the administration of terms and conditions of access, use and disposal, and the tracking and documenting of the recordkeeping actions themselves, as well as the history of the use of the records.[46]

However, the term agent is far more inclusive than authors and creators in diplomatics and archival science respectively, who operate at a specific

---

custodial responsibility for Commonwealth records, in all formats, that have been selected as national archives. National Archives of Australia, *Custody Policy for Commonwealth Records*, March 2000.

45 The relationship of 'mandate' with agents and business used in the models developed by the Recordkeeping Metadata Project drew on the work of the University of Pittsburgh, 'Functional Requirements for Evidence in Recordkeeping Project', in particular on the warrants for recordkeeping in organisational contexts, and on Sue McKemmish's exploration of the broad social mandates for personal recordkeeping found in sociology, creative writing and reflective narratives. See also Chapter 1 on the warrant and regulatory model for recordkeeping which noted that the notion of the mandate does not appear to conflict with the notion of a juridical community or communities of common interest.

46 Sue McKemmish and Glenda Acland, 'Appendix 4, Recordkeeping Metadata (RKM) Elements Draft Version 2.0: Briefing Notes, 4 March 1999', in Proceedings (unpublished), Budapest, Hungary, 8-12 March 1999. [Emphasis added].

level only, and in which the differentiation is closer to formal 'legal' actors, for example the author is the legal or physical person who has the authority to issue the record.[47]

> Agents may be social entities (e.g. organisational bodies or other social drivers such as motherhood), persons, legal and other such instruments. They may operate at any level in a hierarchy and may be responsible for creating, controlling and managing records, or they may be engaged in their use. Examples include intelligent agents (such as in electronic systems which undertake discretionary decisions), organisational positions, organisational units or work groups, organisations, social institutions (including social constructs such as motherhood or friendship), persons or families. The layers defined in this entity are Persons or Actors (who carry out the transactions), Organisational Units or Work Groups (responsible for the activity), Organisations or Corporate Bodies (mandated to carry out the function), and Social Institutions (associated with ambient functions in the sense of high level societal purposes).[48]

In the final iteration of the project, mandates were differentiated by their 'external' and 'internal' nature; they establish responsibilities and provide the motive for their execution.

> People do business in social and organizational contexts that are governed by external mandates (e.g., social mores and conditioning, laws, regulations, standards, best practice codes, professional ethics) and internal mandates (e.g., corporate culture, policies, administrative instructions, delegations, authorities). Mandates establish in both formal and informal ways who is responsible for what, and govern social and organisational activity and recordkeeping behaviours. Authentic records of social and organisational activity provide evidence of that activity and function as corporate and collective memory. They also provide authoritative sources of value added information as they capture not only the content, but also the context of the interactions they document. And they account for the execution of the mandate - internally and externally, currently and over time.[49]

The Recordkeeping Metadata Project clearly links agent behaviour to rules, whether these are legal, business or social, and places less emphasis on the character traits of personal agents, their intentions which may not be definable in terms of acts based on rules alone. Mandates have limitations

[47] InterPARES 1 Project, Authenticity Task Force, *Template for Analysis*, 7 Nov. 2000, pp. 1-6.

[48] McKemmish and Acland, 'Appendix 4, Recordkeeping Metadata (RKM) Elements Draft Version 2.0: Briefing Notes'.

[49] Sue McKemmish, Glenda Acland, Nigel Ward and Barbara Reed, 'Describing Records in Context in the Continuum: the Australian Recordkeeping Metadata Schema', *Archivaria*, vol. 48, Fall 1999, p. 13.

in terms of ethics, where ethics is defined as separate from social mores, and each action has a unique ethical aspect. Many ethical theories do not consider rules or social mores as ethical drivers as they are subject to change, while ethical action is specific to the demands of each individual action. However, motivation for action can be identified by rules only within a deontological model of ethics, that is, it is one's duty to follow a legal rule.

The notion of rules and standards that control the behaviour of agents is a 'neopositivist' deontological model, in this respect no different from rules that govern actors in diplomatics. Rules are predictable and more suited to routines in systems, and for modelling purposes. However, humans are not (as yet) machines. Can any metadata capture the individual act and its intention anyway? The courts surmise intention from circumstantial evidence. If metadata captures the changed relationship between the actors evident in and through transactions, to some extent this evidences intention, if intention is construed by outcome.

At the first dimension in the records continuum there is room to interpret an actor-rule-intention-act; while at the systems level there is a series of acts over time that may or may not be consistent with the actor-rule-intention-act. External mandates for acting virtuously or motivating the act (for example, professional ethics) are one acceptable position in virtue ethics.[50] It could be argued that the 'external mandates' are internalised into business-social-legal rules, rather than being separate from the rules; that is, they can be traced to external mandates, but as motives for action the individual at the transaction level must choose to apply them. Thus choice, essential for ethical behaviour, must be available for recordkeeping action. Mandates alone do not adequately take account of the notion of a reciprocal right-duty evidenced by the record.

4.6 The records continuum, diplomatics and recordkeeping participants: an extended regulatory model

Within the records continuum model the identity of recordkeeping participants for the purpose of attributing responsibility is found in the identity axis, at all four dimensions.[51] The actor in the records continuum

[50] John McDowell, 'Virtue and Reason', in *Virtue Ethics,* eds Roger Crisp and Michael Slote, Oxford University Press, Oxford, New York, 1997, pp. 141-162.

[51] The relevance of identity to trustworthy records is covered in Chapter 2.

model is linked to authorities and responsibilities that support an act, and is an 'instrument' in a transaction.[52] This is also reflected in the Monash Recordkeeping Metadata Project's 'agent' and its relationship with mandated responsibilities. Diplomatics distinguishes between author, writer, originator,[53] and addressee/recipient at the document level and archival science adds the 'creator', the archival 'fonds' or the entity ('structural' provenance). The record as an instrument for attributing responsibility for action is also essential to the Kantian and the jurisprudential-diplomatics differentiation of event and act (see 4.1.2 above, 'Moral action and intention: the recordkeeping dimension'). Recordkeeping metadata needs to capture the elements of person identity and relationships between persons in order to establish rights and obligations in relation to recordkeeping transactions. The record is both evidence of rights and obligations and is itself 'a thing as relationship'.

If we return to the conceptual aspects of both recordkeeping research models, we can in fact extend them in ways that provide methods for analysing legal and ethical responsibilities, that are particularly suited to legal and social relationships.

4.6.1 'Identity' elements in recordkeeping and related legal rights and duties

The assignment of legal responsibilities to 'persons', is an indication of their property rights in records, or to the data or intellectual content in records, or what they can do with the information. If we add third parties, who have an interest in legal relationships, we can come up with a useful matrix to identify recordkeeping participants in any legal system.[54] In

[52] The identity axis at the first dimension of the records continuum is particularly significant as this is where the actors in the initial communication are identified, and their responsibilities begin. Their responsibilities continue across all dimensions. Frank Upward, 'Structuring the Records Continuum, Part One: Postcustodial Principles and Properties', *Archives and Manuscripts*, vol. 24, no. 2, Nov. 1996, endnote 31.

[53] Maria Guercio, in *Archivistica Informatica: I Documenti in Ambiente Digitale*, Carocci, Rome 2002, p. 33 notes that 'originator': name of the person assigned the electronic address in which the record has been generated and/or sent was a new element added to diplomatics by the University of British Columbia, *The Preservation of the Integrity of Electronic Records Project* and adopted by InterPARES 1. See Template for Analysis, 7 November 2000.

[54] The first three terms are from diplomatics, which considers legal actors involved in the creation of records as fact, as well as from the terms actor and agent

ethics all the categories would also be moral agents as defined above. The model is summarised below:

* *Writer/actor/physical person:* human person at the desk/work station acting in his/her own right in relation to other persons; witness to the facts; relevant to reliability of facts in a record.
* *Author/record creator/agent:* legal actor/juridical 'person' or position having the capacity/authority to act legally in his/her own right; the will to act (the juridical act); the actor who undertakes an act which creates, modifies or maintains a situation; an entity/corporate body capable of acting legally. The author can only be established by knowing the legal system; juridical agency/agent with mandated functions must be known. Note: author and creator are separate entities in diplomatics and archival science respectively.
* *Recipient or addressee:* the person for whom the record is intended/directed; may, or may not be the recipient of the action.
* *Third party*: A person who is not part of the original transaction and thus an independent outsider who may authenticate the record, seek access to, or use the record or data therein either for themselves or on behalf of another third party.[55] This party may be vicariously liable for the transaction. The author and the addressee are the first and second party if they are the actors of the action. The relationship of the third party with other parties in the transaction may be removed by varying degrees, for example a regulatory watchdog; an archival authority, or a signature certification authority. A distinction between trusted third parties and other third parties needs to be made.
* *Record or data subject:* the person(s) who is (are) the subject of or referenced in a record or document; in the subject matter of the document. May have no involvement in the action of the record. In some cases may have provided the data, or be the same person as the recipient.

'Authorship' as authority is important to both the reliability and the ownership of the record. Authorship can also be defined by the moral permission given by a community. It is linked to authority and

found in the records continuum model and RKMS, and the remainder have been developed by the author.

55 'One who is a stranger to a transaction or proceeding', from *Osborn's Concise Law Dictionary*, 8th edn, eds Leslie Rutherford and Sheila Bone, Sweet and Maxwell, London, 1993, p. 323.

competence, the sphere of functional responsibility entrusted to an office or an officer within the juridical system; the legal person responsible for the action. Authorship is also relevant to ownership; that is, records created or received by an organisation or a legal entity are owned by the organisation or entity; a record sent to someone is in the 'possession' of the recipient, which may or may not equate with ownership.[56] This may however be different from the ownership of intellectual property of the record. Copyright law may stipulate who is an author for copyright purposes, and owners of moral rights may be the authors of the work as opposed to the owners of the economic rights.[57] Ownership also affects control over access to the information in the record, although this could be overridden by statute. Thus the author, for legal purposes, may be different from the author identified from the analysis in diplomatics or archival science.

4.6.2 Third parties and legal relationships

Third parties are not part of the jurisprudential legal relationship model. The exception is where a contract exists for the benefit of third parties.[58] Trusted third parties have always existed, such as the notaries and trustees. Rights of the recipients of the action or data subjects have also impinged on the one-to-one notion of a legal relationship.

The legal actors that have been added to the matrix (third parties and record subjects) reflect changed business and legal realities, such as the accretion of individual human rights in the last decades of the twentieth century. In the web environment they may operate as intermediaries or trusted third parties. These relationships will determine rights and liabilities of the legal persons participating in the action of the record. In turn these records support the rights and obligations of the persons involved in the action.

---

[56] The data subject, that is, the person referenced in the document is not the owner of the record (unless the author was writing about himself) but could under certain circumstances exercise access rights to the content in the document either via statute or common law. These distinctions are relevant to the ownership of data and records. See 5.1, 'Property as a legal and social relationship'.

[57] See *Copyright Amendment (Moral Rights)* Act 2000 (Cth).

[58] Simon Fisher, 'General Principles of Obligations', in *The Law of Commercial and Professional Relationships,* ed. Simon Fisher, F.T. Law & Tax, South Melbourne, 1996, p. 15.

5 PROPERTY, PRIVACY, ACCESS AND EVIDENCE AS LEGAL AND SOCIAL RELATIONSHIPS

If we apply the law of obligations as defined in Chapter 3 to the relationships between parties in business transactions, recordkeeping provides evidence of the duties and obligations that arise from those relationships, and also whether the obligations have been met. The same body of law also provides bonds between participants and other stakeholders in records processes, for example third parties who need evidence of the transaction for legal or other purposes. The duties and obligations of recordkeeping participants include rights and obligations pertaining to ownership, access and privacy, as well as those of third parties, which in turn are evidenced by records providing proof of the existence of the rights and/or obligations. Legal and social relationships provide a way of focusing on the participants (physical and legal) in business and recordkeeping processes and their rights and obligations (ethical and legal), their associated property, contractual and access rights and obligations, and the evidence that records provide of those rights and obligations.

5.1 Property as a legal and social relationship

In the notion of legal and social relationships, property is a relationship between legal and moral persons, a 'right-duty thing' (thing as obligation, not as a material object, see 5.1.1 below) in which records provide evidence of the relationship, and its concomitant rights and obligations. Simon Fisher argues that the law of property, together with the law of obligations, promotes the interests of property owners, including owners of the records themselves. The rights of non-property holders to gain access to and in some cases to amend records that form part of a legal relationship can also be analysed in terms of duties and obligations, whether found in statutory or non-statutory law in common and civil law systems.

Property can be defined as power over resources, which creates relations between members of a society. It is a right to a flow of income, whether from rent, interest, profits, labour, service or goods. Thus it is not restricted to land or objects, for example when professions transform a service into income-yielding property.[1] Property in its many manifestations is a vexed question in ethical theories because it has been laid down as a requirement for 'reasonable' thinking. Essentially it means that one needs material resources to make reasoned decisions.

In the liberal democratic view one cannot pursue private interests without 'things' as vehicles for action, and private control.[2] A private property system is one in which rules governing access to and control of things assign them to particular individuals. The beneficiaries of property may not own it; they may depend on trust to have the interest upheld.[3]

5.1.1 Thing as material object and as obligation in property law

Property and ownership are complex legal concepts that have been characterised in Roman and common law systems through the nature of 'thing'.[4] The jurisprudential notion of thing has not always carried with it the restricted meaning of being the material object itself, but rather the thing, as the object of a right or duty, is a legal relationship. For example, a trademark may be a mark but is also a legal relation, that is, a thing with rights and obligations arising out of its first appropriation. A broader definition of thing by some jurists is 'any unity with economic value', for

---

[1] Harold Perkin, *The Rise of Professional Society: England Since 1880,* London, New York, Routledge, 1989, p. 9.

[2] John Charvet, *The Idea of an Ethical Community*, Cornell University Press, Ithaca, New York and London, 1995, p. 198.

[3] Perkin, *The Rise of Professional Society: England Since 1880*, p. 124.

[4] 'Thing' originally meant a matter before a court; its residual use in evidence law is as 'document or thing', see for example in Australia, *Evidence Act* 1995 (Cth), s 146(1)(a), 'This section applies to a document or thing'. Michael Buckland in, 'Information as Thing', *Journal of the American Society for Information Science*, vol. 42, no. 5, June 1991, pp. 351-360, distinguishes information-as-thing as a tangible object, such as the document or data, from information-as-knowledge which is intangible, and cannot be touched or measured. Information as thing is extended to objects and events that are 'informative'. Using Buckland's typology a record is a thing from which one can infer knowledge in the form of rights and obligations.

example land or a service.[5] Things which have an economic value include copyrights, trademarks, and trade secrets, and in addition things can include bonds, rents, and services, none of which are material objects. Things of no direct economic value include corporeal integrity and the power to enter personal relations.[6] Thus certain kinds of legal things represent a right.

Based on the evolution of the Roman law division of *res mancipi* and *res nec mancipi* the common law system has divided property into real and personal; real property or immovables include land and fixtures, while personal property or movable property is all other than real property, which includes chattels such as things that are tangible, corporeal, such as a physical record, and things in action ('choses in action') which are assignable things (assignable in law and in equity) and are intangible, incorporeal things.[7] They cannot be possessed; they are merely evidence of the legal relation. It is in the personal property law of the common law system, that a thing as an object takes part in a property relationship.

Bruce Welling, in *Property in Things in the Common Law System,* defines property as a legal relationship, that is, a person that is a holder of a form of property is in a relationship with a person that is not a holder. There is also a third person (usually the state) that acknowledges the holder of the property and can suppress the use of the property by a non-holder. Property and thing are not the same concepts.[8] Some, but not all property is

---

[5] Albert Kocourek, *Jural Relations*, 2nd edn, The Bobbs-Merrill Company, Indianapolis, 1928, p. 307. The Roman law of things was divided into *res corporalis* (land, chattels) and *res incorporalis* (servitudes, choses in action).

[6] Ibid., pp. 324-326.

[7] Ibid., p. 316. The Anglo-American division of real and personal property is the most extensive one used in law since the first property division in Roman law of *res mancipi* (for example agricultural substances and land) and *res nec mancipi* (for example money, clothing, tools). The next classification which came into use in Roman law and in the civil law of Europe was that of *res mobiles* (movables) and *res immobiles* (immovables). This classification attempted to state a natural difference in material substances, a categorisation synonymous with the division of the law of chattels and of land. Although the classification of movables and immovables can apply only to material substances, the law attempted for various purposes, for example taxation and rights, to give a local situation to 'thing' elements which in their nature have no situs.

[8] Bruce Welling, *Property in Things in the Common Law System*, Scribblers Publishing, Gold Coast Queensland, 1996, pp. 8-9; p.15. Welling disagrees with the common law lawyers that have made property and thing synonymous. He believes that people held property in things in the early common law only.

held in things. In contrast with the Roman concept of thing as obligation, 'thing' in common law is defined as 'a material object, a body; a being or entity consisting of matter, occupying space.'[9] For Welling there are four types of property in things: possession, right to immediate possession, ownership, and security interest.[10]

Property in the common law system denotes the relationship between a person and a thing while Roman law makes property an obligation, which is a relationship between two persons.[11] In the common law view the closest personal property concept to the Roman law of things are 'things in action' or 'choses in action' which are intangible property; a right that is 'owned' but cannot be physically transferred. They include shares and negotiable instruments which exist only through evidence of a right, that is records that prove the existence of the right, in any form, electronic or otherwise.[12]

Simon Fisher argues that the Australian law of property rests on the same principle as Roman law. In Roman law, the law of property is a category concerned with relations between people and things. He says:

> It is futile to speak of 'property' as a legal object (or *thing*) unless one can simultaneously point to those legal persons who are said to have an interest in property. The most important interest in property is 'ownership'. The concepts of 'property' and 'ownership' are an important part of the legal matrix underpinning the archival enterprise because a record (that is, a document produced in the course of practical activity) is itself a 'thing' in which legal persons (whether natural or juridical) have a relationship with.[13]

The obligation is not to a thing as object but between persons who are in a legal relationship with the thing. Ownership is an intangible thing which arises from the relationship between two persons and a thing. Thus property is a legal relationship. Rather than someone 'owning' a record, they have obligations arising from ownership. Rather than concentrating

---

[9] Ibid., p. 1.

[10] Ibid., p. 44.

[11] Simon Fisher, 'General Principles of Obligations', in *The Law of Commercial and Professional Relationships,* ed. Simon Fisher, F.T. Law & Tax, South Melbourne, 1996, p. 19.

[12] A share exists only through proof of the right to the share; for example, a record of the share certificate is not the property itself, but evidence of a right to property. 'Things in action' are both obligations as well as items of property. Ibid., 18-20.

[13] Simon Fisher, 'The Archival Enterprise, Public Archival Institutions and the Impact of Private Law', *Archives and Manuscripts*, vol. 26, no. 2, Nov. 1998, p. 331.

on the record as object, it is 'the thing as relationship', or Kocourek's 'thing as a right', that is evidenced in the record that is the subject of ownership.

On the basis of the legal and social relationship model, it is possible to go further than Fisher's record as a thing as an object of obligation, to consider the record as a 'thing-persons-property relationship', that is both the right-duty thing itself and evidence of the property relationship; the evidence that the rights of ownership convey, that is to create, copy, keep, destroy the thing, and the duty of others not to interfere with the enjoyment of the ownership.

In summary, the common law system classifies intangible things as a form of personal property, whereas civil law systems classify them as obligations. Although the common law system defines the record as a physical object rather than as an obligation, it still forms the object of a legal relationship. It is therefore possible to define a record as a right-duty thing or obligation in both the civil and common law systems.

5.1.2 Ownership in common law systems

The common law never developed a theory of ownership, because its remedies for property matters were based on possession.[14] Property in a thing is the state's ability to restrict access to the thing. Ownership is also a form of property in things. A holder of ownership of a thing either holds possession of the thing which no one is at liberty to interfere with, or

[14] In common law, ownership as a term first appears in the nineteenth century. Possession, not ownership, had to be proved to get access to a common law remedy for property matters. This was partly due to the lack of documentary evidence of ownership. Thus written records have been important to proving ownership in a thing. Welling, *Property in Things in the Common Law System,* p. 11, footnote 21. Possession is both a fact and a right (claim). So long as possession operates on the basis of the claim to possess, the right of ownership remains incomplete. Ownership is the ultimate right of possession. The law does not deal with ownership apart from possession. Kocourek, *Jural Relations,* p. 328. Ownership and possession were originally regarded as inseparable concepts, with the possessor considered the owner. The separation of ownership and possession arose from owners having a right against the whole world, while the possessor held the right against whole world but one person, another claimant. There is also consensual possession where possession is by the owner's consent; without consent there may be adverse possession which may become ownership. William Edward Hearn, *The Theory of Legal Duties and Rights: An Introduction to Analytical Jurisprudence,* F.B. Rothman, Littleton Colorado, 1990 (1883), pp. 189-190; p. 197.

holds, or will, when a contract expires hold, right to immediate possession of the thing, while someone else holds possession or right to immediate possession after transfer.[15]

The right of ownership is not a single right and lawyers have had difficulties in defining it. The great tort lawyer, Antony M. Honoré, in his essay, 'Ownership', in *Oxford Essays in Jurisprudence*, identifies a full set of rights over things an individual may be endowed with. This includes the right to possess, use, consume or destroy, modify, manage, rent out and alienate.[16] William Hearn also concentrated on the rights of ownership, which included 'the right to possess, the right to use, the right to produce, the right to waste, the right to disposition, whether during life or upon death, and the right to exclude all other persons from any interference with the thing owned',[17] thereby avoiding using property as a form of ownership. For Hearn, property was defined as the thing owned, and ownership as the right over the property.

Rights of ownership place obligations on others; the right of exclusion places a duty on others not to enjoy the object of ownership.[18] The owner has a residuary right in the thing owned. 'Such a residuary right or interest exists once one subtracts from the totality of the rights in the property concerned the rights asserted, claimed or enjoyed by others'.[19] The exclusion of ownership does not necessarily exclude all property rights. Ideas cannot be owned, but one can have a property right to the idea. They are a subset of property rights.[20]

Proof of possession and custody (as detention)

Possession is a form of property in things. Possession is also a relationship. The record as thing may be possessed or may provide evidence of intention to possess. Possession comprises a *physical* and *mental* element. Case law includes the critical factor of intention. Possession is proved by the

---

[15] Welling, *Things in the Common Law System,* pp. 30-35.

[16] Antony M. Honoré, 'Ownership', in *Oxford Essays in Jurisprudence*, ed. A.G. Guest, Clarendon Press, Oxford, 1961, pp. 107-147. Property may lead to inequality as persons compete, or use their different talents to acquire ownership, but the initial starting point is equality, that is, the principle of just deserts. Thus property may not be an equalising right.

[17] Hearn, *The Theory of Legal Duties and Rights,* p. 186; pp. 200-202.

[18] Ibid., p. 194.

[19] Fisher, 'The Archival Enterprise', p. 331 defines a residuary right of ownership in his interpretation of *Campbells Hardware & Timber Pty Ltd v CSD* (Queensland) (1996) 96 ATC 4348 at 4352.

[20] Kocourek, *Jural Relations,* p. 320.

coexistence of physical control and the manifested intent to exclude others. The person with physical control is said to have detention of that property. Detention is a form of custody. Detention of the property, personally or by a custodian, with the intention of keeping it for one's own use, is possession of that property. It denotes the power of exclusive access to the object and power of exercising control over it, in time and space. One has to have immediate physical contact, but the concept of detention need not be restricted to direct contact.[21] There needs to be evidence of intention to possess.[22] The required degree of control varies with the nature of the thing. As possession is a relationship, the claimant must manifest the intent to exclude others from interfering with the thing. If interference is proven it may result in damages, not necessarily transfer of property to the claimant.[23]

Legal possession and actual possession

In the classical view of the European jurist Savigny, acquisition and possession rests on two elements: 'animus' (the will to control) and 'corpus' (immediate power to control). In continuance of possession the control at will is considered sufficient. According to Kocourek, possession can exist when one does not have the thing with one. One can possess a car even if it is not with one.[24] Using the same reasoning, one can possess a record without physical possession.

In law the test of possession is persons having *a thing in their power* even if not owning it, for example bailees (see bailment below). Possession is an element of power. Rights of an owner depend on the continuing existence of the thing, not necessarily in their physical detention/ possession.[25]

---

[21] Detention required direct physical contact under Roman law. In Roman law delivery made by a seller to the buyer's servant would only give the servant detention and the master possession. In common law the servant also has possession. Ibid., pp. 362-363.

[22] The intent in possession may be indefinite (no limiting condition) or specific, where there may be an intention to transfer possession on the occurrence of an event, for example a payment of money. Hearn, *The Theory of Legal Duties and Rights,* p. 187.

[23] Welling, *Things in the Common Law System,* pp. 26-29.

[24] Kocourek, *Jural Relations,* p. 400.

[25] Originally possession meant detention, but possession became identified with facts needed for possessory remedies. Many statutes use the term possession, for example weapons in a person's possession and deal with an intent to use or

Fisher divides possession into possession *in fact* and possession *in law*.

> As possession in fact, 'possession' means the situation where the possessor of something (usually mobile property such as 'goods' or records) has the use and occupation of which the subject matter of the possessory relationship is capable: see *Gray v Official Trust in Bankruptcy* (1991) 29 FCR 166 at 171. By comparison, legal possession is the state of being in possession in the contemplation of the law: *Gray v Official Trustee in Bankruptcy* (1991) 29 FCR 166 at 171. Legal possession is that degree of possession which is recognised and protected by law: *Horsley v Phillips Fine Art Auctioneers Pty Ltd* (1996) 7 BPR [97557] at 14,371 per Santow J. Legal possession is also known as possession in law: see *Horsley* at 14,371. Two evidentiary propositions support the general utility of legal possession. These are: (1) possession in fact is prima facie evidence of possession in law; (2) possession in fact, with the manifest intent of sole and exclusive dominion, always imports possession in law: *Gray v Official Trustee in Bankruptcy* (1991) 29 FCR 166 at 171. Once again, the concept of possession is important to the archival enterprise and that it is particularly so when records are loaned or used by people. The term used for the transfer of possession is delivery. The test the legal system in Australia uses for deciding whether possession has passed is whether the person in possession has the requisite mix of intention and control over the thing.[26]

The distinction of *possession in fact* (de facto possession) and *legal possession* (de jure possession) is not universally held.[27] Kocourek also supports a right to possession over physical possession.[28] Where the notion of possession without physical possession and rights of possession as intention and 'control' are particularly relevant, is in the digital environment.[29]

---

use them. Detention would be a more appropriate term according to Kocourek, *Jural Relations,* p. 402.

[26] Fisher, 'The Archival Enterprise', p. 333. 'The possession of a material object is the continuing exercise of a claim to the exclusive use of it'. Kocourek, *Jural Relations,* p. 361, footnote 2, quoting Salmond.

[27] Ibid., pp. 364-366.

[28] Ibid., p. 372. The right of possession is presented as a jural thing. The object of possessory rights is to create an infra-jural relation of a human being to a material object, which involves power under normal conditions to make unlimited use of that object. According to this view the right to possession is determined by rules of law not by physical possession.

[29] See discussion in Chapter 7.

Cessation of property in a thing

Property in a thing ceases to exist when the thing itself is destroyed. Without the 'thing', property is meaningless.[30] Decomposition and transmutation of a thing becomes a new thing, for example a work of art that is based on a theme from another work or the alteration of a record.[31] Property in a thing also ceases to exist when the owner of the property dies. The thing continues (because it is an object in common law).

Property in things is commonly acquired, transferred and disposed of by transaction, which includes purchase or sale, gift, and bailment.[32] In addition to the record as a thing that can be possessed, evidence of ownership transferred at the time of contract, the intention to transfer, dates of purchase or transfer and other rules that trigger the transfer of property, are all elements that must be captured in records.

Bailment and possession

Welling has defined bailment as:

> … a transaction whereby possession of a thing is transferred upon agreement that possession of the same thing, perhaps in an altered state, will be transferred back to the transferor or on to someone else as agreed.[33]

Bailment consists of an agreement and a transfer of property. The property transferred is possession of a thing. The agreement proposes a future transfer of possession of the thing, either to a third party or back to the transferor. Bailment can involve transfers of possession by contract or

---

[30] Welling, *Things in the Common Law System,* p. 79. The owner may sue the destroyer for damages.

[31] Ibid., pp. 81-84, p. 95. The doctrine of accession is the process whereby a thing becomes either worked into a different type of thing or combined with one or more things to form a composite unit. The property in the original thing ceases to exist when the reworked product is no longer identifiable as the same item (for example grapes turned into wine or an image reworked digitally), based on physical identity only. A visual specification test has changed to a relative value test which determines a transfer of property by examining labour added to original thing. The owner of the principal thing gets the ownership of the combined thing.

[32] Ibid., p. 233. A gift is also a transaction, a non-contractual transfer of a form of property from one person to another. It is similar to other forms of transfer that are not transfers of sale such as a trust or deed. A gift requires proof of transfer; a donor's intent without consideration is hard to prove, thus proof of delivery is important.

[33] Ibid., p. 283.

by gift. The main issue in property is when does an acquisition or disposition take place.[34]

'Possession' is the essence of bailment, as ownership does not pass to another person directly. Bailment is applied to possessory interest in tangible personal property and rights and duties associated with it.[35] If bailment is applied to non-tangible objects it could be invoked to protect the rights of data owners of electronically transferred 'things', however contract is the more common form for arrangements of this kind (see 5.2.1 below, 'Rights-obligations of recordkeeping participants in personal property law').

It appears that when the notions of possession and ownership are analysed they are less concerned with actually having a thing as object physically in one's hands than with the notion of possessory rights. If this is the case then evidence of possessory rights, including the intention to possess, that arise from a legal relationship as a right to possession or as a duty not to take possession, should apply equally in the online environment.

Although an ethical element appears less obvious in personal property law that deals with exclusive possession, ownership and economic rights, property as an obligation, at least in deontological ethics, includes a notion of restriction on complete control over the thing owned.

5.2 Recordkeeping and property as a legal relationship

As analysed above the legal concepts of property, ownership and possession have a number of ramifications for recordkeeping. Ownership of a record itself depends on the properties of a record, its content and its documentary form, and its context, that is, who authored or created it, all of which determine a range of ownership or possessory rights which may include control over access and/or reproduction, sale of, as well as destruction of the record. When records were made and kept in a physical tangible medium, the common law approach has been to define them as

[34] Ibid., p. 273 and p. 346. Bailment is often incorrectly used to cover situations where one person holds possession while another person holds ownership or a right to immediate possession.

[35] Fisher, 'General Principles of Obligations', pp. 30-31. 'A relationship between two parties (the bailor and the bailee) in which ownership or property in choses in possession remains vested with the bailor and possession of the chose passes to the bailee under the process of delivery which can be actual, symbolic or constructive.'

chattels not as obligations that could be bought and sold as material property. Intellectual property, on the other hand, has always been concerned with the protection of the way an idea is expressed in a material form.

Property concepts have been evident in archival and records legislation. Simon Fisher argues that property law has always been a 'privatising' element in archives law and practice, for example the definition of a record in terms of government property.[36] In Australia what has been termed 'first generation' archival laws and also related laws such as Freedom of Information, use the language of custody, possession, and ownership of records.[37] Under the *Archives Act* 1983 (Cth) s 27, ownership of Commonwealth records remains with the Commonwealth and only the custody of the records is transferred to the archival authority. As both the archival authority and the government agency are the same legal person, ownership cannot in fact pass from one government agency to another.[38] This transfer has been interpreted as physical custody, but the issue of possession as control (legal possession: see above) could apply to records not in the physical custody of the archives.[39] An archival authority may need to gain possession of records of outsourced functions. If the

[36] Fisher, 'The Archival Enterprise', p. 337.

[37] Chris Hurley, 'From Dust Bins to Disk-drives and Now to Dispersal: the State Records Act 1998 (New South Wales)', *Archives and Manuscripts,* vol. 26, no. 2, Nov. 1998, pp. 390-409. The differences between custody, possession and ownership are illustrated by the metaphor of the gentleman's suit of clothes, and the roles of different persons who take possession and custody of the suit and who actually owns it. See Chris Hurley, 'Appendix 2: From Dustbins to Disk-Drives: A Survey of Archives legislation in Australia', in *The Records Continuum: Ian Maclean and Australian Archives First Fifty Years,* eds Sue McKemmish and Michael Piggott, Ancora Press in association with Australian Archives, Clayton, 1994, pp. 206-232.

[38] '... records are usually owned by the Crown in right of the polity which created them or which received them in the course of official duties, and there is no legal reason why it is necessary to distribute ownership of records as between different governmental agencies. Although there may be sound administrative reasons why records management responsibilities are vested in archival institutions, these do not alter the incidence of ownership of records unless the owner of the records is a separate legal person to the archival institution'. Fisher, 'The Archival Enterprise', p. 332.

[39] The review of the *Archives Act* 1983 (Cth) indicates that a physical interpretation of custody is not appropriate for a strategy of distributed custody of records. See Australian Law Reform Commission, *Review of the Archives Act 1983*, Draft Recommendations, Paper 4, December 1997, AGPS, Canberra, 1997.

outsourced body is considered a separate legal entity from government, bailment and contract law may provide a preferable means of enforcing obligations in relation to control over the records. On the other hand, constructive possession may be relevant if the outsourced function is carried out by a legal entity that is not separate from government.

The relevance of bailment law to public archival bodies exists where an owner of records deposits these in an archive on a temporary basis, or even on a long term basis, but without the intention of transferring ownership of the records. Admittedly, as Fisher points out, this may be rare in archival practice, but the possibility remains that a bailment can be created of documents, and could apply to records held in a distributed environment.[40] Another application of the law of bailment is where documents are deposited or loaned by an institution to another person.[41]

Given the notion of intent to possess, that is, to possess an object does not require it to be physically with the claimant, possession could still be an appropriate legal term in the electronic world in relation to record ownership.

5.2.1 Rights-obligations of recordkeeping participants in personal property law

Property concepts have provided a micro-level view of records, concentrating on the role of documents as data or 'trace' rather than records as evidence maintained within a system. For example in the national archival legislation of the United States and the United Kingdom, any data can be a record regardless of physical format.[42] In Australian law, documents and

---

[40] 'If a bailment is created, the owner of the archived material is called the "bailor" and the archivist the "bailee". Even if there is no bailment between an owner of documents and the archivist, there can be one between the archivist (as the *owner* of documents) and the *user* of archived material, so long as possession of that material is transferred to the user.' Fisher, 'The Archival Enterprise', pp. 358-359, endnote 21.

[41] Ibid., pp. 333-334.

[42] In the United Kingdom, the *Public Records Act* 1958 (UK) s 10(1) Interpretation, '"public records" has the meaning assigned to it by the First Schedule to this Act and "records" includes not only written records but records conveying information by any other means whatsoever'. The *Federal Records Act,* 44 U.S.C. 3301, defines 'federal records' to include 'all books, papers, maps, photographs, machine-readable materials, or other documentary materials, regardless of physical form or characteristics, made or received by an agency of the United States government under federal law or in connection with the transaction of public business and preserved or appropriate for preservation

records have generally been defined as property,[43] that is, as material or tangible corporeal objects rather than as an obligation or a right which excludes the record's nature as a representation of an act which may be incorporeal.[44] If 'record as thing' in property law is limited to a material tangible object, an electronic record as a 'non-material object' may be

by that agency or its legitimate successor as evidence of the organization, functions, policies, decisions procedures, operations, or other activities of the government or because of the informational value of data in them'. The InterPARES 1 Project, Findings of the InterPARES Project, *Global Industry Research Team Report*, CENSA, 2001, p. 8, found that '… U.S. regulatory agencies, the U.S. Code of Federal Regulations, and U.S. congressional code define records and electronic records to be any information in any format that is stored for later evidential, business, or historical purposes. They thus equate with records, all evidence or data of any type created by anyone anywhere within the business. They also do not associate records with the business processes they relate to, nor do they include the archival requirement of the record to be "fixed and set aside under the care of a qualified custodian with the responsibility of ensuring the ongoing authenticity of the record."'

[43] Statutory definitions of documents and records have centred on their physical characteristics rather than their function. For example in the former *Evidence Act* 1898 (NSW) s 14A, a 'document' is defined as 'books, maps, plans drawings and photographs', while in the same Act in relation to business records s 14CD(1) defines a 'document' as 'any record of information'. This latter definition of document has been adopted in the *Evidence Act* 1995 (Cth) and (NSW). The *Acts Interpretation Act* 1901 (Cth) s 25(c) includes in its definition of a document 'any article or material from which sounds, images or writings are capable of being reproduced with or without the aid of any other article or device'. The definition of writing is also related to being perceptible in a visible form. The *Archives Act* 1983 (Cth) s 3(1) defines a record as 'a document (including any written or printed material) or object (including a sound recording, coded storage device, magnetic tape or disc, microform, photograph, film, map, plan or model or a painting or other pictorial or graphic work) that is, or has been, kept by reason of any information or matter that it contains or can be obtained from it or by reason of its connection with any event, person, circumstance or thing'.

[44] '"Materiality" is a vital component of a law of property, particularly as it relates to corporeal property such as paper-based records. Modern archival practice has moved well beyond the material form of the record although the law of property is closely wedded to concepts such as "possession" which depend on the materiality of the thing possessed'. Fisher, 'The Archival Enterprise', p. 358, endnote 17.

excluded.[45] However the law has begun to consider the processes that bring an electronic record into existence and to re-assess some fundamental legal principles in the light of that knowledge. For example, Canadian and Australian evidence laws have been drivers in creating a perceptible shift in the legal understanding of a record as a medium-based physical entity to a purpose view, which is much more in keeping with the understanding of a record from a recordkeeping tradition.[46]

Generally archives and records legislation has defined a public record either via a process or a property test.[47] The Australian Law Reform Commission's review of the *Archives Act* 1983 in May 1998, opted for a provenance and process approach in lieu of a property approach to ownership of records, which links ownership to the organisation on the basis of the government activity it undertakes; that is records created or received by a government agency in the conduct of its affairs, including electronic information that is used for practical activity.[48] In the *State*

---

[45] The non-materiality of electronic records has led to classifying them in law as intangible objects and therefore not subject to property law. See Fisher, 'The Archival Enterprise', p. 340.

[46] See Chapter 2.

[47] 'A definition referring to the origin of records (i.e. to provenance) tends to reflect the professionally accepted definition of records (pare. 15), rather than a definition that refers to ownership. The last type, however, which has been linked with the British concept of "undisturbed custody" of records as the basis for their evidential value, is used where the intention is to include historical manuscripts and other documentary property belonging to the State.' Eric Ketelaar, *Archival and Records Management Legislation and Regulations: A Ramp Study with Guidelines,* UNESCO, Paris 1985.

[48] Australian Law Reform Commission, *Australia's Federal Record, A Review of the Archives Act 1983,* Report No. 85, May 1998, AGPS, Canberra, 1998, p. 98, recommendation 24, opts for a provenance definition of a record. It defines a record as follows, 'the term "record" should be defined as "recorded information, in any form, including data in computer systems, created or received or maintained by an organisation or person in the transaction of business or the conduct of affairs and kept as evidence of such activity"'. The *Archives Act 1983* s 3(1) defines a 'Commonwealth record' as (a) a record that is the property of the Commonwealth or of a Commonwealth institution; or (b) a record that is deemed to be a Commonwealth record by virtue of a regulation under sub-section (6) or by virtue of section 22; but does not include a record that is exempt material or is a register or guide maintained in accordance with Part VIII. Australian Law Reform Commission, *Review of the Archives Act 1983*, states 'the use of a property based definition such as that in s 3(1) is not universal in archival legislation. The most common alternative is an administrative provenance definition, such as was proposed in the original

Records Act 1998 (NSW), s 3(1), record means 'any document or other source of information compiled, recorded or stored in written form or on film, or by electronic process, or in any other manner or by any other means'. In s 3(1) of the Act, a 'State record' means any 'record made and kept, by any person in the course of the exercise of official functions in a public office, or for any purpose of a public office, or for the use of a public office, whether before or after the commencement of this section', which is a process test. A process test avoids the common law question of 'materiality', and is based on the record's purpose.

In addition to the 'purpose' view of a record as an alternative to property, a record as a thing, other than as a material object, control over, rather than immediate possession, and property as an obligation, are concepts that are more suited to a non-material or 'virtual' world, because they are based on alternative understandings of property law. Property as obligation supports the duty of maintaining the inviolability of records, as exemplified in archival legislative provisions which disallow the alteration or destruction of records without archival approval or under other law.[49] In addition to the record as an object of property, the record may provide evidence of property ownership, including an intention to possess. Recordkeeping participants may be both property owners and/or holders of evidence of property rights (the latter may be an archival body).

'Intellectual property' is the broad term given to bundles of rights under law to protect and reward creative and economic investment in the creation of intangible products covering a diverse range of subjects which are the product of human industry and creativity, ingenuity, knowledge, skill and labour, and which are susceptible to commercial exploitation.[50] Colin Golvan's more expansive definition of intellectual property includes the protection of confidential information, trade secrets, passing off and trade

---

drafting instructions for the Archives Bill in 1974. The suggested formula was "all records of any kind made or received by any Australian [ie Commonwealth] Government agency in the conduct of its affairs". However successive drafts of the Bill in 1974-75 moved from a provenance definition through a custodial definition ("a record that is held in official custody on behalf of the government") to the present property definition'.

[49] See for example *Archives Act* 1983 (Cth) s 26, and the *State Records Act* 1998 (NSW) s 21(1)(d). Fisher, 'The Archival Enterprise', p. 355.

[50] Julia Baird, 'Introduction to Some Intellectual Property Issues in Information Technology', in *Computers and the Law, 94/42, Papers Presented for the Continuing Legal Education Department of the College of Law on 6 July 1994*, Sydney, CLE Department of the College of Law, Sydney, 1994, pp. 1-28.

practices protection.[51] Copyright is a category of intellectual property concerned with the protection of ideas or the way that ideas are expressed. It is a form of personal property which can be bought, sold (assigned), rented (licensed), or passed onto heirs like any other property. As intangible products they are closer to representing notions of records as evidence of rights rather than as physical objects.

Copyright law: an example of rights and duties

Copyright has been designed to protect 'the form of expression' of ideas not the ideas themselves (there is a limited protection for ideas under copyright law), principally by controlling the copying and reproduction of 'creative works' which, subject to case law, generally require minimal creativity. In the United Kingdom and the United States the courts have interpreted facts as not sufficiently creative to be protected by copyright law.[52]

The copyright owner has a number of exclusive rights to do and to authorise others to do specified acts in relation to 'protected works and other subject matter'. Copyright includes rights that prevent third parties from making uses of intellectual property they do not own. If the third party does use or copy another person's intellectual property without

---

[51] Colin Golvan, *An Introduction to Intellectual Property Law,* Federation Press, Sydney, 1992. p. vii. Originally the concept of intellectual property was only applied to copyright and was contrasted with 'industrial property' which covered patents, industrial designs and trademarks. Now all these areas are considered to fall within the ambit of intellectual property.

[52] The US Supreme Court in *Feist Publications Inc v Rural Telephone Service Co Inc* 499 US 340 (1991) rejected a breach of copyright for data from a telephone directory's white pages, stating that facts cannot be copyrighted, and that lists of names, addresses and telephone numbers in alphabetical order, are not sufficiently creative to qualify for copyright protection. The *Feist* case concluded that data in a telephone directory is not protected by copyright because it fails the test of originality. The Australian case *Desktop Marketing Systems Pty Ltd v Telstra Corporation Limited* [2002] FCAFC 112 (15 May 2002) supports copyright of facts on the basis of the 'industrious collection' test for subsistence of copyright. 'The reasons in Feist provide no ground for concluding that Telstra's various forms of labour (collecting/receiving, verifying, recording, computer-aided assembling) should not suffice to attract copyright protection.' From Black CJ, Reasons for judgment. In the Australian case the originality of facts depended on how much work or 'industry' went into producing them, while in the United States, the claim of copyright protection of facts was rejected on the basis that they were found not to be sufficiently original to warrant protection.

permission the legal term is infringement. There are certain statutory exceptions for non-copyright owners. These are referred to as 'fair dealing' in Australia, and as 'fair use' in the United States.[53] In addition to 'economic' rights there are 'moral' or natural rights which are personal to the author. Both sets of rights are recognised in the *Berne Convention for the Protection of Literary and Artistic Works*.[54] Moral rights protect the work from distortion, mutilation and denigration and require that credit be given when the work is used. Moral rights legislation includes the right of attribution which helps to protect the author's ideas; the right not to have falsely attributed another's name to a work or to an altered work; and the right of integrity which is the right not to modify a work in a way that is prejudicial to honour and reputation, or create contextual misuse that is prejudicial to the author.[55]

Copyright must be expressed in a 'material form' but it is independent of the ownership of the object itself. It is a good example of a right-duty thing, that is, it is not the material object itself that is owned, but the way it is presented. Material form 'includes any form (whether visible or not) of storage from which the work or adaptation, or a substantial part of the work or adaptation can be reproduced'.[56] Material form is analogous to the archival concept of documentary form that carries information in its structure, which is separate from the medium on which it is stored. Copyright protects the arrangement or structure of the work and is therefore dependent on the integrity of the work.

---

[53] Unlike the position in Australia, in the United States a person can use fair use for a purpose other than one of the listed purposes. Australian Copyright Council, *Access to Copyright Material in Australia and the US,* Information Sheet G087v01, Australian Copyright Council, Strawberry Hills, NSW, September 2004, p. 4.

[54] 'Independently of the author's economic rights, and even after the transfer of the said rights, the author shall have the right to claim authorship of the work and to object to any distortion, mutilation or other modification of, or other derogatory action in relation to, the said work, which would be prejudicial to his honor or reputation.' WIPO, *Berne Convention for the Protection of Literary and Artistic Works,* 9 September, 1886, art. 6, bis (1), S. Treaty Doc. No. 27, 99th Cong., 2d Sess. 41 1986.

[55] For example, in Australia: *Copyright Amendment (Moral Rights) Act* 2000 (Cth); in Canada: *Copyright Act* R.S. 1985, c. C-42, ss 12(1) and (2), 14(1) and 28(2) and in the United States (which limits moral rights to visual art): *Visual Artists Rights Act* 1990 (VARA). In Europe moral rights are more broadly protected by ordinary copyright law.

[56] Galvin, *An Introduction to Intellectual Property Law*, p. 5.

Copyright distinguishes between authorship and ownership; the creator/author is generally the first owner of copyright. As noted in the previous chapter, the definitions of author and creator do not equate with their archival definitions. Statutes in different jurisdictions will vary as to definitions of copyright authors and owners and their rights regarding reproduction, distribution, transmission, performance, adaptation, copying and in what form (for example electronic), what material form is being protected (literary or other work), and what is a direct or authorising infringement.

Intellectual property law provides a good example of balancing rights and obligations of interested parties. Balancing the interest of the creators (or producers) and users (consumers) of intellectual property with the interest of the community as a whole is a central tenet of copyright law. The concept of public interest is an essential element of the web of legal relationships in the legal and social relationship model and clearly includes intellectual property. The ethical aspect of intellectual property is particularly evident in moral rights legislation that upholds the integrity of a work, and is based on a duty of respect for the reputation of the author.

Copyright law affects recordkeeping participants in relation to establishing authorship and ownership, including transfer of ownership of copyright, right of access to records protected by copyright and protecting the integrity of the content in its material form. Recordkeeping agent metadata or intrinsic elements of documentary form which identify 'authors' and 'creators' and their intentions are essential to providing evidence of authorship and copyright ownership, as much as for the identity and reliability of the evidence regarding these matters.

Contract law has also become important to intellectual property arrangements involving electronic information delivery. Contracts permit one or more third parties to use (license) the intellectual property on payment of a fee, which is often based on the amount of usage. Rather than selling the intellectual property, the owner licenses it. It is equivalent to renting out property. Contracts allow the owner to keep the copyright. However outside of contracts, copyright law automatically applies for infringements of owners' rights.[57]

---

[57] Most intellectual property matters never reach a court hearing. Minor infringements are ignored, as owners of copyright feel uncertain about pushing their rights in court. Copyright has succeeded in preventing illegal copies in large profitable markets and is seen as protecting big commercial interests rather than the interests of individual creative persons. See Lance Rose, *Netlaw: Your Rights in the Online World,* Osborne McGraw-Hill, Berkeley, 1995, p. 88.

Intellectual property is therefore relevant to legal and social relationships in which the record is the 'form' protected by copyright, but more importantly it also provides evidence of the identity of the 'author' and 'user' in relation to a copyrighted work, which by definition includes the record's context and structure.

5.2.2 Ownership rights in records

Ascertaining ownership rights in records

There is a complex array of relationships relevant to the ownership of even a single document. In fact, given the nature of ownership, property and possession, it is preferable to speak in terms of ownership rights in a document, linked to its creation and use. The complexities are compounded by legal definitions of documents, information and records and the different functions they all perform. For example, under present Australian copyright law, records, archives and databases as compilations are 'literary works', and records are defined within the category of an unpublished original 'literary work'.[58] The author of a literary work (other than in an employment situation and certain other exceptions) is the owner of the copyright in the work, in the absence of an agreement to the contrary.[59] Intellectual property only protects the form in which data is expressed, rather than the data itself, which means that individual data in a record would not have copyright protection, unless it is found to be 'original'.[60]

Relevant issues in common law include the fact that information per se has not been regarded as property and 'statements' are treated separately from a document or a record in which they are recorded. While physical records have been defined as 'chattels', ownership of the chattel may not give rights over the intellectual content of the record. 'Replevin' and the recovery of 'stolen records' are legal methods for regaining control over records. However they are notions based on physical possession of the record which may be difficult to apply in the electronic world.

---

[58] Australian government records are unpublished original 'literary works'. See case law on Crown copyright in Simon Fisher, 'Government and Rights Protection in Commercial Contexts', in *Government Law and Policy, Commercial Aspects*, ed. Bryan Horrigan, The Federation Press, Leichhardt, NSW, 1998, pp. 150-151.

[59] In Australian law in most employment situations, employees do not hold copyright in their work. See *Copyright Act* 1968 (Cth) s 35(2) and (6).

[60] See footnote 52 above.

The matrix in Chapter 4 provides a number of actors that can be used to assist in the analysis of ownership rights in a record, to avoid confusing access or privacy rights with ownership. A commonly held assumption is that anything recorded about an identifiable person must be 'owned' by that person. Email in recent times is a good example of the erroneous belief of 'employee ownership' which is confused with the right to privacy.[61] Records that organisations create in the course of their business that contain personal details are not 'owned' by the data subject or record writer (usually the employee) but by the legal author. The data subject or the record writer may have a right of non-disclosure of that data (privacy rights) or an access right to it (under Freedom of Information), but not a proprietary right. In establishing 'ownership rights' to records many issues need to be considered. These include legal concepts of ownership in the legal system in which the recorded action took place (see 5.1 above, 'Property as a legal and social relationship'), which may involve more than one jurisdiction; the 'form' or structure in which records are required to be captured by the legal system, and the business context in which the recorded action took place. Ownership also depends on the 'competencies' (authority) of the parties to the action; their public or private character which determines what areas of law apply and the nature of their relationship, for example records may be held in fiduciary trust on behalf of a client; and whether the information has been provided under a statutory obligation, a personal favour, a subpoena, a contract, or as an employee duty or under payment. Generally, outside of the employer-employee relationship, ownership of the content remains with the author, that is, the person who created the work. A work copied or reproduced by a third party without the permission of the author could be an infringement of the intellectual property of that author.

---

[61] The right of employees to email privacy and the need of businesses to access email they 'own' as records, are examples of the confusion between ownership and privacy rights. See Monash University, *Electronic Mail Recordkeeping Protocol*, 2001. Para. 5.1 relates to authorised university staff's right to inspect email on university servers. It differentiates between Monash business and private business. Email that is official in nature is university business, created and owned by Monash (including intellectual property rights). Personal privacy for Monash staff as employees applies to them as data subjects, not as record creators. In diplomatics terms they are only writers. However, the distinction between record creator/author/writer and data subject is not universally held. According to some European interpretations if an employee chooses to use an official email system for private correspondence it does not change the private nature of that correspondence. See Chapter 2, footnote 128.

In different organisational contexts it may be necessary to make specific decisions about identifying ownership of proprietary information.[62] Rather than legislating proof of ownership of data or a record, the law provides various rights to have it protected from other interests. In addition to property law, areas of law relevant to exercising ownership rights over ideas, data, records or products, include contract, trade practices legislation, trade secrets, torts (breach of confidentiality, trespass), and equity (breach of fiduciary duty). Trademarks, patent and copyright law may be used to protect unauthorised access to records from competitors. Otherwise copyright provides limited protection for information in records for businesses. Property law is less likely to be applied to electronic records because if its dependence on possession of a record as object.

Confidential information and ownership in ideas

The property right in confidential business information is usually based on a contractual agreement between the employer and employee and/or the employer and a service provider. If there is no contract, tort or equity law may apply. A breach of confidence in tort needs to demonstrate a duty of confidentiality to the claimant on the part of the person alleged to have breached the confidentiality, although it also covers information that has accidentally fallen into hands for which it was not intended.[63] A remedy in the tort of breach of confidence provides a means of protecting ownership of ideas in records. It is however only enforceable if certain conditions are met. These conditions include a relationship which has to have a quality of confidence or secrecy, there has to be restricted dissemination of the idea, the parties need to be aware of the confidentiality, that is the nature and manner of communication, and that there was or may be an unauthorised use of the information.[64]

---

[62] In Australia and Canada, the government through the legal entity of the Crown, owns copyright in public records and government publications. In the United States copyright law does not extend to any work of the United States government. In a medical context in Australia a doctor may not own the patient record if he/she is an employee. See Livia Iacovino, Ethical-Legal Frameworks for Recordkeeping: Regulatory Models, Participants and their Rights and Obligations, PhD Thesis, Monash University, Melbourne, 2002, Chapter 9 for examples of ownership in specific contexts.

[63] Moira Paterson, *Freedom of Information and Privacy in Australia: Government and Information Access in the Modern State,* LexisNexis Butterworths, Chatswood, NSW, 2005, pp. 17-18.

[64] Smith, Graham J.H. and contributors (eds), *Internet Law and Regulation: A Specially Commissioned Report*, F.T. Law & Tax, London, 1996, p. 23. See

In a government context in the British parliamentary tradition, access to information acquired by virtue of office includes obligations of confidence to the Crown as employer, as well as to persons who supply the information.[65]

Trade secrets and ownership in ideas

Information a business does not want competitors to know of or revealed may be protected as a trade secret. A trade secret is defined through case law. 'The cases indicate that the term means a device or a specific formula used in business which gives a person an opportunity to gain an advantage over competitors who do not have access to it'.[66] To be a trade secret there has to be a substantial element of secrecy in the sense that the information must be difficult to obtain by others except by improper means. The information does not have to be technical, and can cover marketing strategies. It can be classified as a harm to a business (tort), and remedies include an injunction to stop information being used and claims for damages through courts can be instituted. Courts protect trade secrets when the owner or the company makes sure, usually through a contract, that all those with access to the information agree to keep it secret. Once information becomes public the company cannot sue anyone who learns about it afterwards for further disclosing the information. The information has lost its status as a trade secret. Contract law provides the strongest protection for a trade secret and for commercial confidentiality.[67]

Recordkeeping systems are vital to establishing proprietary interests in data and records (in particular data on owners, on consultants and employees including confidentiality agreements, evidence of assignment of copyright, and other contextual information which support authorship).

---

also Tina Cockburn, 'Personal Liability of Government Officers in Tort and Equity', in *Government Law and Policy, Commercial Aspects,* ed. Bryan Horrigan, The Federation Press, Leichhardt, NSW, 1998, pp. 383-384.

65 Ibid., p. 383.

66 W.B. Lane and Nicolee Dixon, 'Government Decision Making: Freedom of Information and Judicial Review', in *Government Law and Policy, Commercial Aspects,* ed. Bryan Horrigan, The Federation Press, Leichhardt, NSW, 1998, p. 108.

67 Rose, *Netlaw: Your Rights in the Online World,* p. 114. In the United States lawsuits on breaching confidentiality obligations are common because businesses cannot sustain the loss of valuable information.

5.3 Access rights as legal and social relationships

5.3.1 Access as a property relationship

Generally access rights in the recordkeeping context have been dealt with as separate from property rights. However Fisher points out that access is also a kind of property relationship. 'Whatever the form of the "record" (whether materialised or immaterialised, paper-based or electronic), the access regime affecting records draws in part on the language of ownership and of property law (as well as the law of obligations) to facilitate its operation.'[68]

Access has been expressed as a separate right to ownership, for example in Freedom of Information (FOI) laws, and yet it is *a* right of ownership, which owners give up. Ownership is a form of control over information and how it is used. Secrecy (and the sacred nature of matters for some groups), privacy, confidentiality, permissions, and freedom of information, are all ideas about restricting access and use to allowable circumstances or on the other hand compelling access, that is forbidding someone from denying access when it is asked for. Negative rights of access include unauthorised access, including alteration of data, and unauthorised interception of electronic information.[69] Determining who can see something and under what conditions is access policy governing use. It is this meaning of access that is of relevance in determining the rights and obligations of recordkeeping participants, within legal and social relationships.

5.3.2 Copyright and access

In the definitions of ownership provided by Hearn, Welling and others, access was considered as a right of ownership. Thus the rights of copyright owners have been used to deny access to records and have had significant effects on the rights of those seeking information from records. It has become one of the most contentious issues in the area of privacy rights in

[68] Fisher, 'The Archival Enterprise', p. 332.

[69] In Australia unauthorised access to electronic records has been addressed in computer crime legislation. See Gordon Hughes, 'Reassessing Victoria's Computer Crime Laws', *Law Institute Journal*, vol. 75, no. 7, Aug. 2001, pp. 50-55.

patient data with attempts to do away with any form of property right by the creator of the record.[70]

In terms of third parties providing access to copyrighted works, there are special copyright exemptions for archives and libraries for the provision of copies of records to users, and educational statutory licences for copying.[71] Duration of copyright in unpublished works which includes records as literary works may be perpetual with exceptions for copying.[72]

5.3.3 Government obligations and access to public records

Statutory rights of access to government records (FOI, privacy, and archival/recordkeeping legislation) compete with a right to personal privacy and the need to ensure certain kinds of information are kept secret.

Archival access

In Australia and the United Kingdom statutory schemes within government for giving public access to records began with access arrangements for older records through archives and records legislation. This has found expression in the thirty-year rule which has been adopted by most national archival regimes. Archival institutions are legal actors with rights and responsibilities to a number of persons (also with Crown immunities in Westminster systems), which include the public and other government bodies. However in relation to transactions between the public and

[70] National Electronic Health Records Taskforce, *A Health Information Network for Australia, Taskforce Report*, Commonwealth of Australia, July 2000, Part 5 'Difficulties associated with Electronic Health Records'.

[71] See Australia, *Copyright Act 1968* (Cth) Part VB, 'Reproducing and communicating works by educational and other institutions'; Canada and the United States respectively, Canadian Intellectual Property Office, Copyright Circular No. 13, *Exceptions for Libraries, Museums and Archives,* September 1999, and 17 *Copyright Act* U.S.C. s108.

[72] In Australia copyright begins to run with publication. A copy of a work made available as a result of an archives or library provision is not considered published in relation to copyright duration. Australian Copyright Council, Information Sheet G23, *Duration of Copyright,* February 2005, 'Unpublished literary, dramatic and music works'. The Australia/US Free Trade Agreement (AUSFTA) includes a range of provisions which required changes to the Australian Copyright Act. These included changes to the period of copyright protection (in general, from author's life plus fifty years to life plus seventy years). Australian Copyright Council, Information Sheet G087v01, *Access to Copyright Material in Australia and the US,* September 2004.

government agencies, that is the 'business of government', archival institutions are third parties, as they are not the parties in the transaction, except in their own business transactions.

Freedom of Information legislation

Access to government records via FOI is a notion based on political and legal rights. There are a number of reasons why citizens have a legal right to government information in democratic societies. Firstly citizens cannot make reasoned choices within the political process without access to information that documents government actions. Secondly they need to know their rights and obligations which require access to records in which they are the subjects of the action. FOI promotes greater government transparency and accountability which counteracts government secrecy, a feature of all bureaucracy, identified by the German sociologist and organisational theorist Max Weber in the late nineteenth century.[73] Public access rights have to be considered in terms of the impact of administrative law on recordkeeping in terms of accountability, that is administrators being required to provide reasons for decisions, the reality of political interference in watering down access rights, and the relationship of accountability and recordkeeping as crucial in the areas of privacy and access.

The United States enacted the Freedom of Information Act in 1966, while in Australia, the passing of the Commonwealth Freedom of Information Act 1982 formed part of a range of reforms in the area of administrative law designed to improve government accountability.[74]

---

[73] Max Weber, *Economy and Society: An Outline of Interpretative Sociology*, eds Guenther Roth and Claus Wittich, trans. Ephraim Fischoff [and others] [Wirtschaft und Gesellschaft], New York, Bedminster Press, 1968. As Sweden had Freedom of Information laws since 1766, Weber's theories did not actually initiate them, nor did he advocate them. However, his understanding of bureaucracy and its inherent secrecy provides one of the best theoretical justifications for Freedom of Information laws.

[74] Administrative law deals with the legal means of curbing the administrative powers of ministers of state, and includes concepts of natural justice and fairness. For a summary of the background to Freedom of Information and its origins in Australia, and comparisons with other countries, see Australian Law Reform Commission, *Freedom of Information,* Issues Paper 12, AGPS, Sydney and Canberra, 1994, Chapter 2.

Australia was the first national Westminster style government to enact FOI legislation.[75]

FOI has generally applied to the public sector only. In Australia, under FOI citizens have an enforceable statutory right of access to documents in government, that is, government must grant access to documents on request and if access is denied the citizen may apply to a court or tribunal which can review the decision and order the release of the documents if it thinks fit. The overall approach is similar in each jurisdiction in Australia, and similar models are found in other countries.[76]

FOI Acts usually specify how access must be applied for and the time limit within which a request must be handled, how access must be given, for example the right to inspect a record, make a copy, or charges incurred. In the case of electronic records, one is often entitled to have the data in a human readable form.[77]

Access may be not only to 'official' records, but also to work diaries, note books and paintings. In the *Freedom of Information Act* 1982 (Cth), as long as they are created or received by an officer of the agency, they are a document of the agency for the purposes of the FOI Act. It is a provenancial rather than a property definition.[78] There are usually various review mechanisms if access is denied.[79]

---

[75] Canada enacted FOI at the federal level in 1983 (*Access to Information Act* 1983), Ireland in 1997 (*Freedom of Information Act* 1997), and the United Kingdom in 2000 (*Freedom of Information Act* 2000).

[76] Freedom of Information legislation is found in all Australian states, the Australian Capital Territory and the Commonwealth. Many of the Acts are a result of government enquiries into corruption. There are variations in the legislation but generally they are modelled on the Commonwealth Act. See: *Freedom of Information Act* 1982 (Cth); *Freedom of Information Act* 1982 (Vic); *Freedom of Information Act* 1989 (NSW); *Freedom of Information Act* 1989 (ACT); *Freedom of Information Act* 1991 (Tas); *Freedom of Information Act* 1991 (SA); *Freedom of Information Act* 1992 (Qld); *Freedom of Information Act* 1992 (WA).

[77] *Freedom of Information Act* 1982 (Cth) s 20, Forms of access.

[78] Definition of 'document of an agency' in *Freedom of Information Act* 1982 (Cth), 4 Interpretation, document includes: (a) any of, or any part of any of, the following things: (i) any paper or other material on which there is writing; (ii) a map, plan, drawing or photograph; (iii) any paper or other material on which there are marks, figures, symbols or perforations having a meaning for persons qualified to interpret them; (iv) any article or material from which sounds, images or writings are capable of being reproduced with or without the aid of any other article or device; (v) any article on which information has been stored or recorded, either mechanically or electronically; (vi) any other record of

Freedom of Information and archival access

The interrelationship of archival/records and freedom of information legislative regimes, and which laws take precedence, must also be taken into account in relation to access rights to records. For example, in the Commonwealth of Australia, the Australian Security Intelligence Organisation (ASIO) is an exempt body under the FOI Act, but not under the national archives law; thus ASIO records that are more than thirty years old are open, subject to some continuing exemptions, but records that are less than thirty years old cannot be accessed under FOI.[80]

In Australia the basic difference between FOI and archival access schemes has been twofold. First, FOI involves making a request which is acted upon by agency staff, who have to identify the documents which satisfy that request, whereas archives' clearance procedures may 'release' records automatically after a period of time, for example thirty years, whether or not anyone wants to see the document. Access-examined records are available on demand and may be searched by the applicant personally who is able to decide for herself/himself whether or not the documents are of interest. Again the archival agency is a third party, while access under FOI is usually provided by the agency responsible for the record, which may or may not have authored the record. In terms of the legal relationship model there is therefore likely to be an external party involved in access provision, for example the archival authority for government records more than thirty years old.

Freedom of Information and commercial confidentiality

FOI has recognised a need to protect commercial information held by government, balanced with the right of the public to know how government is involved in business. For example, in Australia commercial information is protected as third party information under FOI law. The *Freedom of Information Act* 1982 (Cth) s 43(1) has a number of self-contained exemptions to prevent disclosure of information supplied to government by outside persons and organisations. The information is protected either as a business and commercial interest, supplied in confidence, as a trade secret exemption, or as information of a commercial

information; or (b) any copy, reproduction or duplicate of such a thing; or (c) any part of such a copy, reproduction or duplicate.

[79] For example, *Freedom of Information Act* 1982 (Cth), s 54 Internal review; s 55 Applications to Administrative Appeals Tribunal; s 56 Application to Tribunal where decision delayed; and s 57 Complaints to Ombudsman.

[80] *Freedom of Information Act* 1982 (Cth) Schedule 2, s 7, Pt I, Exempt agencies.

value that may adversely affect a business or profession. The third party affected is consulted, and if the information is released and the affected party opposes the disclosure, an appeal using 'reverse FOI' may be pursued.[81]

5.3.4 Access rights to private and corporate records

Private records are considered personal property, and thus access to the non-owner is a privilege. Under common law, access to private records is usually only available via a subpoena or a pre-discovery order, unless there is a contractual obligation or a proprietary right of access to particular data or information. In other cases specific rights may be available under statute.

Case law generally indicates the difficulty in gaining access to a private record. For example, in *Breen v Williams* (1996) 186 CLR 71, the High Court of Australia maintained that the patient record remained the property of the doctor, and the patient had no right of access to their clinical records. This is an example of a proprietary right being used to prevent access to information about the data subject.

The right of access to information is as much an issue of social justice as a legal one, so that the denial of access is often seen as an issue of equity. In the networked environment where more and more information is being bought and sold, particularly government information outsourced to private hands, the notion of commercial ownership of information is winning the day.[82]

5.4 Privacy and legal and social relationships

Privacy, like intellectual property, is another example of balancing the needs among a number of participants: the record creator, the recipient of the communication, the record subject(s), the researcher, the preserver and other third parties including the recordkeeping professional with the public interest needs of law enforcement and other agencies. All recordkeeping participants have legal obligations to protect information about individuals

[81] Lane and Dixon, 'Government Decision Making: Freedom of Information and Judicial Review', pp. 106-118.

[82] See Chapter 6. For a detailed discussion on outsourcing government activities in the Australian context see Iacovino, Ethical-Legal Frameworks for Recordkeeping, pp. 369-393.

in records under statute and common law, which may be distinct from their moral duties. The statutory obligations are found in freedom of information, privacy and recordkeeping legislation, and common law duties of confidentiality, contractual and other special relationships, balanced with the correlative rights of access to information by the record subject or a third party. In addition to legislation, recordkeeping and other professionals adhere to principles of confidentiality in relation to records under their control through their professional codes and through the implementation of access policies.[83] The protection of privacy is a fundamental principle in recordkeeping practice.

Privacy in the recordkeeping context is concerned with personal data that is captured in a record, or that can be linked in such a way as to identify a person. The linkage issue is of particular concern in a network system. The record subject's informed consent to the collection, use and disclosure of his/her personal information is an essential element of privacy protection and must be obtained by all recordkeeping participants.[84] However, the business model of professional service reinforced by competition policy has in some instances moved the onus of professional responsibility from an individual onto the business, for example to disclose or not to disclose personal information.[85]

5.4.1 Definitions of privacy

Privacy is recognised in international conventions as a human and a legal right. The *International Covenant on Civil and Political Rights* 1966[86]

---

[83] For example, International Council on Archives, *The International Code of Ethics for Archivists*, 6 September 1996, Code 7.

[84] Consent depends on the capacity of the person to consent 'unambiguously', and therefore have moral agency. On consent by a patient in the medical context, see Bernadette McSherry, 'Ethical Issues in Health*Connect's* Shared Electronic Health Record System', *Journal of Law and Medicine*, vol. 12, no. 1, Aug. 2004, p. 63.

[85] For example, the *Information Privacy Act* 2000 (Vic) s 68 makes the employer not the individual employee responsible for breaches of privacy, and the *Privacy Act* 1988 (Cth) defines a recordkeeper as the agency.

[86] The Department of Foreign Affairs and Trade, *International Covenant on Civil and Political Rights*, Australian Treaty Series, 1980, no. 23 (Reprint), AGPS, Canberra, 1998. The covenant is an international instrument based on the 1948 directive of the United Nations, *Universal Declaration of Human Rights*, Article 12. See Australian Human Rights Centre, *Universal Declaration of Human Rights*, 1948 and Council of Europe, *European Convention on Human*

provides a definition of privacy which emphasises personal integrity and dignity. Two clauses in the covenant relevant to privacy are:

- no one shall be subjected to arbitrary and unlawful interference with his privacy, family, home or correspondence, nor to unlawful attacks on his honour and reputation; and
- everyone has the right to protection of the law against such interference or attacks.

The *International Covenant* provides a definition of privacy in terms of personal autonomy, integrity and dignity. In 1969 a distinguished jurist, Sir Zelman Cowen, later a Governor General of Australia, wrote 'a man without privacy is a man without dignity; the fear that Big Brother is watching and listening threatens the freedom of the individual no less than prison bars.' [87] Although he was concerned with listening devices he also feared the 'womb to tomb' dossier and the potential harm of inaccurate, out of date or incomplete information. Cowen expressed the need for personal space and anonymity that must be balanced with participation in society, and therefore the acceptance that absolute privacy could not exist.

Privacy must also be distinguished from confidentiality which is both an ethical principle and a legal duty not to disclose personal information received in confidence. However, the duty of confidentiality may be overridden by statutory duties to disclose or public interest disclosure in common law.[88] In the United Kingdom, case law has expanded the duty of confidentiality to information which has wrongfully fallen into the hands of a person who had no right to it.[89] In *R v Department of Health Ex Parte Source Informatics Ltd* it was found that even the disclosure of de-identified patient data without patients' consent breached confidentiality, unless a high public interest value in disclosure could be demonstrated.[90]

Rights, as amended by Protocol No. 11, Council of Europe Treaty Series, No. 5, Strasbourg, 1998.

[87] Zelman Cowen, 'The Private Man', *The Institute of Public Affairs*', vol. 24, no. 1, January-March, 1970, p. 26-27.

[88] Law Book Company, *Laws of Australia* (Lawbook on Line), LBC Information Services, North Ryde, NSW, Chapter 4, Privacy, para. 93 (accessed April 1998).

[89] Paterson, *Freedom of Information and Privacy in Australia*, p. 17.

[90] In a 1999 English Court of Appeal case, *Source Informatics Ltd* requested permission from the UK Department of Health to allow general practitioners and pharmacists to provide it with statistical information on their prescribing habits, extracted from their patient data, in order to sell the information to drug companies. The request was dismissed on the grounds that the disclosure would be a breach of confidentiality even if the data were de-identified, unless *Source*

On the other hand, privacy is a much wider concept than confidentiality. It is concerned primarily with an individual's ability to exercise control over his or her own identifiable personal data, based on the ethical principle of autonomy that requires a self-determining individual to be a free moral agent.[91] Rights in relation to privacy are therefore principally about controlling information others hold about an identifiable person and include:

- access to and correction/amendment of personal data, and
- how, why and by whom it is collected, handled, stored, transferred and re-used, whether it is held in a database, a recordkeeping system, and/or a network server.

The identity of parties to the transaction or information which makes it possible to infer the identity of the data subject would constitute personal data, subject to its ambit in privacy legislation.

The right to privacy in the legal relationship model includes the duty not to disclose, and thus diminishes the right to free speech. The balancing of the right of access to personal information by third parties with the obligation to protect it, like the protection of intellectual property and the right to access creative works, is at the heart of modern privacy law.

5.4.2 Recordkeeping principles: conflicts with privacy

Recordkeeping concerns regarding privacy centre on records that may need to be retained to ensure that the rights and obligations of those affected by the business transaction are protected, and that the related identity metadata are also retained. Long term corporate and collective

---

Informatics Ltd could demonstrate a high public interest value in the disclosure, for example for medical research. As the disclosure was not found to be in the public interest the application for judicial review was dismissed. If the English case is followed, a confidential relationship at least between a healthcare provider and patient continues to protect patient information from third party disclosure, where a patient has not consented to other uses, unless there is a demonstrable public interest in its disclosure. Whether or not the data is de-identified the potential harm to the patient arises from the breach of trust caused by the lack of consent for uses of personal information other than that for which it was intended. See *R v Department of Health Ex Parte Source Informatics Ltd* [1999] 4 All ER 185, in Medical Law Reporter, *Journal of Law and Medicine,* vol. 8, Aug. 2000, pp. 27-30.

[91] Moira Paterson, 'Health*Connect* and Privacy: A Policy Conundrum', *Journal of Law and Medicine*, vol. 12, no. 1, Aug. 2004, p. 81.

memory also depends on reliable and authentic evidence. In this context privacy law does not always accommodate recordkeeping principles of reliability and authenticity over time. It may not take account of the record's functional context and the effect of the lapse of time on de-sensitising personal information.[92] Instead it encourages the deidentification or the destruction of records containing personal information no longer required for their immediate use, the deletion of inaccurate information, and anonymous transactions.[93]

The deletion of inaccurate personal information can in fact lead to the absence of evidence of the incorrect data used in further action.[94] It is therefore preferable that the correction is made via a notation rather than by deleting the inaccurate data.[95] These issues have been of concern to archivists internationally, and in countries that form part of the European Union, in particular.[96] In Italy, specific legislative action to allow for the retention of personal data that is in the public interest, and the adherence to

---

[92] The archival notion of 'lapse of time', which varies for categories of records has been one of the major arguments supporting the eventual disclosure of personal information to third parties.

[93] The 'deletion principle' is found in the Australian Privacy Charter Council, *Australian Privacy Charter*, 1994. It appears in the *Privacy Act* 1988 (Cth) as amended, in NPP 4.2.

[94] Danielle Laberge, 'Information, Knowledge and Rights: The Preservation of Archives as a Political and Social Issue, *Archivaria*, vol. 25, Winter, 1987-88, pp. 44-50. This article provides a case study on the destruction of young offenders' judicial files to protect their privacy, which led to the lack of evidence of their mistreatment. Her conclusion is that the potential abuse of individuals requires the retention of personal data and related program details, at least for the life of a person, in order to redress both individual and collective wrongs.

[95] Of particular relevance in the light of record integrity is the retention of amended personal information, in Australia's *Freedom of Information Act* 1982 (Cth) s 50(3): 'To the extent that it is practicable to do so, the agency or Minister must, when making an amendment under paragraph (2)(a), ensure that the record of information is amended in a way that does not obliterate the text of the record as it existed prior to the amendment'.

[96] In Sweden, the *Personal Data Act* 1998 s 3 defines personal data as, 'all kinds of information that directly or indirectly may be referable to a natural person who is alive'. There is also a specific provision to allow personal data to be retained for longer than necessary for its original purposes. Section 9 states that: 'Personal data may be kept for historical, statistical or scientific purposes for a longer time than stated in the first paragraph (i)'. Para (i) states that 'personal data is not kept for a longer period than is necessary having regard to the purpose of the processing'.

ethical codes for both archivists and researchers using personal data appears a possible model to follow.[97]

5.4.3 The transaction model and privacy protection

One way of looking at the handling of personal data in Privacy Acts from within a recordkeeping perspective is a transactional rather than a collection model.[98] The transaction model is a recordkeeping approach which is particularly appropriate to legal and social relationships. In a data collection model all personal data passes from one person (natural or corporate) to another. It passes from a data provider to a data collector to a data controller to a recordkeeper; terms used in the OECD *Guidelines on Privacy* and in privacy legislation.

In a transaction model the transmission of data between two parties involves communication between them in the course of transacting 'business'. Each party would keep copies of its outgoing communications as well as the communications which it receives from the other party. Each party is both a data provider to the other and a data controller of information provided by the other, all of whom have responsibilities for protecting personal data.

Recordkeeping metadata such as an identification number and other personal identification details that may be kept separately in an electronic system from the informational content gathered on an individual, together may comprise identity that 'can reasonably be ascertained' about an individual and which constitute personal information as defined by most Privacy Acts.[99] Even in paper recordkeeping systems, personal data that

---

[97] Paola Carucci, 'Privacy and Historical Research in Italy', *Archivum,* vol. XLV, 2000, pp. 161-169. The requirement for the destruction of personal data under privacy law has been modified in Italy by decree 281/1999 which allows the preservation of personal data for historical, scientific and statistical research. Health and sensitive personal data are restricted for seventy years, and other sensitive data for forty years. For records that are less than thirty years old, application on an individual basis is available, with an ethical code for both the researcher and the archivist to abide by. Although decree 281/1999 has been repealed by 196/2003 (30 June 2003), the provisions dealing with historical, scientific and statistical research have remained substantially the same.

[98] I would like to acknowledge Chris Hurley for the useful distinction that he made between 'transaction' and 'collection' privacy models while giving guest lectures at Monash University in the Bachelor of Information Management, in 1996.

[99] Graham Greenleaf, 'Privacy Principles: Problems in Cyberspace - Likely Areas of Controversy and Interpretation', in Papers from *The New Australian Privacy*

would further identify an individual may be found in related control records, and not on the face of the record. It is the linking of identifying data at the system level that may infringe personal privacy. At the same time the metadata is part of the identity and integrity of the record. The transaction view of privacy highlights time-bound elements of the record essential to its authenticity. From a recordkeeping view, identifiable personal information within a business transaction, either in relation to parties to a transaction or record subjects, or other third parties who may also hold authentication information relevant to the record's reliability, are elements of identity essential to the reliability and authenticity of the record both at the time of creation and over time. Privacy Acts do not operate within a transaction model, but a collection model that makes the assessment of their impact on recordkeeping over time problematic.[100]

5.4.4 Statutory and legal remedies for the protection of personal privacy

Data protection regimes that aim to protect personal privacy are based on the OECD *Guidelines Governing the Protection of Privacy and Transborder Flows of Personal Data* which provides the internationally accepted definition of personal data as '... any information relating to an

Landscape, Faculty of Law, Continuing Legal Education, The University of New South Wales, 14 March 2001, pp. 9-11. In Australia 'personal information' is broadly defined in the *Privacy Act* 1983 (Cth) Part II, s 6 as 'information or an opinion (including information or an opinion forming part of a database), whether true or not, and whether recorded in a material form or not, about an individual whose identity is apparent, or can reasonably be ascertained, from the information or opinion.' Greenleaf interprets the definition to include other sources than those that are immediately apparent, for example a person's identification data (ID). The ID number and identifying details may be kept in a separate database from a record that only consists of the ID number and the relevant action data. In fact the person metadata (ID number and identifying details) should be inextricably linked to the record, even if for access purposes they are not linked. Greanleaf in fact suggests a definition based on 'any information which enables interactions with an individual on a personalised basis'.

[100] Livia Iacovino, 'Identity, Trust and Privacy, Some Recordkeeping Implications in the Context of Recent Australian Privacy Legislative Initiatives', in *Convergence, Joint National Conference, Conference Proceedings*, the Joint National Conference of the Australian Society of Archivists and the Records Management Association of Australia, 2-5 September 2001, Hobart, 2001, pp. 71-90.

identified or identifiable individual (data subject)'.[101] The European Union Directive 95/46/EC states that '"personal data" shall mean any information relating to an identified or identifiable natural person ("data subject"); an identifiable person is one who can be identified, directly or indirectly, in particular by reference to an identification number or to one or more factors specific to his physical, physiological, mental, economic, cultural or social identity.'[102]

Privacy regimes vary as a result of differences between juridical systems, government policy, and the timing of legal enactments in relation to privacy. In Australia statutory rights of access to, and protection of personal privacy in government and private sector records are found in FOI, privacy and records/archives legislation, thus requiring an understanding of the privacy provisions of all three statutory regimes in all Australian jurisdictions.[103] The general approach in Australian Privacy Acts is to create rights in those laws, but to implement them through FOI laws.[104] Privacy legislation in Australia does not follow a uniform model law.[105]

---

[101] OECD, *Guidelines Governing the Protection of Privacy and Transborder Flows of Personal Data,* OECD, 1980, Annex to the Recommendation of the OECD Council, 23 September 1980, Part 1 General, Definitions, b.

[102] The European Parliament and the Council of the European Union, *Directive 95/46/EC On the Protection of Individuals with Regard to the Processing of Personal Data and on the Free Movement of Such Data,* 24 October 1995, Chapter I, General Provisions, Article 2 Definitions, (a). Countries that are members of the European Union use similar definitions of personal data, but there are some significant differences. For example Italy extends its definition of personal data to legal persons, bodies or associations thereby protecting corporate privacy (Article 1 c).

[103] The intersection of Freedom of Information and Privacy Acts in Commonwealth legislation is found in the *Freedom of Information Act* 1982 (Cth) s 41 which protects privacy in the 'personal information' exemption. 'Personal information' cannot be disclosed if considered unreasonable and related to a third party. There is also an amendment right in ss 47A and 50(3) to have incomplete, incorrect, out of date and misleading information corrected. There are also privacy provisions in all Australian state FOI Acts under 'personal affairs' exemptions and some states have their own privacy acts. For a detailed analysis of the Australian privacy regimes, see Iacovino, 'Identity, Trust and Privacy, Some Recordkeeping Implications in the Context of Recent Australian Privacy Legislative Initiatives', and Paterson, *Freedom of Information and Privacy in Australia: Government and Information Access in the Modern State,* pp. 22-30.

[104] The Australian Law Reform Commission's review of the *Freedom of Information Act* 1982 (Cth) in 1995 concluded that the Act had been the main

In the European Union the emphasis has been on reconciling archival and privacy laws[106] as Freedom of Information laws have been of more recent origin except in Scandinavian countries. In the United Kingdom the enactment of Freedom of Information in 2000 followed closely on the Data Protection Act 1998.

The United States clearly distinguishes Freedom of Information from privacy legislation. The federal *Privacy Act* of 1974 (5 U.S.C. Sec. 552a) regulates the collection, maintenance, use and dissemination of personal information. It prohibits disclosure of individual information to a federal agency or person, except with written approval by the affected person. There are, however, several exceptions to this rule. Individuals may have access to their own records, and can request amendments to correct inaccuracies. Many individual states and industry sectors have their own

---

vehicle for access and amendment of personal information rather than the Privacy Act, and that the destruction of incorrect personal information was generally not implemented. The review also considered whether to remove the privacy provisions from FOI legislation and place them into the *Privacy Act* 1988 (Cth). Australian Law Reform Commission, *Open Government: a Review of the Federal Freedom of Information Act 1982,* Report 77, Australian Government Publishing Service, Canberra, 1995.

[105] Most Australian state privacy legislation, for example, *Information Privacy Act* 2000 (Vic) follows the Commonwealth model, with the exception of New South Wales's *Privacy and Personal Protection Information Act* (NSW) 1998. However health privacy legislation is inconsistent across Australian jurisdictions. See Moira Paterson and Livia Iacovino, 'Health Privacy: The Draft Australian National Health Privacy Code and the Shared Longitudinal Electronic Health Record', *Health Information Management Journal,* vol. 33, 2004, pp. 5-11. The impetus for extending privacy legislation to the private sector in both Australia and Canada arose from the 1998 implementation of EU *Directive 95/46/EC* restricting personal information from member countries to other countries unless adequate privacy safeguards were in place. Rather than enacting new legislation the Australian federal government extended its existing public sector legislation to the private sector by incorporating national privacy principles (NPPs) into the Principal Act, the *Privacy Act* 1988 (Cth).

[106] See Marina Giannetto, 'Principi Metodologici e Deontologie Professionali nel Codice Degli Archivisti e Degli Storici', in *La Storia e la Privacy, Dal Dibattito alla Publicazione del Codice Deontologico*, Proceedings of a Seminar in Rome 30 November 1999, Central State Archives and the Bianchi Bandelli Association, Ministry for Cultural Property and Affairs, General Management of the Archives, 2001, pp. 55-90; Decree 281/1999 of 30 July 1999, pp.92-125. See also footnote 97.

privacy laws.[107] In contrast to the European Union, Australia and Canada, the United States has not sought to regulate the information practices of private organisations through legislation.

Some common law jurisdictions have developed a tort of privacy. There is no common law tort of privacy in the Australian legal system, although recent case decisions are moving in this direction.[108] This contrasts with the United States and New Zealand which have recognised a broadly defined right of action in tort for invasion of privacy. Common law therefore plays an important part in protecting privacy rights in these two jurisdictions.

5.4.5 Privacy persistence: records/archival legislation

Privacy regimes focus on consent to the collection, use and disclosure of personal information in its immediate context,[109] while archival regimes focus on preservation of authentic records for general public disclosure, which may include personal information once it has lost its sensitivity. Within a records continuum reading, privacy is addressed not only in terms of how personal information is captured, used and disclosed, but also when it is destroyed or preserved and made accessible, both during the life and after the death of an identifiable person. Highly personal records, for example tax, social security and medical records, rarely survive beyond their statutory limits of retention, and thus archival legislation also protects privacy through authorised destruction. For these reasons restricting access to current information of a personal nature has a different dimension to retention and access to records that have lost their personal sensitivity.

Unlike some EU countries (the United Kingdom and Sweden) and the Canadian federal privacy law where privacy is limited to living persons, in Australia there has not been a clear determination on when privacy ceases. For example, does it persist after death and for how long?[110] In Australia,

---

[107] Robert Gellman, 'Does Privacy Law Work?', in *Technology and Privacy: the New Landscape,* eds Philip Agre and Marc Rotenberg, MIT Press, Massachusetts, 1998, pp. 193-218.

[108] Paterson, *Freedom of Information and Privacy in Australia: Government and Information Access in the Modern State,* pp. 17-19. Protection under the common law for privacy in Australia is available in relation to trespass, nuisance, defamation, and breach of confidentiality.

[109] The principle that personal information should only be used or disclosed for its primary or original purpose addresses the objective of Articles 6(1)(b) and 7 of the European Directive *Directive 95/46/EC*.

[110] However, in some state privacy laws, limits of time are placed on the protection of privacy, for example in the *Privacy and Personal Protection Information*

archival/records legislation for the public sector has adequately protected personal information for the lifetime of the person by restricting access to information that has continuing sensitivity beyond thirty years.[111] In the private sector there is no exemption for records of a profit-making private archive or a business entity wishing to provide access to older records unless they are *deposited* in a designated public institution.[112] Presumably the assumption behind this exclusion is that these records will have been de-identified or destroyed well before they are thirty years old and those of long term value will have been transferred to a public institution.

Act 1998 (NSW) s 4.3 (a) 'personal information' does not include 'information about an individual who has been dead for more than 30 years.' In the case of personal health information in a state archive, the *State Records Act* 2000 (WA) s 49(2) sets a hundred year limit to protecting personal medical information from disclosure.

[111] In the *Privacy Act* 1988 (Cth) s 6(f), Commonwealth records as defined by subsection 3(1) of the *Archives Act* 1983 (Cth) that are in the open access period for the purposes of that Act are exempt and do not have to be in archival custody. See definition of a record in the open access period in the *Archives Act* 1983 (Cth) s 3(7) 'a record is in the open access period if a period of 30 years has elapsed since the end of the year ending 31 December in which the record came into existence'. Privacy continues to be protected through the *Archives Act* 1983 (Cth) under s 33(1)(g): 'Information or matter the disclosure of which under this Act would involve the unreasonable disclosure of information relating to the personal affairs of any person (including a deceased person).'

[112] *Privacy Act* 1988 (Cth) s 6(1) Interpretation "'record'...does not include: ...(e) anything kept in a library, art gallery or museum for the purposes of reference, study or exhibition or (f) Commonwealth records as defined by subsection 3(1) of the Archives Act 1983 that are in the open access period for the purposes of that Act; or (fa) records (as defined in the Archives Act 1983) in the custody of the Archives (as defined in that Act) in relation to which the Archives has entered into arrangements with a person other than a Commonwealth institution (as defined in that Act) ...' See also *Information Privacy Act* 2000 (Vic), s 11 (1)(b)-(d), *Health Records Act* 2001 (Vic) s 15 and the *Health Records and Information Privacy Act* 2002 (NSW) s 4(3) c 'personal information' exemptions for private records that are more than thirty years old, if they are deposited in a public institution as defined by their respective legislation. In the case of *Information Privacy Act* 2000 (Vic) and *Health Records Act* 2001 (Vic) private records held by any 'not-for-profit' organisation are exempted regardless of age.

5.4.6 Other mechanisms of control over privacy

In addition to statute and common law there are codes and guidelines that complement privacy legislative regimes, for example direct marketing codes of practice, and insurance and internet industry information privacy principles.[113] Data sharing protocols, which specify responsibilities of the sharing partners, also complement legal regimes for privacy.[114]

The role of trusted third parties in protecting privacy over time should not be overlooked. In the public sector this has been in part the role of government archival authorities. In the private sector a balance between destruction and protection of privacy may hinge on protecting individual rights in case of litigation. Technology can also be used to protect personal information without destroying it. For example, 'redactibility' which allows a version of the record that has had the personal data removed for research use still ensures the integrity of the original record.[115] A recordkeeping system which is designed to be secure, time bound and linked to retention and access procedures, should provide adequate privacy protection for the data subject, while ensuring that any rights of the data subject are protected without the need to delete the personal information once it has served its purpose.[116]

If records are handled by professionals (business and recordkeeping) who understand both their legal and ethical duties, and as confidential relationships, privacy is much more likely to be protected than by

---

[113] Nigel Waters, *'A Comparative Analysis of Australian Privacy* Laws *with Special Reference to the Concept of "Adequacy" for the Purposes of the European* Union *Data Protection Directive', in Papers* presented *to* The New Australian Privacy Landscape, *Faculty of* Law, *Continuing* Legal *Education, The* University *of* New *South* Wales, 14 *March* 2001 (*no pagination*).

[114] *United Kingdom, Department for Constitutional Affairs,* Public Sector Data Sharing: Guidance on the Law, N*ovember* 2003. *A data sharing* protocol *is a formal agreement between organisations that are sharing* personal *data. It explains why data is being shared and sets out the* principles *and commitments organisations will adopt when they collect, store and disclose* personal *information about members of the* public.

[115] *David* Bearman, Electronic Evidence: Strategies for Managing Records in Contemporary Organizations, *Archives and Museum Informatics, Pittsburgh, 1994, '*Appendix: *Functional Requirements for Recordkeeping Systems, Requirement* 13, *Redactable*', p. 304.

[116] *The Commonwealth of Australia, Attorney-General's Department,* Privacy Protection in the Private Sector, *Discussion Paper, Sept. 1996 Office of Information and Publishing, Attorney-General's Department,* Barton, *ACT, recommended adding the deletion* principle *to the Information Privacy Principles.*

legislation alone.[117] However it will still depend on the ethical behaviour of those who control the identifiable data. Recordkeeping controls on unauthorised disclosure of private details of identifiable persons must be secured if the recordkeeping profession is to argue for the continued retention of personal information beyond its immediate use. Trusted third parties, from archival authorities to professional and industry regulators, as well as the users, contribute to the web of trust that protects personal information.

Technology, for example record redaction, and mediated trust through business, recordkeeping professionals and other trusted third parties, can support privacy based on recordkeeping principles that keep, rather than de-identify, the metadata relating to the author, recipient and/or record-subjects so that the transactions are reliable and authentic. The right of access to personal information needs statutory backing; however the accuracy of the information depends on reliable record creators, and keeping the metadata that identifies their professional competencies and their delegations. In the online environment the identity of the record creators also provides trust and legal validity to the content of the business transaction.

5.5 Legal relationships and evidence

Evidence defined in relation to its legal meaning includes more than documentary evidence. 'Evidence consists of the testimony, hearsay, documents, things and facts which a court will accept as evidence of the facts in issue in a given case'.[118] Records are, however, in their own right, evidence of business and social activity which are governed by a range of accountability mechanisms, including government authorities, legislation, policy, standards and best practice for recordkeeping.[119] However their legal value is of considerable importance.

> *The evidence of a fact is that which tends to prove it - something which may satisfy an enquirer that the fact exists. Courts of law usually have to find that certain facts exist before pronouncing on the rights, duties and liabilities of the*

---

[117] *Professional ethics and personal researcher undertakings based on a human dignity test are proposed in Eric Ketelaar, 'The Right to Know, the Right to Forget? Personal Information in Public Archives'*, Archives and Manuscripts, *vol. 23, no. 1, May 1995, pp. 8-17. See also Italy footnote 97 above.*

[118] J.D. *Heydon,* Cross on Evidence, *5th edn,* Butterworths, *Sydney, 1996, p. 13.*

[119] *See Chapter* 1.

parties, and the evidence they receive in furtherance of this task is described as 'admissible evidence'.[120]

Within the broader values of recordkeeping to society, legal evidence is only one use of a record. Evidence is essential to enforcing rights and obligations, and to the notion of records as a right-duty thing that evidences a legal and social relationship.

In voluntary relationships evidence that a party assumed the obligation expressly or by implication is needed. Even in involuntary relationships an obligation requires proof of its fulfilment or its failure, for example evidence of action to show one acted with duty of care. This is why intentional action is an attribute of a record. Evidence law, as procedural law, is the overriding legal consideration in demonstrating in court that a right or obligation exists, or what Fisher refers to as the 'remedial' obligation when the substantive obligation, has not been performed.

Even though there is a presumption in Australian and Canadian evidence law that established business practices produce reliable documents, there is no guarantee in advance that they will be admitted or not challenged.[121] Records made subsequent to a duty to an employer are likely to be reliable as they arise from a professional duty, which is important in trustworthy professional relationships.[122] In addition, the ethical behaviour of recordkeeping participants contributes to the accuracy of the record and is therefore more likely to be admissible in legal proceedings.

5.5.1 Recordkeeping obligations arising from the legal process in common law systems

Documents that are relevant to a case may be admitted into court by parties to a case tendering them, by the issue of a subpoena to the adverse party or to a third party to produce documents, the use of interrogatories, search warrants, and discovery.[123] An order for discovery may also be made

---

[120] Heydon, *Cross on Evidence,* p. 1.

[121] See Chapter 2, 'Evidence law and trustworthy records'.

[122] The judgment in the Court of Appeal, *Albrighton v Royal Prince Alfred Hospital* [1980] 2 NSWLR 542.

[123] Discovery in common law originates in equity; it is now ruled by Rules of Court. Through discovery parties to proceedings are able to obtain from each other a written list of documents which may be relevant to the proceedings and which are or have been in the possession, custody or control of the party making discovery. Philip Sutherland, 'Documentary Evidence', in *The Principles of Evidence, 94/43, Papers Presented for the Continuing Legal*

against a person or body who is not a party to the proceedings.[124] It should be noted that one might be in contempt of court if a document is destroyed before a subpoena is issued if it is clearly relevant to proceedings that have commenced.[125]

The legal concepts of access, privacy, ownership and evidence are generic to all relationships. However these concepts can also be used to analyse the rights and obligations of recordkeeping participants - professional and business. Property law can apply to records as right-duty things, which evidence the legal relationship, rather than as mere physical objects. The record as evidence of the intent to possess or of a property right including intellectual authorship, or of a duty, depends on elements of identity. Access and intellectual rights and obligations provide examples of the different needs of recordkeeping participants. Privacy protection has to be balanced with the need to retain identity information over time to establish rights and obligations. Using the rights and obligations approach attributes the responsibility for the creation, documentation and preservation of evidence to a range of parties within a web of relationships, which include the author and recipient, data subjects and third parties, that are equally applicable to the online environment. Other substantive law will only apply to specific kinds of relationships, and these are referenced in the chapters that follow.

Education Department of the College of Law, *9 July 1994, Sydney,* CLE Department of the College of Law, Sydney, 1994, pp. 1-55.

[124] National Archives of Australia in cooperation with the Attorney-General's Department, the Office of Government Information Technology and the Tasmanian Department of Premier and Cabinet, Information Strategy Unit, *Records in Evidence, The Impact of the Evidence Act on Commonwealth Recordkeeping,* Commonwealth of Australia, 1998, 'Compliance with subpoenas and orders for discovery', p. 7.

[125] Chris Hurley, 'Recordkeeping, Document Destruction and the Law (Heiner, Enron and McCabe)', *Archives and Manuscripts*, vol. 30, no. 2, Nov. 2002, pp. 6-25; Camille Cameron, 'The Duty to Preserve Documents Before Litigation Commences', *Archives and Manuscripts*, vol. 32 no. 2 Nov. 2004, pp. 70-89. Also US-InterPARES Project, *Findings on the Preservation of Authentic Electronic Records,* Final Report to the National Historical Publications and Records Commission, 2002, pp. 87-88.

6 LEGAL AND SOCIAL RELATIONSHIPS AS REGULATORY MECHANISMS

Legal and social relationships operate within boundaries established by professions, businesses and communities, a concept found in both the warrant-based and juridical models for recordkeeping regulation. The legal and social relationship model therefore builds on the 'warrant' and 'juridical' regulatory models as outlined in Chapter 1. The model can best be illustrated by examples of specific relationships that identify the legal and ethical rights and obligations of the recordkeeping participants over time by adopting the matrix developed in Chapter 4. Reciprocal rights and obligations are modified by the constraints of policy, professional and industry controls, and technological changes, in particular online business transactions. Ultimately legal and social relationships depend on the trustworthiness and ethical behaviour of individual participants.

6.1 Categories of legal relationships and their economic, technological and political context

Both the civil and common law systems recognise a range of legal relationships the nature of which determines the rights and obligations of the parties concerned. Business transactions that form the basis of a dynamic relationship between the parties involved in a business process are essential to witnessing legal and social relationships.

Legal relationships may also be classed as socio-legal relationships in so far as they have social and moral consequences, as well as legal ones. They include personal relationships arising out of birth, marital status or family, for example the parent-child relationship; public relationships in which a citizen interacts with the government, for example the taxpayer-taxation officer (representing the crown) relationship; commercial relationships involving organisations providing a service to a customer, for example the buyer-seller relationship; and professional relationships which provide a professional service, the oldest legally recognised professional relationship being that of the doctor-patient. The legal system recognises individuals (human beings) and organisations as legal persons in order to recognise them as holders of rights and obligations, and to regulate them, for example as an incorporated company (which could include a succession of human incumbents), unborn persons or an agency. It also gives a legal person a legal 'personality' to identify the sum total of all their rights and duties.[1]

Legal relationships imply a duty to another individual or legal entity which in turn creates a right in the other party (for example, the debtor-creditor relationship; the bank provides a person credit, it has a right to be paid back; the debtor has a duty to pay the money back). In a narrow legal sense, records supporting the bank's claim would include the documents signed by the customer for the loan; the accounting records indicating the amounts paid back and when. The authority of these persons to act is assigned by the legal system. Many legal relationships are founded on social trust and confidentiality, also recognised in law, for example the doctor-patient relationship. In fact it is when trust breaks down that the parties resort to legal remedies. Personal relationships also include legal obligations, whether as a spouse, common law partner, parent or child.

All commercial and professional relationships can be centred on obligations as a composite right-duty 'thing' as relationship as evidenced in records. These include the employer-employee, and the manufacturer-distributor to which general principles of equity and common law are applied. In the common law some categories are so long standing that enforceable rights and obligations are immediately recognisable, such as the doctor-patient, and solicitor-client relationships.

In the online environment new categories of relationships are emerging, for example the Internet service provider and the user (private or business). The legal duties of legally recognised relationships are also constantly evolving. The recognition of new duties is also related to standards of morality, interpreted judicially, for example consumer law in the buyer-seller context. Within the common law system it will be the courts that will examine both general principles and specific commercial and professional rights and obligations, and remedies for their breach.[2]

---

[1] Albert Kocourek, *Jural Relations*, 2nd edn, The Bobbs-Merrill Company, Indianapolis, 1928, Chapter XVII Personateness.

[2] R.E. Cooper, 'Foreword', in *The Law of Commercial and Professional Relationships,* ed. Simon Fisher, F.T. Law & Tax, South Melbourne, 1996, pp. v-vi.

6.1.1 The source of obligations in common law: voluntary and involuntary obligations

Voluntary and involuntary obligations provide the framework for the application of the law of obligations to the common law.[3] Common law obligations include contract, tort, equity, restitution and statutory imposition of obligation in public or private law. Voluntary obligations are the obligations which persons readily assume, the classic example is the entry of two people into a contract. Each of the contracting parties will promise to do something for the benefit of the other and each must consent to enter into that contract. Fiduciary relationships, for example trusts[4] or those of bailment,[5] are also voluntary obligations. By contrast, involuntary obligations require people to act in certain ways or to refrain from acting in certain ways, and so impose duties on legal persons irrespective of their consent or assent.[6] For example, the involuntary obligation on a corporation, in trade or commerce, to not engage in conduct that is misleading and deceptive or which is likely to mislead or deceive.[7] The law of torts and equity also give rise to involuntary obligations. Torts impose liability on an obligor in a tort context that is 'reasonable' and 'sound in principle'. The law of torts compensates an injured party for an injury or loss. A legal obligation in the tortfeasor-obligor relationship arises out of an act or omission between the obligor and the obligee, that is, on something one does *not* do.

Although the common law does not require volition-intention for all actions, and even in contract there may be exceptions to the requirement of intention, evidence of ethical intention is needed in order to assess the ethical responsibilities of recordkeeping participants as moral actors. Therefore both voluntary and involuntary obligations require evidence of intention, for ethical if not legal assessment. The nature of consent between parties, the meaning of title and ownership, of performance and

---

3 The relevance of voluntary and involuntary obligations for diplomatics has been analysed in Chapter 3.

4 Simon Fisher, 'General Principles of Obligations', in *The Law of Commercial and Professional Relationships,* ed. Simon Fisher, F.T. Law & Tax, South Melbourne, 1996, pp. 33-36. Trusts consist either of those which arise expressly as a result of the trustees' intention, or those that are constructed by law.

5 See bailment in Chapter 5.

6 Simon Fisher, 'The Archival Enterprise, Public Archival Institutions and the Impact of Private Law', *Archives and Manuscripts,* vol. 26, no. 2, Nov. 1998, p. 337, and 'General Principles of Obligations', pp. 31-32.

7 For example in Australia, the *Trade Practices Act* (Cth), s 52(1).

non-performance, are supported by records. In addition voluntary obligations, in particular contracting of all kinds, are being increasingly adopted for business online, in particular in relation to intellectual property and other services.[8]

6.2 The legal and ethical nature of professional, commercial and public relationships

The common law has found legal categories for a number of relationships over time. These include contractual, fiduciary, and proprietorial relationships.[9] They protect legal interests such as property or personal rights. Some of these relationships are voluntary; others are involuntary.

Legal relationships as legal concepts deal with 'creatibility', that is, the facts that bring legal relations into existence; 'alterability' which involves the changes when a claim is no longer an enforceable right; and 'destructibility', when legal persons cease to exist so do legal relations. In a business transaction a legal relationship whether personal, public, commercial or professional also creates, modifies or extinguishes rights and duties. The relationship gives rise to obligations, rights, powers, claims, duties, and liabilities. Added to the narrow legal view are the ethical dimension and the community of interest context which includes professional practice controls and other informal sanctions. Examples of these relationships and their regulatory context serve to illustrate how communities of common interest are governed by their own ethical practices and laws (see Fig. 6 Legal and Social Relationship Model: Community of Interest-Enterprise Model). Thus the recordkeeping context must capture the interaction between the 'community of common interest' and its external environment, which includes the economic and social factors within which events and acts trigger recordkeeping transactions, arising from business activities.

[8] See Copyright Law Review Committee, *Copyright and Contract Law*, Issues Paper on the Relationship Between Copyright and Contract Law, 15 June 2001.

[9] Most legal relationships are a hybrid of contractual, fiduciary, and proprietorial elements. They may also have a tort obligation. Other legal elements that are of relevance to all kinds of relationships include property as obligation, personal rights which include privacy and defamation, and the duty of confidentiality.

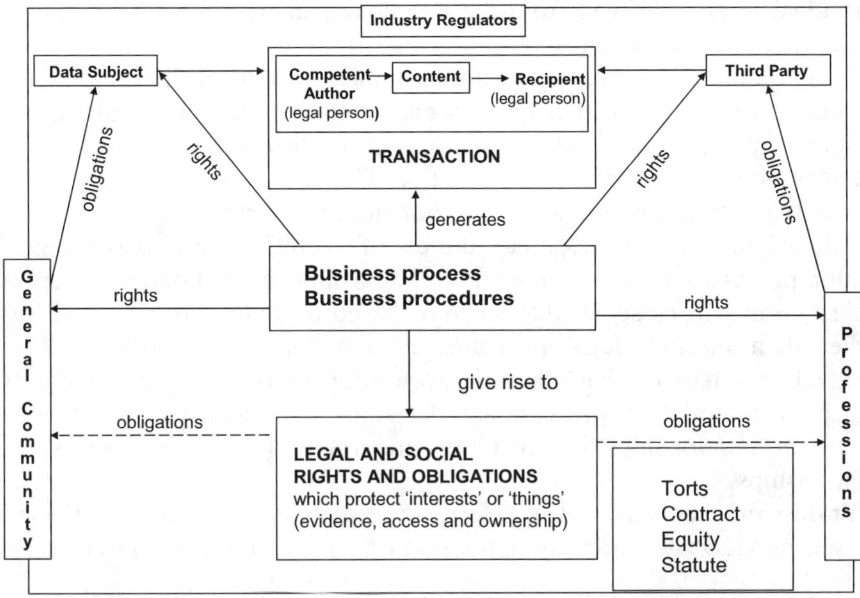

Fig. 6 Legal and Social Relationship Model: Community of Interest-Enterprise Model

6.2.1 Professional relationships

In the 'warrant-based' regulatory model for recordkeeping, professional practices were the most important mandate for creating and keeping records.[10] A community of interest such as a professional one that has developed a set of professional ethical standards and is prepared to critically revise them, provides the individual professional with ethical guidance needed for accountable professional practice, which in turn contributes to trustworthy records as evidence of a right-duty thing as relationship.

The nature of professional relationships is of particular importance, as society has become highly professionalised, that is, one in which the professional ideal of expertise and selection by merit has become the norm. The professional ideal has been justified on the basis of the utilitarian service ideal of the greatest happiness of the greatest number of persons.

[10] See Wendy Duff's research summarised in Chapter 1.

The ideal is also derived from the deontological tradition which equates vocational duty to 'goodness'.[11]

Professional ethics has its roots in a number of ethical theories.[12] These include utilitarianism which focuses on the social good or social harm of actions of professionals, while agent-based or virtue ethics offers a strong set of principles for professional practice. The Aristotelian concept of duty associated with a role or a specific competence in virtue ethics is pertinent to identifying the professional duties of recordkeeping participants.[13] Within professional and commercial relationships, ethical duties in various 'roles' form part of social relationships based on mutual respect and trust rather than through legal pressures of sanctions.[14] Logstrup's 'ethical demand' emphasises that ethics is a question of personal responsibility, which is essential to professional decisions. He identifies power over others in relationships of trust, an important element in professional relationships.[15]

Professional ethics is also a form of discourse ethics as it reflects a consensus view of a profession at a point in time. Cultural relativism may

---

[11] Different ethical stances are also reflected in professional codes. Kantian codes are described in, Nigel Harris, 'Professional Codes and Kantian Duties', in *Ethics and the Professions,* ed. Ruth F. Chadwick, Avebury, Aldershot, Brookfield, USA, 1994, pp. 104-124, and a utilitarian view by Heta and Matti Häyry in, 'The Nature and Role of Professional Codes in Modern Society', in, *Ethics and the Professions,* ed. Ruth F. Chadwick, Avebury, Aldershot, Brookfield, USA, 1994, pp. 136-144.

[12] In Europe professional ethics has a history from Greco-Roman times, through to the Catholic Church's control over professions to its secularisation through education and the craft guilds. Ian Siggens, 'Professional Codes: Some Historical Antecedents', in *Codes of Ethics and the Professions,* eds Margaret Coady and Sidney Bloch, Melbourne University Press, Carlton South, 1996, pp. 55-71.

[13] Alasdair MacIntyre, *A Short History of Ethics: A History of Moral Philosophy from the Homeric Age to the Twentieth Century,* 2nd edn, University of Notre Dame Press, Notre Dame, Indiana, 1998, pp. 93-94. The notion of professional duty evolved from doing one's vocational duty. Professional and personal duty was a unified concept, later separated into distinct personal and professional domains. Duty is an apt term in professional ethics as one is identifying a person's function; for example, a 'good' doctor is performing his duties as a doctor.

[14] Simon Longstaff, 'The Role of Ethics in Commercial and Professional Relationships', in *The Law of Commercial and Professional Relationships,* ed. Simon Fisher, F.T. Law & Tax, South Melbourne, 1996, pp. 89-116.

[15] Knud Ejler Logstrup, *The Ethical Demand*, University of Notre Dame Press, Notre Dame and London, 1997.

affect the ability of the profession to reach a consensus. Within one profession there may be divergent views of professional practice because of religious, cultural or national differences. Universalising one professional ethic within a profession can only be achieved by ongoing dialogue. One has to accept that the more culturally diverse professional members are, the more difficult it is for them to share standards.[16] This is particularly relevant in the online environment where professionals and their clients will be from all parts of the globe and have divergent political, legal and ethical views.

Characteristics of a professional

The characteristics of a professional[17] have generally included exclusivity, highly developed skills and specialised knowledge of a specific domain, several years of formal education and training in a related domain, service to society or a public benefit, governance by a code of ethics or conduct laid down by the profession, a professional association, and a communications network. The importance of the 'collective' aspect of a profession has added to its identity.[18]

A professional maintains that his/her specialist knowledge and education gives him/her an understanding of their field that is not shared outside the profession. Apart from the expertise, service orientation, and altruistic motivation of public duty, ethical standards are expected to be higher than for the general community. Today the term 'professional' is applied to many occupations, but in fact it can be argued that the claim to professional status via special expertise must include ethical obligations to differentiate it from an occupation. It is a matter of degree, but a professional at least aspires to ethical conduct. Professionalism also involves the acceptance of a number of legal responsibilities, including duty of care (see also 6.2.2 below, 'Professional liability').

---

[16] Jennifer Jackson, 'Common Codes: Divergent Practices', in *Ethics and the Professions,* ed. Ruth F. Chadwick, Avebury, Aldershot, Brookfield, USA, 1994, p. 122. Universalism or universality refers to ethical behaviour that transcends time and place.

[17] The word 'profession' in its Latin form meant a public declaration or vow. It encapsulates the notion of a vow to be 'faithful for something' (special expertise) 'to someone' (client) for his or her benefit and not for one's own. Siggens, 'Professional Codes: Some Historical Antecedents', p. 62; pp. 55-71.

[18] Harold Perkin, *The Rise of Professional Society: England Since 1880,* London, New York, Routledge, 1989, p. 85.

A distinguishing characteristic of a professional is that she/he is meant to act differently from a business person in dealing with clients.[19] The duty of service to the client can run to fellow professionals, to others who stand in some relationship to the client such as family members, or business associates, or even to bystanders, and on occasion to the community as a whole (the public interest component). Each professional relationship has its own ethical and regulatory context, but stands in relation to the others. Conflicts of interest often arise, for example a lawyer who owns shares in the company he/she is representing in a court case, or when the interests of a particular client clash with the broader interest of the public, or some part of it. Most importantly the commitment not only to the client but also to public service is part of the tradition of all professions.[20] The focus on the nature of each relationship brings us back full circle to ethical theories and ethical duties in various 'roles' (professional, personal, citizen, customer).

Trust and professional relationships

Concepts of trust essential to legal and social relationships are central to the nature of professionalism. An element of trust is essential to a profession if it does not want to be seen merely as a monopoly. The duty of confidentiality recognised in common law and equity, is found in most professional deontological codes, and has deep roots in Western legal systems. It is recognised particularly in the health and legal professions, as a duty that must be upheld by the professional so that the patient or client will provide truthful information upon which the professional can serve the best interests of the client. It thus contributes to the reliability of the content in the record.[21]

Professional relationships are client-centred. The basis of a professional relationship is the trust expected by the client arising from the autonomy granted the professional and the requirement of professional competence.[22] The professional offers a service which has to be taken on trust expecting the client to accept his/her valuation of the service, rather than the market

[19] McDowell Banks, *Ethical Conduct and the Professional's Dilemma: Choosing Between Service and Success,* Quorum Books, New York, 1991, pp. 16-17.

[20] Ibid., pp. 17-18. Perkin, in *The Rise of Professional Society: England since 1880,* p. 6, also recognises notions of service, trust and commitment beyond the profession as part of the professional ideal.

[21] See Chapter 8, 'The legal and social relationship model and the Internet: the doctor-patient relationship online'.

[22] Banks, *Ethical Conduct and the Professional's Dilemma,* Chapter 3.

place.[23] Both the professional's right to compensation and authorisation to manage a client's affairs or undertake a service arises from the notion of contract. Thus there is a consensual and contractual element to all professional relationships.[24]

Regulatory mechanisms and professional ethical behaviour

Traditionally professions have used a number of techniques to uphold their professional status, such as limiting membership, requiring continued education, licensing and enforcing codes of conduct. Licensing requires that members of a profession can only practise when they are certified by a body of fellow professionals. The personal moral propriety of actions is often taken into account in relation to fitness to practice as professionals, in particular in health care professions. These mechanisms need to be part of the elements of trust that are linked to a professional's identity to ensure reliable records.

There is a substantial difference between professions such as information professions, and highly controlled professions such as medicine and law where a loss of membership (being 'struck off') may also imply a loss of the right to practice. Regulation and sanctions are highest in professions which can take away the livelihood of its member for unprofessional conduct. For example, legal practitioners have to abide by acts or regulations of the jurisdiction in which they are registered; they may also be required to follow written rules of conduct that impose penalties for non-conformity.[25] Many illegal activities, for example fraud, corruption, or abuse of people's rights, are also professionally unethical, thus acting ethically contributes to overall legal compliance. Unprofessional behaviour is unethical behaviour, and may also be illegal behaviour.

Ethics as either a set of rules, moral codes or norms imposed by a community or a system of personal choice of conduct is particularly relevant to how professional behaviour is regulated. In reference to medical professionals, Ian Freckelton, a legal-medical expert, argues that

---

[23] Perkin, *The Rise of Professional Society: England since 1880,* p. 117. Perkin defines professional service as 'human capital'. 'Human capital' is an investment in personal skill, a rent for a scarce resource. To Perkin's 'human capital' should be added Fukuyama's 'social capital', the value from human networks that have made professionals successful (see Chapter 2).

[24] Banks, *Ethical Conduct and the Professional's Dilemma*, Chapter 8 and p. 111.

[25] In Australia, legal practitioners abide by Legal Practice Acts of the states in which they are registered, but are also required to follow Rules of Conduct (for example the Victorian Barristers' Rules of Conduct.)

their education equips them with a capability for rational decisions, and knowingly misbehaving professionally should be strongly admonished for that reason. Most established professions have well recognised patterns of behaviour, and divergences are easily noticed.[26] A community of common interest, such as a professional grouping, can make unethical behaviour unattractive to its members, in many different ways. The punitive approach to enforcing moral behaviour is often set through sanctions related to professional codes. Freckelton has argued that for a profession to maintain its bone fides it must impose penalties for non-compliance with a provision in a code.[27] These penalties do not imply civil or criminal liability, but rather the imposition of disciplinary measures such as restriction on practice. A strictly 'legal' approach to ethical behaviour has limitations, as a professional may follow the letter but not the spirit of an ethical code.

As Banks states:

> When standards carry legal sanctions, the professional has difficulty in predicting the exact content that these terms will be given by the administrative agencies or courts charged with their enforcement. The professional who wants to be sure to comply will then be led to very cautious practice that is unquestionably within the boundaries of the guidelines. The undesirable consequence of either rule-specific norms or flexible guidelines if they carry serious legal sanctions is more routinized performance and less innovative or risky practice.[28]

Malpractice has led to defensive actions that limit the competent professional. The real risk of relying on codes to make professionals ethical is that they may absolve themselves from responsibility for determining their own duty. More importantly, codes should be used to focus on professional duties and virtues, and as a collective consensus of professional values. The principles enunciated in ethical theories can be married to professional ethics. These include cultivating virtues of integrity and honesty, balancing the rights of and the duties to the client, to society and to fellow professionals, as well as consideration of the 'other person' as a fellow human being.

---

[26] Ian Freckelton, 'The Criminalisation "Solution" to Medical Misconduct', in *Health Care Crime and Regulatory Control,* ed. R.G. Smith, Hawkins Press, Sydney, 1998, pp. 26-47.

[27] Ian Freckelton, 'Enforcement of Ethics', in *Codes of Ethics and the Professions,* ed. Margaret Coady and Sidney Bloch, Melbourne University Press, Carlton South, 1996, pp. 130-165.

[28] Banks, *Ethical Conduct and the Professional's Dilemma,* p. 138.

The practice skills model

The practice skills model identifies major social responsibilities common to all professionals as well as duties of the profession to which one belongs.[29] As identified in Chapter 4, recordkeeping participants include business participants who have generic and specific ethical responsibilities depending on the nature of the social and legal relationship in which they participate.[30] Professional culture is largely determined by standards of acceptable behaviour within specific environments. In addition, the concept of reasonable behaviour and duty of care which form part of the law of negligence in the common law system are re-enforced through professional ethics and professional practice, for example confidentiality, which forms part of every transaction between a patient and a doctor, is an important part of medical ethics.

Professional responsibility, as well as legal liability, will depend on position and competencies. A doctor will require evidence of the procedures followed, advice given to the patient, and protection of confidential information to indicate professional competence. A recordkeeping professional has ethical and legal obligations in relation to the accurate capture and storage of the data in the record, its 'stewardship' as property, its legal destruction, its preservation as an authentic record over time; the protection of personal data from inappropriate disclosure; and providing access to material on equal terms. The ethical dimension of legal and social relationships depends on records as evidence of ethical (or unethical) behaviour, including what is destroyed to cover up unethical or illegal behaviour.[31]

6.2.2 Professional liability

The trustworthiness of records depends in part on the high ethical standards of all players involved in the recordkeeping process. The

[29] Livia Iacovino, 'Ethical Principles and Information Professionals: Theory, Practice and Education', *Australian Academic & Research Libraries*, vol. 33, no. 2, June 2002, pp. 57-74.

[30] Richard O. Mason, Florence M. Mason and Mary J. Culnam, *Ethics of Information Management,* Sage Publications, Thousand Oaks, California, 1995. The doctor-patient example in this chapter illustrates specific and general professional responsibilities.

[31] The 'Heiner affair' in Australia is an example of 'legal' but unethical destruction of records related to an aborted inquiry into the John Oxley Centre, Wacol, Queensland which included evidence of child abuse. See Chris Hurley, 'The Shredding of the "Heiner" Documents: An Appreciation', RIMOS, 1997.

reliability of the professionals' records will depend in part on how accurately they record and keep their transactions, and the procedural controls they adopt.[32] Professionalism, as noted above, also involves an acceptance of a number of legal responsibilities, including 'duty of care'. Ethical behaviour can minimise the possibility of negligent conduct and assist legal compliance.

The professional as a service provider

The provision of a service to a client has been defined as one characteristic of a professional. Is there a difference between a professional service provider and any other service provider? Legally, the concept of a profession is an 'open', not a closed category. Simon Fisher, from a legal perspective, does not find much difference between a professional and a service provider, given the diminished role of professional self-regulation. Although it is disputable that a professional is only a service provider, a 'service provider' has standards of responsibility through duty of care, as part of liability in contract and in the tort of negligence[33] where services, including advice, are provided either for reward or gratuitously. Contracts for service contain an implied promise to exercise 'reasonable care' and 'skill in performance' of relevant services, which are defined in case law.[34] Fisher analyses the liability perspective from *Henderson v Merrett Syndicates* as follows:

> ... the House of Lords ruled in *Henderson v Merrett Syndicates Ltd* that a service provider will be exposed to concurrent liability in tort and contract for negligence where services (including advice) are provided either for reward or gratuitously, but negligently, and the service provider assumes responsibility

---

[32] See Chapter 2.

[33] Tort is 'an injury, other than breach of contract, which the law will redress with damages'. Danuta Mendelson, *Torts,* 3rd edn, Butterworths Casebook Companions, Butterworths, Sydney, 2002, p. 4. Torts have evolved from an intentional wrong among intimates to unintentional injuries among strangers, with less emphasis on who is morally responsible to who can pay compensation. Historically moral judgment was the core of tort law. When a person has suffered a physical injury to person or property and wishes to take legal action to shift the loss by means of the law of torts he/she often relies on the tort of negligence. Harold Luntz and David Hambly, *Torts: Cases and Commentary*, 3rd edn, Butterworths, Sydney, 1992, p. 105.

[34] Ibid., p. 230. Professionals must exercise 'reasonable care' in the provision of professional advice and treatment, as persons professing to have a special skill.

coupled with reliance by the counter-party on the service; then the requisite duty of care will arise.[35]

Statutory law to limit the liability of certain professional services, and at the same time facilitate improvements in standards, has also been enacted.[36] Records can both protect professionals in negligence cases or be used against them, but not keeping records does not necessarily provide a defence.[37]

Negligent misstatement

'Negligent misstatement' or misrepresentation is the provision of specific information construed as advice that intentionally causes damage to the client's economic interests. It is a major area of liability for recordkeeping and information specialists, as well as all professionals and any service provider. The plaintiff needs to show reliance on the statement and that the effects were foreseeable. Liability for 'negligent misstatement' exists whether information is provided on a free or paid basis, and the provider need not have any special skill.[38]

Complaints and malpractice suits take ethics and codes of profession into account in assessing the standards expected of a professional. Principles of duty of care may depend on evidence of professional skill, and even for contracted service providers, there is an expected level of reasonable care and skill. Outsourcing of services therefore does not diminish liability for negligent behaviour of contracted providers.

---

[35] *Henderson v Merrett Syndicates Ltd* [1994] 3 All ER 506 as quoted in Fisher, 'Introduction', in *The Law of Commercial and Professional Relationships,* p. 4.

[36] Ibid., pp. 8-9. See *Professional Standards Act* 1994 (NSW).

[37] See *Syrett v Vorbach* No DCCIV-99-336 [2001] SADC 46, 30 March 2001. Also Ian Freckelton, 'Records as Reliable Evidence: Medico-legal Litigation', *Archives and Manuscripts*, vol. 26, no. 2, Nov. 1998, p. 278.

[38] *L Shaddock & Associates Pty Ltd v Parramatta City Council* (1981) 150 CLR 225; 36 ALR 385 High Court of Australia case 16.2.9c. In *L Shaddock & Associates Pty Ltd v Parramatta City Council (No. 1)* the Council held information required by the plaintiff exclusively. The case demonstrated that special skill was not required for duty of care, and that it was sufficient that one is in 'the business of giving information' to be liable for negligent misstatement. It depends on how much the plaintiff relies on the knowledge. Liability is not based on the expertise but on giving the advice in the course of one's business. See also Martin Davies, 'Special Skill in "Negligent Misstatement"', *Melbourne University Law Review*, vol. 17, June 1990, pp. 484-496.

6.2.3 Commercial relationships

Law and commercial relationships

Many of the issues raised by professional relationships apply equally to commercial relationships, because they also provide professional services. These include business to business relationships, as well as business to individual consumer or purchaser. Business relationships, such as the banker-customer, include the common law duty of secrecy.[39] The shareholder's relationship with the company is one in which the shareholder is both an obligee, that is the company owes obligations to the shareholder but there are some duties that the shareholder owes to the company, so the shareholder is also an obligor.[40] A corporation will also have a fiduciary responsibility to shareholders and is itself a moral agent within 'a web of relationships'. It is important to reiterate that in a legal and ethical relationship, one is both a right and duty holder, not just one or the other.

Ethics and commercial relationships

Businesses are not only economic but also social institutions. The increase in 'socially responsible investment funds' is a reflection of the community's preference for the 'moral organisation'. It is not only company directors who have ethical duties but also the shareholders who as beneficiaries of the company's income may know little or want to about its source of profit.[41] The nature of a corporate body's privileges and obligations within a web of relationships (shareholder, consumers, and general public), and the differences between privileges from obligations and rights, a facet of Kocourek's legal relations model outlined in Chapter 3, provide the

---

[39] The duty of secrecy between the banker and customer has its foundation in *Tournier v National Provincial Union Bank of England* (1924) 1 KB 461 1923 All ER Rep 550, but in Australia there are exceptions, for example under the *Financial Transactions Reports Act* 1988 (Cth) financial institutions are required to disclose details of customer transactions open to suspicion. The duty does not extend to other financial institutions and relates to deliberate not negligent disclosure. Law Book Company, *Laws of Australia* (Lawbook online), Chapter 4, 'Privacy', Section D, 'Other Law Relating to Privacy - Professional Duties' (unpaginated).

[40] Leanne Wiseman, 'Shareholder and Company', in *The Law of Commercial and Professional Relationships,* ed. Simon Fisher, F.T. Law & Tax, South Melbourne, 1996, p. 605.

[41] Perkin, *The Rise of Professional Society: England since 1880,* p. 389.

backdrop to commercial transactions. Thus a company has privileges but also moral and legal obligations.

The classic economic view of 'self-interested morality' is often expounded in order to limit the relevance of ethical behaviour to what are considered as purely business relationships.[42] However self-interested reasons for action are rarely the only moral motivation in business relationships. The communitarian view is that market competitors respect rules if they see them as promoting a common good.[43] A prosperous market economy with effective government regulation still requires individuals to have a sense of common good to preserve their institutions.

A number of ethical theories can be applied to business relationships. These include virtue ethics which has had an impact on business ethical models in the United States.[44] Personal responsibility in the micro approach to business ethics emphasises the virtues necessary for individuals operating in a business context. The individual in the business world does not operate in a social vacuum. The organisation is itself a community in which business roles exist equally within the corporation and outside. Virtue ethics applied to business relationships encourages sellers and buyers to nurture the virtues of loyalty, honesty, and cooperativeness. Within a web of interconnectedness, these virtues would be commercial 'best practice'. Businesses, like professions, have set practices that employees tend to follow. These may entrench bad or good practices. Engaging in interrogating the business practice is an ongoing concern of any business organisation.

Fiona Ritchie defines business ethics in terms of responsibilities to customers, shareholders, employees, suppliers, bankers and to the wider community, and links the development of a code for each of these groups, as well as how to implement and monitor them. In effect it is a relationship model in which the business develops its ethical code in relation to each stakeholder. Adherence to the code is part of the employees' agreement with the company, but directors must also adhere to it.[45]

---

[42] John Charvet, *The Idea of an Ethical Community*, Cornell University Press, Ithaca New York and London, 1995, p. 94.

[43] Ibid., pp. 212-213.

[44] Robert C. Solomon, 'Corporate Roles, Personal Virtues: An Aristotelian Approach to Business Ethics', in *Virtue Ethics, A Critical Reader,* ed. Daniel Statman, Georgetown University Press, Washington, D.C., 1997, pp. 205-226.

[45] Fiona Richie, *Finishing First with Ethics: Bringing Good Business Principles and Sound Ethics Together for Greater Profits and a Better Future,* Business and Professional Publishing, Sydney, 1996, Chapter 2.

The nature of trust built on honest and truthful behaviour in business would also be reflected in the recordkeeping systems. Do they capture the functions of the organisation, the responsibilities to shareholders and the public and the outcomes of actions of the directors?

6.2.4 Public relationships

Law and public relationships

Unlike professional and commercial relationships which are centred on private law obligations, public relationships are those sourced in public law, that is the relations between the state and the citizen, or more accurately, the state and an entire class of legal persons. In European law, public law is superior to private law, and many legal relationships are 'public' that common law characterises as private.[46]

Public sector ethics and public relationships

> When a private citizen is elected as an MP, he assumes a second identity, one composed of a structure of special obligations that are often more demanding and restrictive than the general moral obligations of private life.[47]

Unlike business relationships, there is a perceived view that government has to be moral in its relationships. Politicians themselves argue that government has to appear to be ethical to maintain public confidence in democratic government.[48] Codes need to be adhered to by leaders, but some trust is essential. The trust of public office in the specific context of public life has been central to archival science and to the notion of a reliable record. Like professional relationships, the honour entrusted to political and public sector participants is no longer taken for granted. The informed 'consumer' is as concerned with political probity as with the state of their health. In many countries, the public has become concerned that government be honest and accountable for economic reasons, and

---

[46] Paola Carucci, *Il Documento Contemporaneo, Diplomatica e Criteri di Edizione,* Carocci, Rome 1998 (1987), p. 53.

[47] Maureen Mancuso as quoted in 'Introduction', in *Ethics and Political Practice: Perspectives on Legislative Ethics*, eds Noel Preston and Charles Sampford with C-A Bois, Federation Press, Leichhardt, NSW, 1998, p. 1.

[48] Cheryl Kernot, 'Codes and Their Enforcement: Necessary but not Sufficient for Ethical Conduct', in *Ethics and Political Practice: Perspectives on Legislative Ethics*, Federation Press, Leichhardt, NSW, 1998, pp. 134-142.

business is concerned that its investments go to sound governments.[49] In the international context, multinational organisations from the United Nations to the OECD have initiatives to encourage better behaviour in government, as corruption siphons off billions of dollars, and discourages long-term investment.[50] However, no universal standard of government behaviour has emerged. What is acceptable behaviour in the political and public service context? For example, illegally obtained information may be unacceptable, but a 'leak' aimed at a political purpose may be morally acceptable.[51]

Distinctions need to be drawn between individual ethics of public representatives and their relations with citizens. John Uhr's definition of political ethics fits the legal and social relationship model as it is concerned with the responsibilities of both citizens and elected representatives.

> The study of political ethics concerns the standards of conduct which are appropriate to political life, not only for those in government but also for citizens acting in their civic capacity as electors and participants. The study of legislative or parliamentary ethics concerns the standards appropriate to those elected representatives who hold formal responsibility for law-making within a political system.[52]

In legislative ethics, John Uhr refers to 'the ethics of representation' for politicians, based on roles and responsibilities. The conflict is between the responsibility of the party in power to the parliament/government on the one hand, and of parliament to the electors on the other. In addition to the conflict of interest between personal interests and the abuse of power, 'public interest' conflict with government policy is a major ethical question in public sector ethics. Linking ethics with office in the public sphere parallels the recordkeeping concept of actors and creators whose responsibilities enhance the reliability of the record. In the Westminster

---

[49] Rodney Smith, 'Strange Distinctions: Legislators, Political Parties and Legislative Ethics Research', in *Ethics and Political Practice: Perspectives on Legislative Ethics,* eds Noel Preston and Charles Sampford with C-A Bois, Federation Press, Leichhardt, NSW, 1998, pp. 41-51.

[50] Howard R. Wilson, 'Ethics Counsellor to the Government: The Canadian Experience', in *Ethics and Political Practice: Perspectives on Legislative Ethics*, Federation Press, Leichhardt, NSW, 1998, pp. 82-83.

[51] Smith, 'Strange Distinctions: Legislators, Political Parties and Legislative Ethics Research', pp. 41-51.

[52] John Uhr, 'Democracy and the Ethics of Representation' in *Ethics and Political Practice: Perspectives on Legislative Ethics,* Federation Press, Leichhardt, NSW, 1998, p. 11.

system the concept of legislative office is one of public trust, but there have been few protections against its abuse.

The process of carrying out public duties is the essence of the rights and responsibilities of both the public office and the citizen. In a democracy, elected officials represent the communities who elect them, but they have a wider responsibility: the promotion of the public interest. In a liberal democracy there is minimalist legislative intervention, and thus ethical requirements of good government are also minimal.[53] Communitarians favour greater state action, while the liberal view of democracy limits ethical expectation of public life. Uhr opts for the concept of trustee (of the party represented) in which rulers are trustees of the public interest.[54] Ethics of role is illustrated by the fact that a public servant is paid by the taxpayer to represent the interests of the people. The deontological model is found in codes of ethics that regulate political practice. The lack of trust in politicians echoes the concerns already raised by codifying ethics, that is, it is just another form of legislation.[55]

Virtue ethics with its origin in Aristotelian philosophy of state provides a pertinent application to public ethics in which civic virtues enhance ethical conduct. These include honesty, integrity, probity, and fairness. However liberal democracy places emphasis on its political institutions rather than on individual moral behaviour. Contemporary thinking has refocused on civic virtue as a means of bonding the political community.

Public sector ethics have to be 'institutionalised' in government, that is, they have to be integrated into the management of organisations, accepted by all stakeholders, and related to the purpose of government or for that matter any business activity. The enforcement of codes is not enough; education and training are essential.

6.3 Professional, commercial and government relationships: the economic, technological and political context

All social relationships, and the rights and obligations arising from them, are affected by the economic, technological and political context in which they take place. Professional relationships in particular are changing as a

---

[53] Ibid., pp. 18-19.

[54] Ibid., pp. 12-14.

[55] A.C. Harris, 'Changing Government and Constant Ethics', New South Wales Auditor-General, Paper presented to the NSW Public Sector Corruption Committee Inc, 29 June 1999.

result of greater client autonomy supported by communication technologies. The reliability of the communications between parties in professional, business and government relationships will depend on trust engendered in circumstances where direct physical contact has greatly diminished.

Professionals have been able to control the supply of expertise.[56] As their market control diminishes, professional ideals begin to disappear. Competition policy, technological change, and consumer awareness are also impacting on professional roles and responsibilities, as well as creating new professions.

If professional relationships, which are important to the trustworthiness of records, begin to lose their special characteristics, will the new forms of relationships provide the same level of trust?

6.3.1 A new form of professionalism

Professional society consists of hierarchies of communities of common interest in which professional communities have been very powerful, but are now challenged by new business ideals.[57] To a large extent the arguments centre on professionals having sold out to the corporate world and forgoing their ideals of community service and social justice, historically rooted in the professional tradition. If ethical obligations are not adhered to, the pressure for legal regulation increases.

It is more than ten years since Harold Perkin wrote that 'professionalised society' has been radically altered. He argued that the resurgence of the free market economy has led to a reaction by one set of professionals - the private corporate managers and their allies - against the other - the public sector employees.[58] Perkin concluded that we must strive

[56] For Perkin the essence of property is a right to (or some portion of) the flow of income from the resource owned, and 'professional capital' in that context is a species of property, Perkin, *The Rise of Professional Society: England since 1880,* p. 386.

[57] Ibid., p. 9.

[58] Ibid., p. 469, pp. 518-519. In Perkin's thesis the differences between private and public sector professionals has contributed to the overall decline of professional ideals in terms of their inability to resolve the dispute about equality: equality of opportunity and equality of outcome. The public version of the professional ideal is one in which there is a caring concept of social citizenship. The private sector ideal is one of equal opportunity for those that rise in the corporate ladder and compete within corporations in which the struggle is for the survival

to retain the benefits of professional society without taking an extreme view from either set of professionals. However the private-public distinction is disappearing as the public sector outsources services. The struggle now is with the free market business model and its merger or take-over of the professional model.

6.3.2 Economic context: the free market society

The right to provide exclusively a service, including a professional one, is in conflict with worldwide trends of deregulation and competition policy.[59] Competition has been defined as the 'striving or potential striving of two or more persons or organisations against one another for the same or related objects'.[60] It has been linked to deregulation of private industry and also to the privatisation of public utilities. Competition policy is concerned with promoting efficiency, not with whether a business is ethical or unethical. In a 1978 United States Supreme Court decision professional and business services were differentiated, but not to the exclusion of the former's need to comply with anti-trust laws. Stephens J in a United States Supreme Court judgment *National Society of Professional Engineers v United States* stated:

> We adhere to the view ... that, by their very nature, professional services may differ significantly from other business services, and accordingly, the nature of the competition in such services may vary ... we may assume that competition is not entirely conducive to ethical behaviour, but that is not a reason, cognizable under the Sherman Act, for doing way with competition.[61]

Exclusive control over an area of business activity is fundamental to professionalism. Competition policy through the anti-competitive provisions

---

of the fittest corporation. It is a crude dichotomy as both kinds of 'equalities' exist in the private and public sector.

[59] For example, in Australia, legislation supporting competition policy is found in the competition sections of the *Trade Practices Act* 1974 (Cth) Part IV which follows the United States rather than United Kingdom legislation, and in common law countries derives from the restraint of trade doctrine. Philip Clarke and Stephen Corones, *Competition Law and Policy,* Oxford University Press, Melbourne, 1998, p. 18.

[60] Ibid., p. 98. The 'Chicago School' defined competition in terms of efficiency benefits. Other objectives have been added which include public benefits reflected in the *Trade Practices Act* 1974 (Cth).

[61] Stephens J for the Court, *National Society of Professional Engineers v United States,* 1978-1 Trade Cases 61,990, United States Supreme Court, 1978 as quoted in Clarke and Corones, *Competition Law and Policy,* p. 289.

of Trade Practices Acts threatens this control as professions are seen as monopolies.[62] It has other ramifications, in particular its emphasis on the business element of professional relationships and often the introduction of a third party into the relationship.

The global competitive and deregulatory climate is not conducive to nurturing professionalism or high ethical standards. State intervention changes the professional ideal, and competition policies in particular are anti-professional, for example abolishing licensing which controls professional standards. However, if professions regulate themselves they have to exercise control over unnecessary service.

The free market ideology has led to an increase in consumer protection laws. Although on the one hand professional self-regulation and autonomy have reinforced claims to professionalism, on the other hand the advance in knowledge and technology and how we receive services have reinforced consumers' sense of rights. This has led to a view that the consumer rather than the individual professional alone has a right to be directly involved in professional decisions. Successful cases of professional negligence have also strengthened consumer demands over professionals.

6.3.3 Purchaser-provider model

Free market policies and the introduction of a business view of the client-professional relationship have altered traditional professional relationships. The purchaser-provider model, that is where a contracted provider provides a service to a consumer/purchaser, introduces a third party into the professional relationship. The purchaser-provider agreements between medical insurance funds and hospitals as well as hospital day facilities are an example of the effect of competition policy on the medical profession in Australia.[63] The need to be competitive directs professionals to concentrate

---

[62] In Australia, the 1993 *National Competition Policy* ('Hilmer Report'), singled out the cost to consumers of the anti-competitive practices of professions such as lawyers. See, Independent Committee of Inquiry into Competition Policy in Australia, *National Competition Policy,* 'Hilmer Report', Canberra, AGPS, c1993, as quoted by Clarke and Corones, *Competition Law and Policy,* p. 14 and p. 111. The report found that professional and industry codes often contain restrictions on competition, for example restrictions on advertising, fee competition and working with non-members. In Australia, restraints on competition in codes of ethics are likely to contravene s 45 of the *Trade Practice Act* 1974 (Cth) unless they have been exempted from the Act.

[63] Danuta Mendelson, 'Devaluation of a Constitutional Guarantee: The History of Section 51(xxiiiA) of the Commonwealth Constitution', *Melbourne University*

on making a profit, the very thing they are asked to balance with their duties to the welfare of the client.

In the legal relationship model as formulated by Fisher and Kocourek, the traditional professional relationship is well illustrated by the professional as the 'dominus' and the client as the 'servus' (see Fig. 3). However, in the expansive view of legal relationships as social relationships with an ethical dimension, the relationship represents not just the individuals concerned, but the group, community or industry they form part of. In the provider-client relationship, unlike the provider-customer relationship, the power is tilted in favour of the provider. A provider-customer or consumer relationship removes the personalised element in the professional relationship despite the increased rights of the consumer. Once 'consumer' replaces 'citizen', 'patient', or 'student', a purely commercial relationship displaces a governmental, medical or mentoring relationship; an amorphous uniform relationship develops that leaves only contractual and commercial expediency. The 'consumer' purchases a product, which could be their pension, medical treatment or education. The duties of the professional shift to shareholders or other stakeholders wanting a slice of the profit. The market economy tends to homogenise all relationships, but this should not dispel other aspects of a professional relationship. Groups working together develop common interests within a market economy, such as the professional ideal, and the fundamental rights of consumers need to sit within that ideal.

6.3.4 Technological context

> The introduction of a new technology or innovation into a society expands the range of behaviours possible by its members and thereby increases the size of the domain of ethics. More unethical behaviour as well as praiseworthy and normal behaviour is now possible.[64]

The delivery of electronic services via the web has implications for professional practice, which include the greatly increased risk to privacy, the fraudulent manipulation of data, and the ease with which records can be reproduced without attribution. Other issues include applying ethics globally in the networked environment, and whether virtual corporations will engender loyalty. Despite legislation globally from copyright digital agenda acts, privacy and electronic signature/transactions acts, the legal

Law Review, vol. 23, no. 2, 1999, pp. 308-344, in particular, Section VIII, The Purchaser-Provider Agreements.

[64] Mason, Mason and Culnam, *Ethics of Information Management,* p. 12.

system tends to trail technology and thus ethical guidance is the only solution.

The importance of social, economic and technological change in terms of professional and other social relationships, and the rights and duties that emanate from these relationships, cannot be underestimated in the capture of recordkeeping metadata on authors, participants and the regulatory context. Ethical outlooks and service to society in the professional are still at the core of what clients want from their doctor, lawyer, teacher, dentist, and accountant. Residual confidential and fiduciary relationships that have been reduced by contractual and statutory obligations still play an essential part in providing trust in professional and business relationships.

A professional relationship arises within a web of obligations; each communication or encounter with a client or other party has an ethical dimension based on trust. It has been the shift in the balance of power between the professional and the client that has altered the relationship at the transactional level. The special aspects of the professional-client relationship need to be retained if professionalism and its ethical dimension are to have continuing relevance. This is not going to be an easy course of action in the current social and economic environment in which the 'provider-consumer relationship' appears to envelop all professional and business relationships.

Three legal relationships that illustrate the legal and ethical rights-obligations of the parties involved in a professional, commercial, and public sector relationship are the doctor-patient, buyer-seller, and government-citizen.[65] The three relationships also manifest themselves in the online context and have only commenced to harness the 'trust elements' that have been essential to their 'offline' existence. However, the examples indicate that the provider-consumer relationship is inadequate as a regulatory tool because it does not differentiate between roles in different professional activities, nor the legal obligations within those relationships. This is not to deny that the service provider per se is not regulated, but it is a narrower set of legal and ethical rights and responsibilities.

[65] The juridical context is essential to understanding the recordkeeping implications. For the Australian regulatory context of the three examples on which this chapter is based see Livia Iacovino, Ethical-Legal Frameworks for Recordkeeping: Regulatory Models, Participants and their Rights and Obligations, PhD Thesis, Monash University, Melbourne, 2002, Chapter 9.

6.4 Doctor-patient relationship

> Possibly the Western therapeutic tradition is unusual in holding to a model of healer-patient relationship which is regarded as (ideally at any rate) a confidential relationship between two individuals.[66]

The relationship between the person who is ill and the healer, has been described by Susan Budd and Ursula Sharma, a psychoanalyst and medical anthropologist respectively, as having two components: the diagnostic knowledge and the treatment that the expert offers, and the relationship within which it is offered. The relationship is not just a means of delivering treatment but an aspect of the healing itself, and is referred to as the healing bond.[67] In alternative medicine the patient may actively participate in or jointly find a cure with the healer.[68] The legal framework in most Western countries has until recently excluded other forms of medicine.

The commitment of the healer, the patient's obligations, the sharing of the responsibility with other healers, institutional arrangements, responsibility to the employer, and the pastoral aspect as opposed to the contractual one, all form part of the doctor-patient relationship. The relationship may be event-specific, that is a patient may consult a different doctor on every visit, although many patients prefer to consult the same doctor. In some national health systems, the United Kingdom for example, every individual is assigned to a doctor.

The international and domestic movement towards patient rights and the accountability of the health care profession provide an important backdrop to the need for reliable and authentic records. Legislation and the courts have supported patient autonomy.[69] On the other hand, the doctrine of clinical autonomy, which gives the doctor the right to decide on a patient's treatment, has been at times an impediment in the criticism of medical

---

[66] Susan Budd and Ursula Sharma, 'Introduction', *The Healing Bond: the Patient-practitioner Relationship and Therapeutic Responsibility,* eds Susan Budd and Ursula Sharma, London, New York, Routledge, 1994, p. 14.

[67] Ibid., p. 1.

[68] Mary Douglas, 'The Construction of the Physician: a Cultural Approach to Medical Fashions', in *The Healing Bond: the Patient-practitioner Relationship and Therapeutic Responsibility,* eds Susan Budd and Ursula Sharma, London, New York, Routledge, 1994, pp. 23-41.

[69] Peter MacFarlane, 'Doctor and Patient', in *The Law of Commercial and Professional Relationships,* ed. Simon Fisher, F.T. Law & Tax, South Melbourne, 1996, p. 342.

conduct.[70] Together with online diagnosis, the orthodox doctor-patient relationship is likely to undergo change.

In applying the legal and social relationship model to the doctor-patient example, it will be evident that as a legal relationship it only involves two parties, the doctor and the patient. Within a community of common interest model, a legal relationship operates within a web of relationships, which includes the public interest factor. In fact a distinction is made by medical commentators between individual therapeutic responsibility between the practitioner and his/her client, and collective therapeutic responsibility, that is, the formal rules or advice promulgated by the practitioner's profession which regulate doctor-patient encounters.[71] The ethical and moral aspects are prominent in the doctor-patient relationship.

The legal aspects of the doctor-patient relationship are also relevant to other professional relationships, in particular in relation to professional legal liability and negligence. However both statutory and case law have also to be understood within policy frameworks, such as competition policy (see 6.3.2 above 'Economic context: the free market society').

6.4.1 Identity and trust within communities of common interest: the medical context

The general community's level of trust in the professional capacity of the doctor is provided by the medical registration board's control over the profession. Most health regulatory bodies require applicants at the time of entry to demonstrate a test for good character.[72] How far does trust derive from the medical registration process? In relation to professional ethics,

[70] 'Clinical autonomy, held inviolable until recent strong challenges, states that all doctors have the right and responsibility to decide about appropriate diagnosis and treatment of their patients. The doctrine also states that where a judgment does have to be made, as for example, in a court of law where damages for bad practice are being claimed, the only people who can judge the appropriateness for the clinical actions taken are other doctors.' Margaret Stacey, 'Collective Therapeutic Responsibility: Lessons from the GMC', in *The Healing Bond: the Patient-practitioner Relationship and Therapeutic Responsibility*, eds Susan Budd and Ursula Sharma, London, New York, Routledge, 1994, pp. 120-121.

[71] Ibid., p. 107.

[72] Andrew Dix, 'Disciplinary Regulation', in *Health Care, Crime and Regulatory Control,* ed. Russell G. Smith, Hawkins Press, Sydney, 1998, pp. 48-58.

the therapeutic responsibility develops (or should develop) via education and role models, rather than legal controls.[73]

The doctor's professional identity is highly controlled through regulations regarding registration and practice. A medical board holds validation details which are usually publicly available. These elements include name, registration status, registration number, address, medical qualifications, and current conditions, restrictions or limitations on practice. The registration may place conditions on what areas a doctor is professionally competent to perform. The registration process indicates that the doctor is a professional practitioner and that he/she has the authority to 'act' as a doctor. These 'competencies' or permissions are central to diplomatics and recordkeeping theory on the reliability of the record creators. The doctor in his/her professional capacity, and the legal and ethical duties that are upheld within the regulatory system in which she/he operates, give a certain level of credibility to the content of the data in the medical record. The sanctions, both legal and moral, also contribute to the reliability of the data. The registration data is recordkeeping metadata on the author (diplomatics) or actor-agent (RKMS). The identification information held by the medical board, as the certification authority, underpins the reliability of doctor-patient transactions, so that they are as 'truthful' as professionally possible. Within the medical community the registration board acts as a trust channel, a third party to which a patient can turn for verification of the professional credentials and for unsatisfactory service.[74] The processing of health data in relation to a health event should only be undertaken by a professional or a person who owes a duty of confidentiality to the patient, essentially continuing to place the trust with the reliable professional.[75]

---

[73] There are many formal and informal ways medical practitioners are monitored, from peer review to legal action. Doctors in Australia, and in many other countries, have registration requirements to ensure they are professionally qualified and that they conduct themselves professionally. Medical boards are under a legal duty to investigate complaints that are made to them about medical practitioners. The imposition of a sentence in a disciplinary context is as much to protect the public, as it is to punish the professional. Freckelton, 'The Criminalisation "Solution" to Medical Misconduct', p. 31, footnote 4.

[74] For example *Medicare,* the Australian government health rebate scheme, holds a Medicare identifier of the doctor, linked to a provider number which is also a source of verification of a service and a method of checking for overservicing.

[75] Data protection legislation in Europe often defines the healthcare professional as the data processor, see *Data Protection Act* 1998 (UK) Schedule 3, cl 8, as referenced in, Meredith Carter, 'Introducing Health Information Privacy in Victoria', *Privacy Law and Policy Reporter*, vol. 7, no. 7, Dec. 2000, pp.

The identification of the patient had been far less rigorous, unless he/she has a special status, for example a pensioner. The doctor identifies a patient from the information he/she provides, but government health rebate records verify details if needed. There is implied trust on the part of the doctor in relation to the patient's identity, as the verification processes available are not undertaken unless a problem arises. Complaints handled by a medical board mainly deal with a breach of trust in the relationship. The sanctions are harsh; for example a doctor is removed from the register and deprived of his/her livelihood.

Modern clinics operate on the basis of a private patient often consulting with different doctors and fracturing a one to one relationship. However, generally the transactions are on a one to one basis; they may be infrequent over many years or frequent. The use of many different health service providers has been one of the arguments in favour of a shared patient electronic record which would provide a composite summary of the patient's treatment by a number of practitioners over a period of time and available anywhere.[76]

The reliability of the information in the medical record is upheld through the controls on the right of the medical practitioner to practise his/her profession. The degree of truthfulness of the information provided by the patient depends on the non-disclosure of the information provided to the practitioner, that is the duty of confidentiality. The protective controls on disclosure have to be replicated in the online environment if records are to be trustworthy.

Recordkeeping person metadata: the doctor-patient context

Clinical patient case notes created and kept by individual medical practitioners have been in use over the millenia. In hospitals, traditionally, patient information was entered into registers, which recorded the same data for each person. These evolved into case files when it was realised that different data was needed for different people depending on their

130-131. In Australia healthcare providers are not specifically defined in the *Privacy Act* 1988 (Cth). Instead a health service provider is an 'organisation' which includes an individual that provides a health service. This means that hospitals and health networks as 'organisations' allow a broad spectrum of health professionals to process health information.

[76] National Electronic Health Records Taskforce, *A Health Information Network for Australia, Taskforce Report*, Commonwealth of Australia, July 2000, is discussed further in Chapter 8.

unique medical conditions.[77] Database technology has provided for patient information to be logically brought together as needed. However single dossiers continue to be created by hospitals and private practices, and are referred to loosely as medical or patient records.

In Australia both the federal and Victorian privacy and health records legislation make a distinction between health information held by a health service provider and that held by other organisations, with different retention periods for both. A transactional view focuses on a clinical relationship, and other medical information would be viewed in the context in which it was created, for example the employer-employee relationship. The legislative focus on the medical information per se is not a recordkeeping transactional view.

Applying the Fisher model of a composite right-duty of both parties which fits a 'business' record transaction view of the doctor-patient relationship, the following is the basis of a matrix of the rights-obligations entity from the doctor's viewpoint (see Fig. 7, Doctor-patient Relationship: Legal-ethical-recordkeeping Obligations).

[77] In the United Kingdom, before the introduction of the National Health Service in 1948, hospitals would have a volume for each doctor for each year in which he/she would list his/her patients alphabetically by name for each episode of illness. Thus one patient could have his/her treatment record scattered throughout the register depending on the number of episodes of care. Different hospital departments also kept their own records, with the patient's detailed record of hospital interaction and ancillary supporting documentation to clinical treatment scattered between specialised hospital sections. The patient unit system adopted in the United Kingdom, United States, Australia and elsewhere in the 1950s was centred on the patient as the unit for record compilation and identification in which all documents relating to an episode of care in a hospital were linked to the patient's unit number. Bernard Benjamin, *Medical Records*, 2nd edn, William Heinemann Medical Books Ltd., London, 1980, pp. 8-29.

* *Writer/actor/physical person*: doctor/health care provider.
* *Author/record creator/agent*: doctor/hospital/medical facility (Note: author and creator are separate entities in diplomatics-archival science).
* *Recipient/addressee*: patient (of action); another doctor/hospital (of communication).
* *Third party*: medical insurance body; patient's family; pathology provider; drug prescription provider; other medical facilities; medical researcher (de-identified records); individual researchers (identified records); and a medical archive. A distinction between trusted third parties and other third parties needs to be made.
* *Record or data subject*: patient/consumer.

Legal and social relationships, such as the doctor-patient, operate within communities of common interest, that is the medical community, and thus have both general and specific recordkeeping metadata requirements. The nature of the relationship, for example its quality of confidentiality and its contractual aspects, are dependent on recordkeeping metadata which identifies and authorises the doctor and the patient.

Event	'Visit' to the doctor.
Activity	Treatment of patient; assessment of medical state and application of expert knowledge to a patient's symptoms.
Processes	Communication is usually verbal; written assessments are kept or sent to other practitioners by the treating doctor.
Rights and obligations of the parties involved	Patient privacy and confidentiality. Doctor's therapeutic privilege. Health insurance obligations.

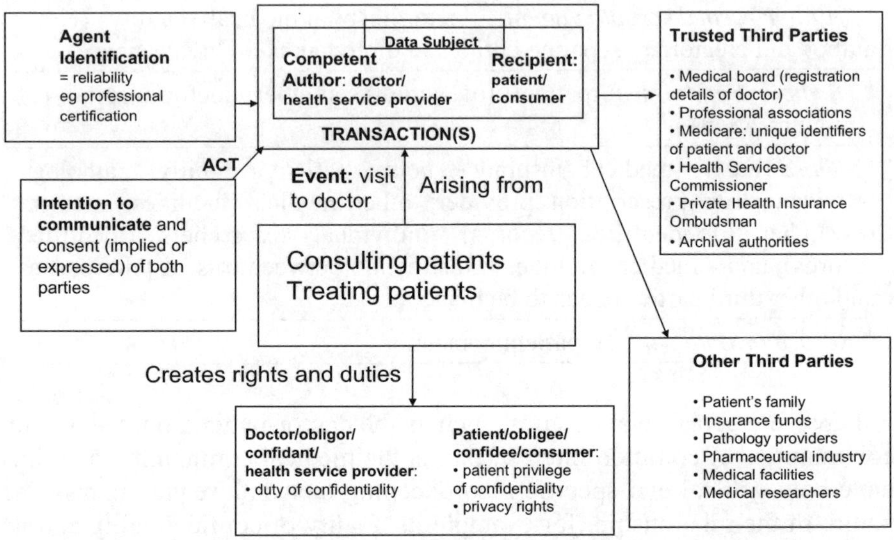

Fig 7. Doctor-Patient Relationship: Legal-Ethical-Recordkeeping Obligations

Rights and obligations of the parties no longer involve the evidence from the records of the doctor alone; the health fund providers are part of the responsibility chain. Legal and ethical rights and obligations need to be linked to the relevant activities, processes and transactions. The authentication data regarding the identity of the doctor and the patient have to be resolved in relation to privacy law. Case law supports the need for quality healthcare records linked to procedures.[78]

6.5 Buyer-seller relationship

The buyer-seller relationship, whether business to business, or business to consumer, is the ideal legal relationship within the current economic

[78] Freckelton, 'Records as Reliable Evidence: Medico-legal Litigation', pp. 278-284.

paradigm, in which government competition policy encourages market forces to control the economy.[79]

The relationship is the classic 'open system' one, where trust mechanisms have been in place for centuries through commercial law. It is another illustration of the web of relationships that depend on trust and the identity of the participants, in which reliable and authentic records both as right-duty things (object as obligation) and record as process are required.

At the level of buyer-seller interaction it would be difficult to argue that the relationship has an ethical dimension beyond a common end of profit or purchase. Given the idea of a web of interconnectedness of relationships, the buyer and seller are in fact subject to a regulatory and ethical environment, which includes consumer codes, government controls of financial transactions, and 'honest' contracts.

6.5.1 Identity and trust within communities of common interest: the business context

If viewed as an atomic relationship, the buyer-seller relationship excludes the notion of public interest and the wider business in which it operates, as well as consumer protection. The trust requirement would emanate from the constituencies from which the buyer and seller work within, for example banking or other business sector. Business participants may be regulated through professional and industry associations, depending on the market sector of the sales, which operate in tandem with legal requirements. The buyer-seller relationship is more than a set of rights and duties that arise from the act of transacting a sale.

Recordkeeping person metadata: buyer-seller context

Applying the Fisher model of a composite right-duty of both parties which fits a 'business' record transaction view of the relationship, the following is the basis of a matrix of the rights-obligations entity from the seller's viewpoint (see Fig. 8, Seller-buyer Relationship: Legal-ethical-recordkeeping Obligations).

---

[79] Competition policy is relevant to the buyer-seller in the area of price fixing, and prohibited conduct including exclusive dealing and third line forcing. Clarke and Corones, *Competition Law and Policy,* p. 329.

* *Writer/actor/physical person*: seller.
* *Author/record creator/agent*: seller/manufacturer/corporate entity.
* *Recipient/addressee*: buyer; (physical or legal person).
* *Third party*: insurance companies; credit card companies; other business facilities; consumer protection bodies; individual researchers; a business archive. A distinction between trusted third parties and other third parties needs to be made.
* *Record or data subject*: may be recipient (buyer).

The right-duty of both parties from the buyer's viewpoint is summarised below.

* *Writer/actor/physical person*: buyer.
* *Author/record creator/agent*: buyer/corporate entity.
* *Recipient/addressee*: seller; physical or legal person.
* *Third party*: insurance companies; other business facilities; consumer protection bodies; individual researchers; a business archive. A distinction between trusted third parties and other third parties needs to be made.
* *Record or data subject*: may be recipient.

If the transaction is to ensure trust, identity metadata on both the seller and buyer must be linked with a sale, and identify the business context also.

Event	Sale.
Activity	Delivery of goods.
Processes	Verification of payment; quality control of goods.
Rights and obligations of the parties involved	Right to possession (buyer). Right to payment (seller).

Consumer and contract law support the need for fair commercial transactions. The buyer-seller relationship is part of a wider web of consumer protection mechanisms which provide trust and truthfulness necessary for reliable records.

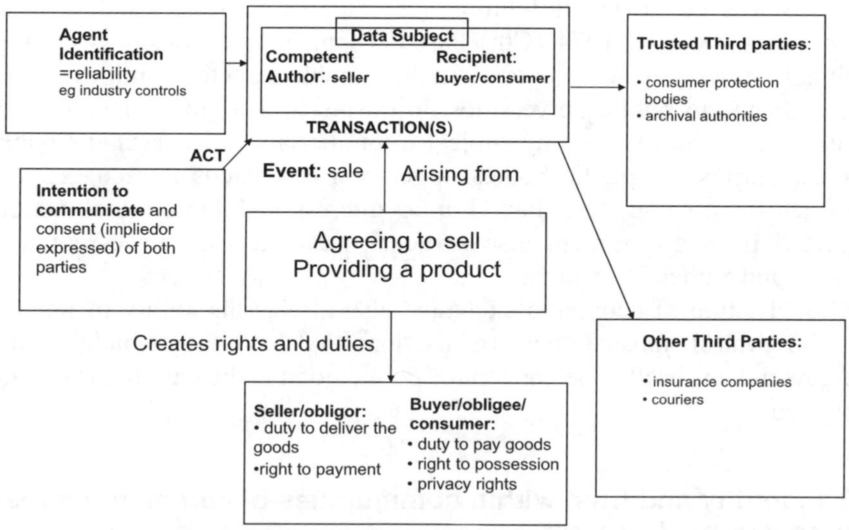

Fig. 8 Seller-Buyer Relationship: Legal-Ethical-Recordkeeping Obligations

6.6 Citizen-government (state) relationship

The intermeshing of private and public law differentiates the government-citizen[80] relationship from other legal relationships.[81] The way services are provided by government, worldwide, has undergone dramatic change. Many countries have redefined government in terms of its commercial

[80] The legal status of citizens is a complex one. A citizen is generally a legally recognised natural person of a sovereign state, either by birth, marriage or naturalisation depending on the laws of that state. Non-citizens, including residents, also have a relationship with the state but depending on the laws of the country in which they reside they may not have the same private rights as a citizen, (for example voting rights, holding public office or accessing social security).

[81] 'Private law is all law besides public law. In modern terms, "public law" includes constitutional law, administrative law, criminal law and taxation law'. Fisher, 'The Archival Enterprise, Public Archival Institutions and the Impact of Private Law', p. 334. See also Fisher, 'General Principles of Obligations', p. 16.

dealings, private-public sector regulatory regimes work across government and business on an equal footing, for example in Australia the *Trade Practices Act* (TPA) 1974 (Cth) Part IV applies to all business entities, including the business operations of public sector entities, from governments, to public universities, to hospitals. The government-citizen relationship is no longer only subject to public law.[82] However the public interest purpose of public bodies in relation to citizens is recognised in both legislation and case law. Public interest and high moral actions expected from government also serve as trust mechanisms essential to reliable and authentic records.

Globalisation of economic exchange also affects the ability of government to control transnational organisations that have larger budgets than the government itself. The concept of public good is difficult to define in a global context.

6.6.1 Identity and trust within communities of common interest: the government context

A political community of common interest consists of citizens, government-elected officials, public employees, and private entities. Trust in the government context has been articulated in recordkeeping theory in terms of procedural controls over record creation and the public standing of its officers, and has its antecedents in Roman law. The politicisation of the public service throws into question the credibility of public office founded in law. A relationship of trust between the citizen and state, unlike the doctor-patient relationship, has not been a private one. Privacy and confidence are private law rights that are applied differently in the public sphere.

Recordkeeping person metadata: the citizen-government (state) context

How government delivers its services impacts on the ethical and legal rights of citizen and state. The legal personality and identity of the entity performing a government function are crucial to its liability and its obligations, particularly in the commercialised government context. Metadata that captures the statutory charter, objectives, community service obligations, executive decisionmaking of government officers are relevant to the

[82] Private sector accountability mechanisms include industry ombudsmen, consumer protection laws, including trade practices legislation, and tort liability.

degree of governmental control over its activities and whether public trust can be extended to private enterprise performing public functions.[83] This data should be available to the citizen transacting if it is to trust the content of the records. The gap between what the legal and political institutions are meant to do and what they actually do is manifested in the records, to the extent that record creators and keepers are legal as well as ethical agents. High level policy context, the fourth dimension of the records continuum, is essential to rights and obligations. However operational records on which citizens rely to make decisions are equally important. At the level of a business transaction the relationship is manifested as an author, record creator or agent relationship. In diplomatics the elements of person identity are found in the documentary context, that is, a government agency as the creator or author, and a public officer as the writer.

Trusted third parties

Archival authorities have played an important part as trusted third parties, in particular in the public sector. Legislative activity in the records area reflects the changing direction of archival authorities into standard setting bodies that monitor the totality of record activity within the government sector.[84]

Other third parties

In the government context, the citizen-state relationship operates in a web with other government agencies, non-government bodies, and businesses, all with different rights and obligations.

Recordkeeping person metadata and the citizen-state relationship, is complicated by those government corporations that have a separate legal personality from the government (see Fig. 9, Citizen-government

[83] Bryan Horrigan, 'Contemporary Sources and Limits of Crown Immunity, Governmental Liability and Legislative Invalidity', in *Government Law and Policy, Commercial Aspects,* ed. Bryan Horrigan, The Federation Press, Leichhardt, NSW, 1998, p. 312.

[84] Hurley, Chris, 'From Dust Bins to Disk-Drives and Now to Dispersal: The State Records Act 1998 (New South Wales)', *Archives and Manuscripts*, vol. 26, no. 2, November 1998, pp. 390-409. See also Ted Ling, 'Setting Standards: Archival Legislation and Recordkeeping Principles', in *Convergence, Joint National Conference, Conference Proceedings*, the Joint National Conference of the Australian Society of Archivists and the Records Management Association of Australia, 2-5 September 2001, Hobart, pp. 93-99.

Relationship: Legal-ethical-recordkeeping Obligations). From the view of a citizen:

* *Writer/actor/physical person*: citizen.
* *Author/record creator/agent*: citizen.
* *Recipient/addressee*: physical or legal person: government agency; corporate entity.
* *Third party*: outsourced service provider; contractor; private entity. A distinction between trusted third parties and other third parties needs to be made. Trusted third party: for example a government archival authority.
* *Record or data subject*: may be the recipient.

As a transaction the matrix can be reversed with the public office as the creator.

* *Writer/actor/physical person*: public officer.
* *Author/record creator/agent*: Executive entity (Crown or its representative government agency).
* *Recipient/addressee*: citizen or organisation.
* *Third party*: outsourced service provider; a government archive. A distinction between trusted third parties and other third parties needs to be made.
* *Record or data subject*: may be recipient.

An example of a business transaction is as follows:

Event	A tax payment.
Activity	Taxation.
Processes	Verifying identity of taxpayer and accuracy of data provided.
Rights and obligations of the parties involved	Right to payment (government). Duty to pay (citizen).

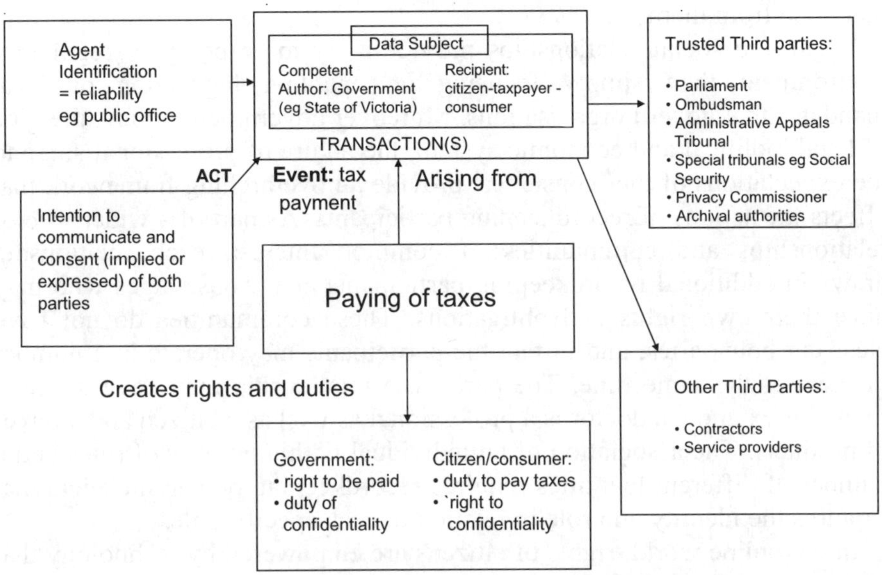

Fig. 9 Citizen-Government Relationship: Legal-Ethical-Recordkeeping Obligations

This chapter has surveyed a range of legal relationships, the nature of professional, commercial and public relationships, and their ethical and legal regulation, professional ideals, the threats to that ideal, and professional negligence. Professional relationships, as legal and social relationships, are constrained by external factors, which diminish their autonomy and self-regulation important to professionalism. The move away from self-regulation for the 'old professions', consumer demands for a greater involvement in professional relationships, decreased trust in professional performance, more remote relationships due to technology, impact on the rights and obligations of the professional, as well as third parties and service providers, as recordkeeping participants. Commercial relationships also depend on trust and ethical behaviour.

The three examples demonstrate the validity of the language of legal relations as a means of understanding the regulatory framework for recordkeeping when records are conceived as both objects that encapsulate a right-duty and as the product of processes. For example the extent of privileges, rights, obligations, immunities and liabilities of legal personalities, and types of legal relationships (fiduciary, contractual, confidential, or proprietorial), are essential to the legal rights and liabilities that arise from them.

Legal and social relationships provide a far more complex regulatory environment than simply focusing on enabling legislation or legal mandates that govern organisations. Moreover government policy, the type of legal, political and economic system, the nature of professionalism, and the expectations of the 'consumer' provide an overarching framework that affects the actions of recordkeeping participants. As part of a wider web of relationships and communities of common interest, each relationship draws in additional recordkeeping participants at various stages who may have their own rights and obligations. These communities do not have clear-cut boundaries, and in fact the participants may operate in a number of them at the same time. The party in a relationship may have multiple roles, for example a doctor is a professional as well as a citizen and a buyer of products. The association of an individual with a number of roles and a number of different identities requires recordkeeping person metadata that captures the identity and role in relation to each specific role.

In the online world, rights of citizens are empowered by technology that governments have difficulty in controlling. The 'buyer' can choose from an array of products and avoid the middleman merchant, and the patient can equip himself/herself with knowledge before consulting a doctor. This 'empowering' element of the 'servus' tips the balance to the consumer, but at the cost of other rights, such as privacy and confidentiality. However the power of the record to support a social relationship has not changed.

7 RECORDKEEPING REGULATORY MODELS IN THE WEB ENVIRONMENT

Juridical and warrant-based regulatory models for recordkeeping[1] are predicated on regulation pertaining to a specific juridical context or an industry or professional community, which in the online environment depends on a combination of codes of conduct, legal action and technical solutions that have gradually emerged to protect privacy, copyright owners, provide access to users, and to give legal validity to transactions. The records continuum provides a framework in which the Internet legal regulatory models outlined below can be incorporated into recordkeeping models.[2] The OECD and a number of other international bodies have provided voluntary principles on Internet regulation which have guided national approaches.[3] The convergence of law internationally supports the 'pluralisation of collective memory' of records outside of their organisational context in the same way that recordkeeping standards provide a universal language for recordkeeping practice. The necessity for closed networks for particular industries provides validity to communities and professions that operate within their own standards of trust where the legal accountability of the organisation and its corporate memory is the strongest.

---

[1] See Chapter 1.

[2] For example, conceptually an intranet operates at the third dimension, that is the organisational or corporate level, and the Internet at the fourth dimension, that is the institutional or collective level of the records continuum model.

[3] OECD, Directorate for Science, Technology and Industry, Committee for Information, Computer and Communications Policy, *OECD Input to the United Nations Working Group on Internet Governance*, OECD, 2005. For an example of Australian Internet regulatory models see Livia Iacovino, Ethical-Legal Frameworks for Recordkeeping: Regulatory Models, Participants and their Rights and Obligations PhD dissertation, Monash University, Melbourne, 2002, pp. 406-411.

7.1 Regulation of the Internet

Regulation has been defined throughout this book not merely as the law made by parliament and the courts, but also social controls or normative systems other than the law proper. The role of ethics and codes of conduct are of particular relevance to Internet 'self-regulation' models.[4]

Ethicists and jurists over the centuries have failed to achieve a consensus on whether humans act only in their own self-interest and whether benevolent behaviour towards others is 'natural' or learned. It is therefore highly unlikely that a simple answer to these questions applies to human behaviour in the Internet context, where the pressure points for ethical motivation and action may operate differently. The image projected of the Internet through advertising is that of a 'cash nexus' society.[5] However users are too varied to allow for generalisation about their habits. What bonds the users are the same social bonds that tie in other contexts, the same interests and values of communities, in which profit, as Peter Singer would express it, is only one motivation.

For democracy advocates, the Internet was not envisaged as developing into a global universal community or market place, but as a multiplicity of communities that would revitalise civic life, a parallel of universalism and particularism, rather than Marshall McLuhan's picture of a global village with universal moral standards.[6] Law in cyberspace was expected to evolve on the basis of communities with distinct rule sets and self-governance. Both the warrant and juridical models include the notion of self-regulatory communities with quasi-legal systems which conform to an Internet self-regulatory model.

In the short history of the Internet, arguments over its regulation have been both social and legal. Many users of the Internet originally argued against its 'regulation' because they saw its value as a tool for improving

[4] Peter Leonard, 'Ethics in Cyberspace', *Internet Law Anthology*, ed. Peter Leonard, Prospect Intelligence Report, Prospect Publishing, Sydney, 1997, pp. 140-141. The Australian government report, *The Global Information Economy: The Way Ahead*, July 1997, advised on a non-regulatory, market-oriented approach which suggested clarifying existing legislation rather than introducing an overarching piece of legislation.

[5] Donna Gibbs, 'Cyberlanguage: What it is and What it does', in *Cyberlines: Languages and Cultures of the Internet,* eds Donna Gibbs and Kerri-Lee Krause, James Nicholas, Melbourne, 2000, p. 18.

[6] Ingrid Volkmer, 'Universalism and Particularism: The Problem of Cultural Sovereignty and Global Information Flow', in *Borders in Cyberspace: Information Policy and the Global Information Infrastructure,* MIT Press, Cambridge, Mass., 1997, pp. 48-83.

equality, and human and political rights.[7] The Open Internet Policy Principles of the Parliamentary Human Rights Foundation promoted the use of the Internet as a means of supporting political freedom, but also recognised the continued existence of national legal systems that are cognisant of international conventions.

> The Internet does not exist in a legal vacuum. For the most part, existing laws can and should regulate conduct on the Internet to the same degree as other forms of conduct. Such laws may differ from country to country, but should conform with the applicable binding human rights obligations contained in the Universal Declaration of Human Rights, the International Covenant on Civil and Political Rights and the European Convention on Human Rights.[8]

Self-regulation by cyberspace participants in which the territorial nation state would have restraining powers is one of the earliest notions of Internet regulation. Physical proximity, the legitimacy of law-making within a geographic border and boundaries as signposts that new rules apply when one moves into another space, no longer held sway. An event on the Internet was considered to take place everywhere and nowhere.

Despite the fact that both domestic law and international conventions do apply to the Internet, a popular belief has been that, in fact, it is 'uncontrolled'. Chris Reed, an Internet legal specialist, has termed the notion of the uncontrolled Internet as the 'cyberspace fallacy'. The fallacy derives from the depiction of the Internet as a jurisdiction in which none of the existing rules and regulations apply, a virtual space that expands and contracts as different networks connect and disconnect from each other, and the geographic locations where the activities occur are fortuitous, dictated by the current configuration of the Internet.[9] This outlook can be refuted by the fact that all actors in an Internet transaction have a real-world existence, and are located in one or more legal jurisdictions. The view has been fuelled by the confusion between the applicability of law

---

[7] Parliamentary Human Rights Foundation, *Open Internet Policy Principles of the Parliamentary Human Rights Foundation*, PHRF Conference, Brussels Belgium, 23 November 1996, 'Preamble'.

[8] Ibid.

[9] John Perry Barlow, '"Selling Wine Without Bottles", The Economy of Mind on the Global Net', 1996. In Barlow's thesis cyberspace is a new jurisdiction in which existing rules do not apply. A 'law of cyberspace', or special 'cyberlaw', analogous to the law merchant ('lex mercatoria') was envisaged as a distinctive area of law. See also David R. Johnson and David G. Post, 'The Rise of Law on the Global Network', in *Borders In Cyberspace: Information Policy and the Global Information Infrastructure,* MIT Press, Cambridge, Mass., 1997, pp. 3-47.

and the apparent lack of its enforcement on the Internet, with a conviction that there is an absence of law. In the view of Chris Reed, the Internet rather than being unregulated, is the most heavily regulated place in the world, as all the laws including legal precedents of every country may be in theory relevant.[10]

Technical reasons why the Internet has been difficult to control are due to the technologies that underlie it. It is a decentralised system of many networks based on an open standard Internet protocol which makes it difficult for anyone to block or monitor information originating from many users.[11] Governments, for example Singapore, have been unsuccessful at control over the content distributed on the web, due to regulatory arbitrage, which allows moving an activity to a jurisdiction which is favourable to non-control.[12]

Legal approaches to Internet regulation follow principles that have already been developed to solve disputes when it is unreasonable to apply legal jurisdiction (see below). Proposals for regulation of the Internet have included delegating authority to self-regulatory organisations, establishing net-based law-making institutions or adapting existing ones, for example the World Intellectual Property Organization.[13] The creation of network standards, for example content filters, still leaves a role for the state.[14] The function of international public and private law which requires a choice of forum and choice of law, or alternatively relying on international agreements, have also been relevant to regulating Internet activity.

---

[10] 'Introduction' in Chris Reed, *Internet Law: Text and Materials*, Butterworths, London, 2000.

[11] Sharon Eisner Gillett and Mitchell Kapor, *The Self-Governing Internet: Coordination by Design*. Prepared for Coordination and Administration of the Internet, Workshop, Kennedy School of Government, Harvard University, September 8-10, 1996.

[12] A. Michael Froomkin, 'The Internet as a Source of Regulatory Arbitrage', in *Borders In Cyberspace: Information Policy and the Global Information Infrastructure,* MIT Press, Cambridge, Mass., 1997, pp. 129-163. Arbitrage is defined in the financial context, as the difference in pricing between two counterparties and exploiting the difference for profit, for example, tax havens. The distributed enterprise may use a safe harbour scheme for tax purposes for particular activities. Reed, *Internet Law,* p. 237.

[13] Johnson and Post, 'The Rise of Law on the Global Network', pp. 16 and 24.

[14] Joel R. Reidenberg, 'Governing Networks and Rule-Making in Cyberspace', in *Borders In Cyberspace: Information Policy and the Global Information Infrastructure,* MIT Press, Cambridge, Mass., 1997, p. 96.

7.1.1 Jurisdiction: legal boundaries

Jurisdiction, that is the power of the courts over persons, things and disputes, is geopolitically-based.[15] In the physical world the laws of a particular jurisdiction only have effect within the boundaries of that jurisdiction. Internet transactions are not limited to geographical or political boundaries; national laws apply to some part of their activities. In Internet activity overlaps in national laws are pervasive and encourage law breaking. Even when jurisdiction applies to a matter, a court may not be able to enforce the judgment. Execution of a 'foreign' judgment through judgment recognition depends on recognition treaties, and even then assets (forfeiture) to execute the judgment must be found. The extent to which conventional courts have jurisdiction to adjudicate civil disputes and prosecute crimes on the Internet may require an international criminal court or a private international arbitration panel where the conventional courts cannot operate. Personal jurisdiction, an international law mechanism, requires that a person be present when tried, in particular in criminal trials. Henry Perritt's jurisdiction model for the Internet involves the use of admiralty-maritime law *in rem*, where a wrongdoer does not have to be in the custody of the court to be tried, and compensation for the aggrieved party is pursued through interests held by the wrongdoer. Perritt introduces the concept of a virtual presence in a state.[16] The weaknesses with these early approaches to regulating cyberspace are that they attempt to replicate the existing legal processes.

Where do Internet transactions take place?

On what basis can a national government claim to apply its laws and regulations to Internet activities which originate in a different jurisdiction? How far, if at all, is it possible to resolve the conflict between differing national laws where the only effective means of compliance is to limit information flows across national boundaries?

---

[15] Jurisdiction is also used broadly to include the power of government to legislate in relation to particular persons or circumstances, to adjudicate by subjecting persons to dispute resolutions, and compelling compliance with laws. See Gaye L. Middleton and Jocelyn A. Aboud, 'Jurisdiction and the Internet', in *Going Digital 2000, Legal Issues for E-commerce, Software and the Internet*, eds Anne Fitzgerald et al., 2nd edn, Prospect Media, St. Leonards, New South Wales, 2000, pp. 245-246.

[16] Henry H. Perritt, Jr., 'Jurisdiction in Cyberspace: the Role of Intermediaries', in *Borders In Cyberspace: Information Policy and the Global Information Infrastructure,* MIT Press, Cambridge, Mass., 1997, pp. 164-202.

Principles have been established via private international law, or conflict of laws, by deciding if a relevant element of a transaction can be localised in the jurisdiction in question. Where did each element of the transaction take place? Chris Reed states:

> The problem with cyberspace is that its constituent elements, the human and corporate actors and the computing and communications equipment through which the transaction is effected, all have a real-world existence and are located in one or more physical world legal jurisdictions. These corporeal elements of cyberspace are sufficient to give national jurisdictions a justification for claiming jurisdiction over, and the applicability of their laws to, an Internet transaction.[17]

'Localisation' in the physical world is defined by where the human actor was situated when the act was performed. For corporate actors in multiple jurisdictions there are various presumptions about place. For example, in contract, place or location of performance is agreed upon as part of the contract. There are exceptions if one of the parties is a consumer. Other factors for localisation include habitual residence of person, principal place of business, place where contract was performed, place where the steps necessary for the conclusion of the contract were taken, and place where an advertisement or invitation to enter into the contract was received. For tortious claims, jurisdiction is where damage occurred.[18]

In diplomatics and rules of evidence, probative value increases with the closeness of the act of documentation to the act itself. Time and place in law vis-à-vis the record is based on the process of executing the act. If physical place is where the transaction occurred, applicable law, according to Chris Reed, is every jurisdiction or else applicable law has no obvious connection with the parties or the substantive transaction.[19] Reed argues

---

[17] Reed, *Internet Law: Text and Materials,* p. 188.

[18] This has been upheld in *Dow Jones Inc. V Gutnick* [2002] HCA 56 10 December 2002. The case decided that the State of Victoria was the place of publication of material that contained defamatory content, even if it was uploaded in the United States. The place of publication is essential to ascertaining where the tort of defamation can be invoked and where the court has jurisdiction. The *Dow Jones Inc. V Gutnick* case indicates that in Australian courts domestic laws are likely to be applied to Internet legal transgressions. In the United States, case law indicates that where a website is outside the territory of a relevant court, carrying on active business with residents of the jurisdiction will attract the jurisdiction of that court. For a discussion on jurisdiction, see Andrew Sorensen and Matthew Webster, *Trade Practices and the Internet*, Lawbook Co., Pyrmont, NSW, 2003, pp. 137-149.

[19] Reed, *Internet Law: Text and Materials,* Chapter 7 Cross-border law and jurisdiction. Local law has been applied successfully in a defamation case in

that localisation is meaningless on the Internet. However, from a recordkeeping view a storage 'space' for the recordkeeping system or where the transactions have been captured whether on a server, hard disk or other storage device, over which an organisation or individual has 'control', is necessary to run a business.[20] Reed is mainly concerned with multiple copies of data on different servers, rather than viewing them from a transactional perspective in which case each 'copy' is the 'original' of the respective records of the organisation.

Enforceability in the Internet environment

The distinction between applicability and enforceability is fundamental to the development of Internet law. Convergence of national laws is one answer to enforceability, but in areas such as free speech it may be

---

Australia. See *Dow Jones Inc. V Gutnick* [2002] HCA 56 10 December 2002. Although an Australian case has no binding authority on other common law countries, it could be followed in the United Kingdom or other common law countries. The case opens up worldwide liability through foreign legal proceedings. See Andrew P. Sparrow, *The Law of Internet & Mobile Communications: the EU and US Contrasted*, tfm Publishing, Harley, England, 2004, pp.139-140.

[20] Where and when a record resides on a server has been defined in the Australian *Electronic Transactions Act* 1999 (Cth) s 14(3) and (4). 'Where the addressee has given specific directions and the electronic communication is transmitted in accordance with those directions, subclause (3) says that the communication is received when it enters the designated information system. As it is expected that a person who has designated an information system will regularly check that information system for messages, the provision effectively deems the communication to have come to the attention of the addressee as soon as it enters the designated system. In all other cases subclause (4) operates to state that the electronic communication will be received when it comes to the attention of the addressee. *The term "comes to the attention of the addressee" does not mean that a communication must be read by the addressee before it is considered to be received.* An addressee who actually knows, or should reasonably know in the circumstances, of the existence of the communication should be considered to have received the communication. For example, an addressee who is aware that the communication is in their electronic mail "box" but who refuses to read it should be considered to have received the communication' [emphasis added]. Australia, Senate, *Electronic Transactions Bill 1999,* Revised Explanatory Memorandum, 30 June 1999, pp. 39-40.

impossible to reach a consensus. Ultimately enforceability is required if law is to have 'normative force'.[21]

Essentially the unenforceability of the law in the Internet context arises from its trans-jurisdictional nature, that is, all laws applicable to an activity in every jurisdiction may apply in the Internet context. There are two types of enforceability issues: laws and regulations which are, in practice, unenforceable, because the court has no effective jurisdiction over the defendant, generally laws relating to criminal offences, and laws and regulations which are in theory enforceable, but where the cost of the enforcement outweighs the benefits of enforcement, usually private matters.

Industry practice and community expectations have also played a role in regulating cyberspace.[22] For example, to reduce uncertainty with respect to personal jurisdiction, choice of law and venue in civil cases, Perritt recommends the adoption of international arbitration.[23] Communities of suppliers and consumers can adopt their own rules on intellectual property infringement and other matters and apply rules through arbitration machinery agreed upon by the community. Conduct can be judged according to norms developed by the users of the network, and violations are adjudicated by a system of arbitration, with monetary penalties or exclusion from network participation. For example, the terms of service between the service provider and the subscriber are contractual and can operate as an arbitration agreement. The arbitration awards would be enforced worldwide under the New York Convention, or by excluding wrongdoers from the services.[24] Criminal matters require a public

---

21 If a law is either unenforceable or unenforced it loses its normative effect as law. Lon Fuller, *The Morality of Law*, revised edn, Yale University Press, New Haven, London, 1969, Chapter 11 as quoted by Reed, p. 252.

22 Perritt suggests adapting legal 'restatements' of common law, a traditional American Law Institute practice, to cyberspace based on evolving online industry practice. See Perritt, 'Jurisdiction in Cyberspace: the Role of Intermediaries', pp. 190-191.

23 Regular courts may enforce the arbitration agreement, by 'compelling arbitration'. There has to be an arbitration agreement in which rules of evidence are written into the agreement, cost allocation, and reference to rules of procedure issued by bodies sponsoring the arbitration, such as United Nations Commission on International Trade Law (UNCITRAL). General commercial law rather than substantive law may be applied. 'Arbitration is a dispute resolution process in which a binding decision is made by one or more private individuals under an agreement entered into by the disputants'. Perritt, 'Jurisdiction in Cyberspace: the Role of Intermediaries', p. 185.

24 Ibid., pp. 184-188.

international court. The current International Court of Justice only handles disputes between nations. An international criminal court may be an avenue, but has many stumbling blocks.[25] The arbitration approach to jurisdiction in cyberspace is similar to the juridical model, that is, it is based on a set of rules sanctioned and enforced by a community with common interests.

International law includes private and public international law (also referred to as transnational law). There are no real sanctions for breaches of public international law. In fact legal positivists deny that international law has the status of law, although it has moral and political force. In most countries it needs to be incorporated into local law. Private international law is part of the local law, and includes whether any state has legal jurisdiction between citizens or between citizens and states; whether a state can enforce a judicial determination (recognition and enforcement) and the body of rules that will be applied to resolve any issues that arise (choice of law). Private international law is relevant to the Internet, and civil remedies are easier to enforce as most Western legal systems accept legal orders of foreign countries that have jurisdiction, although approaches to recognition and enforcement of foreign judgments differ from country to country. A court has jurisdiction even if a person is only briefly in its territory. However apart from commercial-contractual obligations, other areas such as product liability are difficult to enforce if a country does not have similar laws. Generally no state can exercise its own laws in another state without the agreement of the other state. Extradition, when one state requests another to apprehend and surrender to it a person, is complex, therefore activities online that are deemed criminal need to be assessed by domestic laws of all states.[26] Rather than broadening the role of international courts, new laws, in particular in the copyright area, have gone ahead.

Self-regulation schemes, particularly for private rights, already exist for privacy and other rights. They are backed by sanctions for non-compliance, for example loss of the 'seal' from the 'group' or schemes

[25] An international criminal court under the United Nations came into force on 1 July 2002. Its focus is war crimes, and therefore only computer crimes of serious magnitude are likely to be included. The United States has been one of the countries that dragged its feet on establishing such a court, wanting immunity from prosecution for its military from any international criminal court.

[26] John Goldring, 'Netting the Cybershark: Consumer Protection, Cyberspace, the Nation-State, and Democracy', in *Borders in Cyberspace: Information Policy and the Global Information Infrastructure,* MIT Press, Cambridge, Mass., 1997, pp. 334-354.

linked to legislation. Consortia of Internet Service Providers and Internet Watch Groups use the 'seal of approval' approach. Effective enforcement involves self-regulation coupled with alternative enforcement resolution.[27]

The trend for enforcement in the Internet environment is being resolved by identifying infringements that are likely to arise in any jurisdiction, and applying local laws. This approach is slowing building a common body of Internet law.[28]

7.1.2 Convergence of national law

> In the longer term, the Internet and the commercial and non-commercial activities carried out by means of it will impose substantial pressure on national legislators to eradicate the differences between their own laws and those of other states ...[29]

A national government can try to enforce its laws on Internet activities emanating from foreign jurisdictions in its own country, but enforcement in another country is another matter. Governments may apply the principles of 'comity' which require that a state should not claim to apply its legislation to persons within another state unless it is reasonable to do so. Legislators attempt to maintain comity by applying their laws only to activities undertaken within the state. It is a form of localisation, but uses different triggers. Rather than localising Internet activities, comity is maintained by accepting 'country of origin' regulation, coupled with an appropriate degree of harmonisation or convergence of national laws.[30]

Home country or 'country of origin' regulation, adopted by the European Union, is the only regulatory model so far attempted that Reed believes is capable of resolving the conflicts between multifarious and overlapping claims by national jurisdictions to regulate Internet activities.[31]

---

[27] Reed, *Internet Law: Text and Materials,* pp. 267-268.

[28] Reidenberg, 'Governing Networks and Rule-Making in Cyberspace', p. 96.

[29] Reed, *Internet Law: Text and Materials,* p. 271.

[30] Ibid., p. 204. Reed's examples are taken from heavily regulated activities such as banking and finance. Having a permanent establishment in the relevant jurisdiction is the primary trigger for the application of financial services regulation, and for income tax liability. A website hosted on a server where the server is a business asset is treated as part of the enterprise (if the website were hosted by an independent ISP there would be no permanent establishment). The concept of a permanent establishment has to be modified radically, as many websites are not located in the jurisdictions where they do business.

[31] See Stephen Weatherill, 'The Regulation of E-Commerce under EC Law: the Distribution of Competence between Home States and Host States as a Basis

By mutual agreement two states, or a group of states collectively, provide that activities of an organisation which is established and regulated in one state (the home state) may be carried out in another (the host state) without any requirement for prior authorisation from or supervision by an appropriate regulatory body in the host state. The basis of this agreement is an assessment by all participating states that the others operate systems of authorisation and/or supervision which are adequate to achieve the aims of the home state's regulatory system. The laws of the host state will apply to the appropriate aspects of individual transactions undertaken in the state, for example the law of contract.[32] The essence of country of origin regulation is the acceptance by the host country that the home country provides an adequate and broadly equivalent level of regulatory oversight.[33] Online actors can be regulated in their home country by the mechanism of an international convention, implemented into national law by the states who are parties to the convention.

In conclusion, the best means for achieving global regulation is through the convergence of national laws, which conform to international laws, conventions, treaties or model laws.[34] There are two different methods for converging law. One involves an international treaty that binds parties to certain matters that must be included in new laws or require laws to be

for Managing the Internal Market', in *E-commerce Law: National and Transnational Topics and Perspectives*, eds Henk Snijders and Stephen Weatherill, Kluwer Law International, The Hague, London, New York, 2003, pp. 9-25. See also Sparrow, *The Law of Internet & Mobile Communications: the EU and US Contrasted*, pp. 71-72.

[32] Reed, *Internet Law: Text and Materials,* pp. 217-218. An example of an approximation style national scheme is the European Union's 'single passport' for banking services. A credit institution established in, and regulated by one country, is free to provide banking services in all other countries. There are comparable schemes for financial, insurance and electronic signature services.

[33] Ibid., p. 221. Home and host country regulation does not have to be the same, just broadly equivalent.

[34] For example, the international legal principle of *jus cogens* requires a general universal law that has to be adhered to before an international treaty can pass, that is, an international consensus on an area must apply universally. Behaviour that is universally unacceptable, for example, genocide, provides the parameter for deciding on priorities in areas to regulate. Enforcement is through the extension of the principles of territoriality, strengthening international criminal law, and implementation nationally of agreed principles. Viktor Mayer-Schönberger and Teree E. Foster, 'A Regulatory Web: Free Speech and the Global Information Infrastructure', in *Borders In Cyberspace: Information Policy and the Global Information Infrastructure,* MIT Press, Cambridge, Mass., 1997, pp. 244-247.

amended. International conventions already exist for intellectual property, privacy and commercial law. The 'convergence' of law in areas of universal concern on the Internet, such as pornography and privacy, provide a working model. The European Union data protection schemes are based on national or 'home country' regulation, that is, each country has to have an adequate level of protection, and is also applied to non-European Union countries that trade with the European Union. Home country regulation is far less workable where there are conflicts between national laws.[35] The alternative approach is the 'model law' which is based on existing rules together with new rules added by experts, and approved by representative governments. They are sufficiently similar to provide uniform standards of conduct, with local variations if needed, for example the United Nations Commission on International Trade Law (UNCITRAL), which is the basis of national electronic transactions legislation.[36] The 'model law' has been the trend followed in major areas of concern such as electronic commerce. National jurisdiction is still meaningful, but global approaches provide an essential umbrella for areas of universal concern.

7.1.3 Recordkeeping and web 'business' transactions

Recordkeeping functionality in web-based systems has been slow to emerge.[37] The current web context is characterised by the 'one-stop shop' websites, for example portals acting as a single entry into the Internet or into an intranet. 'Intranets' and 'extranets' are used by businesses to

---

[35] Publishing information that contravenes the laws of foreign countries is possible, if the website is hosted elsewhere. Reed, *Internet Law: Text and Materials,* pp. 231-232. However, *Dow Jones Inc. V Gutnick* would now have to be taken into account.

[36] Goldring, 'Netting the Cybershark', pp. 340-351.

[37] The National Archives, United Kingdom, *Management of Electronic Records on Websites and Intranets: an ERM Toolkit*, Dec. 2001; National Archives of Australia, *Policy and Guidelines for Keeping Records of Web-based Activity in the Commonwealth Government*, revised January 2001. Initial studies on websites found that there were no provisions to capture web records into a recordkeeping system. See Richard Barry, 'Factoring Web Technologies into the Knowledge Management Equation ... for the Record', in *Intranets: Problems and Opportunities for Recordkeeping, Proceedings Conducted by the ACT Branch of the Records Management Association of Australia at Parliament House, Canberra, 10-11 March 1999,* ed. Anthony Eccleston, Records Management Association of Australia, ACT Branch, Canberra, 1999, p. 10.

demarcate the use of the Internet for specific types of functions, often on industry or 'communities of common interest' lines, for example banking, retail, and health.[38] Intranets are also used within an organisation as a vehicle dedicated to carrying out core business including recordkeeping. Electronic service delivery online includes government business to business activity, and an increasing requirement to identify website owners and consumers for business transactions.

While security is a continuing thorn in the side for all businesses using the web, recordkeeping software now exists that creates an enduring audit trail of each customer's web session exactly as the user saw it, and can be 'archived' as a record.[39] However as a record must be intentionally created for a 'business' purpose, and form part of a business process, only transactions that are needed for business should be captured. The process is essentially no different from the kinds of recordkeeping metadata that must be captured to create a reliable record. The record has to identify the parties to the transaction, and capture other metadata on time and place, in order to resolve any dispute about what someone saw on the website when the transaction occurred. This includes evidence of what a consumer saw in cases of misleading advertising and other consumer law issues. Therefore evidence of action has to be incorporated into website functionality, or specifically the intranet has to operate as part of the recordkeeping system of an organisation.

What legal liabilities ensue from the nature of recordkeeping related to doing business on the Internet? Legislation to facilitate the use of the web

---

[38] 'The intranet is the use of internet technologies within an agency deployed on an internal network based on open WWW technologies'. The intranet and the Internet can use the same server. By selective extension an intranet becomes an extranet. Extranets are external intranets that allow an organisation to permit selected customers or suppliers to securely connect via the web to carry out electronic commerce or other transactions. However public access websites are also used for business transactions, so the distinction between extranets and the Internet is blurred. See Barry, 'Factoring Web Technologies into the Knowledge Management Equation ... for the Record', pp. 9-12.

[39] 'Webcapture' is a software product which creates an enduring audit trail of each customer's web session, 'exactly as the user saw it', for dispute resolution purposes. This still allows the customisation of the page for each user. It has potential for recordkeeping online if linked to appropriate metadata. David Braue, 'Seeing Is Believing for Online Dealers,' *The Age*, 2 March 2001. Vignette is the distributor of 'Webcapture'. See also the Indiana University Electronic Records Project, Phase II, 2000-2002, which addresses the capture of electronic records from transaction-based systems by using portal technology and a workflow engine.

for commerce so that electronic transactions are legally acceptable, supports the creation and capture of records. For example, in the *Revised Explanatory Memorandum* to the Australian federal Electronic Transactions Bill 1999 (Cth) an 'electronic communication' is defined as 'a communication of information by means of guided and/or unguided electromagnetic energy. The term "communication" should also be interpreted broadly. Information that is recorded, stored or retained in an electronic form but is not transmitted immediately after being created is intended to fall within the scope of an "electronic communication"'.[40] Therefore an intention to transmit the communication makes it a valid communication for the purposes of the Act. The definition below of transaction includes non-commercial ones and its broad meaning would capture all kinds of communication over the Internet.

> 'Transaction' is defined to include transactions of a non-commercial nature. This term is intended to be read in its broadest sense of doing something, whether it be conducting or negotiating a business deal or simply providing information or a statement. It should not be read narrowly to confine it to contractual or commercial relationships. Nor is it limited to the actual transmission of the information. The purpose of this definition is to clearly include within the meaning of transactions any transactions with or by the government. For example, it includes activities of government agencies in their role as service providers and it includes instances where citizens furnish information to a government agency. This definition is intended to remove any doubt about the broad meaning of the word and is not intended to limit the existing breadth of the legal meaning of 'transaction'.[41]

The relevance of consent to electronic communications is expressed as:

> 'Consent' includes consent that can reasonably be inferred from the conduct of the person concerned. This term is used in clauses 9, 10 and 11 in provisions that state a person must consent to receiving information in the form of an electronic communication. While consent would clearly be demonstrated by a person's express statement of consent, the purpose of this definition is to ensure that express consent is not required in every case and that *consent can be inferred from, for example, a history of transactions or previous dealings*. However, when determining whether consent can be inferred from a person's conduct it will be necessary to look at the circumstances of the electronic communication, including the express statements of the person.[42]

---

[40] *Electronic Transactions Bill 1999,* Revised Explanatory Memorandum, p. 21.

[41] Ibid., p. 23. The term 'transaction' as defined in cl 5 of the Electronic Transactions Bill 1999.

[42] Ibid., p. 20. [Emphasis added]

As established in previous chapters, intention and consent are also important to legal liability and to moral responsibility. The *Electronic Transactions Act* 1999 (Cth) requires evidence of implied consent to continuous dealings and therefore supports capturing communications systematically in recordkeeping systems, not just as one-off unrelated communications. Systematic capture of communications is an essential recordkeeping function.

Controls over domain names also have recordkeeping implications as they affect identity ('owners' of a website), and their reputation.[43] The reliability and the authenticity of the website creators are essential to the credibility of the records. Domain names provide a provenancial source, thus registries of domain names, owners, registration details are record-keeping metadata essential to networked records.[44]

A record in the Internet context is more than just any kind of electronic information or data, with the notion of 'communication' over the Internet as pivotal to the recognition of record transactionality. The adoption of the terms 'electronic communication' (from information technology) and 'transaction' (from business) in Australian electronic commerce legislation are examples of this change.

---

[43] No one has been regarded as the 'owner' of the Internet, however the management of domain names and a number of other areas that originated in the United States are now assigned by the Internet Corporation for Assigned Names and Numbers, a non-profit public benefit corporation. It is responsible for both formal and informal procedures, coordinates domain-name assignments, Internet Protocol addresses, and root server management. These areas do impinge on legal regulation in particular the control over domain names, trademark and 'brand' connections. Milton Mueller, Commentary, 'ICANN and Internet Regulation', in *Communications of the ACM*, vol. 42, no. 6, June 1999, pp. 41-43.

[44] The authenticity of actual sites is an issue that has been tackled by the Australian government. Paul Twomey, 'The Information Economy and Electronic Recordkeeping: An Australian Perspective', in *Archives at Risk: Accountability, Vulnerability and Credibility*, Australian Society of Archivists Conference Proceedings, 29-31 July 1999, Brisbane, ASA Inc., Canberra 2002, pp. 33-36.

7.2 Ownership, privacy, access, evidence and recordkeeping on the web

Different countries have taken diverse paths in relation to regulating the Internet.[45] Some countries have passed technology-specific legislation, for example United States digital signature legislation, while other countries have technology-neutral law or 'electronic equivalencies', for example Australian electronic commerce and copyright law, so that both the tangible old world product continues to be protected as well as the new one. Changes in evidence law have been supportive of recordkeeping concepts and these have been endorsed in the electronic commerce frameworks. Electronic commerce, privacy and intellectual property legislation are also examples of where there are existing global frameworks that accommodate divergences in national jurisdictions.

7.2.1 Ownership and web 'business' transactions

There are a number of approaches that can be taken to the issue of ownership of records in the web environment. These include replacing property concepts with process or provenance definitions for establishing ownership over records, as discussed in Chapter 5. Other approaches are analysed below.

Personal property law

The legal concepts of ownership, previously tied to the material or tangible form of a record, is a major legal issue on the Internet, due to the legal classification of personal property law on the basis of a corporeal-incorporeal dichotomy.[46] Some property lawyers suggest replacing the term 'record', which has been aligned to its physical container or medium such as paper, with electronic 'information', as a more appropriate means of controlling a thing that is intangible. Case law has been reluctant to treat

[45] Chapter 5 covered the issues of ownership, privacy, access and evidence of records and the areas of law which are used to claim ownership or invoked when proprietary information has been 'stolen', sold, or copied. This chapter analyses some of the ways that proprietary information, privacy, access and evidence are, or could be, protected in records in the Internet environment.

[46] With some exceptions, property concepts such as possession, custody and control have applied only to a tangible material object. See Simon Fisher, 'The Archival Enterprise, Public Archival Institutions and the Impact of Private Law', *Archives and Manuscripts*, vol. 26, no. 2, Nov. 1998, p. 354.

information as property, for example when electronic data is deleted or modified it has not been considered as theft or damage to property. Instead unauthorised access must be proven.[47]

Chris Reed presents a picture of 'dematerialised' communications which never produce physical objects.[48] He argues that each computer by passing on copies of documents makes traditional legal distinctions of originals and copies meaningless. However, from an archival science perspective, it can also be argued that like paper records, 'copies' of a digital document may be in multiple locations. It is the document's insertion into the recordkeeping system or linked by an 'archival bond' to related documents that makes it a record. Within a recordkeeping perspective of legal and social relationships it has been argued that the record is a 'right-duty' thing as relationship which is both an object and the result of a process, which transcends issues of physicality. In a number of evidence laws, a 'document' has been extended to include all forms of recorded information[49] that eliminates the materiality-immateriality distinction.

The law of obligations

As property is a legal relationship, the law of obligations would appear to provide another way of protecting property in electronic networked records. Instead of a relationship between a person and an object (the record) that exists in personal property law, the relationship is between two persons and their duties and rights in respect of ownership. This model has merit in the Internet world where legal and social relationships are being

---

[47] Reed, *Internet Law: Text and Materials,* p. 149, footnote 8, refers to *Cox v Riley* (1986) 83 Cr App Rep 54 in which the defendant was convicted of criminal damage when he deleted computer programs stored on a magnetic tape; the damage was to the storage medium. The case was considered conceptually problematic and was later overturned by the *Computer Misuse Act* 1990 (UK) s 3, by substituting a new offence of 'unauthorised access' to a computer with intent to modify its contents, and thus avoiding property terms.

[48] Ibid., p. 148. See also Thomas Hoeren, 'Electronic Commerce and Law: Some Fragmentary Thoughts on the Future of Internet Regulation from a German Perspective', in *Legal Aspects of Globalization: Conflict of Laws, Internet, Capital Markets and Insolvency in a Global Economy*, eds Jürgen Basedow and Toshiyuki Kono, Kluwer Law International, The Hague, London, Boston, 2000, pp. 35-47.

[49] See Chapter 2, 'Rules of Evidence and Trustworthy Records' and the definitions of documents in the Australian *Evidence Act* 1995 (Cth), Dictionary, Part 1, as 'any record of information'; the *Acts Interpretation Act* 1901 (Cth) s 25 and the *Archives Act* 1983 (Cth) s 3(1).

redefined. As the law of obligations is a private law concept, it applies to private transactions which are the dominant form of interchange on the Internet. It can be developed further in the online context if rights and duties pertaining to ownership are tied to specific legal and social relationships.[50]

Reconceptualisation of property: intention, control and ownership

Fisher provides an exposé of the property term 'possession' as interpreted via case law.[51] It has two dimensions: 'intent' (legal possession) and 'control' (actual/de facto possession), which are used to identify who has possession and how it is realised in practice. These understandings of possession are concepts that can apply in relation to 'control' over networked electronic records through the notion of the 'intent to possess' as control. However, Fisher also points to the fact that possession and ownership do not change between entities that are the same legal person, for example in a Westminster system the archival authority and other government agencies are the same legal person, that is, the Crown. An archival authority cannot gain possession, only custody of a government agency's records, unless possession is split along the lines of 'intent' and 'control without immediate physical possession'. Custody therefore remains an important property tool for archival preservation.

Ownership is not only based on physical possession. An alternative concept associated with 'custody' of records, encompasses rights over records by a third party, the records however remaining in the physical possession of the creator. This is recognised in relation to access to records under Freedom of Information laws when the government outsources particular activities; the records are considered to be in the possession of the government agency, even if physically with the outsourcer. It is termed 'constructive possession'.[52] A contract could also assign ownership rights

---

[50] See Chapter 8, 'Legal and social relationships online: the medical, consumer and government context'.

[51] Chapter 5 on legal and actual possession introduced the notion of possession without physical possession and rights of possession as intention and 'control' which are particularly appropriate in the digital environment. See Fisher, 'The Archival Enterprise', pp. 332-333 and Albert Kocourek, *Jural Relations*, 2nd edn, The Bobbs-Merrill Company, Indianapolis, 1928, p. 372.

[52] W.B. Lane, 'Government Decision Making-Freedom of Information and Judicial Review: Accessing Government Information', in *Government Law and Policy, Commercial Aspects,* ed. Bryan Horrigan, The Federation Press, Leichhardt, NSW, 1998, p. 121 and Madeline Campbell, 'FOI Access to

in records held by an Internet service provider or computer host to another party.

Property law could remain a powerful control tool over recordkeeping in the Internet context if it could divest itself of the materiality-immateriality dichotomy. The distinction is really a red herring. As Frank Upward has suggested, what really matters is the 'intent' to have a recordkeeping system (Fisher's 'intent to possess'), while the logical design of the system and its implementation (physical) is 'control'. Materiality remains within the physical implementation tasks, but 'control' resides with the 'intent' taken account of in the design of the system.[53] Intent and control are inextricably connected. The disappearance of recordkeeping containers which stem from a physical sense of object is similar to computer 'objects'. However there are still electronic containers in the form of electronic documents. A digital object can have layers of contextual data that include authorship and access rights that can be redacted for different users, and it is independent of the media on which it is stored. In fact the core object and its related parts that give it meaning are logically connected by software, thus it is a 'thing-object as relationship'.

Metadata-encapsulated objects have physicality; they should be able to be 'bailed' or controlled through constructive possession. For example, 'control' is adopted in the *State Records Act* 1998 (NSW) s 6 in relation to the record owner (the state) and the person in possession of the record. The provision enacts that a person has 'control' of a record if she/he has possession or custody of it, whether directly or personally, or indirectly or remotely through another person, thus resorting to property concepts that may involve either bailment or constructive possession.[54] The provision retains property concepts because possession is important to control.

Control is really intent to possess. Archival institutions could be implementation sites, and claim physical possession. In the 'virtual

---

Electronic Records', in *Playing for Keeps,* ed. Stephen Yorke, Australian Archives, Canberra, 1995, p. 191. Constructive possession within Freedom of Information legislation has been a difficult legal argument to adopt in terms of ownership.

[53] These ideas grew out of a discussion on the materiality-immateriality dichotomy with my Monash colleague, Frank Upward, in 1998-99, an expert on the application of postmodernist thought to recordkeeping concepts and practices. The ideas have potential for further development. Upward's argument is that the physical recordkeeping containers now need to be viewed logically and that the operational sites for recordkeeping are the new physicality. The immateriality-materiality division has been reshuffled. In his postmodern form of phrasing, the old duality is replaced by a variable dualism.

[54] Fisher, 'The Archival Enterprise', pp. 343-344.

archives' location is still relevant. Storage of and responsibility for control over the records over time, and their ownership, have to be attributed and managed.

A separation of de facto possession from legal possession is endorsed in the International Records Management Standard. It supports the arrangement of records that are physically stored in one location but owned by another person or entity.

> Records systems should be capable of supporting alternative options for the location of records. In some cases, where the legal and regulatory environment allows this, records may be physically stored with one organization, but the responsibility and management control reside with either the creating organization or another appropriate authority. Such arrangements, *distinguishing between storage, ownership and responsibility for records, are particularly relevant for records in electronic records systems.* Variations in these arrangements may occur at any time in the systems' existence and any changes to these arrangements should be traceable and documented.[55]

Distributed custody or distributed management provides for electronic records that may never be physically transferred to an archival agency even if they are under the legal custody of the archives.

Despite Fisher's elucidation of the division of property into intent to control as a form of possession, property law still distinguishes ownership and control. Another approach has been to simply replace the concept of ownership associated with a document as object with 'control' or 'custodianship' of networked records. Some medical information managers propose custodianship as a means of control over content and use of personal medical information, with access principles based on rights of the data collector, intellectual rights of the provider and rights of the general community to the patient information.[56]

Given property law's entrenchment in material and immaterial distinctions, it is being jettisoned for rights of access and control by different parties to networked records. Fisher's 'intent' (legal possession) and 'control' (actual/de facto possession) are not distinguished. The law of obligations rather than common law property concepts have been adopted to some extent by the move to access rights of different parties. The need to distinguish between ownership, access and storage - where records are held and who owns them - is essential to web transactions.

---

[55] ISO, *International Records Management Standard,* ISO 15489-1, section 8.3.4, 'Distributed Management'. [Emphasis added.]

[56] NSW Health Department, *Ethical Management of Health Information,* Discussion Paper, Better Health Care Centre, Gladesville, NSW, Nov. 1999, p. 13.

Common law rights and property

Simon Fisher has suggested that common law rights found in torts, equity and contract may protect 'intangible property', but are largely untested. The use of the tort of conversion as it applies to rights over incorporeal property, such as money, may apply to electronic data, and the tort of 'spoliation of evidence' that is, seeking damages for intentionally destroying records, could apply to records in any form.[57] Trespass also has application to interfering with electronic information.[58]

7.2.2 Intellectual property and web 'business' transactions

Intangible personal property, protected through intellectual property, in particular copyright, patents and trademarks, has been the major developmental area in Internet regulation. Copyright, in particular, because of its obvious connection to the content on the Internet, may provide a

---

[57] Danuta Mendelson, *Torts,* 3rd edn, Butterworths Casebook Companions, Butterworths, Sydney, 2002, pp. 118-119. Mendelson's explanation of 'spoliation of evidence' is as follows: '… The Privy Council in *The Ophelia* [1916] 2 AC 206 extended the operation of the [spoliation] maxim to the negligent destruction of evidence. The maxim has been recognised in Australia (*Ford v Andrews* (1916) 21 CLR 317 at 324; *McHale v Watson* (1964) 111 CLR 384 at 398). In the United States, *Smith v Superior Court* 198 Cal Rptr (Ct App 1984) was the first to establish an independent tort of spoliation of evidence, which safeguards the interest of the parties to a civil litigation in preservation of evidentiary material against an unreasonable interference with it. Although the majority of cases so far have involved spoliation of objects, the advent of shredding machines, and, more recently, the widespread use of electronic records and their potential for destruction of documents that may be vital to the outcome of civil litigation should help the recognition of this cause of action in Australia.' See also US-InterPARES Project, *Findings on the Preservation of Authentic Electronic Records*, Final Report to the National Historical Publications and Records Commission, 2002, pp. 87-88.

[58] Trespass to goods is the unjustified interference with or denial of the owner's right to possession of the goods. Chris Reed interprets trespass to apply only to the server (= goods) on which the website is stored, as the website is 'intangible'. Reed, *Internet Law: Text and Materials,* pp. 69-70. In footnote 5, p. 69 he refers to an alternative view of trespass based on theories of property which include unauthorised access to the website. Trespass only provides a remedy against interference with goods or land which adversely affect the plaintiff's right of possession. If trespass is developed to encompass the transient interference with the land or goods involved in accessing a website, the person making the link is not trespassing, only the viewer.

preferable legal means of ownership of electronic records rather than concepts of personal property already discussed.[59] For recordkeeping professionals it is more likely that evidence and contract law will remain the cornerstone of the legal issues relating to transactions on the Internet, but copyright law is also increasingly relevant (see below).

Intellectual property, in the electronic information industry has included databases, individual items in a database, computer software and even inventive hardware.[60] An electronic recordkeeping system is likely to be classed as a database. However, intellectual property presents difficulties as rights prevent others from performing certain acts in respect of the protected 'work'. Copyright protects the form of expression, not the ideas or the data in the work. The form and the expression are no longer united in electronic products. The 'rights' rather than the property are 'intangible' and the item protected needs to have a 'material form', such as a film, or a literary work. The text of a web page is protected in different 'forms', as a literary work, graphic images as artistic work, sound and video as sound recording and as film, and the whole as a compilation (a literary work).[61] Despite difficulties with enforcement, there is no question that copyright does subsist in transactions on the Internet.[62]

With Internet access, records, like other information resources, are likely to be accessible directly from the creating agencies or archival authorities by remote users. 'Transmission', 'copying', and 'reproduction' occur simultaneously (which are rights of the copyright owner), when online public access is available. This means that copyright law applies to access where it did not for its analogue counterpart. Access to records that may have been free in the paper world when access and copying were separate activities, now has to be paid for as part of copyright permissions.

'Internet' copyright law: the international context

Intellectual property has an existing international framework which provides protection outside the country of creation of a 'work' at least for the signatories of the *Berne Copyright Convention* to which many

---

[59] Graham J.H. Smith et al. (eds), *Internet Law and Regulation: A Specially Commissioned Report*, F.T. Law & Tax, London, 1996, p. 13.

[60] Charles Oppenheim, *The Legal and Regulatory Environment for Electronic Information,* 2nd edn, Infonortics Ltd, Calne, 1995, p. 3.

[61] Reed, *Internet Law: Text and Materials* p. 73.

[62] Edward A. Cavazos and Gavino Morin, in *Cyberspace and the Law,* MIT Press, Cambridge, Mass., London, 1994, p. 56.

countries belong.[63] It is an international right and therefore of particular importance to online copyright protection. The treaties between member countries usually provide national protection which means that the law of the country where the work is used is applied.[64] The international treaties only cover minimum standards, and domestic copyright law differs substantially from country to country.[65]

However, with the Internet, there has been uncertainty about where a work is 'used'. It could be where it is uploaded onto a website, or where it is downloaded, or perhaps in other countries along the way. As recent court cases suggest, the question of which country has jurisdiction over the Internet is a source of debate around the world. The relationship between the location where the work was originally posted and the place where the infringement has occurred is relevant. Jurisdiction is decided on the rules of conflicts of laws in each country (see jurisdiction above). Because of the diversity of copyright schemes there may be difficulty in a consensus on the model to follow in a single international copyright law.[66]

The Internet has brought together both restrictive and permissive copyright regimes, that is, those that protect and control the distribution of intellectual products and those that consider it inefficient to do so.

---

[63] One hundred and sixty states are parties to the *Berne Copyright Convention* as of April 2005. In 1994 the Berne Convention was incorporated into a major international treaty as TRIPS (Trade Related Aspects of Intellectual Property), which is administered by the World Trade Organization and has mechanisms for breaches via trade sanctions. See Brian Fitzgerald, 'International Initiatives Concerning Copyright in the Digital Era', in *Going Digital 2000, Legal Issues for E-commerce, Software and the Internet*, eds Anne Fitzgerald, et al., 2nd edn, Prospect Media, St. Leonards, New South Wales, 2000, p. 90.

[64] If a copy is made of an article published by an American author in Canada, then Canadian copyright law applies. It is possible to have a treaty that applies protection one would receive in one's home country. This is the principle of reciprocity. Ibid., pp. 87-89. Trade agreements also affect domestic copyright law, for example the Australia/US Free Trade Agreement (AUSFTA). See Australian Copyright Council, *Access to Copyright Material in Australia and the US,* Information Sheet G087v01, September 2004.

[65] Jane C. Ginsburg, 'Putting Cars on the "Information Superhighway": Authors, Exploiters and Copyright in Cyberspace', in F. Hugenholz, *The Future of Copyright in a Digital Environment,* Information Law Series, no. 4, The Hague, Kluwer Law International, 1996, pp. 189-220.

[66] 'Editorial', *The Copyright & New Media Law Newsletter: For Libraries, Archives & Museums,* vol. 5, issue 1, 2001. See also Masato Dogauchi, 'Law Applicable to Torts and Copyright Infringement through the Internet', in *Legal Aspects of Globalization,* pp. 49-65, in which he suggests that a single set of copyright laws is difficult but should be pursued through the WTO.

Localisation of piracy in information products has moved to anywhere in the world. Bringing more countries into an international regime is posited as a solution.[67] The 1996 World Intellectual Property Organization (WIPO) treaties referred to as the 'internet treaties' were precipitated by issues of enforcing copyright law in relation to content communicated via the web.[68] They required countries adhering to the Berne Convention to amend their copyright legislation to conform with the articles of the treaties.[69] The most relevant changes in the treaties have related to Article 8, referred to as the right of 'making available to the public' which specifically covers uses of copyright in online services and Articles 11 and 12 that deal with technological circumvention obligations. The articles provide an example of where the Internet and other communication technologies have called for a new approach to copyright law.

The disagreements among the Berne convention countries over the 1996 WIPO *Treaty on Intellectual Property in respect of Databases* is a recent example of the difficulties of international agreement on intellectual property.[70] One of the controversial issues here was the new *sui generic* right for databases as a whole to be a separate category, apart from protection for individual content such as an image, which would prevent the use of a substantial part of the database for fifteen years, renewable when significantly updated. In theory a database would be protected forever. Compilations of data presently receive protection under copyright in the selection and arrangement of data. The data itself has generally not

[67] Dan L. Burk, 'The Market for Digital Piracy', in *Borders in Cyberspace: Information Policy and the Global Information Infrastructure,* eds Brian Kahin and Charles Nesson, MIT Press, Cambridge, Mass., 1997, pp. 205-234.

[68] World Intellectual Property Organization, *WIPO Copyright Treaty,* adopted by the Diplomatic Conference on December 20, 1996, WIPO 1996.

[69] An example of the implementation of the World Intellectual Property Organization (WIPO) treaties is the Australian *Copyright Amendment (Digital Agenda) Act* 2000 which together with the *Copyright Amendment (Moral Rights) Act* 2000 amended the Commonwealth *Copyright Act* 1968. These amendments include statutory moral rights, amendments to the fair dealing provisions, and the introduction of a new transmission right.

[70] World Intellectual Property Organization, *Basic Proposal for the Substantive Provisions of the Treaty on Intellectual Property in Respect of Databases to be Considered by the Diplomatic Conference Geneva, December 2 to 20 1996,* 30 August, 1996. WIPO proposed that facts or data in a database could be copyrighted. The extension of ownership over facts, with strict liability for infringement placed onto Internet Service Providers, would override fair use and free competition. It would increase monitoring and privacy interference, and protect large database operators.

been given copyright protection but case law has varied significantly on the matter.[71] The 1992 European Commission Directive on Database Protection has gradually been adopted in European Union member countries. The protection of data itself as a form of intellectual property is a major change to copyright law. The extension of copyright to cover data would have some effect on ownership of the content in records if they are classed as a database for the purposes of copyright law.

International copyright reforms indicate a continuing protection of material in non-interactive form, with new rights to cover transmission of material over the Internet. Increased protection has continued to favour copyright owners at the expense of users, compounded by licensing agreements and other forms of contract that modify exceptions granted under copyright law.[72]

Infringement and enforcement of copyright

The new right of communication makes works that are digitally transmitted without the owners' authorisation an infringement of the communication right (Article 8 of WIPO). Generally copyright infringements are due to unauthorised transmission or downloading of protected data or programs.

---

[71] The concept of copyright arising from 'added value' to facts through creative effort, has not been interpreted consistently by the courts. In the United States, names, addresses and phone numbers have not been given copyright protection. If copyright in facts is accepted in the United States, it would overturn the 1991 US Supreme Court decision in *Feist Publications Inc. v Rural Telephone Service* 499 US 340 (1990), as discussed in Chapter 5, footnote 53. In an Australian case regarding originality of facts, English rather than American precedents were used. In *Desktop Marketing Systems Pty Ltd v Telstra Corporation Limited* (2002) FCAFC 112, Telstra argued that compiling a telephone directory database required intelligence and effort while DTMS argued that it was only a collection of data. The judge used English precedents that have interpreted timetables as original works, and made it clear that database rights subsisted in the telephone directory. In the Netherlands in *KPN v Denda* a telephone directory was given copyright protection on the basis of the substantial investment in its production. See Dirk Visser, 'The Database Right and the Spin-off Theory', in *E-commerce Law: National and Transnational Topics and Perspectives*, eds Henk Snijders and Stephen Weatherill, Kluwer Law International, The Hague, London, New York, 2003, pp. 105-110.

[72] For a comment on the US situation, see US-InterPARES Project, *Findings on the Preservation of Authentic Electronic Records,* p. 86.

One must first establish that there is a copyright 'work' involved, and that it has been infringed.[73]

The notion of copying from the 'original' is nonsensical, as the copy is identical to the 'original', in terms of its content. However, original in its recordkeeping definition means the one that has all its meaningful elements, including its recordkeeping metadata. In the amended Australian Copyright Act to copy or to reproduce are used synonymously. The copyright concern is that an exact copy of something belongs to someone else; the issue of being a corrupted copy is relevant to an authentic record and contravenes the creator's moral rights of integrity.

The exclusive right of authorising any communication to the public, 'making available' provides the proprietor with a potential remedy, that is, the person making it available is the infringer. Reed claims that many of the lacunae in law relating to commercial Internet activities can only be filled by laws such as unfair competition and trade reputation, based on concepts of wrongful behaviour rather than property concepts. One can also use contract law, and identify the user or the rightful owner of an electronic publication via electronic signatures. Technological approaches to copyright protection are also relevant to enforcement (see below).

Technological protection of copyright

Technological means of protecting intellectual property have evolved from an early focus on encrypted content to the use of intellectual objects with controls over use. Locking out users include the use of password protection and hardware devices. Legal liability for circumvention of these devices is considered critical to copyright on the Internet.[74] There are concerns on how fair dealing can apply if all copyrighted material is protected by technical means.[75] The WIPO Articles 11 and 12 introduce a requirement for effective legal remedies for the removal of any technological means of circumventing copyright. However, the WIPO articles on technological circumvention of copyright may also affect 'the ability to make copies when migrating from one storage technology to another, and to reformat,

[73] Gordon Hughes and David Cosgrove, 'The Internet - Legal Questions', *Law Institute Journal*, vol. 69, no. 4, April 1995, pp. 326-327.

[74] In Australia, the *Copyright Amendment (Digital Agenda) Act* 2000 s 16B prohibits the removal or alteration of electronic rights management information. Copyright management information is also agent and use metadata.

[75] David Brennan, 'Simplification, Circumvention, Fair Dealing and Australian Copyright Law', in *Going Digital 2000, Legal Issues for E-commerce, Software and the Internet*, eds Anne Fitzgerald, et al., 2nd edn, Prospect Media, St. Leonards, New South Wales, 2000, p. 106.

thereby creating derivative works when moving from one software technology to the next.'[76] From a recordkeeping perspective technological circumvention provisions may present an obstacle to long term digital preservation which can only be a reproduction of an original work and may include migration of proprietary software and record metadata. Where copyright legislative exemptions for archival preservation exist they are frequently based on a custodial model that requires the archives instituition to have physical custody of the copyrighted work for the exemptions to apply.[77] The preservation of an electronic record must be considered at the time of a record's creation when it is unlikely to be in the physical custody of an archival organisation rather than after the expiration of copyright, for example, seventy years after the author's death.[78]

The prohibition on circumventing the technological devices in the United States is found in the *Digital Millennium Copyright Act* 1998 (US) s 1201(a)(1)(A) which provides that 'no person shall circumvent a technological measure that effectively controls access to a work protected under this 'title'. Excluded are works that the Librarian of Congress determines.'[79] The purpose of the exemption by the Library of Congress is to ensure that particular classes of works to which users are, or are likely to be, adversely affected in their ability to make noninfringing uses due to the prohibition on circumvention of access controls are allowable.[80] The Act

---

[76] US-InterPARES Project, *Findings on the Preservation of Authentic Electronic Records,* p. 84, (quoting from Committee on Intellectual Property Rights and the Emerging Information Infrastructure, *The Digital Dilemma: Intellectual Property in the Information Age*, National Academy Press, Washington DC, 2000, p. 119.)

[77] Ibid., p. 85; Filip Boudrez and Sofie Van den Eynde, *Archiving Websites,* State Archives of Antwerp, Antwerp-Leuven, 2002, p. 91.

[78] An exception for libraries and archives in the US in the last twenty years of copyright protection would be of little use for preservation. US-InterPARES Project, *Findings on the Preservation of Authentic Electronic Records,* p. 86.

[79] Brennan, 'Simplification, Circumvention, Fair Dealing and Australian Copyright Law', p. 116.

[80] For example, October 28, 2003, the Librarian of Congress, on the recommendation of the Register of Copyrights, announced the classes of works subject to the exemption from the prohibition against circumvention of technological measures that control access to copyrighted works. These included: '(3) Computer programs and video games distributed in formats that have become obsolete and which require the original media or hardware as a condition of access. A format shall be considered obsolete if the machine or system necessary to render perceptible a work stored in that format is no longer manufactured or is no longer reasonably available in the commercial marketplace.' United States Copyright Office, *Rulemaking on Exemptions from*

targets circumventing an access control mechanism to a work rather than the unauthorised use. However, in many cases access and security measures may be inseparable.[81] In Australia only the manufacture and supply, but not the use, of a circumvention device or service are proscribed by the *Copyright Act* 1968 (Cth). A circumvention device or service may be supplied for certain 'permitted purposes' which include copying by libraries and archives. The Australia/US Free Trade Agreement (AUSFTA) requires Australia to amend its provisions to operate as in the US, in particular the introduction of sanctions against circumventing a technological protection measure, and limitations on exceptions for circumvention.[82] While legal conformity provides for greater consistency between countries that are parties to a trade treaty such as AUSFTA it may also remove Australian provisions that are more advantageous to the preservation of records.

'Rights management information' (RMI) in the WIPO treaties provide sanctions for deliberate removal or tampering with copyright identification information electronically attached. The use of technology to protect copyright by fencing out unauthorised users has involved rights management software of two kinds. One that manages the rights, that is, the transactions dealing with the use of a digital object some of which need full identity disclosure, and the other that reduces 'usage' uncertainty.[83] Rights systems maintain data on the identity of the record creators. These systems duplicate recordkeeping metadata. The 'rights community' could also be analysed in the relationship model in terms of the copyright owner and the user, and other rights such as privacy.

Prohibition on Circumvention of Technological Measures that Control Access to Copyrighted Works, The Recommendation of the Register of Copyrights.

[81] Liong Lim, 'US Digital Millennium Copyright Act', *Internet Law Bulletin*, vol. 2, no. 1, Feb. 1999, pp. 11-14.

[82] Australian Copyright Council, *Access to Copyright Material in Australia and the US.* US court decisions on copyright have been in many instances quite different to Australia.

[83] Peter Higgs, 'Privacy Implications of On-line Intellectual Property Protection', in Papers from *The New Australian Privacy Landscape*, Faculty of Law, Continuing Legal Education, The University of New South Wales, 14 March 2001. Here the term 'rights' is used in relation to the rights of owners of copyright (rather than rights of users), who want their work protected which may lead to privacy infringement of users.

7.2.3 Web access to public records

Governments around the world have improved public access to government information via the Internet, by developing information locator systems which direct users to sources of relevant government information. From the users' perspective all government information whether a record or not will be available through a common user interface.

David Roberts, in 1995 in *Documenting the Future*, described future networked access to documents themselves: users login as 'guest users' with access rights and restrictions, data will be secured with 'firewalls' to separate them from publicly accessible parts, and applicants use the retrieval tools of the agency's recordkeeping system with necessary security safeguards, therefore reducing time and cost for the agency.[84] This scenario assumed that governments would release the records, provide safeguards, and secure the records as time bound into the future and make decisions on archival requirements. Networked access to an agency's records for the public user has not been implemented, and archival authorities are beginning to take custody of electronic records. Electronic access to government data, will involve some continuum in access, and consideration of bringing the access provisions of all legislation dealing with it together, that is, the public right to know as expressed in FOI and the right to privacy in privacy legislation. However, at present access in FOI, archival, and privacy legislation in many jurisdictions is often fragmented, and at times conflicting.

Which government records are made available will depend more on political will rather than the technology of the Internet. This is clearly visible in the watering down of FOI legislation in many countries due to security fears,[85] and the privatisation of government activities which have led to the reduction of the ambit of FOI.

7.2.4 Privacy and web 'business' transactions

There are good arguments for stronger privacy legislation for Internet electronic transactions. These include:

---

[84] David Roberts, *Documenting the Future, Policies and Strategies for Electronic Recordkeeping in the New South Wales Public Sector,* The Archives Authority of New South Wales, Sydney, 1995.

[85] Moira Paterson, *Freedom of Information and Privacy in Australia: Government and Information Access in the Modern State,* LexisNexis Butterworths, Chatswood, NSW, 2005, p. 8.

- the compilation of customer profiles derived from online contracts;
- unauthorised access to, distribution of and tampering with personal data in electronic networks with the possibility of destroying or interfering with the data (which means the record's integrity is threatened); and
- global data matching and surveillance of users of networks by government and between governments, law enforcement agencies and commercially-interested parties using private data dispersed amongst providers.

The relationships between the traditional players, and their respective rights and duties, may not translate into the online world. Contract and licensing have been used to bypass privacy, as well as copyright, defamation and censorship laws, but government contractors should be required to abide by privacy legislation.[86] There are often limitations in the privacy legislation in its application to the Internet, for example in Australia personal information is defined as '... an individual whose identity is apparent' (*Privacy Act* 1988 s 6) when identity is not apparent but may reside in the log of web access held on a server.[87]

In the European Union the scope of the definition of personal data is extremely wide, but the interpretation in relation to individual member states varies. For example, under Belgian data protection law 'personal data' is every piece of information regarding an identified or identifiable natural person. Data is identifiable if someone, the data controller or a third party, is able to link the data to a natural person using any reasonable means. An IP address is personal data as it is reasonably possible for an ISP to determine an 'identifiable' person to whom it belongs, even though the archivist may not be able to achieve this. The Netherlands has not taken the strict Belgian interpretation of identifiable personal data; it does not consider that in all cases IP addresses are personal data. The Dutch view is that the body processing the personal data has to have the ability to identify an individual via his/her IP address. An archivist could argue that, unlike the ISP, he/she does not have additional information to identify a person.[88]

---

[86] Gordon Hughes, 'Our Rapidly Expanding Privacy Obligations', *Law Institute Journal*, vol. 75, no. 6, July 2001, p. 58. Government contracts in Australia have to be consistent with the privacy regulations of Commonwealth agencies.

[87] Graham Greenleaf, 'Privacy Principles - Irrelevant to Cyberspace?', in *Internet Law Anthology*, ed. Peter Leonard, Prospect Intelligence Report, Prospect Publishing, Sydney, 1997, pp. 129-138.

[88] Boudrez and Van den Eynde, *Archiving Websites*, pp. 78-79.

Privacy: international context

The 1980 OECD *Guidelines on the Protection of Privacy and Transborder Flows of Personal Data*, the 1985 *Declaration on Transborder Data Flows* and the 1998 *Ministerial Declaration on the Protection of Privacy on Global Networks* represent international instruments on the collection and management of personal information.[89] Ensuring privacy in Internet transactions is a key consideration internationally. For mechanisms to be effective international regulations and agreements, not domestic, are an imperative. Without international consensus privacy in networks will not work.

> With increasing globalisation of e-commerce, privacy protection is rapidly becoming a transnational issue. As we do more and more transactions on-line, and as organizations contract out more and more functions - often offshore - we can no longer protect our privacy with purely domestic laws. Also, even where privacy regulations address wholly domestic activities, the standards expected are drawn from comparative international experience.[90]

The OECD in 1998 highlighted privacy as a fundamental requirement to give people confidence in the digital marketplace. It concluded that governments have fundamental responsibilities in this area, and that much is expected from, and dependent on, private sector initiatives.[91] Privacy is an area where international convergence is the model. However, there is considerable variation in how privacy is interpreted in online contexts. With the notable exception of the United States, privacy legislation has expanded in the last two decades. The United States 'Safe Harbor' arrangement with the European Union is a self-regulatory scheme which provides certain privacy safeguards and requires US companies that intend to receive personal data from EU countries to be registered within the scheme.[92] However it is not considered a suitable model by privacy advocates.

---

[89] OECD, Information Security and Privacy documents, 2005.

[90] Nigel Waters, 'A Comparative Analysis of Australian Privacy Laws with Special Reference to the Concept of "Adequacy" for the Purposes of the European Union Data Protection Directive', in Papers presented to *The New Australian Privacy Landscape*, Faculty of Law, Continuing Legal Education, The University of New South Wales, 14 March 2001 (no pagination).

[91] OECD, Ministerial Declaration on the Protection of Privacy on Global Networks, OECD Conference, *A Borderless World: Realising the Potential of Global Electronic Commerce,* Ottawa, 7-9 October 1998.

[92] The operation of Article 25 of the Data Protection Directive (95/46/EC) requires that member states take measures to prevent any transfer of personal data to a country that the European Commission finds provides inadequate privacy

Australian privacy law has drawn from external jurisdictions and international agreements and is a good example of international legal models that operate across borders.[93] The *Privacy Act* 1988 (Cth) is based on the OECD principles, and like intellectual property has an international context that is important in terms of Internet developments. The extension of Australian privacy law to the private sector brought Australia in line with international approaches. In relation to its international obligations, the *Privacy Amendment (Private Sector) Act* 2000 (Cth) has within its main objects focused on Australia's international obligations.[94] The national principles of particular relevance to the Internet are the option to remain anonymous when entering transactions (NPP8) and controls on transfers of personal information out of Australia (NPP9).[95] The extra-territorial operation of the Act covers personal information overseas if there is an organisational link with Australia, but it only covers Australians.

---

protection. An alternative transfer method from EU countries to other countries is under EU model clauses. Sparrow, *The Law of Internet and Mobile Communications: The EU and US Contrasted*, pp. 12-38.

[93] Hughes, 'Our Rapidly Expanding Privacy Obligations', p. 60. In fact the European Commission undertakes adequacy assessments of national privacy laws, and did not consider the amendments to the *Privacy Act* 1988 (Cth) as adequate for data transfers to Australia from Europe.

[94] *Privacy Amendment (Private Sector) Act* 2000 (Cth) s 3.

[95] Graham Greenleaf, 'Privacy Principles: Problems in Cyberspace - Likely Areas of Controversy and Interpretation', in Papers from *The New Australian Privacy Landscape*, Faculty of Law, Continuing Legal Education, The University of New South Wales, 14 March 2001, p. 7. There are some transactions where anonymity may be desirable. Pseudonyms have been suggested as a preferable principle to anonymous transactions as certification authorities could hold the real names separately to prevent their disclosure. Transfers of personal information out of Australia are exempted from obtaining consent in s 9(e)(ii) of the *Privacy Act* 1988 (Cth). The EU position is found in *2002/58/EC on Privacy and Electronic Communications,* '(9) The Member States, providers and users concerned, together with the competent Community bodies, should cooperate in introducing and developing the relevant technologies where this is necessary to apply the guarantees provided for by this Directive and taking particular account of the objectives of minimising the processing of personal data and of using anonymous or pseudonymous data where possible. (33) Member States should encourage the development of electronic communication service options such as alternative payment facilities which allow anonymous or strictly private access to publicly available electronic communications services, for example calling cards and facilities for payment by credit card.' *Official Journal of the European Communities*, L 201/37, 31.7.2002. See also Michael Kirby, 'Privacy in Cyberspace', *University of NSW Law Journal*, vol. 21, no. 2, 1998, pp. 323-33.

As with other Internet legal issues if one country does not protect privacy, it becomes unenforceable across borders. Even if principles are the same, substantive differences may apply to different categories, for example a consumer may have to consent or follow opt-in or opt-out provisions. Standards may be insufficient, for example many American companies agreed to adhere to the OECD standards but few changed their practices. A detailed voluntary international privacy code adopted by merchants and consumers with specific responsibilities, along with rights of consumers, some oversight of the activities, as well as practical remedies such as auditing and electronic dispute resolution mechanisms, are required. Adjudication can be implemented through private sector arbitration, but may still not meet the adequacy test of the European Union.[96]

Privacy and access policy for Internet transactions

The management of access on the Internet, and privacy in particular, involves control over to whom information is released, and how it is construed or to what use it is put, and how long it is retained. Policy decisions should precede technological solutions. Examples of Internet privacy policies include private arrangements. In the United States negotiated privacy between user and provider is available by paying a higher price for greater privacy. User privacy in user-provider agreements arrange that the provider will only review messages if there is some suspicion of illegality.[97]

The World Wide Web Consortium has developed a standard that compares a user's privacy preference with that of a website enabled with the standardised privacy policy. This approach relies on the truthfulness of the policy, and for organisations to 'opt in'.[98]

---

[96] Robert Gellman, 'Conflict and Overlap in Privacy Regulation: National, International, and Private', in *Borders in Cyberspace: Information Policy and the Global Information Infrastructure,* eds Brian Kahin and Charles Nesson, MIT Press, Cambridge, Mass., 1997, pp. 255-282.

[97] Lance Rose, *Netlaw: Your Rights in the Online World,* Osborne McGraw-Hill, Berkeley, 1995, pp. 171-185.

[98] W3C, 'The Platform for Privacy Preferences Project (P3P)', 2000, revised 2005, W3C.

Technological and recordkeeping solutions to Internet privacy

Legislation is only one element of privacy protection.[99] A recordkeeping technique to provide evidence of privacy infringements is the use of audit trails or event histories that log or trace who has had access or made any amendments and when to a record.[100] Security controls or 'privacy enhancing technologies' may enhance privacy protection but they cannot guarantee it.[101] For example public key cryptography is designed to ensure security from unauthorised access to personal data on the basis of requiring a third party to control identity certification, but relies on an organisation or person who can be trusted with the keys to the encryption regime. Public key management systems act as trusted mediators between senders and recipients to certify a link between individuals and their public keys. Both the trusted mediators and the keys must themselves be controlled, thus requiring a hierarchical chain of trust. The danger is that if the trusted authority's owner (eg the government or a private organisation) has control over the decryption keys, it can build an extensive identification system and authorise its use. The cryptographic key can also be opened by a court order revealing unnecessary personal information linked to an individual's key. Even with secure key management, a legal warrant may allow law-enforcement agents, employers, or a system owner to have access to keys, thus severely compromising individual privacy.[102] Anonymous remailers

---

99 See also Livia Iacovino, 'Regulating Net Transactions: the Legal Implications for Recordkeeping in Australia', in *Place, Interface, and Cyberspace: Archives at the Edge,* Proceedings of the Australian Society of Archivists Conference, Freemantle, 6-8 August, 1998, Australian Society of Archivists Incorporated, Canberra, 1999, pp. 103-123.

100 Tracking provides an auditable trail of record transactions, ensuring that event histories are part of the record. 'Tracking' is defined in the ISO records management standard as 'creating, capturing and maintaining information about the movement and use of records'. ISO, International Standard ISO 15489-1, *Information and Documentation, Records Management*, Part 1, p 3.

101 'Privacy-enhancing products are those that have been designed in a way that aims at accomplishing the largest possible use of truly anonymous data.' European Commission, Data Protection Working Group, WP37, *Working Document: Privacy on the Internet - An integrated EU Approach to On-line Data Protection,* November 2000, Article 29. See also Philip Agre, 'Beyond the Mirror World: Privacy and the Representational Practices of Computing', in *Technology and Privacy: the New Landscape,* eds Philip Agre and Marc Rotenberg, MIT Press, Massachusetts, 1998, pp. 29-62.

102 See for example, the *Telecommunications (Interception Act)* (Cth) 1901 which, pursuant to a warrant allows access to the encryption key. Natalia Yastreboff, 'Encryption and Australian Government Policy', in *Internet Law Anthology*, ed.

allow identifying elements of communications to be omitted without attribution to any recipient, and together with encryption, one can be totally anonymous. However, a blanket approach of this kind ignores the necessity of identification for record reliability and authenticity purposes.

7.2.5 Evidence in web 'business' transactions

If laws of evidence are particularly prone to their cultural origins, in the global context there is an opportunity for securing universal approaches across legal systems. The Internet raises questions about the legal status of documents as evidence outside national boundaries. The contractual nature of many business transactions necessitates that their evidential qualities be present. At this stage, there is insufficient case law to know how the courts will deal with records as evidence from the Internet.

The Internet is a packet switching network; data can be broken up and routed to their destination along the most suitable path. As the message is reconstructed at its point of destination, interception and alteration may occur during its transmission, endangering the integrity of the communication. In addition, security in a recordkeeping context means ensuring that records retain their integrity over time. For these reasons, the evidential issues relevant to electronic transactions on the Internet are often submerged under discussions on security, encryption and electronic signatures. Secure systems adopting encryption technologies are central to the success of the Internet for recordkeeping. National governments have all developed technologies for this purpose, not often without controversy.[103] The most important issue is the need for businesses and archival authorities to be able to decrypt data, an essential issue for records to be accessible over time.[104]

Peter Leonard, Prospect Intelligence Report, Sydney, Prospect Publishing, 1997, pp. 108-115; David J. Phillips, 'Cryptography, Secrets, and the Structuring of Trust', in *Technology and Privacy: the New Landscape*, pp. 243-276.

[103] The Australian Taxation Office, *Tax and the Internet,* in August 1997 raised a number of recordkeeping issues, including the acceptance of encryption of the data content. Australian Taxation Office, *Tax and the Internet,* Discussion Report of the ATO Electronic Commerce Project, AGPS, Canberra, August 1997.

[104] National Archives of Australia, *Recordkeeping and Online Authentication and Encryption,* Archives Advice 64, September 2003/Revised May 2004; National Archives of Australia, *Recordkeeping and Online Security Processes:*

Laws of evidence: International context

The ability of systems linked to the Internet to retrieve transactions with all their contextual attributes is uncertain, but is being addressed by new technologies. Recognition of the need to maintain evidence, including the completeness of data that forms part of an Internet transaction for potential legal proceedings, has been recognised internationally by the OECD, and is provided for in their *Guidelines for the Security of Information Systems*, including provision for the diverse rules of admissibility in legal systems of different countries.[105] In addition, the Electronic Transactions and Signature Acts in many countries are modelled on the international UNCITRAL model.

The laws of evidence are relevant to the admissibility of documents and records as evidence by the courts, that is, they are the rules which determine what and how records may be introduced into legal proceedings. Electronic information, used in the course of a business or social activity, functions as a record, and may be admissible as evidence.[106] Therefore the admissibility of Internet transactions would appear to be covered in jurisdictions which include rules of evidence that include business and computer records provisions.[107]

Not withstanding the probability that Internet transactions would be legally admissible, the view expressed by a Canadian expert group on law, audit and archives is that electronic transactions need legislative certainty

---

Guidelines for Managing Commonwealth Records Created or Received Using Authentication and Encryption, May 2004.

[105] OECD, *Guidelines for the Security of Information Systems and Networks: Towards a Culture of Security*, May 2004.

[106] Conni Christenssen, 'The Intranet/Recordkeeping Technical Interface', in *Intranets: Problems and Opportunities for Recordkeeping',* Proceedings conducted by the ACT Branch of the Records Management Association of Australia at Parliament House, Canberra, 10-11 March 1999, ed. Anthony Eccleston, Records Management Association of Australia, ACT Branch, Canberra, 1999, p. 19.

[107] Two features of Australian federal evidence legislation which are particularly relevant to transactions on the Internet are the abolition of the original document rule, and provisions for easier proof of, and presumptions about, business and official records, and the use of email, fax and other means of communication. The presumptions opened the way for the admissibility of Internet transactions endorsed in the Attorney-General's Electronic Commerce Expert Group report. Electronic Commerce Expert Group, *Electronic Commerce: Building the Legal Framework, Report of the Electronic Commerce Expert Group to the Attorney General,* 31 March 1998, Recommendation 9, p. 112.

in the normal course of business. This view has in fact been endorsed in most countries.[108] For example the United States, Canada and the European Union member countries have opted to enact specific legislation for electronic communications and contract via electronic signature and electronic commerce legislation.[109] In Australia the technology-neutral *Electronic Transactions Act* 1999 (Cth) is centred on ensuring that electronic communications have legal validity, in particular, but not exclusively, in contractual circumstances.[110] It establishes the basic rule that a transaction is not invalid because it took place by means of an electronic communication and is based on two principles: functional equivalence (also known as media neutrality) 'that transactions conducted using paper documents and transactions conducted using electronic communications should be treated equally by the law and not given an advantage or disadvantage against each other', and technology neutrality that ensures 'the law should not discriminate between different forms of technology for example, by specifying technical requirements for the use of electronic communications that are based upon an understanding of the operation of a particular form of electronic communication technology'.[111]

---

108 National Archives of Canada, *The Keeping of Business Records for Law, Audit and Archives: A Report on the Experts' Meeting*, June 10-11, 1999, Ottawa, Ontario, NAC, Canada, June 1999, p. 3.

109 See Jos Dumortier, 'Directive 1999/93/EC on a Community Framework for Electronic Signatures', pp. 33-65 and Arno R. Lodder, 'Directive 2000/31/EC on Certain Legal Aspects of Information Society Services, in particular Electronic Commerce, in the Internal Market', pp. 67-93, in *eDirectives: Guide to European Union Law on E-Commerce*: *Commentary on the Directives on Distance Selling, Electronic Signatures, Electronic Commerce, Copyright in the Information Society, and Data Protection,* eds Arno R. Lodder, Henrik W.K. Kaspersen, Kluwer Law International, Dordrecht, 2002. For a discussion of the Italian digital signature legislation, see 'La Gestione Informatica nell'ordinamento Giuridico Italiano' in Maria Guercio, *Archivistica Informatica, I Documenti in Ambiente Digitale,* Carocci, Rome 2002, pp. 155-221. On Canadian and US electronic signature and online contract laws, see *E-Commerce in the World: Aspects of Comparative Law*, coordinated by Jean-Pierre van Cutsem, Arnaud Viggria, Oliver Güth, Bruylant, Brussels, 2003, pp. 156-168 and pp. 320-325, respectively.

110 The *Electronic Transactions Act* 1999 (Cth) is based on the recommendations of the Electronic Commerce Expert Group, which reported to the Attorney-General in March 1998. See also *Electronic Transactions Act* 1999 (NSW) and *Electronic Transactions Act* 1999 (Vic) which are modelled on the Commonwealth Act.

111 *Revised Explanatory Memorandum, Electronic Transactions Bill 1999,* 'General Outline', p. 1.

Legislation supports the need to be able to recreate records, not just data.[112] The *Electronic Transactions Act* 1999 also requires that records be accessible for as long as the record needs to be in existence (see ss 9, 11 and 12) ‘at the time the information is given, it must be reasonable to expect that the information would be *readily accessible so as to be useable for subsequent reference*’.

> ... The readily accessible requirement ensures that others will be able to access the information contained in the electronic communication and that transactions are not subsequently vitiated by a lack of access to the information … The notion of readily accessible is intended to mean that information contained in the electronic communication should be readable and capable of being interpreted. Similarly, it is intended that software necessary to allow the information to be read should be retained. This may be the version of the software used to create the message or subsequent versions of the same or different software that is capable of rendering the information readable. The concept of useable is intended to cover use by both humans and machines. It is intended to deal with the useability of information, which is more than just the receipt of the electronic communication.’[113]

Thus the *Electronic Transactions Act* 1999 (Cth) supports authentic Internet records. Other legal, business and societal requirements continue to operate for ascertaining how long to keep the communication. However the Act does at least provide a minimum record retention requirement in electronic form. European electronic and digital signature legislation does not address record authenticity; rather it emphasises detailed rules for transmission in time but not over time.[114]

In terms of legal enforcement in the Internet context, current approaches as outlined in this chapter include the further development of international law both public and private, the application of international model laws and treaties which have been adapted to local conditions by their adoption into domestic legislation (for example, the UNCITRAL model used for the national Electronic Transactions Acts, and the OECD and European Union directives on privacy and national privacy legislation), or simply enforcing domestic laws by claiming breaches occurred within one’s jurisdiction. Self-regulation models have also provided an alternative to increased

---

[112] For example in Australia, in relation to s 262A of the *Taxation Act* 1936 (Cth), Draft Taxation Ruling 97/D4 covers computerised recordkeeping system controls and specifies that data collected and how it has been used must be able to be recreated.

[113] *Revised Explanatory Memorandum, Electronic Transactions Bill 1999,* p. 26.

[114] InterPARES 1 Project, *Italian Research Team Report*, 2001, prepared by Maria Guercio, p. 1.

legislative regulation. Thus the combination of self-regulation and traditional legal sanctions are likely to work best with electronic information which is no longer confined to one jurisdiction.

Ownership, access, privacy and evidence have also needed adjustment to the Internet. There are international frameworks now established for intellectual property, electronic commerce and privacy, and national changes are slowly moving to accommodate these international trends. The risks of not creating reliable and authentic records that may need to be retrievable with all their recordkeeping features over time will continue to be the central issue for recordkeeping regulation.

Electronic transactions legislation can be applied to recordkeeping at the micro-level of business transactions, but not as evidence of legal and social obligations within a community of common interest. Thus the model advocated for identifying the legal obligations of recordkeeping participants online follows the school of legal thinking that in recent years has turned to the law of obligations for legal analysis, but has not itself extended this approach to the Internet.

8 LEGAL AND SOCIAL RELATIONSHIPS: AN ALTERNATIVE INTERNET REGULATORY MODEL

Evolving Internet regulatory models have much in common with the 'self-regulation' and ethical controls of communities of common interest, which continue to depend on the identity and trust of recordkeeping participants. Legal and social relationships within communities of common interest provide an alternative regulatory model for recordkeeping regimes, and a viable tool for identifying the rights and obligations of participants, in particular in relation to ownership, access and evidence in Internet 'business' transactions. The legal and social relationship cyberspace model focuses on the rights, obligations and liabilities of Internet legal and social actors in recordkeeping transactions, with reference to professional, governmental and business relationships online.

The Internet's features have presented new challenges to record authenticity in terms of storing and preserving 'the record' that may be on many servers anywhere in the world. International and general standards for recordkeeping are important in the global environment, as they have been developed to be context-neutral.[1]

8.1 Internet as community and the relationship model

The legal and social relationship model can be applied to the Internet as a community in which the reliability of commercial transactions, rely not only on the technological and legal solutions, but also social ones. Michael Froomkin makes it clear that no cryptography or digital signature can guarantee that a transaction is from the person it purports to be or was sent exactly when it is purported to have been sent. Froomkin says:

---

[1] For example, InterPARES 1 has requirements for preserving authentic electronic records which leave individual countries to contextualise them, and the Monash Recordkeeping Metadata Schema is also organisational-neutral, so it is applicable to any distributed enterprise using Internet technologies.

> These partly cryptographic, partly social, protocols require new entities, or new relationships with existing entities, but the duties and liabilities of those entities are uncertain. Until these uncertainties are resolved, they risk inhibiting the spread of the most interesting forms of electronic commerce and causing unnecessary litigation.[2]

For Francis Fukuyama the Internet in the 1970s and 1980s operated on the basis of a community of shared values, used mainly by the government and the academic community. The 'open' Internet as a community based on reciprocal moral obligation may be difficult to implement without a set of common values by those using it. He views hackers as 'inadequately socialised'.[3] Moves towards building an international consensus on ethical and legal principles applicable in cyberspace have been addressed in a number of domains, for example through UNESCO.[4] The success in transferring shared ethical norms to Internet participants is a critical factor to the success of both electronic business and social communication.

In the online environment elements of trust found in communities and social relationships are difficult to replicate. Can 'virtual communities' substitute for face to face contact? How will ongoing rights and responsibilities be maintained beyond individual contractual obligations? Moral communities take a long time to form and it is not possible to expect the Internet to achieve the same level of trust that has taken thousands of years to build in earlier societies.[5]

The concept of a legal and social relationship can assist by building on trust, both as an ethical and a commercial concept. A system's security features alone cannot provide trust. It is also built on the ability of persons (corporate or physical) to show that they are trustworthy. It is similar to the trust in a company that has a long-standing good reputation in its business dealings. Re-establishing relationships of trust, not only as legal duties but also ethical obligations, are essential to the regulation of Internet transactions.

---

[2] Michael A. Froomkin, 'The Essential Role of Trusted Third Parties in Electronic Commerce', Version 1.02. 14 Oct., 1996, p. 1.

[3] Francis Fukuyama, *Trust: the Social Virtues and the Creation of Prosperity,* Penguin Group, London, 1995, p. 197.

[4] UNESCO, *Right to Universal Access to Information in the 21st Century,* Infoethics 2000 Congress, Third UNESCO Congress on Ethical, Legal and Societal Challenges of Cyberspace, 13-15 November 2000.

[5] Fukuyama, *Trust: the Social Virtues and the Creation of Prosperity,* p. 195 and p. 321.

8.2 Legal and social relationships online: identity, trust, and authenticity

The concept of a legal relationship is one way of considering how trust (or the lack thereof) affects electronic transactions and how it underpins the Internet as a community. The problem of trust in online transactions is complicated by the number of additional actors that are involved in recordkeeping processes outside of a closed community. It is not just the sender and the recipient that need to be trusted, but also those providing the authentication of the identities to the transaction, as well as network providers and the telecommunications infrastructure. In electronic commerce transactions there are several third parties involved that may interfere in the transaction and this may occur outside of the jurisdiction of the legal system in which the transaction occurs.

In 1998 the Australian Electronic Commerce Group report identified the key issues to facilitate electronic commerce as mechanisms to reliably prove the origin, receipt and integrity of information, to identify the parties involved in the transactions, to assess any associated risk, and the ability to have legal recourse if something goes wrong, regardless of the geographic location of the parties involved. The report found that commercial relationships have worked in a bounded context, for example within the banking community because of commercial practice, and that the lack of a pre-existing relationship between two parties transacting on the Internet prevents electronic commerce developing.[6] The requirement of pre-existing trust is also the basis of social relationships. The transactional perspective of recordkeeping involves author-actor (sender) and recipient identity that may or may not be part of a pre-existing relationship, that is the sender-recipient are not known to each other. Relationships built around author and addressee in particular, have reappeared in the 'web of trust' authentication technologies.[7]

Although global markets are a feature of electronic commerce, closed electronic markets also use Internet technologies, for example the stock exchange or the pharmaceutical industry. The 'whole of government' online, from business to business, as well as business to consumer, is based

---

[6] Attorney-General's Electronic Commerce Expert Group, *Electronic Commerce: Building the Legal Framework,* Report of the Electronic Commerce Expert Group to the Attorney-General, 31 March 1998.

[7] Clifford Lynch, 'Authenticity and Integrity in the Digital Environment: An Exploratory Analysis of the Central Role of Trust', in *Authenticity in a Digital Environment*, Council on Library and Information Resources, Washington, D.C., 2000, pp. 32-50.

on the level of trust that exists between citizen and state. These are either 'closed' or 'semi-open Internet systems'. Professional relationships operate as 'closed' intranet systems for reasons of confidentiality. Industry groups continue to operate as communities bound by their own regulatory frameworks, which can be identified using the juridical or warrant-based recordkeeping models. The 'closed' intranet system is preferable for most business contexts (see below: Accreditation schemes).

The nature of legal and social relationships is also indicative of which Internet technology best provides for retaining trust and reliability that must be captured and retained by recordkeeping systems. Legal and social relationships applied to the Internet context require identity and trust to continue to operate within communities of interest. These communities already have their own mechanisms of control, such as professional authorities that provide certification of professional identity, that need to be integrated into networked systems.

8.2.1 Authentication technologies

With the commercialisation of thc Internet, protecting person identity has become a key issue. Encryption, originally used to ensure the integrity of the message,[8] moved to authenticating the participants in transactions by adopting electronic signatures.[9] However, electronic commerce models

[8] Richard C. Barth and Clint N. Smith, 'International Regulation of Encryption: Technology Will Drive Policy', in *Borders in Cyberspace*, Information Policy and the Global Information Infrastructure, eds Brian Kahin and Charles Nesson, MIT Press, Cambridge, Mass., c1997, p. 283. Encryption was adopted by the financial industry in the 1970s for secure payment systems, and the rest of the private sector followed. Encryption has been regulated in the United States to protect foreign intelligence and law enforcement interests.

[9] Electronic signatures are a form of technology which enable the sender of an electronic document to create an electronic signature. When communications are between closed groups the signature is validated by the network operator, while in open communications validation depends solely on the technology. In non-technical terms electronic signature technologies link the information content of the document to some unique information which only the signatory possesses. This might be an encryption key stored in a storage device, for example on a hard disk or a smart card, biometric data, such as the signatory's thumb print, voice and retina print, or hand-written signature metrics. Chris Reed, *Internet Law: Text and Materials*, Butterworths, London, 2000, pp. 154-164.

limit authentication of parties to the immediate transaction.[10] Verifying the authenticity of records 'over time', means that encrypted data has to survive technology migrations. Authentication technologies such as key authentication are software and/or hardware dependent, and encrypted records and signatures may become unreadable without the appropriate software.[11]

Public key cryptography

Public key infrastructure includes public key cryptography, digital signatures,[12] certification authority software, certificates, and staff who enforce policies, procedures and practices.[13] These are the procedural controls necessary for trustworthy records that are also part of recordkeeping and archival practice.

Public key cryptography involves pairs of matching keys: one public and one private. Messages signed with the private key can be validated with the public key, but the public key cannot be used to create a signature for a new message. The signature is kept secret by adopting asymmetric cryptography which uses both a public and a private key. In order to validate a digital signature, the recipient needs to know both the public key of the signatory and the encryption system used to form the signature.

Trusted third party: certification authorities

If the parties have not had previous dealings, the recipient will have no knowledge whether the public key does in fact correspond to the purported

---

[10] The authentication of the parties at the time of the transaction does not mean that the record will remain authentic over time, unless specific measures are taken to preserve the record. See current recordkeeping research in the archives and records community on the preservation of authentic and reliable electronic records over time in Chapters 2 and 4.

[11] Gail L. Grant, *Understanding Digital Signatures: Establishing Trust over the Internet and Other Networks,* McGraw-Hill, New York, c1998.

[12] Digital signatures are electronic signatures which are based on public key cryptography. The European Directive 1999/93/EC covers electronic signatures in its widest term but most of its provisions deal with digital signatures. See Jos Dumortier, 'Directive 1999/93/EC on a Community Framework for Electronic Signatures', in *eDirectives: Guide to European Union Law on E-Commerce*: *Commentary on the Directives on Distance Selling, Electronic Signatures, Electronic Commerce, Copyright in the Information Society, and Data Protection,* eds Arno R. Lodder, Henrik W.K. Kaspersen, Kluwer Law International, Dordrecht, 2002, pp. 33-34.

[13] Grant, *Understanding Digital Signatures,* p. 44.

identity of the signatory. It requires a digital identification certificate issued to an individual by a trusted organisation, a 'certification authority' (CA) that can vouch for an individual's identity. The certificate binds the identity of an individual to a public key. The certificate is stored in a computer by the user, to be incorporated with an electronic signature, using software for this purpose. A certificate will contain a copy of the public key, information specific to a user, information on the issuer, and a validity period. A message with the accompanying certificate provides the evidence from an independent third party that the person named in the certificate did in fact have access to the unique signature data, so long as the public key included in the certificate validates the signature. In the absence of evidence from the alleged signatory that some third party 'forged' the signature, this evidence should satisfy a court.[14] Certificates are used for different web-based applications.[15] A certificate from a trusted CA endorses the rightful owner of the keys. Every time a transaction takes place, a public key is sent to the service provider together with a copy of the digital certificate. If the service provider trusts the CA that issued both the certificate and the key, it should trust the customer. The service provider repeats the process from his/her end, so that each party ends up with a certificate authenticating the other, and the other party's private key.

Digital signatures are also used for authorisation, to ensure a party is sanctioned for a particular function, which protects privacy or confidentiality of the content, data integrity (proof that the object has not been altered), and non-repudiation (protection against someone denying

---

[14] Andrew P. Sparrow, *The Law of Internet & Mobile Communications: the EU and US Contrasted,* tfm Publishing Ltd, Harley, England, 2004, p. 123.

[15] The establishment of third party certification authorities in Australia has included Australia Post (which has since closed its operations as they were not profitable), KPMG and Security Domain. Types of services provided include web server certification where the certification authority (CA) checks the authentication of the company owning the server against national company databases and the domain name registry. An ongoing responsibility of the CA includes monitoring servers that have been authenticated. The certificate once issued sits on the web server as a text file and can be viewed via an icon on the browser. It will state that it has been issued by KPMG and Dun and Bradstreet the company information compiler. Security Domain issues certificates but does not carry out the authentication process. For example the Australian Medical Association sends in a digitally signed request to KPMG and acts as the Registrar, the traditional authorisation role of the 'legal author' of the records. Some organisations act as authentication bodies for their own systems, for example the Australian Taxation Office. Sue Lowe, 'Keys to the Kingdom', *The Age*, 22 September 1998.

they originated a communication or data). For example, credentialing passports depends on a third party (the government) which issues the credentials, trusts in the ability of the third party to authenticate properly, and makes it difficult to forge or modify the credentials.[16] Public key cryptography operates on third party trust, which in archival science emanating from the public records tradition has been the government.

Accreditation schemes

Certification includes a process of identification via a chain of trusted persons, defined as 'Certification Path Discovery and Validation'.[17] English courts have accepted the concept of authentication of message origin via a train of trusted messages.[18]

[16] Grant, *Understanding Digital Signatures,* p. 20.

[17] Reed, *Internet Law: Text and Materials,* pp. 128-131. If an authentication certificate emanates from a CA who is already known to the recipient, and whose public key is in the possession of the recipient, that key can be used to check the validity of the certificate. The recipient's software decrypts the certificate's signature with the CA's public key, and if the result is meaningful this will provide strong evidence that the certificate was issued by the CA, and that the level of identification stated in the certificate has been undertaken by the CA. If the recipient does not know the CA, he can use the CA's own ID Certificate, which is incorporated in the holder's certificate, to check the true identity with the issuer of that ID certificate. If that issuer is also unknown, its identity can be checked via another ID certificate, and so on, that is, as a chain of identity. Whenever a CA is identified, that CA's public key is added to the recipient's list of known CAs. Thus when in future an ID Certificate is encountered which has been issued by that CA, the recipient need undertake no additional checking. There is a limited period of validity for an ID certificate. A certificate could be revoked because of loss of control over a private key or a change of status, for example new employment. The CA issues an electronic notice for revocations (CRL), held in a public repository or with the CA.

[18] In *Standard Bank London Ltd v Bank of Tokyo Ltd* (1995) 2 Lloyd's Rep 169, the defendant communicated with the plaintiff by trusted telexes containing secret codes known only to sender and recipient. Because the parties did not have a trusted telex relationship between themselves, the defendant sent his messages to a correspondent with whom he did have such a relationship, and that correspondent forwarded them to another intermediary who passed them on to the plaintiff. The case was decided on the basis that these messages were properly authenticated as originating from the plaintiff, and the expert evidence (accepted by the court) stated that trusted telex messages were treated by banks as if they were signed by the sending party as standard business practice. Ibid., pp. 129-130.

The authentication infrastructure has both legal and ethical elements. The CA has to be trusted to take proper evidence of the holder's identity if he/she issues ID certificates and the CA has to employ honest staff. There has to be an independent certification that the CA adhered to appropriate technical and operational standards, to verify that the certificate has been assessed as meeting certain security assurance criteria.[19] The emerging trend is to establish voluntary accreditation systems that monitor an accredited CA to ensure continued compliance with standards.[20]

Most accreditation schemes give CAs power to recognise ID certificates issued by foreign CAs as having equivalent legal effect to certificates issued by a domestic, accredited CA. Thus accreditation of CAs is not mandatory but it is essential to have full legal effect.

The global ID Certificate infrastructure is likely to become a fundamental part of the global communications infrastructure and will take into account:

- whether the CA is a fit and proper person to act (an ethical element),
- whether the organisation is financially well-established so as to be able to continue its operations and meet its obligations,
- whether its staff are properly qualified and adequately trained and supervised, and
- whether its technical systems are of sufficient quality, and adequately maintained.

The CA must demonstrate a high level of competence in the identification of applicants for a certificate, the secure generation and management of signature keys, the maintenance of security and confidentiality in respect of its records, and the maintenance of proper records for the required periods of time.[21] These requirements are met from a range of self-regulatory schemes as well as legislation which specifies the accreditation requirements in detail, including auditing the CA.

The CA 'authorises' the act, an essential element in record creation and its reliability, by 'binding' the owner to their authenticators. This is why

---

[19] Ibid., pp. 130-131. Examples of independent certification include the European Commission's certification processes or the 'common criteria certificate' issued by a certification body.

[20] Ibid., p. 130. Accreditation was until recently linked with key escrow for law enforcement purposes. A CA, as part of the accreditation process, was meant to retain a copy of the encryption keys and provide them to law enforcement agencies in prescribed circumstances. This has been criticised widely and is no longer linked to accreditation schemes.

[21] Ibid., p. 133.

licensed third party CAs should operate within a hierarchical structure of checks and balances by other CAs.

Public key infrastructure requirements vary per 'community'. A network of trust consists of a group of CAs that a business decides to trust for the issuance of certificates for a specific purpose.[22] In an 'open system' consumers obtain a single certificate from a third party CA to use with many parties, while in a 'closed system' a special purpose certificate is issued, for example only between the government and a citizen.[23] Roles in cyberspace can be delineated by information tagged to a record; for example, employee identification in a digital certificate provides both the employee's identity and his/her authority much the same way as competencies and delegations are used in diplomatics to identify record 'authors'. Professionals who undertake activities on the Internet can be identified globally with digital certificates tagged to their transactions with clients. Thus current public key technology supports professional, commercial and government relationships 'in time'.

8.3 Internet recordkeeping participants: roles and socio-legal relationships

8.3.1 Participants in Internet regulation

Internet regulation can be analysed in terms of the legal and social relationships of business participants involved in web activities, from the service providers, the users, the parties to the business transactions, trusted third parties and the technical infrastructure. The boundaries of regulation can be delineated by looking at national boundaries, but the international nature of the Internet makes it necessary to keep a global perspective in mind.

---

[22] Grant, *Understanding Digital Signatures,* pp. 39-45; pp. 54-55. A bank account identification process is used to authorise someone to take payments from that account. In a network the bank issues the account holder a certificate via their certification authority. The account holder sends a request for a letter of credit to its bank, signing the request. A bank sends a digitally signed letter of credit to the seller's bank, guaranteeing payment upon receipt of goods. The seller's bank can verify the identity of both the bank and the buyer through their certificates.

[23] Adrian McCullagh and Ian Commins, 'Cryptography: From Information to Intelligent Garbage with Ease', in *Going Digital 2000, Legal Issues for E-commerce, Software and the Internet*, eds Anne Fitzgerald, et al., 2nd edn, Prospect Media, St. Leonards, New South Wales, 2000, pp. 212-213.

The function of a record as a right-duty 'thing as relationship' which encapsulates the rights and obligations of recordkeeping participants does not alter in online transactions. Trusted third parties acting either as intermediaries or as accountability mechanisms have always been essential to record authenticity. However, there are new intermediaries who perform various roles necessary for trustworthy transactions on the web. In theory existing entities can take on these roles, for example in the government sector archival authorities could become certification authorities, registrars of births, deaths and marriages could retain certification certificates, and in civil law systems notaries could take on a similar role in private transactions.[24] The fact that they have not taken on these roles means that authenticity over time may be compromised.

The notion of a legal person that has the capacity to act legally does not change in the online environment. Legal persons have always been conceptual or 'virtual' personae.[25] What is relevant is the capacity of legal persons to enter into legal relationships. Conceptually the theory of legal relations is not restricted to territorial theories.[26] Even if remedies for actions are different in the online context there are still similar sanctionable legal relations.

8.3.2 Recordkeeping participants as moral agents in the web environment

Ethical theories in the open Internet context are difficult to replicate. For example, the ethical demand depends on one-to-one personal relationships amongst strangers. Virtue ethics depends on closeness and familiarity, which can engender pity and other emotions.[27] Cultural-relativist positions

---

[24] Anne Picot, 'Uncovering the Mysteries of Digital Signatures. A Discussion of What Signatures Really Stand for and How They Should be Managed in the Digital Environment', in *Convergence, Joint National Conference, Conference Proceedings*, the Joint National Conference of the Australian Society of Archivists and the Records Management Association of Australia, 2-5 September 2001, Hobart, p. 259. See the legal status of Internet participants within socio-legal relationships, and Fromkin's 'cybernotary' later in this chapter.

[25] Person (persona) is any entity to which the law attributes a capacity for legal relations. Albert Kocourek, *Jural Relations*, 2nd edn, The Bobbs-Merrill Company, Indianapolis, 1928, p. 76, footnote 3.

[26] Ibid., p. 236.

[27] Michael Stocker, 'Emotional Identification: Closeness and Size: Some Contributions to Virtue Ethics', in *Virtue Ethics, A Critical Reader,* ed. Daniel Statman, Georgetown University Press, Washington, D.C., 1997, pp. 118-127.

can only be sustained if a community remains 'closed'. Ethical relationships could be built up over time in professional relationships, but would not operate for one-off business relationships, or in the government context. Amongst ethical theories, Kant's notion of relations between strangers provides the best adaptation to the online world.

Depersonalisation of responsibility in the electronic world creates a greater need for personal ethical systems. 'Intelligent' agents and computer programs that make 'decisions' for individuals challenge the notion of personal and corporate responsibility as necessary to business actions. No legal system can operate without personal attribution for action. Role, linked to identity, is probably one of the most important issues in the online world (see above in relation to authentication). The issue of deception is both a legal and a moral issue.[28] The Internet provides users with an illusion of power and control and the means to separate themselves from their behaviour.[29] In neo-Kantian thinking a computer system is said to act 'intentionally' but 'not intelligently', and therefore cannot be considered to have self-conscious causality.[30] Ethical theories that support a rational self-conscious control over activity cannot sustain the development of the 'self-managing' record.

8.3.3 Recordkeeping participants as legal actors in the web environment

The notion of legal participants involved in the creation of records can also apply to Internet actors. Even a simple transaction on the web involves many actors.[31] For example, accessing a web page involves the controller of the resource, the resource host, and the user. Many of the activities are not the result of conscious human decisions, but neither are they automatic. The most important aspect is to identify the principal actors and their roles, and the rights and liabilities that flow from these roles.

---

[28] John L. Fodor, 'Human Values in the Computer Revolution', in *Social and Ethical Effects of the Computer Revolution,* ed. Joseph Migga Kizza, McFarland & Company, Jefferson, N.C., 1996, pp. 256-266.

[29] Paul C. Grabow, 'La Technique: An Area of Discourse for Computers in Society', in *Social and Ethical Effects of the Computer Revolution,* ed. Joseph Migga Kizza, McFarland & Company, Jefferson, N.C., 1996, pp. 298-312.

[30] Christine Korsgaard, Professor of Moral Philosophy, Harvard University, 'Human Action and Normative Standards', Guest Lecture, the Australian Catholic University, Christ Lecture Theatre, Melbourne, Friday 14th of July 2000.

[31] Reed, *Internet Law: Text and Materials*, Chapter 2.

There are two basic groups involved in an initial Internet exchange: the parties to the exchange, and the intermediaries or hosts that receive and pass on the packets.[32] Hosts use a common set of protocols, that is, each host accepts to transmit packets addressed to others. The interconnection agreement between any pair of hosts is a private one, and obligations, including charging will differ widely. Multiple actors can have possession and control of data on the Internet.

Infrastructure providers are the communications carriers in Internet transactions. The facilitating infrastructure or intermediaries include transmission hosts, resource hosts or website hosts. The primary controller is the website proprietor, but the resource host retains ultimate control and can delete and prevent access to files subject to the contractual terms of agreement with the subscriber. The web host has possession of the resources and some control over them; someone authors the material and may own the copyright. A user accesses the site and copies material into his/her computer's memory. The server may be under one domain name but a virtual site may link to a set of networks and reside in several countries.[33]

Communication services include the Internet service provider (ISP) that connects to other hosts and provides access, mailbox, and disk space for resource hosting. Directory services and transaction facilitation services include domain name allocation and identity services.

There are a small number of pre-existing relationships, but most are indirect relationships passing through hosts. Internet intermediaries more commonly have no pre-existing relationship with each other. They may provide services to one or more of the parties, including communications services such as access or information storage. Other services include identifying one of the parties.

The following is a useful breakdown of Internet actors.[34]

---

[32] 'Internet Access Categories' as produced by the Internet Society in 1995, quoted in Reed, *Internet Law: Text and Materials*, p. 9.

[33] Ibid., p. 19.

[34] Internet actors and roles are drawn from Graham J.H. Smith et al. (eds), *Internet Law and Regulation: A Specially Commissioned Report,* F.T. Law and Tax, London, 1996, Chapter 1, 'Overview of the Internet', with additions.

Infrastructure/network provider: provides the physical connections; and links to the infrastructure of the Internet, routers, hosts and pipes, that is, telecommunications, governments, and networks.
Service provider/access provider (ISP): provides a range of access services, including client software; dial-up or broadband accounts for home use; mailbox space; permanent connections for commercial use; and web hosting and design.
(Resource) host: provides the storage space accessible via the Internet; the servers; may be involved with placing material on the host; may run newsgroups; and provides domain name server
Administrator: provides Internet protocols and domain names.
Content provider: whoever is placing content on the web; for example companies, individuals; linkages to other sites.
Navigation provider: sifts the content using 'search engines' or provides directories.
Transaction facilitators or intermediaries: provide security and identification of the parties to the transaction; act as trusted intermediaries, for example CAs. See also the 'cybernotary', recordkeeping professionals and archival authorities.

Internet participants include persons (physical or legal) that form part of the transaction or that have rights or obligations as a consequence of that transaction. From a recordkeeping view the list below adapts the Internet actors listed above with familiar recordkeeping actors, as well as new ones or old ones in new guises. The first four entries below are participants that were introduced in Chapter 4.

Competent author: the person having authority to carry out an act; an entity/corporate body capable of acting legally. The identity of the facility or location from which the information has originated, a 'facility identifier.
Recipient/addressee: the name of the person(s) to whom the record is directed or for whom the record is intended.
Third party/ transaction facilitator or intermediary: the 'preserver' or professional registration bodies.
Record or data subject: the person who is the subject of, or referenced in a transaction; that is, referenced in the content or subject matter of the transaction; may have statutory rights of access or privacy and confidentiality protection.
Service provider: the provider of a range of access services, including client software; services include dial-up and broadband accounts for home use; permanent connections for commercial use; may provide additional services such as web hosting and design.
Communications carrier: provider of telecommunications service.
Internet regulators: government authorities; legal and social enforcement mechanisms.

The third party sits outside the transaction but has rights because of the relationship with the first and second parties as a result of the consequences of the transaction. In the Internet context third parties include recordkeeping professionals, or transaction facilitators, that is, authenticators, such as CAs, the 'cybernotary',[35] 'gatekeeper'[36] or archival authorities in their primary role of trusted third parties. The concept of the cybernotary, a

[35] Froomkin, 'The Essential Role of Trusted Third Parties in Electronic Commerce'.

[36] The Gatekeeper's role is 'the creation of a Government Public Key Authority (GPKA) to manage the Government Public Key Infrastructure (GPKI), and oversight the accreditation of certification authority service providers and public key technology products'. 'GATEKEEPER was developed by the Office of Government Information Technology in response to the identified needs of agencies to introduce public key technology to support authentication and identification in Government online transactions. The strategy ensures that this is done under a whole of government framework that ensures interoperability, integrity, authenticity and trust for both agencies and their customers.' Could an archival authority have played the role of gatekeeper? See *Gatekeeper: A Strategy for Public Key Technology Use in the Government,* Office of Government Information Technology, Canberra, 1998.

trusted third party that provides a guarantee or certificate for each transaction has links to that of a legal notary, one the oldest recordkeepers in society, and also a role played by archival authorities as the independent third party for public records deemed of long term value. A cybernotary would also provide a means overcoming the differences between the civil and the common law systems when authenticating online transactions.[37]

In Figure 10 Internet participants are represented in an Internet regulatory model of legal relationships. The use of broken lines in the figure denotes a tenuous relationship between the service provider and the actors involved in the transaction.

A participant on the Internet, defined as moral or legal agent, can have a number of roles. When determining the legal consequences of activities on the Internet, it is important to identify which role the person is performing, for example a service provider may perform the same role as the network provider, host and access provider. It is necessary to identify the role and the legal activity involved. The fact that a telecommunications carrier may also provide Internet services exemplifies the complexity of the legal relationship model when an entity has a number of roles (possibly conflicting) and thus legal obligations to several parties.

[37] 'CyberNotary would be a lawyer able to demonstrate that she has the ability to issue certificates from a trusted computing environment. The hope is that civil law jurisdictions will come to accept a CyberNotary's certification as legally sufficient authentication and recordation of legal acts executed in the United States. If so, a power of attorney or the transfer of corporate shares certified by a CyberNotary in the United States would be recognised and enforced in those jurisdictions, even when an ordinary United States lawyer's or United States notary's certification would not suffice.' Froomkin, 'The Essential Role of Trusted Third Parties in Electronic Commerce', pp. 7-9.

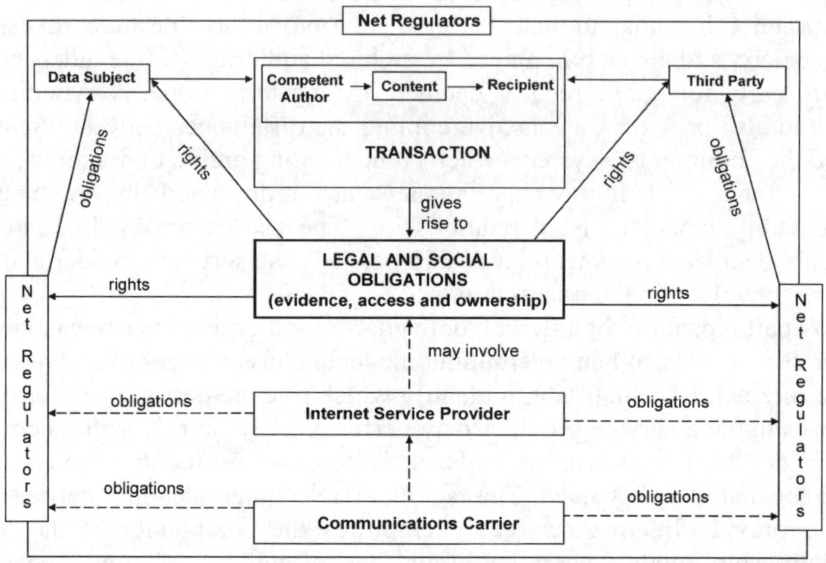

Fig. 10 Legal Relationship Model: Participants in an Internet Transaction

Different actors in an Internet transaction will have different property and access rights. Whether it is the author or the recipient who owns the records, has custody or possession, can provide access to a third party, can retain or destroy records, will also depend on how the legal system views ownership and other rights. In an intranet context, the ownership can be attributed to an organisation, which is likely to be vicariously liable for the content, if it is in breach of a law, unless the act carried out by an employee is outside of the scope of his/her employment.[38] There is therefore a need to identify the legal relationships between Internet actors, for example:

- The relationship between the website owner and the host service provider. A typical service contract between a host and an owner will generally ensure that the owner is liable for content placed on the Internet.

[38] Anthony Willis, 'Intranets and the Law', in *Intranets: Problems and Opportunities for Recordkeeping, Proceedings Conducted by the ACT Branch of the Records Management Association of Australia at Parliament House, Canberra, 10-11 March 1999,* ed. Anthony Eccleston, Records Management Association of Australia, ACT Branch, Canberra, 1999, p. 45.

- The relationship between the end user and the ISP would include the extent of liability the ISP takes for the end user's transactions on the Internet.

How far the actors can be regulated using existing national laws and what other rule sets apply to the enforcement of rights and obligations on the Internet have been slowly emerging.[39]

8.3.4 Proprietary rights of Internet participants

Protecting proprietary information will depend on the nature of the relationship and the activities in which Internet participants are involved. For commercial relationships, a link to the competencies in the organisation, that is, who is responsible for particular activities, is also needed to clarify liability.

In the Internet context the owner's copyright in a 'work' and a record's integrity are threatened when a communication is first transmitted (interception and alteration). From this perspective moral rights legislation is particularly relevant as it seeks to protect the integrity of a work. In diplomatics the 'moral rights' author is the 'writer' rather than the author of the work as defined in legislation.

The ISP has obligations to prevent copyright breaches and to protect rights of the author to communicate to the public.[40]

8.3.5 Privacy rights and obligations of Internet participants

Protecting intellectual property in cyberspace can conflict with access and privacy rights and a proper balance needs to be struck between these competing rights. For example ISPs and content providers have to be aware of any infringing copies and show that they have taken reasonable steps to stop these copies being transmitted. They may have to compromise the privacy of their clients in order to comply with this aspect of copyright.

Legal and social relationships based on trust and the duty of confidentiality have been a major source of protecting the privacy of parties to a transaction. In the online environment participants in an

---

[39] See Chapter 7.

[40] David Brennan, 'Simplification, Circumvention, Fair Dealing and Australian Copyright Law', in *Going Digital 2000, Legal Issues for E-commerce, Software and the Internet*, eds Anne Fitzgerald, et al., 2nd edn, Prospect Media, St. Leonards, New South Wales, 2000, p. 108.

Internet transaction may be strangers, however if identities are known then trust between parties increases. The link between identity and trust is based on having access to knowledge about the person with whom one is dealing; trust increases if moral views, professional standing, and reputation of the organisation represented are known. Contract and other laws serve as a backup when trust fails.

Personal information is at risk when it is transmitted either in the form of identification of parties to the transaction (record identity), record/data subject identification (record identity and integrity), and third parties holding information about parties to the transaction or record/data subjects, for example held by ISPs or authentication certificate providers (record identity).[41] For electronic commerce a unique identifier may emerge for a global context. The use of a unique identifier (such as a business number) could be used to link data across networks and depends on trusted third parties.

Privacy needs to take into account players such as ISPs, CAs and archival regulatory authorities operating as trusted third parties, essential to legal and social relationships online.

8.3.6 Evidence for establishing rights and obligations of Internet participants

Electronic commerce legislation may include provisions which support recordkeeping processes and actions online, needed to establish the rights and obligations of parties in a legal and social relationship. For example the Australian *Electronic Transactions Act* 1999 (Cth) includes rules to determine the time and place of dispatch and receipt of electronic communications and their attribution, so that participants in a transaction can be uniquely identified, essential for contract formation but also for recordkeeping reliability and authenticity.

The relevant recordkeeping provisions in the Act include identifying consenting parties to a transaction, that is, the author-authentication link in recordkeeping. For example the document has to be signed. In s 10 the 'signature' must identify that person sufficiently for the purposes of that communication, it must indicate the person's approval of the contents of

[41] *Privacy Act* 1988 (Cth), NPP 7 Identifiers. Organisations must not use as their own identifiers any personal identifiers assigned by the Commonwealth government agencies, and must not use or disclose such identifiers (with exceptions). Certification authorities (CAs) would be limited in how they use or disclose at least some identifiers which they would have a primary purpose in collecting.

the communication, and the signature method must be as reliable as appropriate for the purposes for which the information was communicated.[42] Section 15(1) provides that a person purporting to be the originator of an electronic communication will only be bound by the electronic communication if in fact the electronic communication was sent by that person or with their authority.

Other recordkeeping provisions include creating and capturing the document into a system. Sections 9(1) and (2) allow a person to satisfy a requirement or permission to give information in writing under a law of the Commonwealth by providing that information by means of an electronic communication, subject to the general condition that, at the time the information was given, it was reasonable to expect that the information in the form of an electronic communication would be 'readily accessible so as to be useable for subsequent reference'.[43] There is also a requirement to retain reliable and authentic electronic records that have identifying metadata required by law if it is a 'reasonable' expectation that the electronic communication would be subsequently accessible. Section 12 requires an electronic communication which under Commonwealth law is required to be retained for a particular length of time to be retained in electronic form if it is reliable, that is, it includes information to identify the record, which includes its origin, destination, time of dispatch and receipt. Recordkeeping metadata on time and place of receipt of a transaction is in s 14. Default rules determine when, and from where, an electronic communication is sent and when and from where it is received. Parties may agree to vary these rules to determine the time and place of dispatch and receipt in their dealings with each other.[44]

---

[42] 'The intention of clause 10 is to allow a person to satisfy a legal requirement for a manual signature by using an electronic communication that contains a method that identifies the person and indicates their approval of the information communicated. This method by which a person is identified electronically is commonly called an "electronic signature". However, the choice of a particular method must be as reliable as appropriate in the circumstances. In addition, where a person must provide a signature to a Commonwealth entity the person must comply with any information technology requirements in relation to the signature method. Finally, where the signature is required to be given to a person who is not a Commonwealth entity, that person must consent to the use of that signature method.' From Australia, Senate, *Revised Explanatory Memorandum, Electronic Transactions Bill 1999,* 30 June 1999, pp. 30-31.

[43] Ibid., p. 26.

[44] *Time of dispatch and receipt* in subclauses (1) and (2): '... of dispatch is deemed to occur when the communication enters the first information system outside of the control of the originator. For example, a message sent by the originator may

The *Electronic Transactions Act* 1999 (Cth) requires parties to consent to the transaction, but how this affects other third parties, including archival authorities, is not covered in the legislation. Both evidence legislation and electronic commerce Acts need to be read with archival Acts in relation to preserving records over time.

8.4 Legal liabilities of Internet participants

8.4.1 Proof of identity

The liability of transaction facilitators for incorrectly identifying a person is a key issue in electronic commerce.[45] Chris Reed argues that in the physical world few transactions require formal evidence of identification as a standard procedure. The establishment of specialised third parties whose function it is to issue identification tokens has been an important feature of Internet transactions and has arisen in the context of the signing of electronic documents.[46] In archival science, identity data in archival and registry systems has been a mandatory aspect of record identity.

An order to enforce the signatory's legal obligations by proof of an electronic signature, has to demonstrate that in fact it originated from the purported signatory, and could not have been affected by a third party. In the United States the *Uniform Computer Transactions Act* ss 112 and 213 require the party relying on the attribution of the electronic record to establish attribution. Similar attribution provisions are found in the Singapore *Electronic Transactions Act* 1998 s 3. In Australia the onus is on the addressee to prove that a message was sent by the originator or with

leave his or her system and enter his or her Internet service provider's system from which it is sent, possibly via other systems, to the addressee's information system. In this situation, the time of dispatch is deemed to occur when the communication enters the originator's Internet service provider's system [not when opened and read]. Unless otherwise agreed between the originator and the addressee of the electronic communication, the time of receipt of the electronic communication is the time when the electronic communication enters that information system'. This is in line with the common law postal rule. *Place of dispatch and receipt*. 'Subclause (5) establishes that the dispatch of an electronic communication is deemed to occur from the originator's place of business and receipt of an electronic communication is deemed to occur at the addressee's place of business'. Ibid., pp. 39-40.

[45] Attorney-General's Electronic Commerce Expert Group, *Electronic Commerce: Building the Legal Framework*, p. 84.

[46] Reed, *Internet Law: Text and Materials,* p. 121.

his/her authority as in common law, that is, the addressee needs to authenticate the originator's identity.[47]

Using the certificate to prove identity

An ID certificate demonstrates that the issuing CA holds identification evidence for its holder, but does not prove that it was in fact the holder who sent the certificate to the recipient. The connection between the sender and holder is made by the electronically signed message which accompanies the certificate. Because the ID certificate also contains a copy of the holder's public key, it can be used by the recipient to check that the signature of the message matches the signature in the certificate. If they match, a presumption can be made that the holder of the certificate is also the sender of the message.[48]

Effects of accreditation

In some jurisdictions, only an electronic signature backed by a certificate from an accredited CA is expressly given the same legal effect as a traditional signature.[49] In some instances electronic signatures act merely as evidence of authentication and approval of a message, but are not specifically stated as complying with the law's formal requirements for signatures.

Liability of certification authorities

What is the liability to the holder of an ID certificate issued by the CA if the certificate contains inaccurate information, so that the transaction fails, or the CA discloses private information about the holder or the key? Given the legal consequences of transactions that would otherwise be difficult to identify on the Internet, the liability on the part of the CA is obvious. The holder and the CA are likely to have a contractual relationship; the liability between them would be managed by contract subject to consumer protection laws or controls on exclusion clauses from which the holder

---

[47] Ibid., pp. 124-125 and p. 212.

[48] Ibid., Chapter 6.

[49] Singapore's *Electronic Transactions Act* 1998, ss 18 and 20 as quoted in Reed, *Internet Law: Text and Materials,* p. 132, footnote 8. See also Italian digital signature legislation which states that only a digital signature which has a public key certified by a CA is legally valid. Dumortier, 'Directive 1999/93/EC on a Community Framework for Electronic Signatures', p. 37.

benefits. These elements are clarified in some electronic signature legislation.

The liability of the CA for losses caused by reliance on a certificate which contains incorrect information is defined and limited where a CA is accredited. Losses suffered by a person who relies on the certificate, 'the relying party', may be defined in accreditation regimes. An unaccredited CA would be subject to general law. It may be possible in common law countries to construct a contract on the basis that the CA had made a unilateral offer to the whole world promising certain things to any person who accepted the offer.[50]

What is the duty of care of a CA when issuing a certificate in terms of verifying the person's credibility? The CA owes the relying party a duty to take reasonable care in ascertaining the accuracy of the information contained in the certificate, and if he/she has failed, he/she would be responsible for the relying party's losses. Tortious liability based on the CA's negligence in ascertaining the accuracy of the information in the certificate may ensue.[51]

Statutory liability regimes usually apply only to accredited CAs. These are based on negligence in ascertaining correctness of information. The CA defines liability in a certification policy statement he/she accepts and is strictly liable for failure to comply with published procedures for ascertaining the correctness of the information in the certificate or for the accuracy of the information itself. Generally the liability is limited to the reliance limit in the certificate itself.[52]

Global consensus is emerging that accreditation enhances legal effectiveness, and liability is defined and/or limited. Foreign accreditation needs to be recognised as equivalent to the domestic law where certificates are used. Most liability regimes agree that reliance limits set out in a certificate should be enforced. CAs can then calculate their liability.[53] Third party liability has been limited for identification services, particularly for communications with legal consequences.[54]

---

[50] See case law in Reed, *Internet Law: Text and Materials*, p.132.

[51] Ibid., p. 139. Duty of care requires a sufficient relationship between the CA and the relying party for a duty to arise. Product liability may be more relevant. Even if tortious liability can be established under applicable law, neither contract nor tort liability covers all the losses suffered by a successful plaintiff, and liability is limited to foreseeable losses, to what is stated in the certificate, and direct loss only.

[52] Ibid., pp. 145-146.

[53] Ibid., pp. 146-147.

[54] Ibid., pp. 82-83.

8.4.2 Internet service providers: legal obligations

The difficulties of enforcement of judicial orders over transaction actors in other countries increase the pressure to hold intermediaries liable, in particular if the originators remain anonymous.[55] The ISP as the 'secondary' actor is often easier to identify than the primary actor.[56]

Liability by ISPs for the illegal activities of their clients may depend on the activity. In an Australian defamation case an Internet provider was sued for defamation after allegations that a London academic had a psychiatric illness were published several times on its service. It was settled out of court for A$10,000 without the ISP admitting liability. The author was also sued. It demonstrates that ISPs are potentially liable for copyright across international borders.[57]

A contractual relationship is usually between the communicating party and its ISP, but unfair contract terms and consumer protection laws in many jurisdictions could render the terms void. Most users will have an express contract which will include ISP liability for communication failure; if there is no contract most jurisdictions will imply that the ISP must take reasonable care in the provision of services to its user. The only way other intermediaries owe an express duty is through an implied contract to all participants and this is unlikely. An enforceable contractual obligation for the benefit of a third party might create a contractual duty owed by a transmission host to the customers of those ISPs with which there is an express interconnection agreement, for example if the ISP

---

[55] Henry H. Perritt, Jr., 'Jurisdiction in Cyberspace: the Role of Intermediaries', in *Borders In Cyberspace: Information Policy and the Global Information Infrastructure,* MIT Press, Cambridge, Mass., 1997, p. 166; pp. 179-184.

[56] Brian Fitzgerald, 'Internet Service Provider Liability', in *Going Digital 2000, Legal Issues for E-commerce, Software and the Internet*, eds Anne Fitzgerald et al., 2nd edn, Prospect Media, St. Leonards, New South Wales, 2000, pp. 309-324. See the *Copyright Amendment (Digital Agenda*) Act 2000 (Cth) on ISP and copyright infringement. In the European context, see Cyril van der Net, 'Civil Liability of Internet Providers Following the Directive on Electronic Commerce', in *E-commerce Law: National and Transnational Perspectives,* eds Henk Snijders and Stephen Weatherill, Kluwer Law International, The Hague, London, New York, 2003, pp. 49-57. The UK *Electronic Commerce Regulations* 2002 (EC Directive F12002No2013) include provisions which limit service providers' liability if they unwittingly carry or store unlawful content provided by others in certain circumstances. See Sparrow, *The Law of Internet & Mobile Communications: the EU and US Contrasted,* p. 90.

[57] The ISP did not respond to the request to have the allegations stopped because it did not want to censor the material. David Passey, 'Internet Provider Pays $10,000 Over Libel', *Sydney Morning Herald,* 14 March 1998.

provides a connection to the Internet on a chargeable basis. The ISP has a duty to take reasonable care in forwarding of packets.[58] Proof of breach would be difficult. A tortious duty of care is even less likely to be imposed on the intermediary. The losses are likely to be financial, and a duty of care is only likely if there is a pre-existing (non-contractual) relationship. Even if a particular intermediary did owe a duty to one or other of the communicating parties, it is not foreseeable that the breach of that duty will cause loss. In common law, if there is an insufficient causal link between the breach and the loss, a duty will be unrecoverable.

Liability for copyright infringement

There are three ways an intermediary can be liable for copyright infringement: via copying, possession, or transmission. ISPs may be potentially liable for content they do not control, because they can prevent further dissemination. United States cases indicate that the more an ISP knows about the illegal matter the more liable he/she becomes.[59] Too much control over content may also lead to authorising an infringement.

Copyright law has always recognised 'authorised infringement', that is, a party authorising the act that infringes copyright is liable even if they do not carry out the act themselves. Shared liability between the user and the information provider for breaches of copyright continues to apply on the Internet. In fact the liability of the provider increases with involvement in content selection.[60]

---

[58] Reed, *Internet Law: Text and Materials,* Chapter 4.

[59] 'Netcom case' (*Religious Technology Center v Netcom Online Communications Services* 21 November 1995 ND Cal) deals with liability of a Usenet host. The case involved postings to a Usenet newsgroup on a bulletin board (BBS) connected to the Internet by Netcom, a large Internet Service Provider. A former scientologist posted portions of scientology works to the alt.religion. scientology newsgroup, resulting in an action for copyright infringement. The suit was brought against the former scientologist, the BBS and Netcom. The court considered whether the centre could be held liable for incidental copies made automatically. Netcom was held not to be a direct infringer and not found liable for copyright infringement. Other cases such as in *Playboy Enterprises, Inc. v Frena* the bulletin board owner was found liable for distribution despite the fact that the material had been uploaded by one of the users (see 839 F Supp 1552 (MD FLA, 1993)). From Smith, *Internet Law and Regulation*, pp. 18-19.

[60] Peter Gleeson, 'The Internet, Email and Bulletin Boards: Who's Liable for What?' in *Computers and the Law,* Leo Cussen Institute, Melbourne, May 1996, pp. 1-19.

Copyright owners have been opposed to excluding ISPs from liability. The provision of physical facilities alone excludes liability but not if other Internet services are provided, then the law of authorisation may continue to apply. An ISP and a content provider have to be aware of any infringing copies and show they have taken reasonable steps to stop them. If the Internet host or access provider uses or knowingly permits others to use his/her Internet service to disseminate unauthorised copies of copyright works he/she is in danger of infringement.[61]

Who can be sued for infringement and where did the offence take place? What if there is no copyright protection in that country? For copyright purposes, it is not relevant where the material is published but rather the country where the infringement took place, which is where the material is downloaded. Enforcement requires identifying the infringer which may force the owner of the host computer to disclose the identity of its users.

Despite differences between jurisdictions, most laws impose liability where the intermediary knows or has reason to believe that the information content it transmits is unlawful; and where, irrespective of the intermediary's knowledge, it benefits directly from the transmission.[62]

However, the reasoning is based on physical world transactions where the intermediaries are more closely connected with the parties to the transaction, and have a greater opportunity to assess the respectability of those for whom they act and the nature of their activities. Internet intermediaries can identify the source of the transmission, but in practice this is difficult. Thus the trend is towards granting Internet intermediaries much greater immunities for liability for third party content. Different models across national boundaries create uncertainties. The major problem is the identification of Internet actors, where the geographical and jurisdictional diversity of recipients makes the assessment of liability almost impossible.

Specific copyright liability immunity

The United States' *Online Copyright Infringement Liability Limitation Act*, which is part of the *Digital Millennium Copyright Act* s 512 provides immunity to intermediaries who merely transmit packets, store automatically cached information requested by users, host third party

[61] Ibid., p. 18. In Australia the liability of ISPs was addressed in the Attorney-General's Department and Department of Communications and the Arts, *Copyright Reform and the Digital Agenda*, Discussion Paper, July 1997.

[62] Reed, *Internet Law: Text and Materials,* p. 104.

resources, or provide search and location tools for resources located elsewhere.

ISPs are subject to detailed conditions to have immunity, primarily lack of knowledge, lack of direct financial benefit from the third party activity, and respect for the resource controller's copyright management technologies. Australia also includes a provision for immunity if ISPs take reasonable steps to prevent the infringing act. However, in the United States, ISPs register with the Copyright Office to qualify for limitation from liability for third party claims of infringement.[63]

An additional restriction on copyright immunities in both the United States and the European Union is that an intermediary must not strip out technical rights management information that is used to prove the copyright ownership of the work or to track licensed users.[64]

Other intermediary immunities

Many jurisdictions have introduced extensive statutory and general immunities for Internet intermediaries, to cover copyright infringement and criminal law, as well as civil actions for torts such as defamation.[65]

Immunity is generally lost if the intermediary fails to comply with court orders, such as injunctions to block access or to remove unlawful material,

---

[63] Saba Hakim, 'Copyright and the Liability of ISPs', *Law Institute Journal*, vol. 73, no. 9, Sept. 1999, p. 65.

[64] Reed, *Internet Law: Text and Materials,* pp. 109-110. Australian copyright legislation also prohibits the removal of rights management information. See *Copyright Amendment (Digital Agenda) Act* 2000 (Cth) s 16B on removal or alteration of electronic rights management information.

[65] There is great variation in law on intermediary immunity. The United States, the European Union and Australia have introduced immunities for intermediaries. The German *Multimedia Law* 1998 Art. 5 and the European Union Directive on Electronic Commerce 2000/31/EC OJ L. 178, 17 July 2000, p. 1, provide immunity to both transmission and resource hosts as well as to packet transmitters and cache operators. However, host immunity is lost if the intermediary knows the nature of the information content. Singapore's *Electronic Transactions Act* 1998 s 10 extends immunity to packet transmission and caching, but not to the hosting resource. In Singapore there is liability even if there is no knowledge of the action as the ISP makes a profit from the activity, but in practice it is difficult for the host to monitor clients. Thus European Union and German law is more realistic. From Reed, *Internet Law: Text and Materials* pp. 107-118. Similar principles are set out in the Schedule 5 of the Australian *Broadcasting Services Act* 1992, inserted by the *Broadcasting Services Amendment (Online Services) Act* 1999 which came into force on 1 January 2000.

or he/she exercises positive control over the content, including editing it, or removes copyright management information or if the unlawful nature of the resource becomes known, and he/she does nothing about it. Thus there is overall global consensus on the general principle of intermediary immunity, but variations in implementation.

Privacy and Internet intermediaries

There has been a history of the failure of ISPs to maintain privacy.[66] Privacy obligations imposed on ISPs in Australia are under the *Telecommunications Act* 1997 (Cth). The Act considers participants as either a 'carrier' or a 'service provider', and service providers are either carriage service providers or content service providers. A content service includes a broadcasting service or an online service.[67] Therefore anyone operating a website is a content service provider. Internet (access) service providers are carriage service providers. The primary carriage service provider and the access provider may be different. Access service providers are subject to statutory obligations of confidence on carriers and carriage service providers, but these obligations would not apply to content providers.[68]

'In decisions involving telecommunications carriers, to be a common carrier the entity must not control the content of the message'.[69] Internet service providers and other carriage service providers under the *Telecommunications Act* (Cth) may have different functions, but under the *Copyright Amendment (Digital Agenda) Act* 2000 (Cth) an ISP is defined as a carriage service provider.

Telecommunications providers

An entire regulatory framework for privacy is in place for the telecommunications industry in Australia which places limits on third

[66] RealNetworks, an ISP used software to gather details about customers. No legal action was taken against the ISP. Kate Crawford, 'Net Firm "Abused Personal Details"', *The Sydney Morning Herald*, 3 November 1999.

[67] *Telecommunications Act* 1997 (Cth) s 15.

[68] Patrick Gunning, 'Legal Aspects of Privacy and the Internet', in *Going Digital 2000, Legal Issues for E-commerce, Software and the Internet*, eds Anne Fitzgerald, et al., 2nd edn, Prospect Media, St. Leonards, New South Wales, 2000, pp. 217-224. See *Telecommunications Act* 1997 (Cth) Part 13.

[69] Henry Perritt, *Law and The Information Superhighway*, John Wiley, New York, 1996, p. 49. Telstra, the major Australian telecommunications carrier is both an ISP and common carrier, thus it has two roles.

party access to Internet transactions.[70] Apart from the protection of the conversations between individuals, other personal details held on names and addresses are not allowed to pass between carriage service providers (carriers and service providers, see definition above).[71] Part 13 of *Telecommunications Act* 1997, s 276 prohibits the use or disclosure of information including the contents of the communication and personal particulars of any person, with exemptions for law enforcement purposes. There are also privacy industry codes under Part 6 formulated by the Australian Communications Industry Forum which are registered with the Australian Communications Authority (ACA). When a code or a revision is registered with the ACA, the ACA gains powers under Part 6 of the *Telecommunications Act* to give warnings and directions, and impose civil penalties for failure to comply. The business enterprises that would be subject to the privacy code are not only 'carriers' and 'carriage service providers' (Internet access providers), but also 'content service providers', a term that is applied broadly. Hence there are sanctions for some kinds of abuses of personal data in the telecommunications sector.[72]

In the United Kingdom the *Privacy and Electronic Communications (EC Directive) Regulations* 2003 implement the European Directive *2002/58/EC on Privacy and Electronic Communications.*[73] They deal with

---

[70] Holly Raiche, 'Telecommunications Privacy - the Interaction of the Privacy and Telecommunications Regulatory Systems', in *Papers from The New Australian Privacy Landscape,* Faculty of Law, Continuing Legal Education, The University of New South Wales, 14 March 2001, pp. 1-9.

[71] Nigel Waters, 'A Comparative Analysis of Australian Privacy Laws with Special Reference to the Concept of "Adequacy" for the Purposes of the European Union Data Protection Directive', in *Papers from The New Australian Privacy Landscape*, Faculty of Law, Continuing Legal Education, The University of New South Wales, 14 March 2001.

[72] Roger Clarke, *A History of Privacy in Australia: Current Developments,* 16 December 1999, Xamax Consultancy Pty Ltd, Canberra, 1999. Under the *Privacy Amendment (Private Sector) Act* 2000 complaints for interferences with privacy can go under the telecommunications regime or the Privacy Commissioner. Raiche, 'Telecommunications Privacy - the Interaction of the Privacy and Telecommunications Regulatory Systems', p. 9.

[73] The European Directive, 2002/58/EC on Privacy and Electronic Communications states that log files of ISPs must be erased or made anonymous when they are no longer needed for the purpose of the transmission. Several exceptions are applicable, amongst others, in the interest of national security, defence, public security, and the prevention, investigation, detection and prosecution of criminal offences or of unauthorised use of the electronic communication system. The Belgian Cyber Crime Act obliges ISPs to store all traffic data for at least 12 months. Under the Electronic Communications Regulations (EC

direct marketing and with the limitations on the processing of traffic and billing data, caller identification and directories of subscribers, previously covered in a specific *Telecommunication Directive 97/66/EC*[74] on privacy which supplemented *95/46/EC,* and the *Telecommuncations (Data Protection and Privacy) (Direct Marketing) Regulations* 1998.

Thus the nature of the activity and how the roles of Internet participants are defined in legislation and in different industries affect their liabilities. Their legal and social responsibilities must be contextualised to have meaning.

8.5 Legal and social relationships online: the medical, consumer and government context

Human communities have bonded together on the basis of mutual political, economic and social interests over the millennia. Existing communities of mutual interest are using Internet technologies for business and social interaction. The renewed interest in trusted communities of interest, differing in the level of requisite trust by that community, has implications in terms of the standard of recordkeeping that will be required by new 'bounded' communities. One of the major concerns is that trust may be difficult to cultivate in web relationships amongst 'strangers'. However, the relationships analysed in Chapter 6 clearly indicate that professional,

---

Directive) 2003, which are the UK implementation of European Directive 2002/58/EC on privacy and electronic communications designed for email and Internet uses, retention of traffic data, that is '... any data processed for the purpose of the conveyance of a communication on an electronic communications network or for the billing in respect of that communication and includes data relating to the routing, duration or time of a communication' is only permissible for limited purposes, for example the end of the period during which the bill may be challenged. In the UK the billing purpose is usually six years plus appeals. Sparrow, *The Law of Internet & Mobile Communications: the EU and US Contrasted,* pp. 93-106.

[74] Article 4(1) of Telecommunication Directive 97/66/EC required appropriate security measures for communications services to be applied by the provider of such services. Security is defined to include the confidentiality of the communications. The Directive was designed for telephone and faxes. See Henrik W.K. Kaspersen, 'Data Protection and E-Commerce' in *eDirectives: Guide to European Union Law on E-Commerce*: *Commentary on the Directives on Distance Selling, Electronic Signatures, Electronic Commerce, Copyright in the Information Society, and Data Protection,* eds Arno R. Lodder, Henrik W.K. Kaspersen, Kluwer Law International, Dordrecht, 2002, pp. 126-138.

commercial and governmental relationships have trust elements which are not based only on personal 'knowledge' of the participants but on reciprocal rights and obligations that have evolved over time. Technological tools to ensure trust are unlikely to suffice; yet trust is an essential ingredient for business online. In the legal and social relationship model trusted third parties for professional, commercial and government relationships include professional certification bodies, consumer protection entities, and government accountability bodies. These third parties will continue to provide online trust through authentication processes (see Figure 10A, Legal Relationship Model: Participants in an Internet Transaction: Examples).

Recordkeeping standards that have derived from RKMS, InterPARES and the ISO records management standards provide rule sets in a global environment in which geopolitical legal rule sets have become difficult to apply and enforce. Authenticity standards are contextualised through legal and social relationships, such as the doctor-patient relationship, which operate within communities of common interest, or 'enterprises', for example the medical community. Communities of common interest have both general and specific recordkeeping metadata requirements, and trust channels that operate in a networked context. As legal and social relationships are not tied to organisational structures they provide useful tools for ascertaining rights and obligations in the online environment.

The elements of trust as they relate to recordkeeping, currently captured within professional, commercial and governmental relationships, have not been replaced by technology, but they do require additional regulatory controls. The Australian examples below build on Chapter 6 and include the doctor-patient relationship which operates within the context of the health care 'industry', in which security and person identity issues are central. It operates more securely in a 'closed' intranet system. The buyer-seller and government-citizen relationships function in 'semi-open systems' where trust mechanisms are less communal.

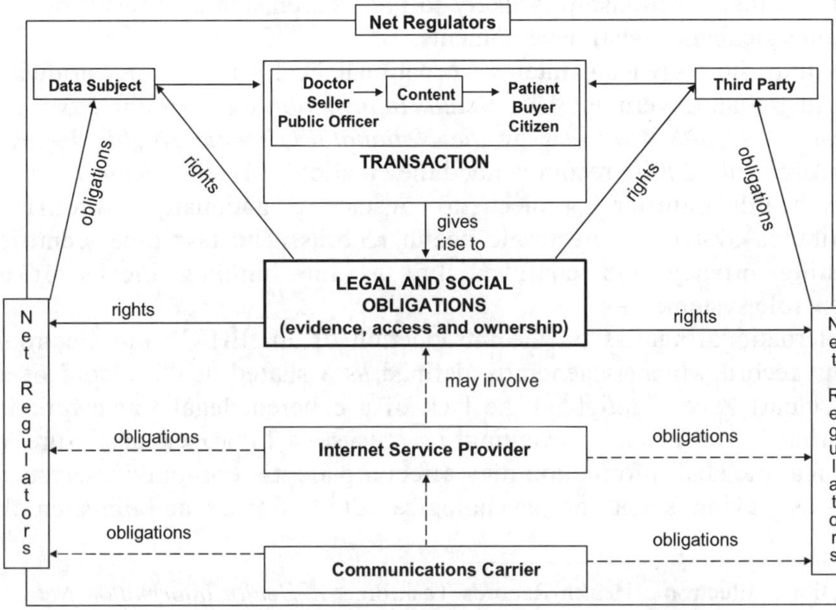

Fig. 10A Legal Relationship Model: Participants in an Internet Transaction: examples

8.5.1 The doctor-patient relationship online

The development of distributed networks, such as the Internet, has made it possible to move many aspects of health care online. In the web environment the integrity, privacy, and confidentiality of electronic medical records becomes of paramount importance. Confidentiality in relationships between health professionals and their clients has a strong ethical basis.[75] The question arises as to whether the traditional ethical approaches are appropriate in the networked environment.

The move to health networking also comes within a 'consumer' centred view of health and the commercialisation of the health industry.[76] The

[75] Ian Kerridge, Peter Saul, and John Mcphee, 'Moral Frameworks in Health Care: An Introduction to Ethics', in *Controversies in Health Law,* eds Ian Freckelton and Kerry Peterson, The Federation Press, Sydney, 1999, pp. 276-289.

[76] 'All About Your Health, Online', *The Age,* 11 May 2000.

doctor-patient relationship is likely to undergo change as a result of both technological and social developments.

Within the increasing interest in national health networks worldwide, the Australian government's *A Health Information Network for Australia: Report to Health Ministers by the National Electronic Health Records, Taskforce* July 2000[77] recommended the creation of Health*Connect,* a joint state health ministers' project, to oversee a nationally coordinated, distributed system of electronic health records. The taskforce identified ensuring privacy and confidentiality as the building blocks of an acceptable system.

International studies on the introduction of an 'EHR'[78] (an electronic health record which is generally defined as a shared health record of an individual) have highlighted the lack of a coherent legal framework for ensuring privacy and preventing its misuse.[79] Improper disclosure of personal medical information may affect a patient's economic interests as well as having social or psychological dimensions,[80] and threaten the

---

[77] National Electronic Health Records Taskforce, *A Health Information Network for Australia, Taskforce Report,* Commonwealth of Australia, 2000. The National Electronic Health Records Taskforce report is a detailed examination of the issues involved in a national approach to electronic health records. It made a series of recommendations to the state Health Ministers on implementing a national health information network, which formed the basis of Health*Connect,* a major Australian electronic health initiative.

[78] There are a number of definitions of an EHR. From an expansive American Institute of Medicine definition which includes not just patient information but also medical databases, to a United Kingdom restricted definition in which the electronic patient record is the record of care mainly held by the institution, that is, a proprietary record. Flinders University, *The Benefits and Difficulties of Introducing a National Approach to Electronic Health Records in Australia,* Report to the National Electronic Health Records Taskforce, Flinders University, Adelaide, April, 2000 (Appendix), in National Electronic Health Records Taskforce, *A Health Information Network for Australia,* Taskforce Report, Commonwealth Department of Health and Aged Care, 2000, p. 7. The major difference between a medical record and the EHR is that the EHR communicates the record outside of the creation framework. For a list of definitions, see ISO/TC 215 *Ad Hoc* Group Report, *Standards Requirements for the Electronic Health Record & Discharge/Referral Plans*, Draft V 2.1, 31 May 2002.

[79] *A Health Information Network for Australia*, Part A, Chapter 4, discusses several major national initiatives. Differences in definitions of an electronic health record reflect varying cultural medical traditions.

[80] Lawrence O. Gostin, Joan Turek-Brezina, Madison Powers and Rene Kozloff, 'Privacy and Security of Health Information in the Emerging Health Care

continuation of an environment where patients are willing to seek timely medical advice.[81] Moreover, medical care is predicated on access to a reasonably complete set of medical records. These systems create, capture and access patients' records across numerous organisations and link or merge them with administrative health systems for billing, government reporting, and statistical analysis. If the EHR is the complete medical record of a person (some definitions focus on family), it will need to be retained for at least the lifetime of the patient to provide continuity of health care. If it is not the complete record, its relationship with the institutional record needs to be clarified. Therefore, the identity of the author of the records, relevant to its reliability and to its ownership, must be provided with technological, legal and ethical safeguards. The loss of accessibility to, and intelligibility of the records, loss of the original functionality of the data during transfer to a new technology or accidental loss due to media failure (the integrity of the records) are of particular concern.[82] The developments in health networks provide an example of the need to apply the results of recordkeeping research to specific domains.[83]

The implementation of a national health network relies on cooperation and participation of patients and the medical community. If a distributed system of electronic health records is implemented, there is a serious risk that the core elements of the doctor-patient relationship, such as trust, will

---

System', *Health Matrix: Journal of Law-Medicine* vol. 5, 1995, pp. 1-36; Chari J. Young, 'Telemedicine: Patient Privacy Rights of Electronic Medical Records', *University of Missouri Kansas City Law Review*, vol. 66, Summer, 1998, p. 921.

[81] Michael Kottow, 'Medical Confidentiality: An Intransigent and Absolute Obligation', *Journal of Medical Ethics,* vol. 12, no. 3, Sept. 1986, pp. 117-122; Paul T. Cuzmanes and Christopher P. Orlando, 'Automation of Medical Records: The Electronic Superhighway and its Ramifications for Health Care Providers', *Pharmacy and Law*, vol. 6, 1997, pp. 19-32.

[82] Livia Iacovino, 'Trustworthy Shared Electronic Health Records: Recordkeeping Requirements and Health*Connect*', *Journal of Law and Medicine*, vol.12, no. 1, Aug. 2004, pp. 40-59; Amy M. Jurevic, 'When Technology and Health Care Collide: Issues with Electronic Medical Records and Electronic Mail', *University of Missouri Kansas City Law Review*, vol. 66, Summer 1998, pp. 809-836.

[83] The need to contextualise recordkeeping research results has been an outcome of both the Monash RKMS and InterPARES 1 recordkeeping projects, that is, generic recordkeeping metadata schema and elements of record authenticity have to be applied to domain-specific needs. Recognition of differences in the application of authenticity is also supported by major information peak bodies, such as the US Council on Library and Information Resources, in *Authenticity in a Digital Environment*, CLIR, Washington, D.C., 2000.

be damaged. The networking of health records provides a good example of the need to work within a community of common interests based on trust, and to analyse the issues in terms of identifying the legal and ethical responsibilities of health participants in 'business' transactions.

Regulation of online health services: international context

When a patient's record is transmitted electronically and stored in a number of databases, to be accessed by other health providers, including hospitals and patients, valid consent from patients is required by medical practitioners, organisations and other third parties. Other issues include the division between ownership and access in the electronic environment, where access controls do not depend on possession of a physical record; the retention and access to patient records for research purposes, the role of the criminal and civil law in relation to misappropriation and misuse of EHRs; and ways in which trust between the doctor and patient are replicated online.

Areas of risk to networked medical records identified by Russell G. Smith include the interception and alteration of confidential communications, online vandalism and terrorism, illegal transfer of funds, unprofessional conduct such as not examining a patient properly or operating in jurisdictions unregistered and the delegation of medical decisionmaking that could also lead to professional liability.[84] If health networking were global, changes to the international registration and special codes of conduct for medical practitioners online would be essential. In principle any cross-jurisdictional control of medical practice would need to take account of Smith's list of risks.

Smith advocates a model that replicates the existing protection mechanisms of the medical profession extended to the international arena, essentially a community of common interest, operating internationally. Legal principles for health networks include applicable rules of conduct and jurisdiction of medical disciplinary bodies; registration of health care providers to be recognised in the jurisdiction in which the patient is physically located at the time the procedure or test takes place; and the health care provider to abide by codes of conduct and rules in the jurisdiction where the patient resides. Security issues include protecting

---

[84] Russell G. Smith, 'The Regulation of Telemedicine', in *Health Care, Crime and Regulatory Control*, ed. Russell G. Smith, Hawkins Press, Sydney, 1998, pp. 190-203. Smith states that no systematic study of the medico-legal risks associated with the use of telemedicine has been conducted. See his examples of risks, pp. 193-197.

any communication which identifies a health care provider or health care user; access controls and passwords; and the use of digital signatures.[85] The European Union has been a model for the control over medicine beyond national borders well before the advent of the Internet. However, the variations in the way medicine is controlled in different countries, even in the United Kingdom which has had a strong government-medicine alliance, has to be taken into account in a global medical treatment context.

8.5.2 Communities of interest trust model: medical community

The Australian Commonwealth Health Taskforce recommended a 'virtual private network', with in-built security measures to protect privacy in order to overcome the otherwise insecure communications over the Internet.[86] The system would be built on top of a public network as a virtual closed circuit for restricted user groups. A 'closed' intranet system is used in many business contexts, with privacy enhancements including encryption across an unsecured network, access controls, and authentication of the identity of the parties to the transaction. But existing security technologies are not adequate and accessibility over time to encrypted material is uncertain.[87] The need for security in online systems is not unique to the medical context. However, for medical records, additional authentication may be required in relation to each transaction.[88] The 'Good European Health Record Project' links a 'responsible' clinician to a health record. Information does not form part of the health record until a clinician has taken responsibility for entering it.[89] This intentional feature of record making is found in archival science and should be incorporated into all definitions of a health record.

Who is ultimately in control of the EHR is of fundamental importance to its preservation. The regulatory framework that is currently in place can

---

[85] Ibid., p. 199.

[86] Private networks were originally built using owned or leased private lines by firms seeking to establish secure communications amongst a 'closed' group of users. See *A Health Information Network*, Appendix E: Network and Communications Considerations, E9: 'A virtual private network (VPN) is a secure, encrypted connection between two or more points across the Internet'.

[87] *A Health Information Network for Australia*, p. 137, and Appendices E 1 and E 8. The Report indicates here and elsewhere that these 'secure' systems are never really secure.

[88] Ibid., Appendix E 4.

[89] Flinders University, *The Benefits and Difficulties of Introducing a National Approach to Electronic Health Records in Australia,* p. 9.

apply to a web environment only if it is a controlled closed system based on current practice, that is, one in which the EHR is under the control of health professionals. Within the community of interest model the health professional is regulated by a number of rights and duties.[90] In a totally open system the state would be able to gain access to information held in a database, and in a distributed environment individual servers would be subject to attack.[91] A cautious approach that builds on existing regulation would provide greater protection for both the patient and the medical practitioner.

Rights and obligations: ownership and access

The concept of 'custodianship' of the medical record has been proffered as a 'new' approach to ownership and access by health information experts. Custodianship it is claimed would provide control over content and use, with principles based on the rights of the data collector (doctor, medical facility), intellectual rights of the provider and the rights of the community. Multiple 'authors' would have ownership claims which would be unworkable, as their consent would be required each time the record was accessed.[92] A statutory right of access by the patient to his/her medical record is a far cry from the patient owning and controlling the record outright.[93]

If participants are analysed within a recordkeeping framework that differentiates the 'legal authors' from 'writers' then it would not be a question as to gaining consent of every contributor to the health record, but only of the legally responsible person. Using the legal and social relationship model, rights and duties can be identified, with the person who is the subject of the collection as having rights and the 'health service provider' having duties to perform (unless exempt). Other common law

---

[90] Elements of trust (confidentiality, privacy and ethics), identity (ownership and access), and authenticity (evidence) within doctor-patient communications are outlined in Livia Iacovino, Ethical-Legal Frameworks for Recordkeeping: Regulatory Models, Participants and their Rights and Obligations, PhD Thesis, Monash University, Melbourne, 2002, pp. 319-353.

[91] Flinders University, *The Benefits and Difficulties of Introducing a National Approach to Electronic Health Records in Australia,* p. 114. The Flinders Report recommends a closed system together with patient control.

[92] NSW Health Department, *Ethical Management of Health Information, Discussion Paper,* November 1999, Better Health Care Centre, Gladesville, NSW Health Department, 1999, p. 13.

[93] Iacovino, 'Trustworthy Shared Electronic Health Records: Recordkeeping Requirements and Health*Connect.*'

rights and obligations unless extinguished by legislation would continue to be relevant. Privacy should be an element of the relationship, that is protected by a number of means, both legal and social.

Duty of confidentiality and medical privacy online

Confidentiality in the doctor-patient relationship is the major ethical and legal concern when patient information is transmitted electronically and accessed by health providers, hospitals and patients. In the proposed health network for Australia, privacy, confidentiality and security are not defined as legal concepts. The *Health Information Network for Australia* report acknowledges that the unconditional trust placed by the patient in his or her healthcare provider that the information supplied will remain confidential is fundamental in the patient's relationship with the provider.[94] The mechanisms proposed to protect confidentiality include identifiers that are not inextricably linked to a name (patient, health provider or facility) except when needed. However, named identifiers are needed to provide the record with its identity and integrity over time. Therefore an inextricable link between an identifier and the record must also be maintained but protected from inappropriate disclosure.[95]

The piecemeal and inconsistent jurisdictional approach to Australian privacy and health legislative initiatives will be challenged by a national health network which will require consistent principles, and the retention of health information for at least the lifetime of the patient.[96]

8.5.3 Recordkeeping person metadata requirements: doctor-patient online

The EHR has been defined as:

---

[94] *A Health Information Network for Australia*, Appendix F2.3, footnote 87 is the only full reference to Hippocratic ideals and its importance in OECD countries.

[95] Health*Connect, Business Architecture v1.9*, Nov. 2004, Version for Comment, p. 30. Health*Connect* developments point to a national health identifier rather than just a Health*Connect* identifier possibly associated with a personal identifier for all government transactions, thus linking health personal data with an ever widening set of transactions between government (frequently via private deliverers) and the individual.

[96] Moira Paterson and Livia Iacovino, 'Health Privacy: The Draft Australian National Health Privacy Code and the Shared Longitudinal Electronic Health Record', *Health Information Management Journal* vol. 33, no. 1, 2004, pp. 5-11.

> a necessary tool for providing person-centred and continuing health care safely and efficiently in the modern information environment. It is not a stand-alone system in a doctor's surgery or in hospital outpatients; rather, it is a longitudinal collection of information about a person's health that is stored at the point of care, and which may be moved or accessed with the individual's specific consent by health professionals at other sites involved in providing care.[97]

The boundary of the electronic medical record in a networked context is problematic. The definition of a health service in the *Privacy Amendment (Private Sector) Act* 2000 (Cth) provides an activity-based definition that is useful in the electronic context.[98]

In terms of recordkeeping in the web environment the terms used in medical informatics of 'encounters' (transactions) and 'episodes of care' (activity-process), form the basic record unit. A 'business' transactional perspective of patient to doctor, doctor to doctor, and health care facility to doctor is central to a record as a right-duty thing, which is missing in an episodic view alone. How does the EHR operate to authenticate the participants? What metadata is required to prove that a person is a medical doctor and the patient is who he/she claims to be? How are identification and competence persistently linked to the transaction?

Relevant person metadata in the online context for the doctor-patient relationship is summarised in the box that follows. It extends the doctor-patient matrix introduced in Chapter 6 from the viewpoint of the medical provider.

---

[97] Flinders University, *The Benefits and Difficulties of Introducing a National Approach to Electronic Health Records in Australia,* p.1.

[98] *Privacy Act* 1988 (Cth) as amended in 2000, s 6 Interpretation, health service means: (a) an activity performed in relation to an individual that is intended or claimed (expressly or otherwise) by the individual or the person performing it: (i) to assess, record, maintain or improve the individual's health; or (ii) to diagnose the individual's illness or disability; or (iii) to treat the individual's illness or disability or suspected illness or disability; or (b) the dispensing on prescription of a drug or medicinal preparation by a pharmacist.

Competent author: doctor/hospital/medical facility. The identity of the facility, location or doctor from where the information has originated: the 'facility identifier' or 'medical provider identifier'(legal author), and the identity of the medical person who has created each piece of information (the 'writer' if not the 'legal author'): the 'medical provider identifier'.
Recipient/addressee: the patient (of action): 'patient identifier'; another doctor/hospital (of communication): 'facility identifier' or 'medical provider identifier'.
Third party/transaction facilitator/ intermediary: authentication authorities such as professional medical bodies; thc Health Insurance Commission.
Data subject: the patient.
Service provider: Health Information Network for Australia.
Communications carrier: provider of telecommunications service.
Internet regulators: government authorities; the Commonwealth Government's 'Gatekeeper'.

Authentication framework

How will the trust between the doctor and patient be replicated online? Patient information is protected from disclosure to third parties by medical practitioners via confidentiality in professional codes and the common law but may be disclosed under statutes. Trusted third party channels could include the registration and practice function found in medical boards. Authentication certificates and digital signature verification would logically be issued via this function, depending on the purpose for which it is used.[99] It would only verify that X is a doctor within the competence of that authority, not his/her reliability in any other capacity. In a wider health network this would also be sufficient unless another role was assumed with added responsibilities on the part of the doctor (that is, as a director or registrar). Channels for international trust for a global health network could be provided by countries that cooperate in professional identify-cation. These channels could build on Mutual Recognition Acts which currently require each Australian state to notify other states if a doctor is registered. Each state could issue a 'good standing' certificate for international practice.

---

[99] Electronic lodgement of Medicare claims adopts digital certificates issued by the Health Insurance Commission to identify doctors under the Gatekeeper program. Stewart Carter, 'Net-based System Paves Way for Use of Digital Medicare Forms', *The Age*, 9 May 2000.

8.5.4 The buyer-seller relationship online

The business to consumer relationship online is an example of a combined legal and self-regulation model. Business to business activity has on the whole more easily adapted to Internet technologies and continued to build on 'closed systems', similar to EDI (Electronic Data Interchange), which operates on exchanges based on prearranged contractual relationships using computer to computer applications in standardised form. Business to consumer transactions over the Internet involve a free form of communication.[100] Legal issues regarding the limits of territorial law are particularly relevant to the buyer-seller if they are transnational transactions.

Regulation of online consumer services

The legal implications of selling goods and services via the Internet include liability for advertising, 'misleading and deceptive conduct', product liability, consumer protection laws (including the law of 'passing off'), and trademarks. It may require defences such as 'due diligence'. Liability may arise under the *Trade Practices Act* 1974 (Cth) s 52 in particular, state and territory fair trading legislation, the laws of negligence and misrepresentation, or breach of contract.[101] However, these laws have limited application outside of Australia. Section 52 covers information on the Internet which originated in Australia, and may be extended to material that originates from elsewhere. Until the courts address the extraterritorial operation of the *Trade Practices Act* 1974 (Cth) s 52 will only apply if the conduct occurred in Australia.[102] Therefore the major problem in the online context is the buyer's rights when goods are bought from outside Australia. However '...provided there is a sufficient jurisdictional nexus between

[100] Smith, *Internet Law and Regulation*, Chapter 8.

[101] Willis, 'Intranets and the Law', p. 50. Promoting a product or service is pre-contractual, regardless of whether one is actually selling or providing it online.

[102] Beth Finch, 'Consumer Protection on the Internet', *Going Digital 2000*, *Legal Issues for E-commerce, Software and the Internet*, eds Anne Fitzgerald et al., 2nd edn, Prospect Media, St. Leonards, New South Wales, 2000, p. 263. Consumer protection provisions contained in the *Trade Practices Act* 1974 (Cth) s 51(1) extend to conduct outside of Australia by companies incorporated or carrying on a business in Australia or by Australian citizens or persons ordinarily resident in Australia.

a relevant e-commerce activity and the territory or people of Australia, then the laws of Australia are likely to apply to that activity.'[103]

International context

Major concerns in Internet commerce centre on the ineffectiveness of national laws, as well as international agreements, in particular deceptive practices. When a consumer purchases a commodity a contract is made, which in theory is a free consensual act. The economic power of the supplier does not provide sufficient protection for the buyer, hence the need for consumer law. Each jurisdiction has its own set form of consumer protection legislation. It is usually not possible to override consumer protection legislation via a contract, as this will override any agreed terms in the contract which contravene the rights and protections granted, including such terms as choice of law or jurisdiction.[104]

A 'cyberjurisdiction model' is the emerging international model for consumer protection with rules drawn from UNCITRAL, International Standards Organisation (ISO), World Trade Organization (WTO) and non-government bodies such as Consumer International. The preference has been for the WTO's rules because it has an adjudicatory system. Extralegal redress includes consumer organisations taking action on behalf of consumers against specific traders and international cooperation measures with the OECD.[105] Cases of long distance fraud have occurred using aliases and anonymous sources.[106] Compliance with international regimes still needs resolution.[107]

---

[103] Andrew Sorensen and Matthew Webster, *Trade Practices and the Internet*, Lawbook Co., Pyrmont, NSW, 2003, p. 6. For a detailed analysis of the extraterritorial operation of the *Trade Practices Act* 1974 (Cth) in the context of electronic commerce, see pp. 137-149.

[104] Lars J. Davies, *A Model for Internet Regulation? Constructing a Framework for Regulating Electronic Commerce,* Information Technology Unit, Centre for Commercial Law Studies, Queen Mary and Westfield College, London, 1999, para 3.10-15.

[105] Finch, 'Consumer Protection on the Internet', pp. 277-280. See the UNCITRAL Model Law on Electronic Commerce.

[106] John Goldring, 'Netting the Cybershark: Consumer Protection, Cyberspace, the Nation-State, and Democracy', in *Borders in Cyberspace: Information Policy and the Global Information Infrastructure,* MIT Press, Cambridge, Mass., 1997, pp. 322-354.

[107] Chris Connelly, 'Financial Services Policy - the Interaction of the Privacy and Financial Services Regulatory Systems', in *Papers from The New Australian Privacy Landscape*, Faculty of Law, Continuing Legal Education, The University of New South Wales, 14 March 2001.

8.5.5 Community of interest trust model: commercial community

Rights and obligations: contracting online

The market and the law have pushed for reliability, trust and non-repudiation of Internet commerce which has created new legislation, for example in Australia the *Electronic Transactions Act* 1999 (Cth) and similar legislation internationally. The *Electronic Transactions Act* provides a 'light handed regulatory regime for the use of electronic communications in transactions'.[108] The Act is centred on ensuring that electronic communications have legal validity, in particular, but not exclusively, in contractual circumstances. It provides coverage for identities of parties essential for contract formation, but does not cover specifics, such as terms and conditions.

Contracting online includes evidence of contract formation, offer and acceptance, requirements of writing, and contractual terms. Issues of time and place of contract, that is, when is it reasonable to believe the contract was received, identity of persons contracting, and payment mechanisms are all required. When a buyer-seller contracts online a contract is formed when one party offers to do or supply something on terms which are accepted finally and unequivocally by the other party, and that acceptance is communicated to the person making the offer. Something of value in legal terms must be given to the person making the offer, usually a payment. The record must capture the terms of the contract and evidence that the buyer read the conditions, for example, a web page offer becomes a binding contract on receipt of a user response requesting to purchase a product, unless it is made clear that it is merely an 'invitation to treat'. Signatures to a contract are a formality for certain kinds of contracts only, but identification of the parties to the contract is required. In contract law when a contract is accepted (or it is reasonable to believe that it has been accepted) has to be demonstrated for it to be legally valid. The time of the contract may be when there is a clear acceptance of an offer or it may be when an order is placed (time is also essential to record identity). The place of the contract is relevant where parties have not agreed on which jurisdiction governs, or where there are no applicable international conventions (place is also essential to record identity). The international

[108] Parliament of the Commonwealth of Australia, Senate, *Revised Explanatory Memorandum, Electronic Transactions Bill 1999,* 30 June 1999, General Outline. The *Electronic Transactions Act* 1999 (NSW) and *Electronic Transactions Act* 1999 (Vic) are modelled on the Commonwealth Act.

dimension of online contracts relates to law of applicability and law of jurisdiction.[109]

A contract witnesses many transactions: the agreement, and the terms and conditions that result from the contract process. A contract has been a prescribed legal record. It is both a record as object and as process. The most important question is whether or not a contract was actually formed, and if so, where that contract was formed and when.[110] The necessity to prove an offer and acceptance between unknown parties accentuates the need for a reliable record.

Trade practices and consumer confidence issues are managed by the *Australian Competition and Consumer Commission*. The *Trade Practices Act* 1974 (Cth) Part 5 contains a range of provisions for protecting consumers and corporations as consumers, including s 52 which deals with misleading and deceptive conduct, prohibits conduct which is misleading or deceptive, or which is likely to mislead or deceive. Sellers are required to tell the truth or to refrain from giving an untruthful impression, including disclosure of relevant information. Section 53 prohibits false claims about sponsorship approval, performance characteristics, accessories, and uses of, or benefits from goods and services. These restrictions apply to electronic transactions and electronically supplied information as well as to physical goods and services.[111]

---

[109] The common law is less concerned with the date of receipt of a message than with when the contract takes effect. Davies, *A Model for Internet Regulation? Constructing a Framework for Regulating Electronic Commerce*, Part 3.4 Rules of Contract Formation.

[110] Ibid., para 3.4.8.1. Differences between civil and common law regimes arise. Davis states that 'The approach within the common law is not so much to ask when a message was received as to ask when does it take effect? This is in line with the general focus of the common law on function as opposed to form but this approach can lead to seemingly strange results. An extreme example of the results of this type of approach can be seen in the postal rule which does not depend on the receipt of a message at all for the message to take effect. The rule simply provides that a message takes effect once it has been sent irrespective of actual receipt.'

[111] See also in this chapter, 8.3.6 'Evidence for establishing rights and obligations of Internet participants', in particular electronic transactions legislation which provides some legislative certainty for consumers, such as the identity of seller and location.

8.5.6 Recordkeeping person metadata requirements: buyer-seller online

Person metadata must identify the buyer and seller, unless anonymous transactions are an option. An authentication framework is essential. Trust and identity have to be verified through individual industries. Elements that communicate trust in websites from the point of view of a consumer include factors that produce a sense of trustworthiness and their relative importance. These do not take into account the evidentiary and recordkeeping aspects but they contribute to trust when a customer uses an unknown website. Commercial relationships depend on experience and habit over time. Other factors include presentation which includes the reliance on 'form' or the formal characteristics of websites, seals of approval, the interaction of effective navigation, a well-known brand and product fulfilment. Security over personal data should be clearly stated. Effective navigation of the site, particularly for less known brands, and fulfilment of promises, also increases trust.[112] Below is an Internet transaction matrix from the seller's viewpoint.

Competent author: seller (physical or corporate person).
Recipient/addressee: buyer (physical person).
Third party: Australian Competition and Consumer Commission; Australian Securities and Investment Commission (Office of Consumer Protection).
Data subject: buyer; other referenced parties.
Service provider: private or commercial ISP.
Communications carrier: provider of telecommunications service.
Internet regulators: Australian Competition and Consumer Commission; World Trade Organization; OECD; International Standards Organisation; Consumer International.

8.5.7 The citizen-government (state) relationship online

In relation to direct citizen transactions with government, access to the Internet for the whole community is essential. The initial dissemination of government Internet resources has been shifted to take up 'online

[112] Cheskin Research and Studio Archetype/Sapient, *E Commerce Trust Study*, Cheskin Research, Jan. 1999.

business', such as paying bills and fines electronically.[113] Internet-enabled applications for citizens are an emerging international trend which is seen as enhancing democratic processes.[114] The national governments of Canada and Australia and some European countries have moved agency to agency, business to business and customer (citizen) services online and adopted 'portals' to link all transactions of one citizen together, without however having resolved the privacy and ethical aspects adequately. In Canada a federated architecture model includes a public key infrastructure with a secure channel including a 'brand' on the 'window' for the citizens to identify the government agency. 'Portals' have been used as a layer between the original record and the information provided using unique identifiers for each citizen. The benefit of the increased accuracy of data linked by a unique identifier has to be balanced against the risk of increased privacy infringements that may occur when personal information from many sources is electronically linked to one person. Together with the legislative and authentication frameworks, government-citizen transactions are now technologically and legally feasible, but may not always be socially acceptable.[115]

---

[113] Australian governments began using the benefits of service delivery on the Internet in 1997. The Office of Government on Line (OGO) 'Internet 2001' initiatives aimed to make all appropriate government services online by 2001. These included Fedlink 1998 (the federal government's intranet), the Shared Systems Suite and Project Gatekeeper. See Dagmar Parer, 'Integrating Information Resources and Services Through the Intranet', in *Intranets: Problems and Opportunities for Recordkeeping, Proceedings Conducted by the ACT Branch of the Records Management Association of Australia at Parliament House, Canberra, 10-11 March 1999,* ed. Anthony Eccleston, Records Management Association of Australia, ACT Branch, Canberra, 1999, pp. 65-77.

[114] Agneta Ranerup, 'Internet-enabled Applications for Local Government Democratisation: Contradictions of the Swedish Experience', in *Reinventing Government in the Information Age: International Practice in IT-enabled Public Sector Reform*, ed. Richard Heeks, Routledge, London, 1999, pp. 177-193. In relation to the Swedish project analysed in this article, the political and economic context was a central element in how government applied its technology.

[115] Tom Dale, 'Overview of the Policy, Legislative and Regulatory Environment and Issues Facing Electronic Commerce Frameworks and Uptake in Australia', Paper presented at *Doing Business Electronically: Electronic Commerce and Recordkeeping*, Recordkeeping Systems and the Records Continuum Research Group, School of Information Management and Systems, Monash University, Canberra, November 1999.

Regulation of online government services

In Australia the Commonwealth government has been presented as the 'e-government' model for private business to follow.[116] E-government has also been extended to many state governments.[117] The idea of integrated citizen-centred services for Australia federally and at state levels was set in the 1998 government industry statement, *Investing for Growth.*[118] The Commonwealth in this statement made a commitment to an appropriate regulatory framework for electronic commerce so that Commonwealth government information and services could go online by 2001. Many government agencies are engaging in business online. In the Commonwealth sector the National Archives of Australia has in fact used electronic commerce as a means of promoting good recordkeeping.[119]

In *Moving to an Electronic Marketplace* the Commonwealth announced the government's strategy for paying all suppliers to government electronically by the end of 2000 and trading with ninety per cent of suppliers to government electronically by the end of 2001. Essentially this is the government as buyer, the business to business relationship. The 'electronic marketplace' uses 'established trading networks, mainly procurement chains, between component suppliers and manufacturers and between government buyers and suppliers. Through global electronic markets these supply chain networks are inter-related through computing networks such as extranets, the Internet or the World Wide Web.'[120] The government marketplace adopts existing EDI closed systems, but open systems of electronic trading are also encouraged. There is a unique supplier and buyer identification system in place.

---

[116] National Office for the Information Economy, *Government Online: The Commonwealth Government's Strategy,* Department of Communications, Information Technology and the Arts, April 2000.

[117] Jackie Bettington and Sally Algate, 'Convergence and Divergence in the Queensland Public Sector', in *Convergence, Joint National Conference, Conference Proceedings,* the Joint National Conference of the Australian Society of Archivists and the Records Management Association of Australia, 2-5 September 2001, Hobart, pp. 351-376.

[118] Department of Industry, Science and Resources, *Investing for Growth*, December 1997.

[119] Steve Stuckey and Anne Liddell, 'Electronic Business Transactions and Recordkeeping: Serious Concerns - Realistic Responses', *Archives and Manuscripts*, vol. 28, no. 2, Nov. 2000, pp. 92-109.

[120] Office for Government Online, *Moving to an Electronic Marketplace*, Discussion Paper, Department of Communications, Information Technology and the Arts, August 1999, Glossary, p. 26, 'electronic marketplaces'.

8.5.8 Communities of interest trust model: public sector community

Rights and obligations

The citizen-government relationship online still operates within the regulatory framework outlined in Chapter 6. Consumer protection as outlined above for the seller-buyer online is equally relevant to a citizen's rights when transacting with a government department online. The *Electronic Transactions Act* 1999 (Cth) also applies to communications of citizens or corporate bodies with government.

8.5.9 Recordkeeping person metadata requirements: citizen-government (state) relationship online

Government business online in Australia operates on the whole within the one jurisdiction so there are no cross border legal issues involved. However, new third parties in the government-citizen relationship include Internet security providers, for example the Australian Taxation Office provides authentication certification for some government agencies within the Government Public Key Authority (PKA) framework. PKA provides a 'closed system' between the citizen and government.

Person metadata in government online transactions requires additional parties from the PKA authentication framework. Below is a transaction matrix from the public office viewpoint.

Competent author: executive entity (Crown or its representative government agency for example a government business enterprise).
Recipient/addressee: citizen or organisation.
Third party: PKA and Internet security providers.
Data subject: may be recipient.
Service provider: government ISP.
Communications carrier: provider of telecommunications service.
Internet regulators: government authorities; legal and social enforcement mechanisms. Government certification authority, for example Australian Taxation Office.

Legal and social relationships online, as exemplified by examples in this chapter, are currently hampered by inadequate authentication frameworks in relation to the trust elements that communities of common interest have been able to provide, although business and technological changes have eroded many of the traditional elements. In addition, the retention and preservation over time of record objects with persistent person metadata is still at developmental stages of research, despite a number of excellent recordkeeping metadata schema and templates of record attributes for record identity and integrity. Without the identification and capture of the competencies and moral motives of the recordkeeping participants, their rights and obligations become more difficult to define. Ownership, access, privacy and evidence of records as right-duty things have evolving frameworks in the international context, but are largely enforced by domestic laws, and notions of jurisdiction of sovereign nation states, albeit within international model laws. Notions of materiality-immateriality dichotomies are still evident in laws where frameworks for the paper record as object parallel the electronic version. Legal and social relationships are analytical tools applicable in the online environment for analysing the extent to which current technology provides trust. Social trust continues to play an essential role.

CONCLUSION

Records provide evidence and memory of social actions, including but not exclusive of those with legal consequences, essential to the notion of a legal and social relationship as a representation of reciprocal rights and obligations. These rights and obligations are the responsibility of both recordkeeping professionals and 'business' participants. The record creator is no longer the 'subject' who relates passively to an external world of 'objects' which include records; nor does the recordkeeping participant stand outside of the world in which he/she lives. Records are logical rather than physical entities, whether they are in paper or electronic form.

New ethical-legal-recordkeeping concepts that emerge include the record not only as a form of property that can be bought and sold, but also evidence of a composite right-duty relationship, that is the record-object is evidence of an obligation. A re-reading of Kant, diplomatics, and positivism, particularly the debate on universality versus relativism, and the notion of will and intention, provide a renewed emphasis on records that are 'deliberately' created. A search for a balance between rule-driven and self-motivated ethical action requires some moral standards that are universal for all times and places, as well as relative values that are sanctioned by communities of common interest. Actions that are evidenced by the record have to be assessed by a set of values that has an authoritative source, not only within its own community, but also outside of it. Alasdair MacIntyre's virtues that are 'those goods which are internal to practices' provide for an authoritative source valid only to those who adhere to the same norms. At the societal level, international human rights, in particular crimes against humanity, are universally unacceptable morally and legally. They are not subject to time limitations and depend heavily on documentary evidence because eye witnesses are often too old to recall details or are no longer alive. Communities must engage in internal examination in relation to global issues to be truly ethical.

Legal and social relationships operate within boundaries established by professions, businesses and communities, a concept found in both the warrant-based and juridical models for recordkeeping regulation. Legal relationships thus form part of the wider class of social relationships recognised in law. The legal relationships selected demonstrate how each participant may have a number of roles and relationships, and corresponding rights and obligations. To ensure the participants are legally and morally accountable, recordkeeping person metadata must capture their identity and competencies in relation to each role. The examples also reveal that policy, professional and industry controls, business models, technology and the expectations of the 'consumer', constrain the actions of recordkeeping participants.

Mandates, warrants and social norms are legal and ethical drivers that need to be closely identified with individual rights and duties within reciprocal relationships between legal and physical persons. Legal and social relationships are argued to be the most important warrant for recordkeeping, both on and offline. Further research on relationships, for example personal ones such as parent-child, could be used to test the legal and social relationship model in relation to personal recordkeeping and as an appraisal tool for all kinds of records.

The notions of rights and obligations, intention, motive and circumstance surrounding human actions necessary for compliance with legal and ethical responsibilities have been noted as major themes in the discourse of ethics and law, as well as of fundamental importance to the purpose of records. The record has been conceptualised as the manifestation of an interrelationship of the act, the persons, their intentions, and the legal and social effects of the act, as understood in law, ethics and archival science. The intentionality of record creation on the part of the recordkeeping participant is essential to responsible and accountable action, even in the digital world where intelligent agents may be programmed to take on the decisionmaking of individuals. How much of the ethical and legal context is captured in recordkeeping metadata also requires further research. If ethical intentions are evidenced by outcome, then the record is the evidence of intention or at least circumstantial evidence of intention, but if outcome is irrelevant to motivation and intention, then records may provide insufficient evidence of ethical action.

Metaphors for the Internet as a 'virtual community' with its own rules need to be carefully drawn as they may overlook existing rules which operate as social and legal constructs of behaviour. The focus on the law of obligations as an area of common concern to two major legal system types, that is, the common law and the civil law legal systems, has been predicated on finding cross-jurisdictional understandings of legal concepts and enforcement models needed for the Internet. The law of obligations is therefore a particularly useful legal concept for online business transactions. Trust in online transactions is complicated by the number of additional actors who are involved in recordkeeping processes outside of a closed community. The relationships of participants on the Internet may appear more complex than their physical counterparts but establishing the relationships between key parties to a transaction are still fundamental to ascertaining their legal and ethical obligations, whether in the online or offline world.

This book has proposed an Internet regulatory model based on legal and social relationships which takes account of the various roles of the participants and their responsibilities in relation to ownership, privacy, access and evidence in national and international contexts. Both nationally and internationally, as promoted by the European Union and international bodies such as the OECD, the trend is towards increased regulation over Internet transactions. Each jurisdiction is developing its own legal norms for Internet regulation within the context of international conventions to provide a secure business environment. However, national security policies, and attempts to curb cybercrime have led to increased surveillance of Internet activity, and pose a serious threat to data protection and privacy. Electronic commerce and incipient industry models still depend on communities of common interest to provide trust. The risks of not creating reliable and authentic records that need to be retrievable with all their recordkeeping features over time will continue to be the central issue for recordkeeping online regulation.

BIBLIOGRAPHY

Agre, Philip, 'Beyond the Mirror World: Privacy and the Representational Practices of Computing', in *Technology and Privacy: the New Landscape,* eds Philip Agre and Marc Rotenberg, MIT Press, Massachusetts, 1998, pp. 29-62.

Alderman, Harold, 'By Virtue of a Virtue', in *Virtue Ethics, A Critical Reader,* ed. Daniel Statman, Georgetown University Press, Washington, D.C., 1997, pp. 145-164.

'All About Your Health, Online', *The Age,* 11 May 2000.

Anscombe, G.E.M., 'Modern Moral Philosophy', *Philosophy,* vol. 33, 1958, reprinted in *Virtue Ethics,* eds Roger Crisp and Michael Slote, Oxford University Press, Oxford, New York, 1997, pp. 26-44.

Attorney-General's Department, *Privacy Protection in the Private Sector,* Discussion Paper, September 1996, Office of Information and Publishing, Attorney-General's Department, Barton, ACT, 1996.

Attorney-General's Department and Department of Communications and the Arts, *Copyright Reform and the Digital Agenda*, Discussion Paper, July 1997.

Attorney-General's Electronic Commerce Expert Group, *Electronic Commerce: Building the Legal Framework,* Report of the Electronic Commerce Expert Group to the Attorney-General, 31 March 1998, Commonwealth of Australia.

__________ *Electronic Transactions Bill 1999,* Revised Explanatory Memorandum, 30 June 1999, <http://www.aph.gov.au/parlinfo/billsnet/6er872.pdf> (accessed Nov. 2005).

Australian Copyright Council, *Access to Copyright Material in Australia and the US,* Information Sheet G087v01, Australian Copyright Council, Strawberry Hills, NSW, Sept. 2004, <http://www.copyright.org.au/pdf/acc/InfoSheets/G087.pdf> (accessed Nov. 2005).

__________ *Duration of Copyright,* Information Sheet G23, Australian Copyright Council, Strawberry Hills, NSW, Feb. 2005, <http://www.copyright.org.au/pdf/acc/InfoSheets/G023.pdf> (accessed Nov. 2005).

Australian Law Reform Commission, *Freedom of Information,* Issues Paper 12, AGPS, Sydney and Canberra, 1994.

__________ *Review of the Archives Act 1983*, Draft Recommendations, Paper 4, December 1997, AGPS, Canberra, 1997.

__________ *Australia's Federal Record, A Review of the Archives Act 1983,* Report No. 85, May 1998, AGPS, Canberra, 1998.

Australian Law Reform Commission and Administrative Review Council, *Open Government: A Review of the Federal Freedom of Information Act 1982*, Report 77, AGPS, Canberra, 1995.

Australian Privacy Charter Council, *Australian Privacy Charter*, 1994, <http://www.anu.edu.au/people/Roger.Clarke/DV/PrivacyCharter.html> (accessed Nov. 2005).

Australian Taxation Office, *Tax and the Internet,* Discussion Report of the ATO Electronic Commerce Project, AGPS, Canberra, August 1997.

Babirak, Milton et al., 'Electronic Commerce in the USA', in *E-Commerce in the World: Aspects of Comparative Law,* eds Jean-Pierre van Cutsem, Arnaud Viggria, and Oliver Gu□th, International Grouping of Lawyers, Brussels, 2003, pp. 309-329.

Baird, Julia, 'Introduction to Some Intellectual Property Issues in Information Technology', in *Computers and the Law, 94/42,* Papers Presented for the Continuing Legal Education Department of the College of Law on 6 July 1994, Sydney, CLE Department of the College of Law, Sydney, 1994, pp. 1-28.

Banks, McDowell, *Ethical Conduct and the Professional's Dilemma: Choosing Between Service and Success,* Quorum Books, New York, 1991.

Barlow, John Perry, '"Selling Wine Without Bottles", The Economy of Mind on the Global Net', 1996, <http://www.eff.org/Misc/Publications/John_Perry_Barlow/HTML/idea_economy_article.html> (accessed Nov. 2005).

Barry, Richard, 'Factoring Web Technologies into the Knowledge Management Equation ... for the Record', in *Intranets: Problems and Opportunities for Recordkeeping,* Proceedings, Conducted by the ACT Branch of the Records Management Association of Australia at Parliament House, Canberra, 10-11 March 1999, ed. Anthony Eccleston, Records Management Association of Australia, ACT Branch, Canberra, 1999, pp. 7-15.

Barth, Richard C. and Smith, Clint N., 'International Regulation of Encryption: Technology Will Drive Policy', in *Borders in Cyberspace*, Information Policy and the Global Information Infrastructure, eds Brian Kahin and Charles Nesson, MIT Press, Cambridge, Mass., c1997, pp. 283-299.

Bearman, David, 'Archival Data Management to Achieve Organisational Accountability for Electronic Records', *Archives and Manuscripts*, vol. 21, no. 1, 1993, pp. 14-28.

__________ 'Electronic Records Guidelines: A Manual for Development and Implementation', in *Electronic Evidence: Strategies for Managing Records in Contemporary Organizations*, Archives and Museum Informatics, Pittsburgh, 1994, pp. 72-116.

__________ 'The Implications of *Armstrong v the Executive Office of the President* for the Archival Management of Electronic Records', in *Electronic Evidence: Strategies for Managing Records in Contemporary Organizations,* Archives and Museum Informatics, Pittsburgh, 1994, pp. 118-144.

Bearman, David, et al., 'The Warrant for Recordkeeping Requirements', in *University of Pittsburgh, Recordkeeping Functional Requirements Project: Reports and Working Papers, LIS055/LS9400*, School of Library and Information Science, University of Pittsburgh, Pittsburgh, 1994.

Benjamin, Bernard, *Medical Records*, 2nd edn, William Heinemann Medical Books Ltd., London, 1980.

Bentham, Jeremy, *An Introduction to the Principles of Morals and Legislation, Jeremy Bentham, An Authoritative Edition by J.H. Burns and H.L.A. Hart; with a New Introduction by F. Rosen, and an Interpretive Essay by H.L.A. Hart,* Clarendon Press, Oxford, 1996.

Bettington, Jackie and Algate, Sally, 'Convergence and Divergence in the Queensland Public Sector', in *Convergence, Conference Proceedings,* the Joint National Conference of the Australian Society of Archivists and the Records Management Association of Australia, 2-5 September 2001, Hobart, pp. 351-376.

Birks, Peter, 'Definition and Division: A Meditation on *Institutes* 3.13', in *The Classification of Obligations,* ed. Peter Birks, Clarendon Press, Oxford, 1997, pp. 1-35.

Black, Henry Campbell, *Black's Law Dictionary: Definitions of the Terms and Phrases of American and English Jurisprudence, Ancient and Modern,* 5th edn, by the publisher's editorial staff, contributing authors, Joseph R. Nolan and M.J. Connolly, West Publishing Co., St. Paul, 1979.

Blanchette, Jean-François, 'Digital Archiving Strategies for the Long Term', in *E-archiving for Posterity, Electronic Record Keeping and Long-term Preservation of Digital Data,* One-Day International Conference, University of Leuven, 26 June 2003, Technologische Instituut, Antwerp, 2003, pp. 1-12.

Boudrez, Filip and Van den Eynde, Sofie, *Archiving Websites,* State Archives of Antwerp, Antwerp-Leuven, 2002, <http://www.antwerpen.be/david/website/teksten/Rapporten/Report5.pdf> (accessed Nov. 2005).

Braue, David, 'Seeing Is Believing for Online Dealers,' *The Age*, 2 March 2001.

Brennan, David, 'Simplification, Circumvention, Fair Dealing and Australian Copyright Law', in *Going Digital 2000, Legal Issues for E-Commerce, Software and the Internet*, eds Anne Fitzgerald, et al., 2nd edn, Prospect Media, St. Leonards, New South Wales, 2000, pp. 105-121.

Brown, R.A., *Documentary Evidence in Australia,* 2nd edn, LBC Information Services, North Ryde, NSW, 1996.

Buckland, Michael, 'Information as Thing', *Journal of the American Society for Information Science*, vol. 42, no. 5, June 1991, pp. 351-360.

Budd, Susan and Sharma, Ursula, 'Introduction', *The Healing Bond: The Patient-Practitioner Relationship and Therapeutic Responsibility,* eds Susan Budd and Ursula Sharma, Routledge, London, New York, 1994, pp. 1-22.

Burk, Dan L., 'The Market for Digital Piracy', in *Borders in Cyberspace: Information Policy and the Global Information Infrastructure,* eds Brian Kahin and Charles Nesson, MIT Press, Cambridge, Mass., 1997, pp. 205-234.

Butterworths Concise Australian Legal Dictionary, Butterworths, Sydney, 1997.

Butterworths Business and Law Dictionary, Butterworths, Sydney, 1997.

Canadian Intellectual Property Office, *Exceptions for Libraries, Museums and Archives,* Copyright Circular No. 13, September 1999, <http://strategis.ic.gc.ca/sc_mrksv/cipo/cp/cp_circ_13-e.html> (accessed Nov. 2005).

Cameron, Camille, 'The Duty to Preserve Documents Before Litigation Commences', *Archives and Manuscripts*, vol. 32, no. 2, Nov. 2004, pp. 70-89.

Campbell, Madeline, 'FOI Access to Electronic Records', in *Playing for Keeps,* ed. Stephen Yorke, Australian Archives, Canberra, 1995, pp. 188-203.

Cane, Peter, 'Retribution, Proportionality, and Moral Luck in Tort Law', in *Law of Obligations: Essays in Celebration of John Fleming*, eds Peter Cane and Jane Stapleton, Clarendon Press, Oxford, 1998, pp. 141-173.

Carter, Meredith, 'Introducing Health Information Privacy in Victoria', *Privacy Law and Policy Reporter*, vol. 7, no. 7, Dec. 2000, pp. 130-131.

Carter, Stewart, 'Net-Based System Paves Way for Use of Digital Medicare Forms', *The Age*, 9 May 2000.

Carucci, Paola, *Le Fonti Archivistiche: Ordinamento e Conservazione,* Carocci, Rome, 1998 (1983).

——— *Il Documento Contemporaneo, Diplomatica e Criteri di Edizione,* Carocci, Rome 1998 (1987).

——— 'Privacy and Historical Research in Italy', *Archivum,* vol. XLV, 2000, pp. 161-169.

Carucci, Paola and Messina, Marina, *Manuale di Archivistica per L'impresa*, Carocci, Rome, 1998.

Cavazos, Edward A. and Morin, Gavino, *Cyberspace and the Law: Your Rights and Duties in the On-Line World,* MIT Press, Cambridge, Mass., London, England, 1994.

Central Computer and Telecommunication Agency (CCTA), *Legal Issues and the Internet, Guideline,* HMSO, London, 1996.

——— *Legal Issues and the Internet, Reference Book,* HMSO, London, 1996.

Certoma, G. Leroy, *The Italian Legal System*, Butterworths, Sydney, 1985.

Charvet, John, *The Idea of an Ethical Community*, Cornell University Press, Ithaca New York and London, 1995.

Cheskin Research and Studio Archetype/Sapient, *E Commerce Trust Study*, Cheskin Research, Jan. 1999, <http://www.gii.com/trust_study.html> (accessed Nov. 1999).

Christenssen, Conni, 'The Intranet/Recordkeeping Technical Interface', in *Intranets: Problems and Opportunities for Recordkeeping',* Proceedings Conducted by the ACT Branch of the Records Management Association of Australia at Parliament House, Canberra, 10-11 March 1999, ed. Anthony Eccleston, Records Management Association of Australia, ACT Branch, Canberra, 1999, pp. 17-22.

Clanchy, M.T., *From Memory to Written Record: England 1066-1307*, 2nd edn, Blackwell, Cambridge Massachusetts, 1993.

Clarke, Philip and Corones, Stephen, *Competition Law and Policy,* Oxford University Press, Melbourne, 1998.

Clarke, Roger, *A History of Privacy in Australia: Current Developments*, Xamax Consultancy Pty Ltd, Canberra, 1999, <http://www.anu.edu.au/people/Roger.Clarke/DV/OzCurrent.html> (accessed Nov. 2005).

Cockburn, Tina, 'Personal Liability of Government Officers in Tort and Equity', in *Government Law and Policy, Commercial Aspects,* ed. Bryan Horrigan, The Federation Press, Leichhardt, NSW, 1998, pp. 340-389.

Connelly, Chris, 'Financial Services Policy - The Interaction of the Privacy and Financial Services Regulatory Systems', in *Papers from The New Australian Privacy Landscape*, Faculty of Law, Continuing Legal Education, The University of New South Wales, 14 March 2001 (no pagination).

Cooper, R.E., 'Foreword', in *The Law of Commercial and Professional Relationships,* ed. Simon Fisher, F.T. Law & Tax, South Melbourne, 1996, pp. v-vi.

Copyright Law Review Committee, *Copyright and Contract Law*, Issues Paper on the Relationship Between Copyright and Contract Law, 15 June 2001, <http://www.law.gov.au/aghome/agnews/2001newsag/999_01.htm> (accessed June 2001).

Council of Europe, *European Convention on Human Rights, as amended by Protocol No. 11,* Council of Europe Treaty Series, No. 5, Strasbourg, 1998, <http://www.coe.int/T/E/Human_rights/echr_eng.pdf> (accessed Oct. 2005).

Council of Europe, Committee of Ministers, *Guidelines for the Protection of Individuals with Regard to the Collection and Processing of Personal Data on Information Superhighways*, Recommendation No. R (99) 5 of the Committee of Ministers to Member States for the Protection of Privacy on the Internet, Committee of Ministers, 23 February 1999, <http://www.coe.fr/cm/ta/rec/1999/99r5.htm> (accessed Oct. 1999).

Cowen, Zelman, 'The Private Man', *The Institute of Public Affairs*', vol. 24, no. 1, Jan.-March, 1970, pp. 26-32.

Cox, Richard and Duff, Wendy, 'Warrant and the Definition of Electronic Records: Questions Arising from the Pittsburgh Project', *Archives and Museums Informatics,* vol. 11, 1997, pp. 222-234.

Crawford, Kate, 'Net Firm "Abused Personal Details"', *The Sydney Morning Herald*, 3 Nov. 1999.

Crisp, Roger and Slote, Michael, 'Introduction', in *Virtue Ethics,* eds Roger Crisp and Michael Slote, Oxford University Press, Oxford, New York, 1997, pp. 1-25.

Cuzmanes, Paul T. and Orlando, Christopher P., 'Automation of Medical Records: The Electronic Superhighway and its Ramifications for Health Care Providers', *Pharmacy & Law*, vol. 6, 1997, pp. 19-32.

Dale, Tom, 'Overview of the Policy, Legislative and Regulatory Environment and Issues Facing Electronic Commerce Frameworks and Uptake in Australia', Paper presented at *Doing Business Electronically: Electronic Commerce and Recordkeeping*, Recordkeeping Systems and the Records Continuum Research Group, School of Information Management and Systems, Monash University, Canberra, Nov. 1999 (unpublished).

Davies, Lars J., *A Model for Internet Regulation? Constructing a Framework for Regulating Electronic Commerce,* Information Technology Unit, Centre for Commercial Law Studies, Queen Mary and Westfield College, London, 1999, <http://www.scl.org/content/ecommerce> (accessed May 2001).

Davies, Martin, 'Special Skill in "Negligent Misstatement"', *Melbourne University Law Review*, vol. 17, June 1990, pp. 484-496.

de Franchis, Francesco (ed.), *Law Dictionary, English-Italian*, 2 vols, Giuffre, Milan, 1984.

Deakin, Simon, 'Private Law, Economic Rationality and the Regulatory State', in *The Classification of Obligations,* ed. Peter Birks, Clarendon Press, Oxford, 1997, pp. 283-304.

Department of Foreign Affairs and Trade, *International Covenant on Civil and Political Rights*, Australian Treaty Series, 1980, no. 23 (Reprint), AGPS, Canberra, 1998.

Department of Industry, Science and Resources, *Investing for Growth*, December 1997, <http://www.isr.gov.au/growth/> (accessed June 2002).

Dix, Andrew, 'Disciplinary Regulation', in *Health Care, Crime and Regulatory Control,* ed. Russell G. Smith, Hawkins Press, Sydney, 1998, pp. 48-58.

Dodge, Bernadine, 'Places Apart: Archives in Dissolving Space and Time', *Archivaria,* vol. 44, Fall 1997, pp. 118-131.

Dogauchi, Masato, 'Law Applicable to Torts and Copyright Infringement through the Internet', in *Legal Aspects of Globalization: Conflict of Laws, Internet, Capital Markets and Insolvency in a Global Economy,* eds, Jürgen Basedow and Toshiyuki Kono, Kluwer Law International, The Hague, London, Boston, c2000, pp. 49-65.

Douglas, Mary, 'The Construction of the Physician: A Cultural Approach to Medical Fashions', in *The Healing Bond: The Patient-Practitioner Relationship and Therapeutic Responsibility,* eds Susan Budd and Ursula Sharma, Routledge, London, New York, 1994, pp. 23-41.

Duff, Wendy, 'The Influence of Literary Warrant on the Acceptance and Credibility of the Functional Requirements for Recordkeeping: A Dissertation Proposal' (Unpublished Draft), University of Pittsburgh, Nov. 1995.

_________ 'Increasing the Acceptance of Functional Requirements for Electronic Evidence', *Archives and Museum Informatics,* vol. 10, no. 4, 1996, pp. 326-351.

_________ 'Harnessing the Power of Warrant', *The American Archivist*, vol. 61, Spring 1998, pp. 88-105.

Dumortier, Jos, 'Directive 1999/93/EC on a Community Framework for Electronic Signatures', in *eDirectives: Guide to European Union Law on E-Commerce*: *Commentary on the Directives on Distance Selling, Electronic Signatures, Electronic Commerce, Copyright in the Information Society, and Data Protection,* eds Arno R. Lodder and Henrik W.K. Kaspersen, Kluwer Law International, Dordrecht, 2002, pp. 33-65.

Duranti, Luciana, 'The Concept of Appraisal and Archival Theory', *American Archivist*, vol. 57, Spring 1994, pp. 328-344.

_________ 'Medieval Universities and Archives', *Archivaria,* vol. 38, Fall 1994, pp. 37-44.

_________ 'Reliability and Authenticity: The Concepts and Their Implications', *Archivaria*, vol. 39, Spring 1995, pp. 5-10.

_________ 'Archival Science', in *Encyclopedia of Library and Information Science,* vol. 59, supplement 22, 1997, pp. 1-19.

Duranti, Luciana, 'The Archival Bond', *Archives and Museum Informatics*, vol. 11, 1997, pp. 213-218.

_________ *Diplomatics: New Uses for an Old Science*, The Society of American Archivists and Association of Canadian Archivists in Association with The Scarecrow Press, Maryland and London, 1998.

Duranti, Luciana and MacNeil, Heather, 'The Protection of the Integrity of Electronic Records: An Overview of the UBC-MAS Research Project', *Archivaria,* vol. 42, Fall 1996, pp. 46-67.

'Editorial', *The Copyright & New Media Law Newsletter: For Libraries, Archives & Museums,* vol. 5, issue 1, 2001.

European Commission, Data Protection Working Group, WP37, *Working Document: Privacy on the Internet - An integrated EU Approach to On-line Data Protection,* Nov. 2000, <http://europa.eu.int/comm/internal_market/ privacy/workinggroup/wp2000/wpdocs00_en.htm> (accessed April 2005).

Finch, Beth, 'Consumer Protection on the Internet', *Going Digital 2000, Legal Issues for E-Commerce, Software and the Internet*, eds Anne Fitzgerald, et al., 2nd edn, Prospect Media, St. Leonards, New South Wales, 2000, pp. 257-280.

Fioravanti, Gigliola, 'Italy's Legislative Framework for Electronic Documentation', in *Authentic Records in the Electronic Age,* Proceedings from an International Symposium, ed. Luigi Sarno, Istituto Italiano di Cultura Vancouver and The InterPARES Project, Vancouver, Canada, 2000, pp. 94-107.

Fisher, Simon, 'General Principles of Obligations', in *The Law of Commercial and Professional Relationships,* ed. Simon Fisher, F.T. Law & Tax, South Melbourne, 1996, pp. 13-50.

_________ 'Introduction', in *The Law of Commercial and Professional Relationships,* ed. Simon Fisher, F.T. Law & Tax, South Melbourne, 1996, pp. 3-11.

_________ 'Preface', in *The Law of Commercial and Professional Relationships,* ed. Simon Fisher, F.T. Law & Tax, South Melbourne, 1996, pp. vii-x.

_________ 'Government and Rights Protection in Commercial Contexts', in *Government Law and Policy, Commercial Aspects,* ed. Bryan Horrigan, The Federation Press, Leichhardt, NSW, 1998, pp. 142-203.

_________ 'The Archival Enterprise, Public Archival Institutions and the Impact of Private Law', *Archives and Manuscripts*, vol. 26, no. 2, Nov. 1998, pp. 328-366.

_________ *Agency Law*, Butterworths, Sydney, 2000.

Fitzgerald, Brian, 'International Initiatives Concerning Copyright in the Digital Era', in *Going Digital 2000, Legal Issues for E-Commerce, Software and the Internet*, eds Anne Fitzgerald, et al., 2nd edn, Prospect Media, St. Leonards, New South Wales, 2000, pp. 87-103.

_________ 'Internet Service Provider Liability', in *Going Digital 2000, Legal Issues for E-Commerce, Software and the Internet*, eds Anne Fitzgerald, et al., 2nd edn, Prospect Media, St. Leonards, New South Wales, 2000, pp. 309-324.

Flinders University, *The Benefits and Difficulties of Introducing a National Approach to Electronic Health Records in Australia,* Report to the National Electronic Health Records Taskforce, Flinders University, Adelaide, April, 2000 (Appendix), in National Electronic Health Records Taskforce, *A Health Information Network for Australia,* Taskforce Report, Commonwealth Department of Health and Aged Care, 2000.

Fodor, John L., 'Human Values in the Computer Revolution', in *Social and Ethical Effects of the Computer Revolution,* ed. Joseph Migga Kizza, McFarland & Company, Jefferson, N.C., 1996, pp. 256-266.

Freckelton, Ian, 'Enforcement of Ethics', in *Codes of Ethics and the Professions,* eds Margaret Coady and Sidney Bloch, Melbourne University Press, Carlton South, 1996, pp. 130-165.

________ 'Records As Reliable Evidence: Medico-Legal Litigation', *Archives and Manuscripts*, vol. 26, no. 2, Nov. 1998, pp. 270-293.

________ 'The Criminalisation "Solution" to Medical Misconduct', in *Health Care, Crime and Regulatory Control,* ed. Russell G. Smith, Hawkins Press, Sydney, 1998, pp. 26-47.

Froomkin, Michael A, 'The Essential Role of Trusted Third Parties in Electronic Commerce', Version 1.02, 14 Oct. 1996, <http://osaka.law.miami.edu/~froomkin/articles/trusted.htm> (accessed Nov. 2005).

________ 'The Internet as a Source of Regulatory Arbitrage', in *Borders In Cyberspace: Information Policy and the Global Information Infrastructure,* MIT Press, Cambridge, Mass., 1997, pp. 129-163.

Fukuyama, Francis, *Trust: The Social Virtues and the Creation of Prosperity*, Penguin Group, London, 1995.

Fuller, Lon L., *The Morality of Law*, revised edn, Yale University Press, New Haven, London, 1969.

Gellman, Robert, 'Conflict and Overlap in Privacy Regulation: National, International, and Private', in *Borders in Cyberspace: Information Policy and the Global Information Infrastructure,* eds Brian Kahin and Charles Nesson, MIT Press, Cambridge, Mass., 1997, pp. 255-282.

________ 'Does Privacy Law Work?' in *Technology and Privacy: the New Landscape,* eds Philip Agre and Marc Rotenberg, MIT Press, Massachusetts, 1998, pp. 193-218.

Getzler, Joshua, 'Patterns of Fusion', in *Classification of Obligations,* ed. Peter Birks, Clarendon Press, Oxford, 1997, pp. 157-192.

Giannetto, Marina, 'Principi Metodologici e Deontologie Professionali nel Codice Degli Archivisti e Degli Storici', in *La Storia e la Privacy, Dal Dibattito alla Publicazione del Codice Deontologico*, Proceedings of a Seminar in Rome, 30 Nov. 1999, Ministry for Cultural Property and Affairs, General Management of the Archives, 2001, pp. 55-90.

Gibbs, Donna, 'Cyberlanguage: What it is and What it does', in *Cyberlines: Languages and Cultures of the Internet,* eds Donna Gibbs and Kerri-Lee Krause, James Nicholas, Melbourne, 2000, pp. 11-30.

Gibson, Anna, 'Overview of the Diplomatic Analysis of Electronic Records within the Canadian Automated Patent System (TechSource)', in *How Do You Know It's the Real Thing?, Preserving Authentic Electronic Records: Preliminary Research Findings*, Proceedings from an International Symposium, 17 February 2001, University of British Columbia, InterPARES and the Italian Government Cultural Office, Vancouver, August 2001, pp. 61-66.

Gillett, Sharon Eisner and Kapor, Mitchell, *The Self-Governing Internet: Coordination by Design*, Prepared for Coordination and Administration of the Internet, Workshop, Kennedy School of Government, Harvard University, 8-10 September 1996, <http://ccs.mit.edu/papers/CCSWP197/CCSWP197.html> (accessed Nov. 2005).

Ginsburg, Jane C., 'Putting Cars on the "Information Superhighway": Authors, Exploiters and Copyright in Cyberspace', in F. Hugenholz, *The Future of Copyright in a Digital Environment,* Information Law Series, no. 4, The Hague, Kluwer Law International, 1996, pp. 189-220.

Gleeson, Peter, 'The Internet, Email and Bulletin Boards: Who's Liable for What?', in *Computers and the Law,* Leo Cussen Institute, Melbourne, May 1996, pp. 1-19.

Goldring, John, 'Netting the Cybershark: Consumer Protection, Cyberspace, the Nation-State, and Democracy', in *Borders in Cyberspace: Information Policy and the Global Information Infrastructure,* MIT Press, Cambridge, Mass., 1997, pp. 322-354.

Golvan, Colin, *An Introduction to Intellectual Property Law,* Federation Press, Sydney, 1992.

Goodpaster, Kenneth, 'Concepts of Corporate Responsibility', in *Just Business: New Introductory Essays in Business and Ethics*, ed. Tom Brogan, Random House, New York, 1984, pp. 292-322.

Gostin, Lawrence O, et al., 'Privacy and Security of Health Information in the Emerging Health Care System', *Health Matrix: Journal of Law-Medicine*, vol. 5, 1995, pp. 1-36.

Grabow, Paul C., 'La Technique: An area of Discourse for Computers in Society', in *Social and Ethical Effects of the Computer Revolution,* ed. Joseph Migga Kizza, McFarland & Company, Jefferson, N.C., 1996, pp. 298-312.

Grant, Gail L., *Understanding Digital Signatures: Establishing Trust over the Internet and Other Networks,* McGraw-Hill, New York, c1998.

Gray, Peter R.A., 'Saying It Like It Is: Oral Traditions, Legal Systems, and Records', *Archives and Manuscripts*, vol. 26, no. 2, Nov. 1998, pp. 248-269.

Greenleaf, Graham, 'Privacy Principles - Irrelevant to Cyberspace?', in *Internet Law Anthology*, ed. Peter Leonard, Prospect Intelligence Report, Prospect Publishing, Sydney, 1997, pp. 129-138.

__________ 'Privacy Principles: Problems in Cyberspace - Likely Areas of Controversy and Interpretation', in Papers from *The New Australian Privacy Landscape*, Faculty of Law, Continuing Legal Education, The University of New South Wales, 14 March 2001, pp. 1-18.

Guercio, Maria, 'Definitions of Electronic Records, the European Perspective', *Archives and Museums Informatics*, vol. 11, 1997, pp. 219-222.

Guercio, Maria, *Archivistica Informatica: I Documenti in Ambiente Digitale,* Carocci, Rome, 2002.

Gunning, Patrick, 'Legal Aspects of Privacy and the Internet', in *Going Digital 2000, Legal Issues for E-Commerce, Software and the Internet*, eds Anne Fitzgerald, et al., 2nd edn, Prospect Media, St. Leonards, New South Wales, 2000, pp. 217-230.

Hackney, Jeffrey, 'More than a Trace of the Old Philosophy', in *The Classification of Obligations,* ed. Peter Birks, Clarendon Press, Oxford, 1997, pp. 123-155.

Hakim, Saba, 'Copyright and the Liability of ISPs', *Law Institute Journal*, vol. 73, no. 9, Sept. 1999, pp. 62-65.

Halsbury's Laws of Australia, Butterworths, Sydney, 1999, vols 5 and 6.

Harris, A.C., 'Changing Government and Constant Ethics', New South Wales Auditor-General, Paper presented to the NSW Public Sector Corruption Committee Inc, 29 June 1999.

Harris, Nigel, 'Professional Codes and Kantian Duties', in *Ethics and the Professions,* ed. Ruth F. Chadwick, Avebury, Aldershot, Brookfield, USA, 1994, pp. 104-124.

Hart, H.L.A., 'Bentham's Principle of Utility and the Theory of Penal Law', in Jeremy Bentham, *An Introduction to the Principles of Morals and Legislation, Jeremy Bentham, An Authoritative Edition by J.H. Burns and H.L.A. Hart; with a New Introduction by F. Rosen, and an Interpretive Essay by H.L.A. Hart,* Clarendon Press, Oxford, 1996, pp. lxxix-cxii.

Harvey, David, 'Class Relations, Social Justice and the Politics of Difference', in *Principled Positions: Postmodernism and the Rediscovery of Value,* ed. Judith Squires, Lawrence and Wishart, London, 1993, pp. 85-121.

Häyry, Matti, *Liberal Utilitarianism and Applied Ethics*, Routledge, London, New York, 1994.

Häyry, Heta and Häyry, Matti, 'The Nature and Role of Professional Codes in Modern Society', in *Ethics and the Professions,* ed. Ruth F. Chadwick, Avebury, Aldershot, Brookfield, USA, 1994, pp. 136-144.

Health*Connect, Business Architecture v1.9*, Version for Comment, Nov. 2004, Department of Health and Ageing, <http://www.healthconnect.gov.au/pdf/BArc1-9.pdf> (accessed Nov. 2005).

Hearn, William Edward, *The Theory of Legal Duties and Rights: An Introduction to Analytical Jurisprudence*, F.B. Rothman, Littleton, Colorado, 1990 (1883).

Heydon, J.D., *Cross on Evidence,* 5th edn, Butterworths, Sydney, 1996.

Higgs, Peter, 'Privacy Implications of On-Line Intellectual Property Protection', in Papers from *The New Australian Privacy Landscape*, Faculty of Law, Continuing Legal Education, The University of New South Wales, 14 March 2001, pp. 1-21.

Hirtle, Peter B., 'Archival Authenticity in a Digital Age', in *Authenticity in a Digital Environment,* Council on Library and Information Resources, Washington, D.C., 2000, pp. 8-23.

Hoeren, Thomas, 'Electronic Commerce and Law: Some Fragmentary Thoughts on the Future of Internet Regulation from a German Perspective', in *Legal Aspects of Globalization: Conflict of Laws, Internet, Capital Markets and Insolvency in a Global Economy,* eds, Jürgen Basedow and Toshiyuki Kono, Kluwer Law International, The Hague; London; Boston, c2000, pp. 35-47.

Honoré, Antony M., 'Ownership', in *Oxford Essays in Jurisprudence*, ed. A.G. Guest, Clarendon Press, Oxford, 1961, pp. 107-147.

Horrigan, Bryan, 'Contemporary Sources and Limits of Crown Immunity, Governmental Liability and Legislative Invalidity', in *Government Law and Policy: Commercial Aspects,* ed. Bryan Horrigan, The Federation Press, Leichhardt, NSW, 1998, pp. 276-339.

Horrigan, Bryan and Fitzgerald, Brian, 'International and Transnational Influences on Law and Policy Affecting Government', in *Government Law and Policy: Commercial Aspects,* ed. Bryan Horrigan, The Federation Press, Leichhardt, NSW, 1998, pp. 2-54.

Hughes, Gordon, 'Our Rapidly Expanding Privacy Obligations', *Law Institute Journal*, vol. 75, no. 6, July 2001, pp. 55-61.

_________ 'Reassessing Victoria's Computer Crime Laws', *Law Institute Journal*, vol. 75, no. 7, August 2001, pp. 51-55.

Hughes, Gordon and Cosgrove, David, 'The Internet - Legal Questions', *Law Institute Journal*, vol. 69, no. 4, April 1995, pp. 326-327.

Hurley, Chris, 'From Dustbins to Disk-Drives: A Survey of Archives Legislation in Australia' (Appendix 2), in *The Records Continuum: Ian Maclean and Australian Archives First Fifty Years,* eds Sue McKemmish and Michael Piggott, Ancora Press in Association with Australian Archives, 1994, pp. 206-232.

_________ 'The Shredding of the "Heiner" Documents: An Appreciation', The Caldeson Consultancy, RIMOS, 1997, <http://www.caldeson.com/RIMOS/heiner.html> (accessed Nov. 2005).

_________ 'The Making and Keeping of Records: (1) What Are Finding Aids For?' *Archives and Manuscripts*, vol. 26, no. 1, May 1998, pp. 58-77.

_________ 'From Dust Bins to Disk-Drives and Now to Dispersal: The State Records Act 1998 (New South Wales)', *Archives and Manuscripts*, vol. 26, no. 2, Nov. 1998, pp. 390-409.

_________ 'Recordkeeping, Document Destruction and the Law (Heiner, Enron and McCabe)', *Archives and Manuscripts*, vol. 30, no. 2, Nov. 2002, pp. 6-25.

Iacovino, Livia, *'Things in Action': Teaching Law to Recordkeeping Professionals*, Ancora Press, Monash University, Melbourne, 1998.

_________ 'The Nature of the Nexus between Recordkeeping and the Law', *Archives and Manuscripts*, vol. 26, no. 2, Nov. 1998, pp. 216-246.

_________ 'Regulating Net Transactions: The Legal Implications for Recordkeeping in Australia', in *Place, Interface, and Cyberspace: Archives at the Edge,* Proceedings of the Australian Society of Archivists Conference, Freemantle, 6-8 August, 1998, Australian Society of Archivists Incorporated, Canberra, 1999, pp. 103-123.

Iacovino, Livia, 'Common Ground, Different Traditions: An Australian Perspective on Italian Diplomatics, Archival Science, and Business Records', *Archives and Manuscripts,* vol. 29, no. 1, May 2001, pp. 118-138.

_________ 'Identity, Trust and Privacy, Some Recordkeeping Implications in the Context of Recent Australian Privacy Legislative Initiatives', in *Convergence, Conference Proceedings*, the Joint National Conference of the Australian Society of Archivists and the Records Management Association of Australia, 2-5 September 2001, Hobart, 2001, pp. 71-90.

_________ Ethical-Legal Frameworks for Recordkeeping: Regulatory Models, Participants and their Rights and Obligations, PhD Thesis, Monash University, Melbourne, 2002.

_________ 'Ethical Principles and Information Professionals: Theory, Practice and Education', *Australian Academic & Research Libraries*, vol. 33, no. 2, June 2002, pp. 57-74.

_________ 'Trustworthy Shared Electronic Health Records: Recordkeeping Requirements and Health*Connect', Journal of Law and Medicine,* vol.12, no. 1, Aug. 2004, pp. 40-59.

_________ 'Recordkeeping and Juridical Governance', in *Archives: Recordkeeping in Society,* eds Sue McKemmish et al., Centre for Information Studies, Charles Sturt University, Wagga Wagga, NSW, 2005, pp. 255-276.

Independent Committee of Inquiry into Competition Policy in Australia*, National Competition Policy,* 'Hilmer Report', Canberra, AGPS, c1993.

Indiana University, *Indiana University Electronic Records Project, Phase 2*, 2000-2002, <http://www.libraries.iub.edu/index.php?pageId = 3313> (accessed Nov. 2005).

International Council on Archives, *The International Code of Ethics for Archivists*, 6 Sept. 1996, <http://www.ica.org/biblio/code_ethics_eng.html> (accessed Nov. 2005).

InterPARES 1 Project, Proceedings, Budapest, Hungary, 8-12 March 1999 (unpublished).

_________ Authenticity Task Force, Template for Analysis, 21 May 1999 (unpublished).

_________ Authenticity Task Force, *Template for Analysis,* 7 Nov. 2000, University of British Columbia, Vancouver, 2000, <http://www.interpares.org/documents/interpares_TemplateforAnalysis_071100.pdf> (Nov. 2005).

_________ Authenticity Task Force, Minutes of Meetings, April 2001 (unpublished).

_________ Authenticity Task Force, *Final Report*, 28 Oct. 2001, University of British Columbia, Vancouver, 2001, <http://www.interpares.org/documents/atf_draft_final_report.pdf> (accessed Nov. 2005).

_________ *Global Industry Research Team Report*, CENSA, 2001, University of British Columbia, Vancouver, 2001, <http://www.interpares.org/book/interpares_book_g_part4global.pdf> (accessed Nov. 2005).

_________ *Italian Research Team Report*, 2001, University of British Columbia, Vancouver, 2001, <http://www.interpares.org/book/interpares_book_g_part4ital.pdf> (accessed Nov. 2005).

InterPARES 1 Project, Preservation Task Force, *Final Report,* 25 July 2001, University of British Columbia, Vancouver, 2001, <http://www.interpares.org/book/interpares_book_f_part3.pdf> (accessed Nov. 2005).

__________ Strategies Task Force, *Report*, December 2001, University of British Columbia, Vancouver, 2001, <http://www.interpares.org/book/interpares_book_g_part4.pdf > (accessed Nov. 2005).

InterPARES 2 Project, *Experiential, Interactive and Dynamic Records,* University of British Columbia, Vancouver, 2002, <http://www.interpares.org/ip2_index.cfm> (accessed Nov. 2005).

ISO, *International Standard ISO 15489-1, Information and Documentation, Records Management,* Part 1: General; *ISO 15489-2, Information and Documentation, Records Management,* Part 2: Guidelines, ISO, 2001.

ISO/TC 215, Ad Hoc Group Report, *Standards Requirements for the Electronic Health Record & Discharge/Referral Plans*, Draft V 2.1, 31 May 2002.

Israelsohn, Cedric, 'Where is the Technology Taking Us? Current Office Technology, Knowledge Management: The Hype and the Reality', Delphi Consulting Australia, Paper presented at *Doing Business Electronically: Electronic Commerce and Recordkeeping*, Recordkeeping Systems and the Records Continuum Research Group, School of Information Management and Systems, Monash University, Canberra, Nov. 1999 (unpublished).

Jackson, Jennifer, 'Common Codes: Divergent Practices', in *Ethics and the Professions,* ed. Ruth F. Chadwick, Avebury, Aldershot, Brookfield, USA, 1994, pp. 116-124.

Johnson, David R. and Post, David G., 'The Rise of Law on the Global Network', in *Borders In Cyberspace: Information Policy and the Global Information Infrastructure,* MIT Press, Cambridge, Mass., 1997, pp. 3-47.

Jurevic, Amy M., 'When Technology and Health Care Collide: Issues with Electronic Medical Records and Electronic Mail', *University of Missouri Kansas City Law Review*, vol. 66, Summer 1998, pp. 809-836.

Kahin, Brian and Nesson, Charles (eds), *Borders in Cyberspace: Information Policy and the Global Information Infrastructure,* MIT Press, Cambridge, Mass., 1997.

Kaspersen, Henrik W.K, 'Data Protection and E-commerce', in *eDirectives: Guide to European Union Law on E-Commerce*: *Commentary on the Directives on Distance Selling, Electronic Signatures, Electronic Commerce, Copyright in the Information Society, and Data Protection,* eds Arno R. Lodder and Henrik W.K. Kaspersen, Kluwer Law International, Dordrecht, 2002, pp. 119-145.

Kernot, Cheryl, 'Codes and Their Enforcement: Necessary but not Sufficient for Ethical Conduct', in *Ethics and Political Practice: Perspectives on Legislative Ethics*, Federation Press, Leichhardt, NSW, 1998, pp. 134-142.

Kerridge, Ian, Saul, Peter, and Mcphee, John, 'Moral Frameworks in Health Care: An Introduction to Ethics', in *Controversies in Health Law,* eds Ian Freckelton and Kerry Peterson, The Federation Press, Sydney, 1999, pp. 276-289.

Ketelaar, Eric, *Archival and Records Management Legislation and Regulations: A Ramp Study with Guidelines,* UNESCO, Paris, 1985.

Ketelaar, Eric, 'The Right to Know, the Right to Forget? Personal Information in Public Archives', *Archives and Manuscripts*, vol. 23, no. 1, May 1995, pp. 8-17.

_________ 'The Difference Best Postponed? Cultures and Comparative Archival Science', *Archivaria,* vol. 44, Fall 1997, pp. 142-148.

Kirby, Michael, 'Privacy in Cyberspace', *University of NSW Law Journal*, vol. 21, no. 2, 1998, pp. 323-333.

Kocourek, Albert, *Jural Relations*, 2nd edn, The Bobbs-Merrill Company, Indianapolis, 1928.

Kolsrud, Ole, 'Developments in Archival Theory', in *Encyclopedia of Library and Information Science,* vol. 61, supplement 24, 1998, pp. 91-108.

Korsgaard, Christine, 'Human Action and Normative Standards', Guest Lecture, the Australian Catholic University, Christ Lecture Theatre, Melbourne, Friday 14 July 2000.

Kottow, Michael, 'Medical Confidentiality: An Intransigent and Absolute Obligation', *Journal of Medical Ethics,* vol. 12, no. 3, Sept. 1986, pp. 117-122.

Kramer, Matthew, *Legal Theory, Political Theory and Deconstruction: Against Rhadamanthus,* Indiana University Press, Bloomington and Indianapolis, 1991.

Kurz, Raymond A. et al., *Internet and the Law: Legal Fundamentals for the Internet User*, Government Insitutes, Rockville, M.D., 1996.

Laberge, Danielle, 'Information, Knowledge and Rights: The Preservation of Archives as a Political and Social Issue, *Archivaria*, vol. 25, Winter 1987-1988, pp. 44-50.

Lane, W.B. and Dixon, Nicolee, 'Government Decision Making: Freedom of Information and Judicial Review', in *Government Law and Policy, Commercial Aspects,* ed. Bryan Horrigan, The Federation Press, Leichhardt, NSW, 1998, pp. 104-139.

Law Book Company, *Laws of Australia* (Lawbook Online), LBC Information Services, North Ryde, NSW (accessed July 2001).

Leal, Fernando, 'Ethics is Fragile Goodness is Not', in *Information Society: New Media, Ethics, and Postmodernism*, ed. Karamjit S. Gill, Springer, London, New York, c1996, pp. 78-89.

Leonard, Peter, 'Ethics in Cyberspace', *Internet Law Anthology*, ed. Peter Leonard, Prospect Intelligence Report, Prospect Publishing, Sydney, 1997, pp. 140-141.

Lim, Liong, 'US Digital Millennium Copyright Act', *Internet Law Bulletin*, vol. 2, no. 1, Feb. 1999, pp. 11-14.

Ling, Ted, 'Setting Standards: Archival Legislation and Recordkeeping Principles', in *Convergence, Conference Proceedings*, the Joint National Conference of the Australian Society of Archivists and the Records Management Association of Australia, 2-5 September 2001, Hobart, pp. 93-99.

Lodder, Arno R., 'Directive 2000/31/EC on Certain Legal Aspects of Information Society Services, in particular Electronic Commerce, in the Internal Market', in *eDirectives: Guide to European Union Law on E-Commerce*: *Commentary on the Directives on Distance Selling, Electronic Signatures, Electronic Commerce, Copyright in the Information Society, and Data Protection,* eds Arno R. Lodder and Henrik W.K. Kaspersen, Kluwer Law International, Dordrecht, 2002, pp. 67-93.

Logstrup, Knud Ejler, *The Ethical Demand*, University of Notre Dame Press, Notre Dame and London, 1997.

Longstaff, Simon, 'The Role of Ethics in Commercial and Professional Relationships', in *The Law of Commercial and Professional Relationships,* ed. Simon Fisher, F.T. Law & Tax, South Melbourne, 1996, pp. 89-116.

Louden, Robert B., 'Kant's Virtue Ethics', in *Virtue Ethics, A Critical Reader,* ed. Daniel Statman, Georgetown University Press, Washington, D.C., 1997, pp. 286-299.

Lowe, Sue, 'Keys to the Kingdom', *The Age*, 22 September 1998.

Luntz, Harold and Hambly, David, *Torts: Cases and Commentary*, 3rd edn, Butterworths, Sydney, 1992.

Lynch, Clifford, 'Authenticity and Integrity in the Digital Environment: An Exploratory Analysis of the Central Role of Trust', in Council on Library and Information Resources, *Authenticity in a Digital Environment*, CLIR, Washington, D.C., 2000, pp. 32-50.

MacFarlane, Peter, 'Doctor and Patient', in *The Law of Commercial and Professional Relationships,* ed. Simon Fisher, F.T. Law & Tax, South Melbourne, 1996, pp. 341-361.

MacIntyre, Alasdair, *After Virtue*, 2nd edn, London, Duckworth, 1985.

_________ *A Short History of Ethics: A History of Moral Philosophy from the Homeric Age to the Twentieth Century,* 2nd edn, University of Notre Dame Press, Notre Dame, Indiana, 1998.

MacNeil, Heather, *Trusting Records: Legal, Historical and Diplomatic Perspectives,* Kluwer, Dordrecht, 2000.

_________ 'Providing Grounds for Trust: Developing Conceptual Requirements for the Long-Term Preservation of Authentic Electronic Records', *Archivaria,* vol. 50, 2001, pp. 56-67.

Mason, Richard O., Mason, Florence M. and Culnam, Mary J., *Ethics of Information Management,* Sage Publications, Thousand Oaks, California, 1995.

Mayer-Schönberger, Viktor and Foster, Teree E., 'A Regulatory Web: Free Speech and the Global Information Infrastructure', in *Borders In Cyberspace: Information Policy and the Global Information Infrastructure,* MIT Press, Cambridge, Mass., 1997, pp. 244-247.

McCulagh, Adrian, 'Ecommerce a matter of TRUST', in *Electronic Commerce: Net Benefit for Australia? The 1998 Information Industry Outlook Conference*, the Australian Computer Society, Canberra Branch, Canberra, 7 Nov. 1998, pp. 15-29.

McDowell, John, 'Virtue and Reason', in *Virtue Ethics*, eds Roger Crisp and Michael Slote, Oxford University Press, Oxford, New York, 1997, pp. 141-162.

McKemmish, Sue, 'Are Records Ever Actual?', in *The Records Continuum: Ian Maclean and Australian Archives First Fifty Years*, eds Sue McKemmish and Michael Piggott, Ancora Press in Association with Australian Archives, Clayton, 1994, pp. 187-203.

__________ 'Constantly Evolving, Ever Mutating': An Australian Contribution to the Archival Metatext, PhD Thesis, Monash University, 2001.

McKemmish, Sue and Acland, Glenda, 'Appendix 4, Recordkeeping Metadata (RKM) Elements Draft Version 2.0: Briefing Notes, 4 March 1999', in InterPARES Project, Proceedings (unpublished), Budapest, Hungary, 8-12 March 1999.

McKemmish, Sue, et al., 'Describing Records in Context in the Continuum: The Australian Recordkeeping Metadata Schema', *Archivaria*, vol. 48, Fall 1999, pp. 3-37.

McSherry, Bernadette, 'Ethical Issues in Health*Connect's* Shared Electronic Health Record System', *Journal of Law and Medicine*, vol. 12, no. 1, Aug. 2004, pp. 60-68.

Mendelson, Danuta, 'Devaluation of a Constitutional Guarantee: The History of Section 51(xxiiiA) of the Commonwealth Constitution', *Melbourne University Law Review*, vol. 23, no. 2, 1999, pp. 308-344.

__________ *Torts,* 3rd edn, Butterworths Casebook Companions, Butterworths, Sydney, 2002.

Middleton, Gaye L. and Aboud, Jocelyn A., 'Jurisdiction and the Internet', in *Going Digital 2000, Legal Issues for E-Commerce, Software and the Internet*, eds Anne Fitzgerald, et al., 2nd edn, Prospect Media, St. Leonards, New South Wales, 2000, pp. 245-255.

Monash University, *Electronic Mail Recordkeeping Protocol*, 2001, <http://www.adm.monash.edu.au/magpie/restrict/rmo/email.html> (accessed April 2001).

Monash University, Department of Librarianship, Archives and Records, Master of Information Management and Systems, *LAR5530 Managing the Records Continuum, Subject Book 1*, Distance Education Centre, Monash University, Churchill, Victoria, July 1997.

Monash University, Distributed Systems Technology Centre, 'W3C Update', Seminar, 17 Nov. 2000, Monash University.

Monash University, School of Information Management Systems, Records Continuum Research Group, *Recordkeeping Metadata Standards for Managing and Accessing Information Resources in Networked Environments Over Time for Government, Social and Cultural Purposes* (RKMS), Monash University, 1998-1999, <http://www.sims.monash.edu.au/research/rcrg/research/spirt/index.html> (accessed Nov. 2005).

__________ *Australian Recordkeeping Metadata Schema (RKMS)*, Version 1.0, 31 May 2000, <http://www.sims.monash.edu.au/research/rcrg/research/spirt/deliver/RKMSGen%2BTechIntro.pdf> (accessed Nov. 2005).

Monash University, School of Information Management Systems, Records Continuum Research Group, with the University of California (UCLA) and National Archives of Australia, *Create Once, Use Many Times: The Clever Use of Metadata in eGovernment and eBusiness Processes in Networked Environments,* Monash University, 2003-2005, <http://www.sims.monash.edu.au/research/rcrg/research/crm/index.html> (accessed Nov. 2005).

Montague, Philip, 'Virtue Ethics: A Qualified Success Story', in *Virtue Ethics, A Critical Reader*, ed. Daniel Statman, Georgetown University Press, Washington, D.C., 1997, pp. 194-204.

Mueller, Milton, Commentary, 'ICANN and Internet Regulation', in *Communications of the ACM*, vol. 42, no. 6, June 1999, pp. 41-43.

National Archives of Australia, *Custody Policy for Commonwealth Records*, March 2000, <http://www.naa.gov.au/recordkeeping/custody/policy.html> (accessed Nov. 2005).

__________ *Policy and Guidelines for Keeping Records of Web-Based Activity in the Commonwealth Government*, January 2001, <http://www.naa.gov.au/recordkeeping/er/web_records/intro.html> (accessed Nov. 2005).

__________ *Recordkeeping and Online Authentication and Encryption,* Archives Advice 64, September 2003/Revised May 2004, <http://www.naa.gov.au/recordkeeping/rkpubs/advices/advice64.html> (accessed Nov. 2005).

__________ *Recordkeeping and Online Security Processes: Guidelines for Managing Commonwealth Records Created or Received Using Authentication and Encryption,* May 2004, <http://www.naa.gov.au/recordkeeping/er/security.html> (accessed Nov. 2005).

National Archives of Australia and the State Records Authority of New South Wales, *DIRKS (Designing and Implementing Recordkeeping Systems) Manual: A Strategic Approach to Managing Business Information*, Commonwealth of Australia 2000, <http://www.naa.gov.au/recordkeeping/dirks/dirksman/contents.html> (accessed Nov. 2005).

National Archives of Australia in cooperation with the Attorney-General's Department, the Office of Government Information Technology and the Tasmanian Department of Premier and Cabinet, Information Strategy Unit, *Records in Evidence, The Impact of the Evidence Act on Commonwealth Recordkeeping,* Commonwealth of Australia, 1998.

National Archives of Canada, *The Keeping of Business Records for Law, Audit and Archives: A Report on the Experts' Meeting, June 10-11, 1999, Ottawa, Ontario,* NAC, Canada, June 1999.

National Electronic Health Records Taskforce, *A Health Information Network for Australia, Taskforce Report*, Department of Health and Aged Care, Commonwealth of Australia, July 2000, <http://www.healthconnect.gov.au/pdf/ehr_rep.pdf> (accessed Nov. 2005).

National Office for the Information Economy, *Establishment of a National Authentication Authority, A Discussion Paper,* 19 August 1998, Commonwealth of Australia, 2000, <http://www.noie.gov.au/projects/consult/neac/disc%5Fpaper%5Fnaadp98.htm> (accessed June 2002).

National Office for the Information Economy, *Government Online: The Commonwealth Government's Strategy,* Department of Communications, Information Technology and the Arts, April 2000, <http://www.govonline.gov.au/projects/strategy/GovOnlineStrategy.htm> (accessed June 2002).

National Public Key Infrastructure Working Party, *Strategies for a Peak Body for an Australian National Electronic Authentication Framework*, Complete Report, March 1998, <http://www.noie.gov.au/publications/1998.htm> (accessed June 2002).

NSW Health Department, *Ethical Management of Health Information,* Discussion Paper, Nov. 1999, Better Health Care Centre, Gladesville, NSW Health Department, 1999.

OECD, *Guidelines Governing the Protection of Privacy and Transborder Flows of Personal Data,* 23 September 1980, OECD, 1980, <http://www.oecd.org/document/18/0,2340,en_2649_34255_1815186_1_1_1_1,00.html> (accessed Oct. 2005).

_________ *A Borderless World: Realising the Potential of Global Electronic Commerce,* Ministerial Declaration on the Protection of Privacy on Global Networks, OECD Conference, Ottawa, 7-9 Oct. 1998.

_________ *Guidelines for the Security of Information Systems and Networks: Towards a Culture of Security*, May 2004, <http://www.oecd.org/document/42/0,2340,en_2649_34255_15582250_1_1_1_1,00.html> (accessed Oct. 2005).

_________ Information Security and Privacy Documents, 2005, <http://www.oecd.org/findDocument/0,2350,en_2649_34255_1_119820_1_1_1,00.html> (accessed Oct. 2005).

OECD, Directorate for Science, Technology and Industry, Committee for Information, Computer and Communications Policy, *OECD Input to the United Nations Working Group on Internet Governance*, OECD, 2005 <http://www.oecd.org/dataoecd/34/9/34727842.pdf> (accessed Oct. 2005).

Office for Government Online, *Moving to an Electronic Marketplace*, Discussion Paper, August 1999, Department of Communications, Information Technology and the Arts, 1999.

Office of Government Information Technology, *Gatekeeper: A Strategy for Public Key Technology Use in the Government,* Commonwealth of Australia, Canberra, 1998.

Office of the Privacy Commissioner, Australia, *National Principles for the Fair Handling of Personal Information,* revised edn, January 1999, Human Rights and Equal Opportunity Commission, 1999.

Onions, C.T. (ed.), *The Shorter Oxford English Dictionary on Historic Principles*, 3rd edn, Clarendon Press, Oxford, 1994.

Oppenheim, Charles, *The Legal and Regulatory Environment for Electronic Information,* 2nd edn, Infonortics Ltd., Calne, 1995.

Oxford English Dictionary, Oxford University Press, New York, 1971.

Parer, Dagmar, 'Integrating Information Resources and Services Through the Intranet', in *Intranets: Problems and Opportunities for Recordkeeping,* Proceedings Conducted by the ACT Branch of the Records Management Association of Australia at Parliament House, Canberra, 10-11 March 1999, ed. Anthony Eccleston, Records Management Association of Australia, ACT Branch, Canberra, 1999, pp. 63-77.

Parliamentary Human Rights Foundation, *Open Internet Policy Principles of the Parliamentary Human Rights Foundation*, PHRF Conference, Brussels Belgium, 23 Nov. 1996, <http://www.cpsr.org/prevsite/cpsr/lists/rre/Open_Internet_Policy_Principle> (accessed Nov. 2005).

Passey, David, 'Internet Provider Pays $10,000 Over Libel', *Sydney Morning Herald,* 14 March 1998.

Paterson, Moira, 'Health*Connect* and Privacy: A Policy Conundrum', *Journal of Law and Medicine*, vol. 12, no. 1, Aug. 2004, pp. 80-90.

__________ *Freedom of Information and Privacy in Australia: Government and Information Access in the Modern State,* LexisNexis Butterworths, Chatswood, NSW, 2005.

Paterson, Moira and Iacovino, Livia, 'Health Privacy: The Draft Australian National Health Privacy Code and the Shared Longitudinal Electronic Health Record', *Health Information Management Journal,* vol. 33, no. 1, 2004, pp. 5-11.

Penner, J.E., 'Basic Obligations', in *The Classification of Obligations,* ed. Peter Birks, Clarendon Press, Oxford, 1997, pp. 91-122.

Perkin, Harold, *The Rise of Professional Society: England Since 1880,* Routledge, London, New York, 1989.

Perritt, Jr., Henry H., *Law and The Information Superhighway*, John Wiley, New York, 1996.

__________ 'Jurisdiction in Cyberspace: The Role of Intermediaries', in *Borders In Cyberspace: Information Policy and the Global Information Infrastructure,* MIT Press, Cambridge, Mass., 1997, pp. 164-202.

Phillips, David J., 'Cryptography, Secrets, and the Structuring of Trust', in *Technology and Privacy: the New Landscape,* eds Agre P and Rotenberg M Massachusetts, MIT Press, 1998, pp. 243-276.

Picot, Anne, 'Uncovering the Mysteries of Digital Signatures. A Discussion of What Signatures Really Stand For and How They Should be Managed in the Digital Environment', in *Convergence, Conference Proceedings,* the Joint National Conference of the Australian Society of Archivists and the Records Management Association of Australia, 2-5 September 2001, Hobart, 2001, pp. 251-259.

Preston, Noel, *Understanding Ethics,* Federation Press, Leichhardt, NSW, 1996.

Public Record Office Victoria, *Victorian Electronic Records Strategy*, Final Report, Public Record Office Victoria, 1998, <http://www.prov.vic.gov.au/vers/pdf/final.pdf> (accessed Nov. 2005).

Raiche, Holly, 'Telecommunications Privacy - The Interaction of the Privacy and Telecommunications Regulatory Systems', in *Papers from The New Australian Privacy Landscape,* Faculty of Law, Continuing Legal Education, The University of New South Wales, 14 March 2001, pp. 1-9.

Ranerup, Agneta, 'Internet-Enabled Applications for Local Government Democratisation: Contradictions of the Swedish Experience', in *Reinventing Government in the Information Age: International Practice in IT-Enabled Public Sector Reform*, ed. Richard Heeks, Routledge, London, 1999, pp. 177-193.

Reed, Barbara, 'Metadata: Core Record or Core Business?', *Archives and Manuscripts,* vol. 25, no. 2, Nov. 1997, pp. 218-241.

Reed, Chris, *Internet Law: Text and Materials*, Butterworths, London, 2000.

Reidenberg, Joel R., 'Governing Networks and Rule-Making in Cyberspace', in *Borders In Cyberspace: Information Policy and the Global Information Infrastructure,* MIT Press, Cambridge, Mass., 1997, pp. 84-105.

Research Libraries Group and Online Computer Library Center, *Trusted Digital Repositories: Attributes and Responsibilities, Final Report, May 2002,* RLG, Mountain View, California, 2002, <http://www.rlg.org/en/pdfs/repositories.pdf> (accessed Nov. 2005).

Richie, Fiona, *Finishing First with Ethics: Bringing Good Business Principles and Sound Ethics Together for Greater Profits and a Better Future,* Business and Professional Publishing, Sydney, 1996.

Roberts, David, Records Management Office, The Archives Authority of New South Wales, *Documenting the Future, Policies and Strategies for Electronic Recordkeeping in the New South Wales Public Sector,* The Archives Authority of New South Wales, Sydney, 1995.

Rose, Lance, *Netlaw: Your Rights in the Online World,* Osborne McGraw-Hill, Berkeley, 1995.

Rosen, F., 'Introduction', in Jeremy Bentham, *An Introduction to the Principles of Morals and Legislation, Jeremy Bentham, An Authoritative Edition by J.H. Burns and H.L.A. Hart; with a New Introduction by F. Rosen, and an Interpretive Essay by H.L.A. Hart,* Clarendon Press, Oxford, 1996, pp. xxxi-lxix.

Rothenberg, Jeff, 'Preserving Authentic Digital Information', in *Authenticity in a Digital Environment,* Council on Library and Information Resources, Washington, D.C., 2000, pp. 51-68.

Saarland University, Institute of Law and Informatics, *The Roman Law Branch of the Law-Related Internet Project,* 2005, <http://www.jura.uni-sb.de/Rechtsgeschichte/Ius.Romanum/english.html> (accessed Nov. 2005).

Schneewind, Jerome B., 'The Misfortunes of Virtues', in *Virtue Ethics,* eds Roger Crisp and Michael Slote, Oxford University Press, Oxford, New York, 1997, pp. 178-200.

Seidmann, Gertrud, 'Personal Seals in Eighteenth and Early Nineteenth Century England and their Antecedents', in *7000 Years of Seals,* ed. Dominique Collon, British Museum Press, London, 1997, pp. 143-160.

Siggens, Ian, 'Professional Codes: Some Historical Antecedents', in *Codes of Ethics and the Professions,* eds Margaret Coady and Sidney Bloch, Melbourne University Press, Carlton South, 1996, pp. 55-71.

Singer, Peter, *A Darwinian Left, Politics, Evolution and Cooperation*, Weidenfield and Nicolson, London, 1999.

Slote, Michael, 'From Morality to Virtue', in *Virtue Ethics, A Critical Reader*, ed. Daniel Statman, Georgetown University Press, Washington, D.C., 1997, pp. 128-144.

Smith, Graham J.H. and contributors (eds), *Internet Law and Regulation: A Specially Commissioned Report,* F.T. Law & Tax, London, 1996.

Smith, Rodney, 'Strange Distinctions: Legislators, Political Parties and Legislative Ethics Research', in *Ethics and Political Practice: Perspectives on Legislative Ethics,* eds Noel Preston and Charles Sampford with C-A Bois, Federation Press, Leichhardt, NSW, 1998, pp. 41-51.

Smith, Russell G., 'The Regulation of Telemedicine', in *Health Care, Crime and Regulatory Control*, ed. Russell G. Smith, Hawkins Press, Sydney, 1998, pp. 190-203.

Solomon, Robert C., 'Corporate Roles, Personal Virtues: An Aristotelian Approach to Business Ethics', in *Virtue Ethics, A Critical Reader,* ed. Daniel Statman, Georgetown University Press, Washington, D.C., 1997, pp. 205-226.

Sorensen, Andrew and Webster, Matthew, *Trade Practices and the Internet*, Lawbook Co., Pyrmont, NSW, 2003.

Sparrow, Andrew P, *The Law of Internet & Mobile Communications: the EU and US Contrasted*, tfm Publishing, Harley, England, 2004.

Squires, Judith (ed.), *Principled Positions: Postmodernism and the Rediscovery of Value,* Lawrence and Wishart, London, 1993.

Stacey, Margaret, 'Collective Therapeutic Responsibility: Lessons from the GMC', in *The Healing Bond: The Patient-Practitioner Relationship and Therapeutic Responsibility*, eds Susan Budd and Ursula Sharma, Routledge, London, New York, 1994, pp. 107-133.

Stapleton, Jane, 'A New "Seascape" for Obligations: Reclassification on the Basis of Measure of Damages', in *The Classification of Obligations,* ed. Peter Birks, Clarendon Press, Oxford, 1997, pp. 193-231.

Statman, Daniel, 'Introduction', in *Virtue Ethics, A Critical Reader,* ed. Daniel Statman, Georgetown University Press, Washington, D.C., 1997, pp. 1-41.

Stocker, Michael, 'Emotional Identification: Closeness and Size: Some Contributions to Virtue Ethics', in *Virtue Ethics, A Critical Reader,* ed. Daniel Statman, Georgetown University Press, Washington, D.C., 1997, pp. 118-127.

Stuckey, Steve and Liddell, Anne, 'Electronic Business Transactions and Recordkeeping: Serious Concerns - Realistic Responses', *Archives and Manuscripts*, vol. 28, no. 2, Nov. 2000, pp. 92-109.

Sullivan, Roger J., *An Introduction to Kant's Ethics,* Cambridge University Press, New York, 1994.

Sutherland, Philip, 'Documentary Evidence', in *The Principles of Evidence, 94/43, Papers Presented for the Continuing Legal Education Department of the College of Law, 9 July 1994, Sydney,* CLE Department of the College of Law, Sydney, 1994, pp. 1-55.

The Australian Human Rights Centre, *Universal Declaration of Human Rights* 1948, <http://www.austlii.edu.au/au/other/ahric/treaties/udhr.html> (accessed June 2005).

The European Parliament and the Council of the European Union, *Directive 95/46/EC On the Protection of Individuals with Regard to the Processing of Personal Data and on the Free Movement of Such Data,* 24 Oct. 1995.

The National Archives, United Kingdom, *Management of Electronic Records on Websites and Intranets: An ERM Toolkit,* Dec. 2001, <http://www.nationalarchives.gov.uk/electronicrecords/advice/pdf/website_toolkit.pdf> (accessed Oct. 2005).

Throsby, Margaret, 'Peter Singer', Radio Interview, ABC Classic FM, 10 AM, 22 August 2001.

Twomey, Paul, 'The Information Economy and Electronic Recordkeeping: An Australian Perspective', in *Archives at Risk: Accountability, Vulnerability and Credibility*, Conference Proceedings, Australian Society of Archivists, 29-31 July 1999, Brisbane, ASA Inc, Canberra 2002, pp. 33-36.

Uhr, John, 'Democracy and the Ethics of Representation', in *Ethics and Political Practice: Perspectives on Legislative Ethics,* Federation Press, Leichhardt, NSW, 1998, pp. 11-46.

UNESCO, *Right to Universal Access to Information in the 21st Century,* Infoethics 2000 Congress, Third UNESCO Congress on Ethical, Legal and Societal Challenges of Cyberspace, 13-15 Nov. 2000, <http://webworld.unesco.org/infoethics2000/index.html> (accessed June 2005).

United Kingdom, Department for Constitutional Affairs, *Public Sector Data Sharing: Guidance on the Law*, Nov. 2003, <http://www.dca.gov.uk/foi/sharing/toolkit/> (accessed Nov. 2005).

United Nations Advisory Committee for Coordination of Information Systems, *Management of Electronic Records: Issues and Guidelines*, United Nations ACCIS, New York, 1990.

United States Copyright Office, *Rulemaking on Exemptions from Prohibition on Circumvention of Technological Measures that Control Access to Copyrighted Works*, The Recommendation of the Register of Copyrights, 28 October 2003, <http://www.copyright.gov/1201/index.html> (accessed Oct. 2005).

University of British Columbia, School of Library, Archival and Information Studies, *The Preservation of the Integrity of Electronic Records* (UBC) Project, 1994-1997, <http://www.interpares.org/UBCProject> (accessed Nov. 2005).

University of Pittsburgh, *Reference Model for Business Acceptable Communications*, 1996, <http://www.sis.pitt.edu/%7Enhprc/meta96.html> (accessed Jan. 1999).

Upward, Frank, 'Structuring the Records Continuum, Part One: Postcustodial Principles and Properties', *Archives and Manuscripts*, vol. 24, no. 2, Nov. 1996, pp. 268-285.

_________ 'Structuring the Records Continuum, Part Two: Structuration Theory and the Records Continuum', *Archives and Manuscripts*, vol. 25, no. 1, May 1997, pp. 10-35.

_________ 'The Records Continuum', in *Archives: Recordkeeping in Society*, eds Sue McKemmish et al., Centre for Information Studies, Charles Sturt University, Wagga Wagga, NSW, 2005, pp. 197-222.

US-InterPARES Project, *Findings on the Preservation of Authentic Electronic Records,* Final Report to the National Historical Publications and Records Commission, 2002.

Vignette, 'WebCapture' software, 2005, <http://www.vignette.com/contentmanagement/0,2097,1-1-1928-4149-1968-4535,00.html> (accessed Nov. 2005).

Visser, Dirk, 'The Database Right and the Spin-off Theory', in *E-commerce Law: National and Transnational Topics and Perspectives*, eds Henk Snijders and Stephen Weatherill, Kluwer Law International, The Hague, London, New York, 2003, pp. 105-110.

Volkmer, Ingrid, 'Universalism and Particularism: The Problem of Cultural Sovereignty and Global Information Flow', in *Borders in Cyberspace: Information Policy and the Global Information Infrastructure,* MIT Press, Cambridge, Mass., 1997, pp. 48-83.

W3C, 'The Platform for Privacy Preferences Project (P3P)', 18 Oct. 2000, W3C, <http://www.w3.org/P3P/> (accessed Nov. 2005).

Waters, Nigel, 'A Comparative Analysis of Australian Privacy Laws with Special Reference to the Concept of "Adequacy" for the Purposes of the European Union Data Protection Directive', in Papers presented to *The New Australian Privacy Landscape*, Faculty of Law, Continuing Legal Education, The University of New South Wales, 14 March 2001 (no pagination).

Weatherill, Stephen, 'The Regulation of E-Commerce under EC Law: the Distribution of Competence between Home States and Host States as a Basis for Managing the Internal Market', in *E-commerce Law: National and Transnational Topics and Perspectives*, eds Henk Snijders and Stephen Weatherill, Kluwer Law International, The Hague, London, New York, 2003, pp. 9-25.

Weber, Max, *Economy and Society: An Outline of Interpretative Sociology*, eds Guenther Roth and Claus Wittich, trans. Ephraim Fischoff [and others] [Wirtschaft und Gesellschaft], New York, Bedminster Press, 1968.

Weeramantry, C.G., *An Invitation to the Law*, Butterworths, Sydney, 1982.

Weinrib, Ernest J., 'The Juridical Classification of Obligations', in *The Classification of Obligations,* ed. Peter Birks, Clarendon Press, Oxford, 1997, pp. 37-55.

Welling, Bruce, *Property in Things in the Common Law System*, Scribblers Publishing, Gold Coast, Queensland, 1996.

Williams, Bernard, 'Morality, the Peculiar Institution', in *Virtue Ethics,* eds Roger Crisp and Michael Slote, Oxford University Press, Oxford, New York, 1997, pp. 45-65.

Willis, Anthony, 'Intranets and the Law', in *Intranets: Problems and Opportunities for Recordkeeping*, Proceedings Conducted by the ACT Branch of the Records Management Association of Australia at Parliament House, Canberra, 10-11 March 1999, ed. Anthony Eccleston, Records Management Association of Australia, ACT Branch, Canberra, 1999, pp. 45-55.

Wilson, Howard R., 'Ethics Counsellor to the Government: The Canadian Experience', in *Ethics and Political Practice: Perspectives on Legislative Ethics*, Federation Press, Leichhardt, NSW, 1998, pp. 81-89.

Wilson, Stephen, 'Current Issues in the Rollout of a National Authentication Framework?', in *Electronic Commerce: Net Benefit for Australia?* The 1998 Information Industry Outlook Conference hosted by the Australian Computer Society - Canberra Branch; Canberra, Australia, 7 Nov. 1998, pp. 5-13.

Wiseman, Leanne, 'Shareholder and Company', in *The Law of Commercial and Professional Relationships,* ed. Simon Fisher, F.T. Law & Tax, South Melbourne, 1996, pp. 605-627.

World Intellectual Property Organization, *Berne Convention for the Protection of Literary and Artistic Works,* 9 September, 1886, Treaty Document No. 27, 99th Congress, Second Session, 41, 1986.

__________ *Basic Proposal for the Substantive Provisions of the Treaty on Intellectual Property in Respect of Databases to be Considered by the Diplomatic Conference Geneva, 2-20 December 1996*, 30 August, 1996, <http://www.copyright.gov/wipo/wipo6.html> (accessed Nov.2005).

__________ *WIPO Copyright Treaty adopted by the Diplomatic Conference on December 20, 1996*, WIPO 1996, <http://www.jus.uio.no/lm/wipo.copyright.treaty.1996/doc.html#10> (accessed Nov. 2005).

Yastreboff, Natalia, 'Encryption and Australian Government Policy', in *Internet Law Anthology,* ed. Peter Leonard, Prospect Intelligence Report, Prospect Publishing, Sydney, 1997, pp. 108-115.

Young, Chari J., 'Telemedicine: Patient Privacy Rights of Electronic Medical Records', *University of Missouri Kansas City Law Review*, vol. 66, Summer 1998, pp. 921-937.

Young, Iris Marion, 'Together in Difference: Transforming the Logic of Group Political Conflict', in *Principled Positions: Postmodernism and the Rediscovery of Value,* ed. Judith Squires, Lawrence and Wishart, London, 1993, pp. 121-150.

Zimmerman, Reinhard, *The Law of Obligations: Roman Foundations of the Civilian Tradition*, Juta & Co. Ltd, Cape Town, 1990.

INDEX

THE ARCHIVIST'S LIBRARY

1. H. MacNeil: *Trusting Records*. Legal, Historical, and Diplomatic Perspectives. 2000 ISBN 0-7923-6599-2
2. L. Duranti, T. Eastwood and H. MacNeil: *Preservation of the Integrity of Electronic Records*. 2003 ISBN 1-4020-0991-7
3. A. Menne-Haritz: *Business Processes*. An Archival Science Approach to Collaborative Decision Making, Records, and Knowledge Management. 2004 ISBN 1-4020-2197-6
4. L. Iacovino: *Recordkeeping, Ethics and Law*. Regulatory Models, Participant Relationships and Rights and Responsibilities in the Online World. 2006 ISBN 1-4020-4691-X